LYSIPPOS

Head of Alexander, Geneva

LYSIPPOS

BY

FRANKLIN P. JOHNSON, Ph.D.

Assistant Professor of Greek in
Duke University

GREENWOOD PRESS, PUBLISHERS
NEW YORK   1968

PREFACE

This book is designed to be a critical consideration of all materials that may be expected, or have been expected, to afford contributions to our knowledge of Lysippos. Most of the topics here discussed have often been discussed previously; and in general I have presented not only my own conclusions, but also the conclusions of others, so that the reader may balance the various arguments (or weigh the various authorities) and form his own opinions.

The usefulness of such a study was suggested to me by Professor David M. Robinson, of Johns Hopkins University, and my dissertation for the doctorate was written under his direction and presented in 1921. It contained ten chapters, to which Chapters III-XII of this book correspond; but all except Chapter VI have been revised very thoroughly, and the first two chapters are wholly new. At all stages of the work I have received a great deal of assistance of all kinds from Professor Robinson. During my two years at the University of Illinois, my work was much facilitated by the funds liberally assigned by Dean Daniels of the Graduate School; and most of the illustrations are reproduced from material owned by that university.

Through the courtesy of Professor Wilhelm Kroll, I saw in 1926 the proofs of Lippold's article on Lysippos, written for Pauly-Wissowa. From it I gleaned two new passages for the appendix, but my study was already in virtually its final form. At about the same time I read Waldhauer's little book on Lysippos, which had been published in 1923. As this is in the Russian language and has not been reviewed, so far as I have observed, in the archaeological journals, it may be useful to give a short account of it.

The book consists of forty-one pages of text and thirty full-page illustrations. There are three chapters: the first (pp. 7-16) deals with "Literary Evidence on Lysippos", the second (pp. 17-39) with existing copies of his works, the third (pp. 40-47) with "Lysippos as an Artistic Personality". The first chapter is devoted largely to a somewhat Spenglerian treatment of the state of the world in the time of Lysippos; in the second various sculptures are ascribed to Lysippos and minutely analyzed; while in the third an effort is made to trace the development of style in these works and so to arrange them in chronological order. As is right in such a book, the author gives little space to disputed questions of fact. His aesthetic analyses of the sculptures are decidedly suggestive, stimulating, and interesting. At the end of his study he assigns the Agias, the "Jason", the Eros, the Herakles Farnese, the Herakles with the hind, of Palermo, to the youth of Lysippos; the apoxyomenos, the seated Hermes, the Naples wrestlers, the Seilenos and Dionysos, the Herakles Epitrapezios, the feminine head in Munich, the Nelidow statuette, the Borghese satyr, the Poseidon (both Lateran and Porcigliano types, apparently) and the Otricoli Zeus, to his maturity; the head of Herakles in the British Museum and the Pergamene "Alexander" to the later years of the artist. There is a good deal here from which one must dissent.

I desire gratefully to acknowledge the courtesy of Mr. James Loeb, who granted permission to use extracts from the translations in the Loeb Classical Library; of the Oxford University Press, which gave similar permission as regards Slater's translation of Statius; and of Macmillan and Company, who allowed quotations from Frazer's *Pausanias,* Jex-Blake's *Pliny,* and Jones's *Ancient Writers on Greek Sculpture.* The other translations have been used without special permission, but the translator's name is always given.

Most of the illustrations are taken, by permission, from the various series of photographs published by

Bruckmann in Munich. Plates 21A and 32B are used by permission of the authorities of the British Museum. I met with the greatest courtesy in getting photographs and information from Mr. Caskey of the Boston Museum, Mr. Xanthoudides of the Candia Museum, M. Merlin of the Louvre, the Hillyer Art Gallery of Smith College, and the museums of Berlin, Dresden, Frankfurt, and Geneva.

F. P. J.

TABLE OF CONTENTS

PAGE

CHAPTER I THE SUCCESSORS OF POLYKLEITOS 3

CHAPTER II EUPHRANOR AND SKOPAS 40

CHAPTER III THE LIFE OF LYSIPPOS 58

CHAPTER IV LITERARY EVIDENCE ON LYSIPPIAN ART;
THE APOXYOMENOS 74

CHAPTER V THE SIGNED BASES; THE POLYDAMAS BASE;
THE HERAKLES EPITRAPEZIOS; THE EROS 92

CHAPTER VI THE DAOCHOS GROUP 117

CHAPTER VII STATUES OF DEITIES 134

CHAPTER VIII OTHER STATUES OF DEITIES ASCRIBED TO
LYSIPPOS BY MODERN SCHOLARS 166

CHAPTER IX THE REPRESENTATIONS OF HERAKLES 190

CHAPTER X LYSIPPOS, COURT SCULPTOR 213

CHAPTER XI MISCELLANEOUS WORKS 230

CHAPTER XII CONCLUSIONS 254

ADDENDA 265

APPENDIX I PASSAGES IN ANCIENT AUTHORS 266

APPENDIX II BIBLIOGRAPHY 322

INDEX 329

PLATES

PLATES

Frontispiece: Head of Alexander, Geneva. (Photograph of the Museum)

1. Doryphoros after Polykleitos, Naples. (*Mon. Rayet,* III, pl. 1)
2. Diskobolos after Naukydes, Vatican. (Brunn-Bruckmann, pl. 131)
3. A. Doria-Pamphili Amazon. (Brunn-Bruckmann, pl. 688)
   B. Berlin Amazon. (Brunn-Bruckmann, pl. 348)
   C. Capitol Amazon. (Brunn-Bruckmann, pl. 349)
4. Statue in Vienna. (Brunn-Bruckmann, pl. 325)
5. Statue found at Antikythera. ('Εφ. 'Αρχ., 1902, pl. VII)
6. Alexander Rondanini. (Arndt-Bruckmann, pl. 183)
7. Head of Alexander Rondanini. (Arndt-Bruckmann, pl. 184)
8. A. Helmeted head found at Tegea. *(Antike Denkmäler,* I, pl. 35, no. 4)
   B. Head of Herakles found at Tegea. *(Le Sanctuaire d'Aléa Athena,* pl. XCIX, A)
9. A. Medici Aphrodite. (Brunn-Bruckmann, pl. 374)
   B. Knidian Aphrodite, copy in Munich. (Brunn-Bruckmann, pl. 372)
   C. Capitol Aphrodite. (Brunn-Bruckmann, pl. 373)
10. Statue found at Ephesos. *(Forschungen in Ephesos,* I, pl. VI)
11. A. Head of Diskobolos after Naukydes, Municipal Antiquarium, Rome.
    B. Head of statue found at Ephesos. (Brunn-Bruckmann, pl. 683)
12. Apoxyomenos, Vatican. (Brunn-Bruckmann, pl. 281)
13. Head of the Vatican Apoxyomenos. (Brunn-Bruckmann, pl. 487)
14. A. Bronze Arm, Boston. (Photograph of the Museum)
    B. Base at Thebes. (Drawing)
    C. Base at Megara. (Photograph)
15. Herakles Epitrapezios, cast in Dresden. (Photograph of the Museum)
16. Herakles Epitrapezios, cast in Dresden. (Photograph of the Museum)
17. Eros, British Museum. (Mansell photograph)
18. Head of Eros, Copenhagen. (Arndt, *Glyptothèque Ny Carlsberg,* pl. 124)
19. Torso of Eros, Hillyer Art Gallery, Smith College. (Photograph of the Gallery)
20. Agias. *(Fouilles de Delphes,* pl. LXIII)

21. A. Statutette in British Museum. *(Select Bronzes,* pl. XX)
    B. Torso in National Museum, Athens. *(Einzelaufnahmen,* no. 722)
    C. Statuette in Frankfurt. (Photograph of the Museum)
22. Zeus of Otricoli. (Brunn-Bruckmann, pl. 130)
23. Zeus, Dresden. (Photograph of the Museum)
24. Poseidon, Lateran. (Brunn-Bruckmann, pl. 243)
25. Poseidon, Candia. (Photographs of Xanthoudides)
26. "Grande Herculanaise". (Brunn-Bruckmann, pl. 310)
27. "Petite Herculanaise". (Brunn-Bruckmann, pl. 558)
28. Head of Ares Ludovisi. *(Einzelaufnahmen,* nos. 254-255)
29. Torso of Ares, Naples. *(Einzelaufnahmen,* nos. 534-535)
30. Lansdowne "Jason", cast in Victoria and Albert Museum. (Photograph of the Museum)
31. Lansdowne "Jason", cast in Victoria and Albert Museum. (Photograph of the Museum)
32. A. Head of "Jason" in Acropolis Museum, Athens. *(Einzelaufnahmen,* no. 734)
    B. Fagan Head, British Museum. *(Marbles and Bronzes,* pl. 25)
33. Seilenos and Dionysos, Louvre. (Brunn-Bruckmann, pl. 64)
34. Head of Seilenos, Museo Nazionale, Rome. (Photograph by Alinari)
35. Hermes, Naples. (Brunn-Bruckmann, pl. 282)
36. Head of Aphrodite, Dresden. (Photographs of the Museum)
37. Herakles Farnese. (Brunn-Bruckmann, pl. 285)
38. A. Herakles, Uffizi. *(Einzelaufnahmen,* no. 346)
    B. Herakles, Villa Borghese. *(Einzelaufnahmen,* no. 2775)
39. Head of Herakles, Villa Borghese. *(Einzelaufnahmen,* nos. 2776-2777)
40. Two statues of Herakles, Palazzo Pitti. *(Einzelaufnahmen,* nos. 231 and 228)
41. Lansdowne Herakles. (Brunn-Bruckmann, pl. 691)
42. Herakles in Louvre, statuette. (Photograph by Giraudon)
43. Alexander Azara. (Arndt-Bruckmann, pl. 181)
44. Alexander Azara. (Arndt-Bruckmann, pl. 182)
45. Head of Alexander, Geneva. (Photograph of the Museum)
46. Head of Alexander, Frankfurt. (Photographs of the Museum)
47. Alexander in Louvre, bronze statuette. (Photograph by Giraudon)
48. A. Bronze Horseman, Naples. (Arndt-Bruckmann, pl. 479)
    B. Statues in Church of St. George, Saloniki. (Photograph)
49. Bust of Seleukos Nikator, Naples. (Arndt-Bruckmann, pls. 101-102)

50. Bust of Socrates, Louvre. (Arndt-Bruckmann, pls. 1038-1039)
51. Bronze Head found at Olympia. (Brunn-Bruckmann, pl. 247)
52. A-B. "Philandridas" head. (Photographs)
    C-D. Head of Youth on stele. (*Einzelaufnahmen*, nos. 698-699)
53. A. Ganymede, Florence. (*Einzelaufnahmen*, no. 323)
    B. Hermes in Geneva, bronze statuette. (*Einzelaufnahmen*, no. 1883)
    C. Head of statue in Berlin. (Photograph of the Museum)
54. Statue in Berlin. (Photograph of the Museum)
55. Beardless Athlete, Dresden. (Photograph of the Museum)
56. Bearded Athlete, Dresden. (Photograph of the Museum)
57. Head in Copenhagen. (Arndt, *Glyptothèque Ny Carlsberg*, pls. 130-131)
58. Meleager, Vatican. (Brunn-Bruckmann, pl. 386)
59. Head of Meleager, Copenhagen. (Arndt, *Gryptothèque Ny Carlsberg*, pl. 100)
60. Wrestlers, Naples. (Brunn-Bruckmann, pl. 354)
61. Dancer, Frankfurt. (Photograph of the Museum)

LYSIPPOS

CHAPTER I

The Successors of Polykleitos

Dipoinos and Skyllis were traditionally pupils of Daidalos and are actually the earliest substantial figures among Greek sculptors. In about 580, as Pliny[1] estimates it, they set out from their home in Crete for the Peloponnesos. Their destination was not chosen lightly, for it was almost the most distant city of the peninsula: it was Sikyon, on the shore of the Gulf of Corinth. The artists were presumably attracted by the liberality of the tyrant Kleisthenes, since so far as we know the city had then no extraordinary prominence in any respect. But from the arrival of the Cretans to the end of the fourth century, Sikyon was second only to Athens among the artistic centers of Greece and "was long the home of all such crafts," as Pliny says; her sculptors and still more her painters reached the highest excellence. Her last great sculptor was Lysippos, the last great sculptor of Hellas.

The labors and the followers of Dipoinos and Skyllis were not, however, confined to Sikyon. There was one other Peloponnesian center which, so far as sculpture is concerned, came to occupy a position fully equal to that of Sikyon: this was Argos. In the fifth and fourth centuries the relations between these two schools were very close, in a way for which neither geography nor history offers an explanation. The cities seem indeed to have been two centers of one school; sometimes coördinate, sometimes affected by the appearance in one town or the other of a great figure.

In the fifth century Peloponnesian sculpture was dominated by the great figure of Polykleitos. Although probably a Sikyonian by birth, he apparently did most of his work as an Argive; it may be that he

[1] *N.H.*, XXXVI 9 (*SQ* 321).

went to Argos to study, though the tradition that made
him a pupil of Ageladas is very difficult to believe.
Probably he was born about 480: he made a statue of
a boy boxer Kyniskos, who won in 464 or 460. The
latest sure date in his career is 418, when he made a
statue of Zeus Meilichios at Argos.[2] His style is well
known through copies of two of his statues, the Doryphoros (Plate 1) and the Diadoumenos, and several
other types are ascribed to him with a near approach
to certainty.

Polykleitos made a special study of the relative
dimensions of the parts of the human body and devised a system of mathematical proportions which an
ideally perfect body would exhibit. The result of his
study is seen in the somewhat heavy but splendidly
strong and virile figures of which we have copies.
Essaying the problem of giving animation to a figure
without definite action, he introduced the "walking
position," and ensured the correct balance of the figure
by the "chiastic" arrangement of the arms and legs.
The statues thus designed were finished with consummate technical skill and exquisite care, and were un-
equalled in formal beauty; but they were said to be
monotonous and to lack "pondus,"—that majesty
which was the crowning glory of Pheidias. The Hera
of Polykleitos was said to be more beautiful than the
Zeus of Pheidias, but it is not recorded that anybody
saw in her a contribution to the grandeur of Greek
religion. But Polykleitos was a very great artist, and
it is not to be supposed that his formalism was pushed
beyond the bounds of sound taste.

It is probable that the most eminent of the Argive
contemporaries of Polykleitos was Naukydes.[3] He is

[2] Pausanias, II 20, 1. His narrative has frequently been doubted,
but with no sound reason. No other marble statue by Polykleitos is
known, but he was probably capable of making one.—The most recent
extended treatment of Polykleitos is by Carlo Anti (*Mon. Ant.*, XXVI,
1920, 502-783).

[3] *SQ* 995-1002. On his chronology see Robert in *Hermes*, XXXV,
1900, pp. 190 ff.

most reliably dated by the fact that his pupil Alypos worked on the great group dedicated by the Spartans after the battle of Aigospotamoi, in 405. The activity of Naukydes must have begun some time before this; so we assume that his two statues of the wrestler Cheimon were made shortly after his victory in 448, as they naturally would be if there were no cause for delay; and that the Hebe by Naukydes, which stood beside the great chryselephantine statue of Hera by Polykleitos in the Argive Heraion, was contemporary with the Hera, i.e. made about 420.

On the base of the statue of a Rhodian pugilist Eukles, Naukydes signs as son of Patrokles.[4] It is not known just when Eukles won; but his grandfather Diagoras won in 464, his uncle Damagetos in 452 and 448, his uncle Akousilaos in 448, and his uncle Dorieus in 432, 428, and 424. To judge from the interval between the victories of Dorieus and those of his older brothers, the mother of Eukles was probably older than Dorieus. One infers that Eukles won somewhat before 400. The lettering seems to belong to the latter part of the fourth century, but it was doubtless renewed, as in several other cases. There is no reason then for separating Naukydes son of Patrokles from the portraitist of Cheimon. Another signature, found on the Acropolis, appears from its epigraphical character to belong to his later years.[5]

The traces on the top of the Eukles base show that both feet rested flat on the base and were nearly parallel. They were rather widely separated and the left was set distinctly forward. We have more satisfying relics of his art in several copies from one of his best works, a diskobolos (Plates 2 and 11, A).[6] Since the

---

[4] Loewy, *Insch. griech. Bildh.,* 86; *Olympia, Ergebnisse,* V, no. 159. On the statues of this family see Preuner, in *Jb. Arch. I.,* XXXV, 1920, pp. 63-65.

[5] Loewy, 87.

[6] Hyde, *OVM,* pp. 76-78, with references; Brunn-Bruckmann, 682-685. Here Sieveking adopts Mahler's idea that there were two sculptors named Naukydes and assigns the diskobolos to the second.

discovery of the true head of this type, the attribution to Naukydes has been very generally accepted. In the forms of the body and still more of the head the influence of Polykleitos is evident, and one who views the statue with the diskobolos of Myron in mind will find in it a good deal of Polykleitan formalism. But it represents faithfully the theme which it is designed to represent and is vastly more expressive of athletic action than any athlete that can be ascribed to Polykleitos. It is clear that Naukydes was no slavish follower, but a first-class sculptor in his own right.

It is frequently stated as a fact that Naukydes was a brother of Polykleitos. This is based on Pausanias II 22, 7, where one reads: τὸ μὲν Πολύκλειτος ἐποίησε, τὸ δὲ ἀδελφὸς Πολυκλείτου Ναυκύδης Μόθωνος. So all recent texts and all of the better manuscripts; but four manuscripts have Περικλείτου instead of Πολυκλείτου. Of these two, M and Mo in Hitzig's notation, are closely related; indeed Mo may be derived directly from M. The other two, Pa and Vb, are descended from a hypothetical archetype but are not related to the first two.[7] It is obvious that Περικλείτου or any similar word would almost certainly be changed to Πολυκλείτου in the context, while the contrary change is almost inconceivable. Moreover, the unparalleled Μόθωνος is generally believed to be corrupt—it must be if Naukydes was son of Patrokles—and this throws suspicion on the whole sentence. The name Perikleitos is not unknown to us, but no sculptor is known to have borne it. Periklytos, however, was a sculptor contemporary with Naukydes, and may well have been his brother, though in view of the uncertainty of the evidence this must remain a hypothesis.

We know but little of this Periklytos. He is mentioned in only one other passage, in which it is stated that he was a pupil of Polykleitos and the teacher of

[7] On the manuscripts of Pausanias see the preface to Spiro's edition.

Antiphanes of Argos.[8] This pupil, however, is a fairly substantial figure.[9] One of his works was a monument in bronze representing the wooden horse of Troy, which the Argives dedicated at Delphi in commemoration of a campaign which took place in 414; the horse was presumably made shortly afterwards.[10] The date can hardly be doubted, though Pausanias refers the monument to a much earlier campaign. The horse has naturally vanished, but there are considerable remains of the basis, from which it can be seen that the monument was one of considerable magnitude: the horse was about two and a half times life-size. Although it is unlikely that so important a commission would be given to an artist who had not proved himself, it must have been among the earlier works of Antiphanes. He had a part in the great Spartan group dedicated after Aigospotamoi in 405, and in a Tegean dedication of 369, and in an Argive dedication which seems to belong to about the same time. These groups merit description.

In the Spartan monument the victorious commander Lysander was represented with Poseidon, lord of the domain in which Aigospotamoi was won, placing a crown on his head. Zeus, Apollo, Artemis, and the Dioskouroi were present, and the prophet Agias and the pilot Hermon. "Behind" these there were twenty-eight figures representing other captains of the Spartans and their allies in the battle.[11] There was a herald also, though Pausanias does not mention him. Altogether there were thirty-seven statues; no other pre-Pergamene monument contained so many.

[8] Pausanias, V 17, 4 (*SQ* 985).

[9] Discussed by Poulsen, *Bull. Dan. Acad.*, 1908, pp. 415 ff.

[10] Pausanias, X 9, 12 (*SQ* 1006). For remains of the pedestal see note *ad. loc.* in Hitzig-Blümner; especially full study, with reconstruction, by Pomtow and Bulle in *Klio*, VIII, 1908, pp. 102-120.

[11] Pausanias, X 9, 7 ff (*SQ* 979); Dittenberger, *Sylloge*[3], no. 115; *Fouilles de Delphes*, III, 1, pp. 24-41; fullest discussion by Pomtow and Bulle in *Ath. Mitt.*, XXXI, 1906, pp. 492-559; Pomtow in *B. Ph. Wo.*, XXXII, 1912, col. 959-968, with reconstruction in sketch.

It may perhaps be regarded as now agreed that these statues stood in a rectangular roofed building, 19.90 m. long and 6.20 m. deep, on the right side of the Sacred Way. On the side next the Sacred Way there was a colonnade, but the number of columns is disputed. In the interior there were at the ends two platforms against the back wall, 5.02 m. long and 3.93 m. deep; these were connected by a bank along the wall, 1.14-1.18 deep. On this tripartite basis, 1.20 m. high, stood the statues of twenty-eight captains at least; if we ascribe any significance to Pausanias's ὄπισθεν we may assume with Pomtow that the nine principal figures were on a separate basis near the colonnade; but no trace of such a basis has been found. Ten bases for the statues of the captains have been preserved, as well as the Lysander base and one which may have borne the statue of Zeus. Besides inscriptions which identify them, the bases have holes for the fastenings of the feet.

These holes vary in length from about 20 to 22.5 cm. It appears that the actual outline of the foot is not clearly perceptible in any case, and the length of the foot can not always be inferred from the length of the hole. In some of the bronzes found in the Antikythera wreck[12] the lead fastenings are virtually as long as the feet to which they belong; while in several bases found at Olympia,[13] the hole is only about two thirds as long as the outline of the foot, which can be seen on the stone. If we may accept this as the usual practice in the fifth century, it follows that the feet of the admirals were 30 cm. long or a little longer. The Doryphoros is 2 metres tall and has feet 33 cm. long; if, as is altogether probable, the admirals were similarly proportioned in the relation of height to length of foot, they would be 1.82 metres to 2 metres

[12] Ἐφ. Ἀρχ., 1902, col. 151, fig. 3; cf. col. 154.
[13] Olympia, Ergebnisse, V, nos. 146, 155, 164, 165.

in height, that is, roughly, from six feet to six feet seven.[14] The size of the bases is as great as would be expected for such figures. Lysander apparently was somewhat but not much larger than the admirals.

The statues of Lysander, Poseidon, and Artemis were made by Dameas of Kleitor. The Lysander stood in the same general position as the Doryphoros of Polykleitos,[15] but with the left foot set a little farther back. Zeus and Apollo were made by Athenodoros of Kleitor, the Dioskouroi by Antiphanes of Argos, Agias by Pison of Kalaureia, and the pilot by Theokosmos of Megara. The two Arcadian sculptors, to whom the most important statues were entrusted, are known to us otherwise only from Pliny, who merely mentions them as pupils of Polykleitos.[16] It is just possible that the base of the Zeus is preserved:[17] a letter Z, which is all that remains of the original inscription, is not easily explicable except as the first letter of Ζάν. The feet were nearly in the position of the Doryphoros, though the left was set farther to the side and not so far back. There are three holes in the stone at the figure's right: one, beside the right toes, could well be for a sceptre or lance; the others would serve for something else, very likely an eagle if the statue really represented Zeus.

Of Pison of Kalaureia we know as little as of the two Arcadians, but that little indicates that he was not connected with Polykleitos: Pausanias says that he was a pupil of Amphion of Knossos.[18] We think of Amphion chiefly as the man who a few years ago leaped into the very front rank of Greek sculptors as

[14] Pomtow (B. Ph. Wo., XXXII, 1912, 962 f.), by a different course of reasoning, makes them smaller.

[15] Fouilles de Delphes, III, 1, p. 28, fig. 8.

[16] N.H., XXXIV 50 (SQ 978).

[17] Fouilles de Delphes, III, 1, p. 39, fig. 18; the base mentioned in note 1 on p. 35 is the same, according to Pomtow (B. Ph. Wo., XXXII, 1912, col. 967, note 11).

[18] Pausanias, VI 3, 5 (SQ 463).

the presumptive author of the charioteer of Delphi; but now he has returned to his obscure station, pupil of Ptolichos who was pupil of Kritios of the Tyrannicides. Theokosmos of Megara is mentioned by Pausanias[19] as the man who began a chryselephantine statue of Zeus in Megara, but was prevented by the outbreak of the Peloponnesian War from finishing it; the statue is thereby dated 428. It appears from Pausanias's description that it was imitated from the Olympian masterpiece of Pheidias,[20] and indeed Pausanias records a tradition that Pheidias collaborated on the Megarian statue. The artistic affiliations of Theokosmos, then, were not with the Peloponnesos. He belonged to a family which produced a number of sculptors[21] and was perhaps the oldest and most esteemed of the sculptors who contributed to the monument.

The twenty-eight figures of the captains are divided by Pausanias into three groups: Teisandros made eleven, Alypos of Sikyon seven, and ten were made by Patrokles and Kanachos. Whether they worked in collaboration or each made some of the ten is not certain, but one assumes the former.

Teisandros is wholly unknown to us except for this group. As for his statues, the base of the Arakos is partly preserved, but the position of the feet can not be discerned, at least from the drawing in *Fouilles de Delphes*.[22] The Kimmerios had a singular position: the weight rested on the right leg, the left foot was set very far back and considerably to the side and rested only on the front part of the foot, and the left hand held a lance which rested on the base far in front of the right foot.[23] The Aiantides,[24] which bore the

[19] I 40, 4 (*SQ* 855).

[20] For possible imitations on coins see Imhoof-Blumer and Gardner, *Numismatic Commentary on Pausanias*, pl. A, 3.

[21] See Preuner, in *Jb. Arch. I.*, XXXV, 1920, pp. 62 f.

[22] *Fouilles de Delphes*, III, 1, p. 29, fig. 9.

[23] *Ibid.*, III, 1, p. 31, fig. 11.   [24] *Ibid.*, III, 1, p. 33, fig. 12.

artist's signature on the base, stood in approximately the position of the Doryphoros, but with the legs reversed.

Alypos was a pupil of Naukydes and made three or four statues of athletes at Olympia.[25] Nothing is known of these statues. In the group at Delphi the statue of Theopompos, which was signed and stood on the same base with the Aiantides of Teisandros, stood with the feet equally advanced but with the weight resting decidedly on the left. Since the attachment for a lance is seen behind, i.e. farther from the front of the base than the left foot, it is probable that the upper part of the body was swung to the man's left. The feet of the Autonomos were in approximately the position of the Doryphoros, but the left one was set farther back.[26] The Apollodoros rested his weight on the left leg, while the right foot was set forward.[27] The size of the hole for the left foot suggests that it was set against some object. Another hole is seen in the rear at the man's right; its size and position suggest that it does not belong to an attribute, but to the left foot of another figure whose right foot would be on an adjoining block.

Patrokles and this Kanachos are mentioned by Pliny as flourishing in the ninety-fifth Olympia (400 B.C.).[28] Kanachos is termed a pupil of Polykleitos by Pausanias,[29] who ascribes to him a statue of a boy boxer, Bykelos, at Olympia. Nothing is known of this statue nor of its date. Patrokles is one of twenty-six artists who, according to Pliny,[30] made "athletes, armed men, hunters, and sacrificers." Presence in this list marks the absolute minimum of notice that could be accorded an artist.

The base of the statue of Komon is partly pre-

[25] Pausanias, VI 1, 3 and VI 8, 5 (SQ 1002 and 1003).
[26] Fouilles de Delphes, III, 1, p. 35, fig. 13.
[27] Ibid., III, 1, p. 37, fig. 15.   [28] N.H. XXXIV 50 (SQ 983).
[29] VI 13, 7 (SQ 984).   [30] N.H., XXXIV 91 (SQ 986).

served, but not enough to permit any conclusions as
to the position of the feet.[31] There is a base that is
pretty well preserved on top but has lost most of the
inscription:[32] a Corinthian stood on it, but we do not
know whether he was Aristophantos, by Alypos, or
Pythodotos, by Kanachos and Patrokles. Whoever he
was, his weight rested on the right leg, and the left
foot was set back on a part of the stone which is now
lost or on an adjoining stone. The figure stood at the
edge of the stone and left room for another figure at
his right. To it probably belong the traces farthest
to the rear on the stone; the right "Spielbein" was
slightly advanced. Apparently other statues were set
on the base at a later period. Finally, the base for the
herald has been preserved.[33] His weight rested on the
left leg and the right foot was set far to the side.
There are other foot-traces on the stone, but they are
said to be different in appearance from those belonging to the group and are supposed to belong to later
statues.

The Spartan group enjoyed some celebrity in later
times;[34] I suppose that they are mentioned more frequently than any other sculptures at Delphi. The
statues acquired a blue patina and people said that they
looked as if they had just emerged from the sea. But
we find no comments on their artistic value and we are
in a poor position to estimate it. The Greeks apparently were fond of aggregations of statues with little
or no relation to one another. One such group, dedicated by Daochos of Thessaly, is pretty well preserved,
as will be seen in a later chapter; but it is probably the
worst there ever was and should not color our notions
of the others too much. Yet it seems impossible that
they could have been very effective, even if the individual figures were excellent.

[31] *Fouilles de Delphes,* III, 1, p. 38, fig. 16.
[32] *Ibid.,* III, 1, p. 36, fig. 14.   [33] *Ibid.,* III, 1, p. 38, fig. 17.
[34] References in Frazer's note, vol. V, p. 264, of his *Pausanias.*

It was found possible to determine the position of the feet for nine bases. In four of these the "Polykleitan walking-motive" appears in a form fairly close to that which is seen in the works of Polykleitos himself. In another case the only difference is that the left foot is set farther back than usual. In two cases the "Spielbein" was set forward, in one it was set flat at the side, and in one it was set at the side and rested on the ball of the foot only. The statues with the "walking-motive" were made by Dameas, Teisandros, Alypos, and possibly Athenodoros (if it was really Zeus); the Kimmerios, with the "Spielbein" far back, was made by Teisandros; two of the others by Alypos and the other two are of unknown authorship.

The period of Lakedaimonian grandeur which was inaugurated at Aigospotamoi did not long endure. In 371 Leuktra was fought; in the winter of 370-369 Epaminondas and his allies invaded Lakedaimon. In memory of this campaign the Arcadians set up at Delphi another group on which Antiphanes worked.[35] This monument consisted of nine statues standing in a row on a long, narrow basis in front of the great Spartan dedication. This position was probably chosen as an affront to the Spartans; but it appears that in fact only the socle of the earlier monument was much obscured by the Arcadian dedication, which itself must have been dwarfed by the proximity of an ensemble so much larger.

At the right end of the line was Apollo. It is evident from the size of the base and of the holes for the fastenings of the feet that he was about a half larger than the other figures: he must have been nearly nine feet tall. His feet were set apart and both turned decidedly outward; the right especially, as though he

[35] Pausanias, X 9, 5-6 (SQ 993); Dittenberger, Sylloge³, no. 160; Fouilles de Delphes, III, 1, pp. 4-9. For the traces of the feet see chiefly Pomtow and Bulle in Ath. Mitt., XXXI, 1906, pp. 474-492; a restoration in sketch, B. Ph. Wo., XXXII, 1912, 963.

had taken a step in that direction. On the stone there are two other places for fastenings, perhaps for a griffin which sat with one paw raised and was visible between Apollo's legs. On the next stone was Kallisto, apparently advancing toward Apollo: it looks as though these two were composed as a group, though Apollo had nothing to do with Kallisto and was present merely as the god to whom the group was dedicated. The two figures were made by Pausanias of Apollonia. He is otherwise unknown: we can not even say from which of many Apollonias he came.

The third figure was Nike. Traces of only one of her feet remain, which pointed straight toward the front. Arkas, son of Kallisto and eponymous hero of Arcadia, stood in the fourth place. He was turned more or less away from Nike and stood approximately in the position of the Doryphoros. At his left are marks of attachment for some object or objects; Bulle suggests a shield. Nike and Arkas were made by Daidalos of Sikyon.

The next two figures represented Apheidas and Elatos, sons of Arkas, and were works of Antiphanes. They were turned somewhat toward each other. Four holes for fastenings show that beside Elatos there was some animal, perhaps a dog. Then came Azan, third son of Arkas, and Triphylos. In each case there is only one clear footprint, though there are several other marks of attachment; it may be that each figure had its left foot set up on some object. Both were made by Samolas, an Arcadian sculptor of whom nothing is known otherwise. The ninth figure, Erasos, was again by Antiphanes. The one remaining footprint points straight toward the front.

Of the four sculptors who contributed to this group, two—Antiphanes and Daidalos—were perhaps the two most eminent Peloponnesian sculptors who were active at the time; the other two, though doubtless somewhat better known than they are now, must have been obscure. It is noteworthy that Pausanias, totally unknown to us and presumably not an Arcadian —no Apollonia in Arcadia is known—was chosen to make the Apollo. Whether there was any artist who designed or supervised the whole group is not clear.

At about the same time Antiphanes worked on a similar group for his own state of Argos in commemoration of the same campaign.[36] Here the legendary heroes of Argos, including Herakles and his ancestors, were represented. The total number is not certain, though estimated by Bourguet at twenty. They stood in a hemicycle opening on the right side of the Sacred Way. Eight inscribed pedestals are preserved, making a continuous series from the left end of the arc to about the middle; and one other, without inscription, which was the next one at the middle. All of these have more or less clear indications of the positions of the feet of the statues which they bore. Apparently the figures were slightly larger than most of those in the Arcadian group.

At the extreme left of the hemicycle stood Herakles. Without regard to the unity of the group, he was turned away from the rest of the line and apparently was occupied with a small animal, perhaps Kerberos, of whose four feet traces are visible. Next to Herakles stood his mother Alkmene. There are traces (two holes of different size) for some attribute on her right. Bulle suggests a thunderbolt, symbolizing Alkmene's association with Zeus; but there seems to be no type of thunderbolt which would be fastened at two places, and as a rule thunderbolts are relatively small objects which are held in the hands and do not touch the ground. (On forms of the thunderbolt see Cook, *Zeus*, II, 1, pp. 764 ff.) It is just possible that

[36] Pausanias, X 10, 5; for the remains see Dittenberger, *Sylloge*³, no. 161, with references; *Fouilles de Delphes*, III, 1, pp. 41-46; for the evidence as to the statues, Bulle in *Klio*, VII, 1907, 415-421.

the attribute belonged to Herakles. On Alkmene's left stood her father Alektryon. He faced the front and held a lance or long sceptre in his right hand. Alkmene apparently was turned slightly toward him.

Between Alektryon and Perseus there is a considerable interval, so far as the holes in the bases are concerned. We can not say whether such an interval appeared in the row of statues or not: it may be that Perseus was stretching out his arm somewhat as in the Cerigotto bronze; in fact he might very naturally display the head of Medusa in this way. At any rate he was turned to his right, with his feet in approximately the position of the Doryphoros, so that his mother Danae, standing close to him and turned toward him, must have been almost directly behind him.

Beyond Danae there is again an interval and then Akrisios, Abas, and Lynkeus are represented in that order. In each one the weight rested on the right leg and the left foot was set back. The three sets of holes look monotonous, but of course the statues may have had considerable variety. The last stone contains also a hole for the right foot of, or for something held by, another figure. In regard to the remaining right half of the hemicycle, the situation is puzzling: three stones and large parts of two others remain, but there are no inscriptions and no traces for fastenings for statues; one slab may have had such a fastening at the edge, which is broken away.[37] Pausanias mentions two members of the group, Danaos and Hypermnestra, who must have stood to the right of the figures that have been mentioned.

The signature of Antiphanes is found on the slabs that contained the figures of Perseus and Danae. As no other signature appears anywhere, it is commonly and perhaps rightly assumed that Antiphanes made all the statues in the hemicycle. We have seen, how-

[37] Bulle's no. 6; at the left in the drawing in *Fouilles de Delphes*, p. 43.

ever, that Perseus and Danae are more or less isolated from the other figures, and it is quite possible that they only were works of Antiphanes. It is just possible that the group was not completed as designed; this might explain the sparse population on the right side of the hemicycle and also the lack of other signatures.

In Sikyon the leading sculptor in the early part of the fourth century was Daidalos.[38]   That he was a son of Patrokles we know both from his signatures and from Pausanias, and the periegete adds that he was his father's pupil.   Patrokles then was a sculptor and without doubt was the Patrokles known to us as one of the artists of the great Spartan monument. Pausanias[39] relates that Daidalos made a trophy to commemorate a victory won by the Eleans over the Spartans in a fight in the Altis, which he dates 401-399 B.C.   The date has been questioned because of the silence of Xenophon in regard to any such battle, though he describes the war of which it would be a part.   But Xenophon might omit events which were without influence on the course of the war, and Elean tradition about their own trophy would probably be right.   If the trophy was set up at once it was the earliest work of Daidalos of which we have record.

Pausanias mentions statues by Daidalos of the Elean sprinter Eupolemos,[40] who won in 396, and of the Elean wrestler Aristodemos,[41] who won in 388. These statues and their bases are lost; but the inscription on the base of a third statue mentioned by Pausanias,[42] representing the Phigalian Tharykidas, is partially preserved and evidently belongs to the first

[38] *SQ* 987-993.   On his chronology see Robert, in *Hermes*, XXXV, 1900, pp. 191 f. and Preuner in *Jb. Arch. I.*, XXXV, 1920, pp. 65-69.

[39] VI 2, 8 and VI 2, 3.

[40] VI 3, 7; Hyde, *De Olympionicarum Statuis*, no. 28.

[41] VI 3, 4; Hyde, no. 25.

[42] VI 6, 1; Hyde, no. 49; Loewy, *Insch. griech. Bildh.*, no. 103; *Olympia, Ergebnisse*, V, no. 161; Preuner, *l.c.*, p. 67.

half of the fourth century. In this case, as the result
of some political or personal happening not known to
us, Daidalos describes himself not as a Sikyonian but,
according to the most likely restoration, as a citizen of
the neighboring town of Phlious. Then there is another signed base at Olympia,[43] of which the dedication is lost. This base was used in the base of a statue
of Zeus which was set up in 124 A.D.; Pausanias
therefore did not see the base, though he may have
seen the statue. This signature also belongs to the
early part of the fourth century. The marks for the
feet of the statue remain, but I have not observed any
illustration or description that indicates their position.
Daidalos also made statues of Timon, who won in a
chariot race, and of his son Aisypos,[44] who won a
horse race and had an equestrian statue. The dates
of their victories are not known. It is evident that
Daidalos was a favorite sculptor with the victors at
Olympia.

We have also a fragmentary epigram from the
statue of a boy pugilist at Delphi.[45] The boy's name
ends in . . . υκων; the obvious restoration is Glaukon, a fairly common name. His father's name was
Taureas; this is not a common name, so one thinks of
the Athenian Taureas, who built the palaestra in which
was laid the scene of the Charmides of Plato, and was
related to Glaukon the father of Charmides. This
Taureas and his son Nisaios were involved in the prose-
cution which followed the mutilation of the Hermes in
415, but escaped. If our boy victor was another son of
Taureas he should have won his victory before 400. But
according to Pomtow—no facsimile has been published—the inscription seems to have been cut by the
same mason who cut the inscription on the Arcadian
dedication of 369; and this would suggest that the

[43] Loewy, no. 89; *Olympia, Ergebnisse,* V, no. 635.
[44] Pausanias, VI 2, 8; Hyde, nos. 17 and 18.
[45] *Klio,* XV, 1917-18, p. 63 (Pomtow).

statue was considerably later than the victory. Finally there should be mentioned a base in Ephesos,[46] now lost, which bore the signature of Daidalos and the name of Euthenos son of Eupeithes. Who he was we do not know, and the lack of a dependable facsimile of the inscription forbids any conjecture as to date. It speaks well for the fame of Daidalos that a statue should be ordered from distant Ephesos.

Except for the Nike in the Arcadian group, evidence of versatility is conspicuously lacking; but Daidalos was evidently regarded as an athletic sculptor of the first order. In this he differs from his Argive contemporary Antiphanes, from whom no athletic statues at all are recorded. In Pliny's sources Daidalos apparently was not prominent: that erudite man does not seem definitely to have distinguished him from the vast and vague figure after which he was named, and gives only "two boys scraping themselves"[47] as his works. It is highly probable that we have copies from at least one of these apoxyomenoi; but that must be discussed in a later chapter.

Kleon of Sikyon,[48] like Daidalos, is known to us largely through Pausanias. Pliny mentions him only as having made statues of philosophers,[49] but Pausanias tells us that he was a pupil of Antiphanes[50] and mentions eight statues by him at Olympia: two of Zeus, one of Aphrodite, and five of athletes. It was customary at Olympia to fine heavily violators of the rules of the festival and to erect statues of Zeus from the fines. In 388 B.C. Eupolos of Thessaly, who tried to win in boxing through bribery, and those who accepted his bribes defrayed the cost of six "Zanes." Pausanias[51] says that two of these were made by Kleon

---

[46] Loewy, no. 88. [47] N. H., XXXIV 76.
[48] SQ 985 and 1007-1013; a recent article in Pauly-Wissowa.
[49] N.H., XXXIV 87. [50] V 17, 4.
[51] V 21, 2-3.

and his signature remains on the base of one of them.[52]
The traces on top of the base show that the feet were
in approximately the position of the Doryphoros. We
have also the base[53] of his statue of the boy boxer
Kritodamos of Kleitor.[54] The date of the victory is
unknown, but the signature is so like that on the base
of the Zeus that the two statues can hardly be separated by a great interval. The position of the feet is
not clear. Alketos[55] was another boy boxer from
Kleitor; Deinolochos[56] and Hysmon[57] were Eleans, the
former a chariot racer and Hellanodikos, the latter a
pentathlete who was represented with jumping-
weights; Lykinos[58] was a boy runner from Heraia in
Arcadia. None of these statues can be dated, nor has
any trace of them been found. The one female figure
of which we hear was an Aphrodite in the Heraion at
Olympia.[59] At Delphi a signature of Kleon has been
found[60] on a base belonging to a statue in memory of
Hagesipolis, king of Sparta, which was set up by his
exiled father Pausanias. Hagesipolis died in 381-380
and the statue was doubtless set up soon after that.

A block which was built into the basis of one of the
late Zanes, and which has already been mentioned as
bearing a signature of Daidalos, had also in another
place the signature of another Sikyonian.[61] The sculptor's name is lost, but . . . ιτου remains of his father's
name. The position of this line renders it improbable
that there was another above it, so Loewy's tempting
restoration Πολυκλείτου must be discarded; and it

[53] Loewy, no. 95; *Olympia, Ergebnisse,* V, no. 637.
[53] Loewy, no. 96; *Olympia, Ergebnisse,* V, no. 167.
[54] Pausanias, VI 8, 5; Hyde, no. 80.
[55] Pausanias, VI 9, 2; Hyde, no. 86.
[56] Pausanias, VI 1, 4-5; Hyde, no. 5.
[57] Pausanias, VI 3, 9-10; Hyde, no. 31.
[58] VI 10, 9; Hyde, no. 100.
[59] Pausanias, V 17, 3.
[60] Bourguet, in *B.C.H.,* XXV, 1911, pp. 162-165.
[61] *Olympia, Ergebnisse,* V, no. 636; Loewy, no. 89b.

appears that the names of the sculptor and his father,
both short, were in one line. Purgold's suggestion,
Κλέων Κρίτου, is very plausible. He thinks that the
signature is somewhat earlier than the two certain signatures at Olympia. The position of the feet of the
statue can be seen on the stone, but so far as I know
no illustration of the top of the stone has been published. It is not clear whether we have here a real
group, made by the two leading Sikyonian sculptors of
the time, or merely two statues set on a single base.

Pausanias[62] saw at Olympia a statue of a Theban
boy wrestler Agenor, which was the work of Polykleitos, "an Argive, not he who made the image of
Hera, but a pupil of Naukydes." "The statue was dedicated by the Phocian confederacy, for Theopompos,
father of Agenor, was a proxenos of the Phocian
nation." There is no evidence as to the date of Agenor's victory; but it is probable that the statue was
erected at a time when friendly relations existed between Thebes and the Phocians. There were no really
cordial relations between the two states until 339-338,
when the Phocian confederacy was reconstituted by
Athens and Thebes. In 335 Thebes was destroyed;
from that year to 316, when the city was rebuilt, there
were probably few statues set up anywhere at the
expense of Thebans. This period would certainly
seem to be the best time for the statue of Agenor,
were it not that Pausanias distinctly names Naukydes
as the teacher of the artist. Naukydes, as has been
seen, can not have lived much after 400, and his pupil
could hardly have been at work after 335. We are
forced then to follow Anti[63] in dating the statue soon
after 371, when the Phocians, in consequence of the
battle of Leuktra, contracted an unwilling alliance with
Thebes. In this case there is a *terminus ante quem* in

[62] VI 6, 2 (*SQ* 1004).
[63] *Mon. Ant.*, XXVI, 1921, p. 653, note 5.

357, when the amphiktyonic decree against the Phocians was passed through the machinations of Thebes; and a probable one in 362, when the Phocians refused to send a detachment for the campaign which led to the battle of Mantineia. Of course there is an element of uncertainty in all this reasoning, since a proxenos might deserve and obtain rewards in any state of international relations; yet it will be agreed that the occurrence is far more likely in a time of friendship.

This is the only passage in which a Polykleitos other than "he who made the image of Hera" is definitely mentioned, but there are several other works, assigned merely to a Polykleitos, which can hardly belong to the great master of the fifth century. The earliest of these is the Aphrodite of Amyklai. Pausanias says that it was dedicated from the spoils of Aigospotamoi (405).[64] Since the great Polykleitos must have been born about 480, he would have been quite old at that time. We know that Alypos, a pupil of Naukydes, was active at that time, so it is probably right to refer the Aphrodite to his other pupil Polykleitos. Mahler indeed suggests that Pausanias misunderstood the inscription on the base of the statue and that it had nothing to do with Aigospotamoi.[65] Pausanias was not incapable of errors, but we have no particular reason for accusing him of this one.

Then there is the statue of the Milesian boy boxer Antipatros.[66] Pausanias relates a perfectly straightforward and credible story of the relations of Antipatros with Dionysios of Syracuse, who tried to have him entered as a Syracusan. Since Dionysios became tyrant in 406/5, the statue must be later than that; the most probable date for it is 388, since we know from Diodoros of the tyrant's particular exertions at Olympia in that year.[67] Anti indeed says that 388 is "anno

---

[64] III 18, 8 (SQ 942). [65] *Polyklet*, pp. 7 f.
[66] Pausanias, VI 2, 6 (SQ 951); Hyde, no. 16. [67] XIV 109.

dal quale datano le relazioni di Dionisio con Olimpia";[68] but I do not know any grounds for the belief that there were no earlier relations. Robert[69] doubts the incident related by Pausanias, for no reason at all; several similar cases are known.[70] Dionysios died in 367; if we consider the bare possibility that the younger Dionysios was meant, the lower limit of possibility for the statue may be brought down to 357, the date of his first exile. The brief and troubled period of his second rule need not be taken into account.

The Zeus Philios at Megalopolis was the work of Polykleitos.[71] A *terminus post quem*, certain except for the possibility that the statue may have been brought from another town when Megalopolis was founded, is 369, when the city began. *Terminus ante quem* there is none. If it were certain that the epithet "had a political significance, referring to the friendship which was to bind the petty Arcadian communities together,"[72] it would be probable that it was made soon after the foundation of Megalopolis; but the cult of Zeus Philios was by no means peculiar to Megalopolis and the epithet apparently had no political significance elsewhere. On the other hand the use of attributes of Dionysos clearly indicates that the god was thought of chiefly as connected with the "friendly feast."[73]

The tholos and theater at Epidauros are ascribed to Polykleitos by Pausanias.[74] Dörpfeld judged from the style of the remains of these buildings that they

[68] *Mon. Ant.*, XXVI, 1920, p. 653, note 5. Hyde in one place (*OVM*, p. 118) says that 388 is given by Africanus; but this seems to be a slip.

[69] *Arch. Märchen*, p. 107 and *Hermes*, XXXV, 1900, p. 187.

[70] Hyde, *OVM*, p. 33.

[71] Pausanias, VIII 31, 4 (*SQ* 1005).

[72] So Frazer *ad. loc.* and Farnell, *Cults of the Greek States*, I, p. 118.

[73] Cf. Farnell, *op. cit.*, I, p. 74.

[74] II 27, 5. For the restoration of the tholos see Kavvadias, in *Sitz. Berl. Akad.*, 1909, pp. 536 ff.

must have been built very late in the fourth century,[75] and Fränkel was led to the same conclusion by an epigraphical study of the building inscription of the tholos.[76] But Kavvadias placed them at about the middle of the century:[77] he was influenced partly by the forms of the letters and partly by the monetary units mentioned in the inscription. This opinion is generally accepted. It is well known that the quality of the buildings is such as to place this Polykleitos in the front rank of Greek architects, however much or little of a sculptor he was.

Of the victor statues at Olympia which are ascribed by Pausanias to Polykleitos there are two which may belong to the younger artist. One of these was set up by the boy wrestler Xenokles of Mainalos in Arcadia.[78] The epigraphical character of the inscription and the form of the base tend to indicate, though they by no means prove, that the statue belongs to the period of the younger Polykleitos. The weight rested on the right leg or was evenly divided; the left foot was very slightly advanced; both feet were turned slightly outward.

The inscription of the Epidaurian boxer Aristion[79] belongs to the middle of the fourth century. As we learn from the precious Oxyrhynchos papyrus, Aristion won in 452. Hence the statue was made long after the victory or the basis, with its inscription, was renewed. The latter hypothesis has received more general indorsement than it deserves. Certainly it is quite possible, but the erection of the statue by the son or grandson of Aristion is equally so; and the younger

[75] Dörpfeld-Reisch, *Das griech. Theater,* pp. 130 ff.
[76] *I. G.* IV, p. 338.
[77] *Fouilles d'Épidaure,* p. 98.
[78] Pausanias, VI 9, 2 (*SQ* 950) ; Hyde, *OVM,* p. 118, with references; *Olympia, Ergebnisse,* V, no. 164; Loewy, 90; Furtwängler, *Masterpieces,* p. 279; Robert, in *Hermes,* XXXV, 1900, p. 187.
[79] Pausanias, VI 13, 6 (*SQ* 947) ; Hyde, *OVM,* p. 117; *Olympia, Ergebnisse,* V, no. 165; Loewy, 92; Robert, *l.c.,* pp. 185 f.

Polykleitos is especially likely to have worked for an Epidaurian family, since his work on the tholos and theater would have made him acquainted with many of the citizens. The base of the statue shows that the weight rested on the left leg or was equally divided; both feet were turned out, the right much more distinctly; the right foot was slightly advanced.

Pliny attributes to Lysippos a portrait of Hephaistion.[80] He mentions that some authorities ascribed the statue to Polykleitos, but considers the suggestion absurd, since he thinks Polykleitos lived almost a hundred years earlier. There are a number of Greek statues that are attributed to two different artists, one much better known than the other; and archaeologists are agreed that the less eminent artist is generally to be accepted as the true author of the work in dispute. The portrait of Hephaistion seems a very clear example of such confusion. It is certain that any Polykleitos who was contemporary or approximately contemporary with Lysippos was far less known than he, even to those who had not, like Pliny, forgotten him altogether. An erroneous attribution to him is, in the circumstances, incredible, and we can be sure that he really made a portrait of Hephaiston,[81] though it is highly probable that Lysippos made another and that Pliny's two authorities referred to two distinct statues. Hephaistion was born in 356, and his statue would probably be later than 340.

Pliny mentions among the works of Polykleitos a Hermes "which was in Lysimachia."[82] Lysimachia ought to mean Lysimachia in Thrace, just as Alexandria means Egyptian Alexandria; and that city was found in 309. It is usually assumed that the statue was taken there from somewhere else, and of course

[80] *N.H.*, XXXIV 64 (App. 1, 3).
[81] So Loeschcke, in *Arch. Zeit.*, XXXVI, 1878, p. 11.
[82] *N.H.*, XXXIV 56.

this is quite possible. Anti[83] conjectures (and supports
the conjecture by a diverting bit of historical reconstruction) that the Lysimachia in question was not the
noted city in Thrace, but the Aitolian town; and thinks
that an existing type of Hermes, which has been shown
to be thoroughly in the style of the elder Polykleitos,
represents the statue mentioned by Pliny.

We have then a series of works extending from
405 to 340 at the earliest, and that is a long time for
the activity of one man. Dittenberger,[84] Fränkel,[85]
and formerly, at least, Dörpfeld[86] thought that there
were three sculptors named Polykleitos. The latest of
the three would be the portrayer of Hephaistion, would
be active after the foundation of Lysimachia, and
would probably be the artist whose signature is found
with that of Lysippos on a base at Thebes.[87] This solution may well be right, though it is not, after all,
impossible that a pupil of Naukydes should be active
after 340. A second Naukydes, to be the master of a
late Polykleitos the Younger, is certainly to be rejected: the chronology of Naukydes offers in itself not
the slightest difficulty, and this solution leaves the
Aphrodite of Amyklai as troublesome as it was before.

Plato tells us that the great Polykleitos had sons
who were sculptors but were "nothing in comparison
with their father."[88] He calls them contemporaries of
the sons of Perikles, who died in 429 in early man-
hood. The sons of Polykleitos then would be born
slightly before 450, as would be expected from the
chronology of Polykleitos. Hippias(?) says that
Polykleitos taught his son to make statues.[89] But nobody says what statues they made or what their names
were. It is probable that they are among the sculptors

[83] Mon. Ant., XXVI, 1920, pp. 567-578.
[84] I.G., VII, 2533.   [85] I.G., IV, p. 338.
[86] Das griech. Theater, pp. 130 ff.; cf. Röm. Mitt., XVII, 1902, p. 339.
[87] Chapter III, pp. 62-64.   [88] Protagoras, 328 C.
[89] Mullach, Frag. Philosophorum Graec., I, p. 551.

who have been mentioned, but identification is not easy. We can not be sure whether they would be Sikyonians or Argives, since Polykleitos was both. Perhaps they are among the obscure pupils named by Pliny:[90] Asopodoros of Argos, Alexis, Aristeides,[91] Phrynon. Kanachos and Teisandros are possibilities. Alypos, a pupil of Naukydes, is improbable; Antiphanes was a pupil of Periklytos and too young besides. Periklytos himself is a possibility, considering the similarity in name, if we are justified in disregarding the corrupt passage in Pausanias which has been discussed.

Naukydes and Daidalos, both sons of men named Patrokles, ought to be related somehow. It is possible that the Patrokles of the Aigospotamoi monument was son of Naukydes and father of Daidalos; but this makes the generations short, so perhaps it is better to consider Patrokles a younger brother or nephew of Naukydes. If we reckon Periklytos to this family also and count the pupils Alypos and Antiphanes and Kleon of Sikyon, the unknown sons and obscure pupils of Polykleitos are left far behind. One would gladly assume a connection between the two families, but it has not been proved. The younger Polykleitos may very probably have been a grandson of the elder; though a pupil of Naukydes, he seems to have been too young to be his son.[92]

Phradmon of Argos is a sculptor who deserves mention here. Pliny gives his *floruit* as 420,[93] mentioning him along with Polykleitos and others; but Pliny's dates are notoriously unreliable and this one has an

---

[90] *N.H.*, XXXIV 50 (*SQ* 978).

[91] Aristeides, according to another passage of Pliny (*N.H.*, XXXIV 72; *SQ* 981) made quadrigas and bigas, and is perhaps the same Aristeides to whom Pausanias (VI 20, 14; *SQ* 982) attributes some improvement in the machinery for starting chariots in the race at Olympia.

[92] For opinions on the relationships of these artists see Robert, in *Hermes*, XXV, 1900, pp. 190-193; Mahler, *Polyklet*, pp. 8 ff.; Klein, *Gesch. d. griech. Kunst*, II, pp. 329-331.

[93] *N.H.*, XXXIV 49 (*SQ* 1015).

obvious explanation in the story according to which
Pheidias, Polykleitos, Kresilas, and Phradmon made
statues of Amazons in competition at Ephesos.[94]
Mahler[95] argued for a much later date on the basis of
an epigram.[96] The epigram appears to have been
placed on the basis of a group of twelve bronze oxen
which were dedicated by Thessalians from spoils
gained in a campaign against the Illyrians. No such
campaign is known to have occurred in the fifth century. Mahler named 356 as the most probable date
for the campaign, but Swoboda places it rather between 345 and 336.[97] Their position, though not universally accepted, seems to be quite sound: the story
of the Amazons rather confirms than contradicts it,
for Pliny notes that the "competing" artists were not
contemporary, while we know that the three others
lived at the same time.

Aside from the cows and the Amazon, only one
work of Phradmon is mentioned: a statue of the
Elean wrestler Amertas, who won as a boy at Olympia
and as a man at Delphi.[98] There is no clue to the date
of either victory. Finally there is a singular line of
Columella,[99] in which Polykleitos, Phradmon, and
Ageladas are named as typical great sculptors.

The Amazon is obviously the only work that we
can hope to identify. In addition to the artists in the
"competition," we know that Strongylion, an Athenian
of the late fifth century, made an Amazon celebrated
for the beauty of her legs (below the knees). The
attempts to assign the existing types of Amazons to
their true authors have been many and discordant: the
Capitoline type has been given to Pheidias, Kresilas,

[94] Pliny, N.H., XXXIV 53 (SQ 946).
[95] Polyklet, pp. 101 ff.
[96] Anth. Pal., IX 743 (SQ 1018).
[97] Jh. Oest. Arch. I., VI, 1903, pp. 200-214.
[98] Pausanias, VI 8, 1 (SQ 1017).
[99] De Re Rustica, X 29 (SQ 1016).

and Polykleitos, the Berlin type to Polykleitos, Strongylion, and Phradmon, the Mattei type to Pheidias, Kresilas, and Strongylion.[100]

According to the vulgate opinion the Berlin type (Plate 3, B) is derived from Polykleitos. This attribution is supported by several considerations. (1) The forms of the body and the positions of the legs are Polykleitan. (2) The number of extant copies and imitations shows that the original was famous; Polykleitos is named by Pliny as the winner of the "contest" and the Berlin type has never been attributed to either of the other great sculptors, Pheidias or Kresilas. (3) The posture of the figure is designed to show its beauty, as would be expected of a formalist like Polykleitos. Other stylistic arguments are adduced by Miss Bieber. The rebels against the traditional view argue: (1) The use of a post to lean on and the resultant languid appearance are unknown in any other work believed to be Polykleitan. (2) Polykleitos, formalist or not, was a great artist, and would not represent a wounded Amazon in a position which would make the wound as painful as possible. Noack indeed believes that the wound was not present in the original; but all the copies have it, and it is methodically indefensible to reject their testimony in favor of the Greek relief at Ephesos. It is possible that the artist wished to show the Amazon's indifference to the wound, but this the-

[100] Fullest recent discussion: Noack, in *Jb. Arch. I.*, XXX, 1915, pp. 131-179 (assigns Capitol type to Polykleitos, Berlin type to Strongylion, Mattei type to Kresilas); also Bieber, in *Jb. Arch. I.*, XXXIII, 1918, pp. 49-75 (supports Furtwängler in assigning Capitol type to Kresilas, Berlin type to Polykleitos, Mattei type to Pheidias). Anti (*Mon. Ant.*, XXVI, 1920, 600-627) follows Bulle in assigning the Capitol type to Pheidias, the Mattei type to Kresilas, the Berlin type to Polykleitos. Klein, in *Jh. Oest. Arch. I.*, XVIII, 1915, pp. 17-39, announced the discovery of a head for the Mattei type, but the head appears to be too small; it is rejected by Bieber, article cited, p. 73, note 2. Its lack of correspondence with the Loukou caryatid (Bieber, p. 74, fig. 15) would not be too serious if the case for it were strong otherwise. Recently a figure said to represent the Mattei type has been found with a head of the Capitol type which apparently belonged to it (Sogliano, in Μουσεῖον, II, 1924, pp. 1-9).

atrical conception would also be unexpected in Polykleitos. (3) The Doria-Pamphili Amazon (Plate 3,
A),[101] attributed by several scholars to Phradmon, resembles the Berlin type in posture and the treatment of
the garment so closely that there must be some close relation between them. A stylistic comparison places it
entirely beyond question that the Doria-Pamphili type
is the older of the two. The theory more or less
frankly proposed by some scholars, that Phradmon was
a stupid and unprogressive fellow and hence, in imitating the Polykleitan Amazon, made a figure of distinctly more archaic style, is almost laughable. The
imitation was certainly the other way about, and it is
improbable that Polykleitos imitated anybody. There
is also a decided resemblance between the Capitol (Plate
3, C) and Berlin Amazons, and here again it is clear
that the Berlin type is the later one: the very genuine
and expressive arms of the Capitol type are altered, by
relatively slight formal changes, into the almost ab-
surdly unfunctional arms of the Berlin type. Is it credible that the Amazon of Polykleitos was a fusion of two
earlier types, with changes which made it inferior, except in purely formal beauty, to both its predecessors?
(4) The abundance of copies is to be explained, as in
the case of numerous Hellenistic Aphrodites and
nymphs, by the generous display of the female body.
This is very much more conspicuous in the Berlin type
than in the other two. (5) The Capitol type resembles the male athletes of Polykleitos as much as would
be expected in view of the difference in subject.

Doubt is justified, but the better conclusion seems
at present to be that of Mahler and Klein: that the
Berlin type is not derived directly from Polykleitos
but from a later and lesser artist who was strongly
influenced by him in matters of form. The leaning

[101] Brunn-Bruckmann, 688-689, with references; Furtwängler, *Masterpieces,* p. 129.

positibn may be due to the direct influence of Praxiteles. The fourth century Argive, Phradmon, is clearly the right man. Noack's attribution to Strongylion seems singularly perverse: there is no reason to expect in him such strong Polykleitan influence; there is no reason to believe that his Amazon was in Ephesos, while the relief found there is strong evidence that the original of the Berlin type stood in the city; and the legs of the Berlin Amazon are a distress to the cultivated eye.

Klein would ascribe to Phradmon the Sisyphos I of the Daochos group.[102] There is a resemblance in position between that figure and the Amazon, and they represent the same general stylistic tendency; but the relation is not close enough to justify attributing the Sisyphos to Phradmon. The most widely copied type which represents this mixture of Polykleitan form with Praxitelean(?) languor is the "Narkissos."[103] Those who wish to keep the Berlin Amazon for Polykleitos would do well to ascribe the Narkissos to him also, but in fact it is usually assigned to his following. Perhaps Phradmon made it, though the head of the "Narkissos" is hardly so Polykleitan as that of the Amazon.

Of the many sculptors who have been named in this chapter, three are known to us through Roman copies from their works: these are Naukydes, Daidalos, and Phradmon. No existing work can be brought into definite connection with any other Peloponnesian sculptor between Polykleitos and Lysippos. There are however several bronzes which in all probability were made by Peloponnesians of that period, and it will not be out of place to consider some of them.

A bronze head of a youth, supposed to have been

[102] Gesch. d. griech. Kunst, II, pp. 339-341. For references on the Sisyphos see infra, p. 00.

[103] Bieber, Die antiken Skulpturen und Bronzen in Cassel, pp. 13 f., no. 11, with references. A good torso of this type was for sale in New York in 1924.

found at Beneventum and now in the Louvre,[104] is a
Greek work of high excellence. Around the hair there
is a very simple garland of wild olive, indicating that
the head belonged to the statue of an Olympic victor.
Behind the garland the hair is represented by flat,
wavy wisps which are very like the hair of the Doryphoros. In front of the garland, however, the locks
are swelling and luxuriant. A difference so decided
must be termed artificial, and one would expect it in
the following of the formalist Polykleitos rather than
in Attic work, though no sure Polykleitan head shows
a closely similar treatment of the hair about the face.
The head is more domed than the head of the Doryphoros, but the head of the Diadoumenos is domed; the
Beneventum head, however, appears to be shorter, from
front to back, than any Polykleitan head. The forms
of the face are distinctly Polykleitan, though the head
is both more charming and nobler than any head
known to be derived from Polykleitos. This is no
doubt partly the difference between copies and an
original. In profile view the head distinctly suggests
the head of the Lemnian Athena; but there is not much
similarity between the two in details; not even in the
mouth. This feature is quite individual, and is to be
regarded as taken from life. The workmanship is not
fine, i.e. delicate, in the highest degree, as is seen in a
comparison with the bronze head in Munich; but that
is not to say that the Beneventum head is inferior. It
indeed deserves second place, at worst, among the
antique heads that are left to us.

It is usual to regard the head as a work of the
Polykleitan school, with Attic influence; Bulle finds

[104] De Ridder, *Les Bronzes Antiques du Louvre*, no. 4, p. 8, pl. I;
Handbook of the same title, fig. 26; Brunn-Bruckmann, 324; Bulle,
*Der schöne Mensch*², pl. 206; Von Mach, *University Prints*, 481; Reinach,
Recueil, pl. 72, p. 58; Mahler, *Polyklet*, p. 130. Fullest discussion:
Michon, in *Mon. Piot*, I, 1894, pp. 77 ff., with plates X-XI: Furtwäng-
ler, *Masterpieces*, pp. 290 f., *Meisterwerke*, p. 507; Hyde, *OVM*, p. 63;
Waldmann, *Griechische Originale*, fig. 119.

the Attic strain predominant. I see nothing in the head that can reasonably be termed Attic rather than Argive, and the Polykleitan character is very strong. The artist who made it, in the neighborhood of 400 B.C., must have been among the most worthy successors of the master.

Before the discovery of the Charioteer at Delphi, the "Idolino" of the Museo Archeologico in Florence[105] was usually reckoned the finest antique bronze statue known, and even now it probably holds second place. It represents a slender boy, who held a phiale or similar dish in the right hand; the left hand was probably empty. The weight rests entirely on the right leg, as is evident from the strong projection of the right hip; the left foot is set a considerable distance to the side and somewhat advanced. The head looks toward the phiale and the "Standbein." The chiastic scheme usual in Polykleitan works is therefore conspicuously absent, but the rhythm of line in the Idolino is considered very beautiful by most observers. A statue of Hermes found at Cyrene[106] represents an original resembling the Idolino in posture, but with the legs reversed, and the resultant rhythm more in the style of Polykleitos. It seems probable that the Idolino was a modification of this original; though it is not impossible that the imitation was in the other direction, and that the artist of the Hermes tried to make a conventional Polykleitan figure out of the production of a more independent sculptor.

[105] Waldhauer, *Lisipp*, fig. 2; Reinach, *Répertoire*, II 588, 2; Milani, *Museo Archeologico*, p. 173, pl. CXLIII; Amelung, *Führer durch Florenz*, no. 268; Brunn-Bruckmann, 274-277; Bulle, pls. 52-53 and 204-205; Von Mach, *University Prints*, 123; Hyde, *OVM*, pp. 141-143, with additional references; Waldmann, *Griechische Originale*, figs. 89 f.; Lippold, *Kopien und Umbildungen*, pp. 125 f. Copy of the head in the magazines of the Vatican: *Arch. Anz.*, 1921, col. 262; *Illustrated London News*, Sept. 9, 1922, p. 380, fig. 14. According to Milani the arms are an antique restoration.

[106] *Cron. B.A.* (*Sup. Boll. d'Arte*), XII, 1918, pp. 29 f.; *A.J.A.*, XXIII, 1919, p. 319; cf. Hyde, *l.c.*

The Idolino has always been regarded as an original, but Lippold now questions this, thinking it improbable that an original of sufficient celebrity to be copied would be found in an unimportant place such as Pesaro. It seems quite possible, however, that wealthy men of taste might have lived there. A copy of a bronze could be mechanically accurate except for the final treatment which, in either original or copy, would be given after the casting; but in this final treatment the hand of the master would be as evident as in any other point, and it is difficult to believe that a masterpiece of craftsmanship such as the Idolino is not an original in the fullest sense.

A technical masterpiece in bronze, representing a nude youth, is likely to come from a school of specialists in bronze and in athletic sculpture: that is to say, from the school or schools of Argos and Sikyon. This assumption is strengthened by a consideration of the head and treatment of the hair, in which Polykleitan character is evident. The posture, as has been seen, and the treatment of the body show a style which is not Polykleitan, and scholars have usually regarded this second influence as Attic, though Furtwängler[107] explained the statue as the work of an artist who continued the traditions of the old Argive school with only moderate influence from Polykleitos. It is in the first place impossible, and in the second place unimportant, to ascertain the exact influences which contributed to the formation of the style of this artist; but it is worth while, for our subject, to note that a sculptor working in the later years of Polykleitos or soon thereafter, and making a statue of the sort in which Polykleitos was particularly expert, and indeed showing clear Polykleitan influence, shows also complete independence of the master in more important respects. We can not be sure that this artist was a

[107] *Masterpieces,* p. 286 (*Meisterwerke,* p. 500).

Peloponnesian; an Attic relief[108] contains a figure of Herakles which seems probably to be imitated from the Idolino, and this is sound, though not conclusive, evidence that the statue stood in Attica. One can not infer, however, that the Idolino is a Herakles; it is in all probability a youthful athlete. The head, which has no nobility and little charm, is a portrait, if this term is properly applied to the Perikles of Kresilas.

A bronze head in Munich[109] represents a boy of perhaps fourteen years. The fillet in the hair indicates that it is an athletic victor; the swollen ear, that the victory was won in boxing or the pankration. Boyish charm has seldom if ever been better expressed in sculpture, and in technical excellence the head ranks very high. In delicacy of treatment it is comparable with the Hermes of Praxiteles. We are reminded that the skill of Polykleitos was effective particularly when "the clay came to the nail," when the final touches were given to the model. As a part of a bronze statue of an athletic victor, the head is likely to be Peloponnesian work, and it has usually been so regarded; but it is difficult to find in it tangible traces of Polykleitan style.

Several works of similar style have been noted. Furtwängler[110] mentioned a head in the Museo Chiaramonti of the Vatican[111] as copied either from the Munich head or from an analogous work by the same artist; Amelung describes it merely as closely related to the Munich head, and it has not appeared in recent

---

[108] Svoronos, Τὸ Ἐθνικὸν Μουσεῖον, II, pls. CI, CXXI, no. 2723, pp. 378-416; Stais, *Marbres et Bronzes*, pp. 240-242; cf. Hyde, *OVM*, p. 142.

[109] Furtwängler-Wolters, *Beschr. d. Glypt.*, pp. 398 f., no. 457; Brunn-Bruckmann, pl. 8; Bulle, *Der Schöne Mensch*², pl. 207; Friederichs-Wolters, no. 216; Furtwängler, *Masterpieces*, p. 291 (*Meisterwerke*, p. 507); Hyde, *OVM*, p. 63, with citations; Waldmann, *Griechische Originale*, fig. 120; Lippold, *Kopien und Umbildungen*, pp. 124 f. and 257 f., note 6; Brunn-Bruckmann, pl. 699, with text by Sieveking; fig. 4 in the text shows the back of the head.

[110] *Masterpieces* and *Meisterwerke, l.c.*

[111] Amelung, *D. Skulpt. d. Vat. Mus.*, I, p. 624, no. 475, pl. 66.

discussions. A statue in green basalt in the Museo Nazionale at Rome[112] has been regarded by many scholars as closely related to the Munich head, though no one has suggested that it is copied from it. The statue represents a boy victor with an olive wreath around his head. Hauser thought the similarity in style sufficient to indicate that this statue was copied from a work of the artist who made the head at Munich; he suggested Kallikles of Megara, and found in the records definite names for both of the boy victors. Anti does not think that so definite a connection between the two works can be assumed;[113] but around the basalt statue he assembles a group of sculptures which are, he thinks, very similar to it, and argues ingeniously for an attribution to Lýkios, the son of Myron. The basalt statue would be a copy of the statue of Autolykos, who won the pankration for boys in the Panathenaic games in 422. Pliny mentions this statue and assigns it, as the text stands, to Leochares; but it had been suggested previously that the true author was probably Lykios. An obvious objection to this theory is found in the fact that an olive wreath, such as is worn by the youth, is not known to have been given as prize at the Panathenaic games: it is the token of victory at Olympia. Besides, it appears that the basalt statue is more closely related to the Munich head than to the other members of the "Lykios" group. Those two works may well be derived from one artist, and Lippold may well be right in suggesting that a head in the Lateran is copied from another work by him.[114]

[112] Paribeni, *Mus. Naz. Rom.*[4], p. 207, no. 498; Helbig, *Führer*[3], II, p. 156, no. 1364; Hauser in *Röm. Mitt.*, X, 1895, pp. 97-119 and pl. I; Brunn-Bruckmann, pl. 700, with text by Sieveking. The head: *B. Com. Rom.*, XLVII, 1919, pl. VI; figs. 4-6 in text to Brunn-Bruckmann, pl. 700.

[113] *B. Com. Rom.*, XLVII, 1919, pp. 59-62.

[114] *Op. cit.*, p. 257, note 6.

A head in black basalt,[115] also in the Museo Nazionale at Rome, is treated by Furtwängler, Bulle, and Amelung as related to the Munich head and the basalt statue in the same way that they are related to each other. Schrader[116] found a great difference between the Munich head and basalt statue on the one hand and the basalt head on the other, and regarded the latter as an example of a type known in several other copies and ascribed by Schrader at that time to Pheidias. It was certainly an error to assign the basalt head to that type; but to separate it from the other two works seems to. be right, though it has not found general acceptance.[117] The similarity of the basalt head to the other two lies principally in time and subject.

According to Lippold a real copy of the Munich head exists at Frankfurt.[118] From this he reasons, as in the case of the Idolino, that the head is not an original but a careful copy made with mechanical accuracy, which would have the same relation to the original that the "galvanoplastic" reproductions of the Munich head have to it. This hypothesis draws some support from the condition in which the bronze was found. The head and neck, in one piece, and the genitals reached Germany. According to report the statue was found complete, but the rest of it was destroyed by the ignorant discoverers. *A priori,*

---

[115] Paribeni, *Mus. Naz. Rom.*⁴, p. 207, no. 499; Helbig, *Führer*³, II, p. 158, no. 1365; figs. 1-3 in text to Brunn-Bruckmann, pl. 700; Paribeni in *B. Com. Rom.*, XXXVIII, 1910, pp. 42-48, pls. III-IV (suggests Daidalos as author).

[116] *Jh. Oest. Arch. I.*, XIV, 1911, pp. 70-74. Apparently neither the basalt head nor the type to which he assigned it is mentioned in Schrader's *Pheidias.*

[117] Anti (article cited, p. 63) agrees. Sieveking (text to Brunn-Bruckmann, pl. 700) assumes one original for the two works in basalt.

[118] Published by Sieveking in text to Brunn-Bruckmann, 699, figs. 1-3, and treated as a sure copy. The arrangement of the hair on the back of the Munich head is so individual that a satisfactory correspondence in this respect would prove derivation from a common original. It may be assumed that such a correspondence exists, though it is not clearly evident in the illustrations.

this is improbable in the extreme; and according to Lippold there was another tradition, according to which no other parts were found. If this is so, obviously it was a herm; and Lippold argues that the original work certainly was not a herm. It is possible, however, that the statue met with some injury which affected the body and not the head, and that then the head was set on a herm. This external evidence is at all events not sufficient to overcome the presumption, founded on the extraordinary quality of the head, that it is a Greek original.

A bronze statue in Vienna (Plate 4),[119] representing an athlete in prayer, is a copy from a work of the late fifth or early fourth century. The posture resembles that of the Idolino: the right leg is the "Standbein," the right arm is raised, and the head is turned to the right. The left leg, however, is not set at the side, but drawn back in approximately the position of the Doryphoros, with the result that the deviation from Polykleitan style is much less marked. The treatment of the body is also more in the Polykleitan manner, though the original of this statue must have been considerably later than the Idolino, and the head is more purely Polykleitan than any other head that is not supposed to be derived from the master himself. Furtwängler tentatively ascribed the original of this statue, as well as the Idolino, to Patrokles; but it seems improbable that the two are derived from one sculptor.

In the Antiquarium at Munich there is a splendid bronze statuette of Zeus or Poseidon.[120] The right

[119] *Jb. d. Sammlungen*, XV, 1894, pp. 103-124 (R. von Schneider) with fine illustrations; Klein, *Gesch. d. griech. Kunst*, II, pp. 341 f. and *Jh. Oest. Arch. I.*, XIII, 1910, pp. 140-143; Von Sacken, *Die ant. Bronzen*, pls. XXI-XXII, pp. 52 f.; Friederichs-Wolters, no. 1562; Brunn-Bruckmann, 325; Furtwängler, *Masterpieces*, p. 290 (*Meisterwerke*, pp. 506 f.); Hyde, *OVM*, p. 131.

[120] Bulle, *Der schöne Mensch*², pl. 59, col. 113; Bulle in Roscher, *Lexikon*, III, col. 2885; Friederichs-Wolters, no. 1750; Furtwängler, *Masterpieces*, p. 299 (*Meisterwerke*, p. 519); Baumeister, *Denkmäler*, II, col. 1393.

hand is new. The position is for the most part that of the Idolino, but the weight is not so completely borne by the right leg, and the position in general is more stable and dignified, as the subject demands. The left arm is raised and the hand held a long sceptre or trident; this of course strengthens the left side and makes the general effect quite unlike that of the Idolino. The hair and beard are heavy and give grandeur to the head.

It may not be out of place to mention here the Zeus in Blundell Hall.[121] It is a fine copy from an original that must have been about contemporary with the Munich bronze statuette. The general position is similar to that of the bronze, but the left leg is drawn back slightly and the head looks straight forward. The body is distinctly less elastic than in the bronze: in this case the original was not made by an artist who was trained in the portrayal of athletes. The head, if not grander or more impressive than that of the bronze, is nobler and more spiritual; if the illustration is not deceptive, it foreshadows the Asklepios of Melos as well as the Zeus of Otricoli. There is an effective "mane" and altogether the head is admirable. Furtwängler suggests Kephisodotos as the author of this type, and that is reasonable enough. Certainly the Blundell Zeus belongs to an artistic current quite different from that of the Munich bronze, which may represent for us the Peloponnesian school of about 375. One might imagine Antiphanes as the sculptor of the bronze.

So much for the idea that we can form of the Peloponnesian successors of Polykleitos. They were not, even the earlier of them, slavish followers of that master, but they made no vital innovations. If we had a number of original works from their hands, we could distinguish the productions of one from those of another by minute study, but we should probably find small differences in ideal or general style.

[121] Reinach, *Répertoire*, I 184, 4; Furtwängler, *Ueber Statuenkopieen im Alterthum* (*Abh. Bayer. Akad. Wiss.*, XX, 1896), pp. 551-555, pls. I and III, 1.

CHAPTER II

Euphranor and Skopas

Euphranor is called "Isthmian" *(Isthmius)* by Pliny[1] and it is usually assumed for this reason that he was a Corinthian. Plutarch, however, calls him an Athenian,[2] and certainly not by mere oversight, for the writer is enumerating Athenians whose achievements brought glory to the city. The scholiast on Juvenal, *Satires* III 17, also speaks of him as an Athenian;[3] but he speaks in the same way of Polykleitos, which disposes of him as an authority. The two signatures of his son Sostratos were found in Attica[4] and Euphranor surely worked in Athens a good deal. Three of his four known paintings were in Athens, the fourth in Ephesos. One of his fourteen known statues is said to have been in Athens; another, Bonus Eventus or Triptolemos, was undoubtedly in Attica, to judge from the subject. Antidotos, the only pupil concerning whom we have any details, is said to have worked at Athens, and Nikias of Athens was pupil of Antidotos.

There was no distinct Corinthian community which went by the name "Isthmus"; the Isthmian sanctuary of course had no citizenry. "Isthmian" then, if connected with Corinth at all, would mean a citizen of a village on the isthmus—which would have a name of its own—or simply of Corinthian territory, in which case it would be an unexpected synonym for "Corinthian." Probably Euphranor was born in some town named, or at least called, Isthmus. Halikarnassos, or possibly a part of it, was so called, according to Stephanos Byzantios, and so was a town in Kos.[5] It is just

[1] *N. H.*, XXXV 128 (*SQ* 1786).   [2] *De Glor. Athen.*, 2 (*SQ* 1109).
[3] *SQ* 1789.   [4] Loewy, *Insch. griech. Bildh.*, 105 and 106.
[5] See Pauly-Wissowa, v. Isthmos, nos. 5-7.

possible that "Isthmian" was a sort of surname, given because the artist had some famous work in the Isthmian sanctuary. At all events our evidence indicates that he was to all intents and purposes an Athenian.

For the chronology of his life we have the statement of Pliny that he flourished in the 104th Olympiad (364-361).[6] This is doubtless drawn from the fact that he painted a representation of a cavalry fight at the battle of Mantineia,[7] which took place in 362. Certainly, Euphranor was not a beginner when he received this commission; but neither was he approaching the end of his career, for some twenty-five years later he made statues of Alexander and Philip in quadrigas.[8] Pliny's brevity leaves us in doubt whether the two works belonged together, but this is probable. At any rate the Alexander would hardly be much earlier than 340, since Alexander was born in 356, and Philip's death in 336 furnishes an almost certain *terminus ante quem*. Euphranor's "Valor and Greece, both colossal"[9] obviously made a Panhellenic monument, which would almost certainly be due to Philip;[10] it was very probably set up just after the congress of Corinth, in 338, at which Philip was chosen leader of united Hellas for the projected attack on Persia. Where? Doubtless at some great Panhellenic center, and not at Olympia, since the Philippeion was erected there at the same time.[11] Perhaps at Delphi; more likely at the Isthmian sanctuary, since the congress was held at Corinth. Hence, possibly, "Euphranor Isthmius." With one work dated 362 and two about 337, we have a good idea of the artist's period of production: we may suppose that he was born between 400 and 390.

[6] *N.H.*, XXXIV 50 (*SQ* 1787).   [7] Pausanias, I 3, 4 (*SQ* 1791).
[8] Pliny, *N.H.*, XXXIV 78 (*SQ* 1798).   [9] *Ibid.*
[10] This is suggested by Klein, *Gesch. d. griech. Kunst*, II, p. 322.
[11] Pausanias, V 20, 9-10.

As has already appeared, Euphranor was both a sculptor and a painter. We find mention of more sculptures than paintings from his hand; but the paintings are much more fully described in the literature that remains to us, and he seems to have been discussed as a painter more than as a sculptor in the sources of Pliny. Only painters are mentioned as his pupils, and his only recorded master was Aristeides of Thebes, who was a great painter and an obscure sculptor if he was a sculptor at all. It seems likely then that painting was the art in which Euphranor specialized; yet his commissions from Philip show that he was considered a sculptor of the first rank. He was especially noted for his versatility.[12] He wrote books on color and on proportion *(symmetria)*. His theories of proportion are reflected in the criticism preserved in Pliny, to the effect that his heads and limbs were too large, his bodies too slender (*fuit in universitate corporum exilior et capitibus articulisque grandior*).[13] His expression of the majesty of heroes *(dignitates heroum)* won commendation.[14] In view especially of his interest in proportion, it is highly probable that Euphranor had some influence on the development of Lysippos, some twenty years his junior.

Among his works there is at least one of which we might expect to recognize a copy, if it be at all well preserved: the "Leto holding in her arms the newborn infants Apollo and Artemis" (*Latona puerpera Apollinem et Dianam infantis sustinens in aede Concordiae*).[15] We have two copies of a group representing this subject[16] and several coin-types seem to be de-

[12] Quintilian, *Inst. Orat.*, XII, 10, 6 (*SQ* 1788).

[13] *N.H.*, XXXV 128 (*SQ* 1802).

[14] *Ibid.*

[15] Pliny, *N.H.*, XXXIV 77 (*SQ* 1798).

[16] Reinach, *Répertoire*, II 417, 6-7; Overbeck, *Gesch. d. griech. Plastik*⁴, II, p. 117; Helbig, *Führer*³, no. 982; Jones, *Palazzo dei Conservatori*, p. 227, no. 31, pl. 85; Mahler, in *R. Arch.*, VIII, 1906, pp. 290-296, discusses the type and ascribes it to the older Praxiteles.

rived from the same original. The subject is not a
common one and the attribution to Euphranor was
very natural. It has been almost abandoned in recent
years, however, because the style of the existing
groups seems too old. They are not really archaic, as
a comparison with the Copenhagen Niobid,[17] whose
position is similar, will show; but 430 is a more reasonable date for them than 360. Of course Euphranor
might have been influenced by an older type, and the
attribution to him is not impossible, but it must be considered improbable. It has been suggested also that
the existing groups are derived from a bronze group
at Delphi which is mentioned by Klearchos of Soloi;[18]
but one gathers that in that group Leto held only
Apollo in her arms. Aside from this, there is nothing
to show that it is not Euphranor's work which is
mentioned by Klearchos.

The Paris of Euphranor seems to have been one
of his most celebrated creations. In it could be per-
ceived at once the judge of the goddesses, the lover of
Helen, and the slayer of Achilles (*omnia simul intel-
liguntur, iudex dearum, amator Helenae et tamen
Achillis interfector*).[19] Figures of Paris are ordinarily recognizable by their Phrygian garb. A figure
wearing the Phrygian cap, represented by many copies
and variants, has been identified by Furtwängler as
the work of Euphranor.[20] But this type is as unlikely
as any statue in existence to call forth the praise quoted
by Pliny: only the most prejudiced eye could see in it
the judge of the goddesses or the slayer of Achilles,
and surely no eye whatever could see the lover of fair-

---

[17] *De antike Kunstvaerker*, no. 398; Von Mach, *University Prints*, no.
109; Reinach, *Répertoire*, II 419, 2.

[18] *Frag. Hist. Graec.*, II, p. 318, no. 46.

[19] Pliny, *N.H.*, XXXIV 77 (*SQ* 1798).

[20] Helbig, *Führer³*, I, no. 369, with citations; Bieber, *Die antiken
Skulpturen in Cassel*, p. 22, no. 26. A new example in Granada: *R.
Arch.*, XVII, 1923, pp. 325-328 (Paris).

haired Helen.   It is altogether probable that the figure
is not Paris at all, but Ganymede.

A seated statue in the Galleria delle Statue of the
Vatican,[21] in Phrygian costume, is very generally regarded as Paris, though the apple in his hand is a
restoration. This has been ascribed to Euphranor by
Amelung and others and the ascription is not impossible; the proportions agree pretty well with those said
to have been used by the sculptor. Yet Miss Bieber's
opinion, that the statue is Hellenistic, is naturally suggested by its appearance; and in its original condition[22]
it must have resembled the original of the seated
Hermes in Naples so distinctly as to suggest strongly
that it was imitated from it, which would hardly have
been true of Euphranor's Paris.   Robert[23] would
identify the "Ares Borghese"[24] in the Louvre as the
Paris of Euphranor. This has never been accepted by
anybody, so far as I know. The "Ares" is in all probability a real Ares belonging to the fifth century.

The famous bronze statue from the Antikythera
wreck (Plate 5)[25] has been identified as the Paris of
Euphranor by Stais[26] and Miss Bieber.[27] The figure is
nude like a Greek athlete, but the identification as Paris
is nevertheless almost sure. The youth, standing quietly,
is holding forth in one hand an object of some significance—otherwise his posture would be ridiculous—
and small and light; lighter than the head of Medusa,
though that is the second best suggestion that has been

[21] Amelung, *Skulpt. d. Vat. Mus.*, II, p. 422, no. 255, pl. 47; Helbig,
Führer,I, no. 186; *Jb. Arch. I.*, XXIV, 1909, pp. 20 f. (Six); *Jb. Arch.
I.*, XXV, 1910, p. 165 (Bieber).

[22] For comments on the restoration see Amelung, *l.c.*

[23] XIX *Hallisches Winckelmannsprogramm*, 1895, pp. 21-29.

[24] Brunn-Bruckmann, 63; Von Mach, *University Prints*, 125; Fried-
ericks-Wolters, 1298.

[25] Hyde, *OVM*, pp. 80 ff., with references; 'Εφ. 'Αρχ., 1902, pls.
VII-XII.

[26] *Marbres et Bronzes du Musée National*, 255.

[27] Article cited, pp. 164-168.

made. An apple fulfils the conditions ideally and it seems that nothing else does. (For a recent suggestion see the *Journal of Hellenic Studies*, XLIII, 1923, pp. 142 f.; although it is sponsored by an eminent scholar, one can not easily read it without laughing aloud.) The figure seems also to belong in origin to the time of Euphranor: even if the statue itself is Hellenistic—it may well be—it doubtless reflects an earlier type. It might easily have received the triple praise accorded to Euphranor's work, especially if we restore a bow in the left hand as we reasonably may; and it might well proceed from an artist who expressed the nobility of heroes with eminent success. But can the proportions of Euphranor, as reported to us, be found in the statue? None too well, it must be admitted. It may be that the restoration is to blame;[28] or it may be that since these proportions, which apparently ought to be so easily recognizable, do not in fact enable us to find any of Euphranor's works, we are justified in forgetting about them; for it is a virtual certainty that some of his works are preserved. At all events the Paris of Euphranor is more plausibly found in the Antikythera statue than in any other.

It has been suggested[29] that the Alexander Rondanini (Plates 6 and 7)[30] in Munich may be copied from Euphranor. In this statue Alexander is a youth of sixteen or eighteen. He is in an unusual position for a portrait: the right leg is raised and the foot is set on an ele-

[28] So Miss Bieber, p. 167. For bitter comments on the restoration see Von Mach, *Handbook*, pp. 319 f.

[29] Amelung, in *R. Arch.*, IV, 1904, pp. 375 ff.; Six, in *Jb. Arch. I.*, XXIV, 1909, pp. 17-20.

[30] Furtwängler-Wolters, *Besch. d. Glypt.*, no. 298; Arndt-Bruckmann, 183-185; Brunn-Bruckmann, 105; Furtwängler-Urlichs, pl. 54; Von Mach, *University Prints*, no. 399; Koepp, *Ueber das Bildniss Alexanders des Grossen*, pp. 16 ff., with fig. and pl. II; Ujfalvy, *Le type physique d'Alexandre le Grand*, pls. 10-11, pp. 84-88; Schreiber, *Studien über das Bildniss Alexanders des Grossen*, pp. 82 f., 208, 272 ff. (questions the identification); Bernoulli, *Die erhaltene Darstellungen Alexanders des Grossen*, pp. 44 ff., fig. 10, pl. V.

vation. The right leg is nearly all new, but enough of the hip is antique to show the raised position. The arms also are new except just below the shoulders, and the restoration of them is uncertain; one can say confidently that the existing restoration, in which the prince anoints his leg with oil, is wrong.

Some justification for the posture should be found.[31] We know that Euphranor made a statue of Alexander, that in all probability it was made in the early youth of the prince, and that he was represented "in a chariot." The beautiful statue in the Palazzo dei Conservatori, as well as numerous vase-paintings, suggest that the Rondanini figure is to be understood as mounting a chariot. This view is not usually accepted, even by those who ascribe the statue to Euphranor; and it is true that the right leg of a figure mounting a chariot ought to be raised higher than it is in this figure. But the copyist, who could not be expected to reproduce the chariot and horses, might naturally make a slight modification which would render the posture less extraordinary. It is generally and rightly recognized that the statue shows no trace of Lysippian style; it can not have belonged to the group by Leochares in the Philippeion, since that figure was simply standing; and it corresponds in all respects to a natural idea of Euphranor's statue. Even the proportions agree tolerably well with those said to have been used by Euphranor, though this matters little in a portrait. The artistic merit of the figure has been considerably overestimated by some critics: the head is better than the body, as would be expected from an artist who specialized in nobility and made no figures of athletes.

Pliny says that Euphranor made a "woman in wonder and prayer" (*mulierem admirantem et adoran-*

---

[31] It should be mentioned that a bronze statuette in the British Museum (Walters, *Select Bronzes,* pl. 60) has one foot raised and is identified as Alexander. But it is surely not copied directly from an original of the fourth century.

tem),[32] Praying persons of uncertain gender are ascribed to Sthennis,[33] who belongs to the second half of the fourth century, but Euphranor is the only sculptor distinctly credited with a praying woman. The Greek attitude of prayer is well known to us and is unmistakably exemplified in a feminine type preserved in at least eight copies.[34] Only one copy is believed to have its own head and that is a portrait, so we have no clue to the head of the Greek original. The weight rests on the left leg; the right foot is set to the side and, at least in some copies, rests only on the ball of the foot. Partly as a result of this the figure has a certain elasticity and alertness which contrast equally with the quiet grandeur of the fifth century and with the graceful ease of Praxiteles. It also helps to make the epithet "admirans" intelligible: the posture of the figure, if not known to be one of prayer, would probably be taken to indicate astonishment. The treatment of drapery is decidedly effective and in my judgment is altogether favorable to an attribution to the time of Euphranor: the lower part of the figure would suggest a period later than Euphranor at least as much as one earlier than he. There is truth in Hekler's observation that "die ganze Figur wie gezeichnet erscheint," which of course strengthens an attribution to a sculptor who was also a painter. The forms of the body are visible through the garment well enough to enable us to judge the proportions fairly well, and they agree with those said to have been used by Euphranor. This attribution, due to Hekler, has every probability in its favor.

Here our account of Euphranor may close. Various scholars have published reconstructions of his

---

[32] *N.H.*, XXXIV 78 (*SQ* 1798).

[33] Pliny, *N.H.*, XXXIV 90 (*SQ* 1347).

[34] Hekler, *Römische weibliche Gewandstatuen*, pp. 134-137 and figs. 5-7; Reinach, *Répertoire*, I 133, 5; 208, 2; 565, 4; II 654, 2; 655, 1; Helbig, *Führer*[3], I, p. 155, no. 241, where Amelung denies the attribution to Euphranor and assigns the type to the end of the fifth century.

work.[35] None of them is convincing in regard to the unity of the groups of works which they include, to say nothing of the attribution of such groups to Euphranor. No thorough study of the affinities of the praying woman has yet been made: such a study might have solid results, especially if the head could be discovered. At present Euphranor is sadly intangible.

There is no literary evidence that would lead us to expect any sort of connection between Lysippos and Skopas of Paros.[36] Modern investigators, however, have found it difficult to distinguish the works of the two artists, and one can hardly deal with Lysippos before forming some notion of the great Parian. To treat Skopas exhaustively would be to double the size of this book and is unnecessary for our purpose, since there is general agreement on the broad characteristics of his style and on several works which illustrate it.

Born in the island of Paros, famous for its marble but not for its sculptors,[37] Skopas studied with no eminent artist, so far as we are informed. An Aristandros of Paros,[38] however, collaborated with Polykleitos (one or the other) in a group dedicated at Amyklai after the battle of Aigospotamoi in 405; and another Parian, Aristandros son of Skopas,[39] was active in Delos in the neighborhood of 100 B. C. In view of the frequent recurrence of names and professions in Greek families, it is usually and reasonably assumed that these four sculptors all belonged to one family and that

[35]Furtwängler, *Masterpieces*, pp. 348 ff.; Amelung, in *R. Arch.*, IV, 1904, pp. 325-347; Six, in *Jb. Arch. I.*, XXIV, 1909, pp. 7-27; Bieber, in *Jb. Arch. I.*, XXV, 1910, pp. 159-173; Willers, *Studien zur griechischen Kunst*, pp. 93 ff.

[36] *SQ* 1149-1189; Urlichs, *Skopas' Leben und Werke* (1863); Collignon, *Scopas et Praxitèle* (1907); Neugebauer, *Studien über Skopas* (1913); Berchmans, in *Mélanges Holleaux* (1913), pp. 17-41.

[37] The existence of an important school there has been suspected. Furtwängler assigned to it the sculptures of the temple of Zeus at Olympia, Schrader several of the maidens of the Acropolis.

[38] Pausanias, III 18, 8 (*SQ* 942).   [39] Loewy, 287-288.

the great Skopas was the son of the first Aristandros and doubtless his pupil. We can not guess under what influence the style of Aristandros was formed nor how old he was in 405. Skopas may have been born about 420, the date which is given by Pliny for his *floruit*. The only sure date in his career is 352-351, when he worked on the sculptures of the Mausoleum.

Pausanias tells us that Skopas was the architect of the temple of Athena Alea at Tegea in Arcadia.[40] The old temple was burned in 395. It may be assumed that Pausanias, who evidently found the local authorities willing to answer his questions, would have given a date for the new temple if there had been any considerable delay in building it. On the other hand a thorough study of the remains of the temple has led the French scholars to suggest 360-330 as the period within which it was built.[41] Hook clamps are used (as they are, however, in the tholos at Delphi, which was probably built very early in the fourth century), and in many features the temple resembles the tholos at Epidauros. Clemmensen has noted also close resemblances between the Tegea temple and the temple at Nemea,[42] and has concluded that Skopas is the architect of the latter edifice also; he thinks that there can be no great difference in date, though the Tegea temple was probably built first. This conclusion, if sound, must render us still more reluctant to accept the traditional date for the Tegea temple, because the temple at Nemea has always been regarded as later than any other Doric temple in Greece. One finds however that the Tegea temple is not so wide in proportion to its length, and that its columns are not so slender (though Clemmensen suggests that there may have been a mistake in calculating the height of the columns at

[40] VIII 45, 4-5.

[41] Dugas, Berchmans, Clemmensen, *Le Sanctuaire d'Aléa Athéna à Tégée*, pp. 127 f.

[42] Clemmensen, in *B.C.H.*, XLIX, 1925, pp. 1-12.

Tegea). These are two of the principal indications of
a late date for the Nemea temple, and it seems possible
that the similarities between the two buildings are the
result of imitation rather than of common authorship,
and that the temple at Nemea is considerably later.
Yet no one, forming his opinion from the remains
alone, would place the temple at Tegea as early as 390.
From the other point of view, since Skopas was still
active in 350 it is not likely that he was very famous in
390; yet the construction of an important temple would
certainly not be entrusted to a beginner. Still 360
seems late, to say nothing of 330.

In glancing over the catalogue of Skopas's works
one is struck by the variety in it. In the first place
by the geographical variety: works by him are recorded at Tegea and Gortys in Arcadia and also in
the two Peloponnesian centers of sculpture, Argos and
Sikyon; there were several in Attica and others in
Megara and Thebes; Samothrace, Chryse in the Troad,
Ephesos, Knidos, and Halikarnassos were embellished
by his talent; and the greatest of all his works, at least
in size, seems to have been made for a temple of
Poseidon in Bithynia. It is usual to assume that the
home of Skopas, for such time as he had one, was
Athens, and this is probably true: his works seem to
have been more concentrated there than in any other
place, and traces of his style are evident in Attic grave-
steles. But his work at Tegea and at other places in
the Peloponnesos was apparently earlier.

More important than the variety in place is the
variety in theme. He made a Herakles, a presumably
nude male hero; a nude Apollo, an Ares, a Dionysos;
Eros, Himeros, and Pothos; an Apollo in long robes;
an Athena, an Artemis, a Hekate, two Furies, a Hestia, maidens carrying baskets; two Aphrodites, one of
them nude, a frenzied Maenad; two groups of Asklepios and Hygieia; a battle scene and a hunting scene

in the gables of the temple at Tegea, and a vast assemblage of marine deities, besides his architectural sculptures at the Mausoleum and the Ephesian temple. So far as we know he never attempted to represent the majesty of Zeus or of Hera and he never made a statue of an athlete, but with these exceptions his range of subjects was as wide as the Greek traditions permitted. He apparently had no special fondness for any type or subject. Polykleitos was a specialist in athletes, Pheidias in Athenas, Praxiteles in feminine charm and youthful male figures, but one can not name the specialty of Skopas. The Hestia and the maidens carrying baskets would presumably be dignified figures of substantially fifth century type; so perhaps the Athena,[43] the Hekate and the Artemis. The two Furies and the Maenad would be full of tempestuous passion and the nude Aphrodite, if not the other, would be primarily sensuous. The list of male figures shows a similarly wide range.

Pausanias was much impressed by the temple at Tegea, as are modern students who can know it only in shattered fragments. All three orders were employed in it and its decoration was rich. Obviously Skopas was an original and brilliant architect. Pausanias does not say that Skopas had anything to do with the sculptures of the temple; but since he was primarily a sculptor, and since the sculptures of the temple that have been found possess a very vigorous and individual style which surely recurs in some of the sculptures of the Mausoleum, it is not questioned

[43] Furtwängler once (*Masterpieces*, pp. 305 f.) assigned the fascinating Athena Rospigliosi to Skopas; later (*Sitz. Bayer. Akad. Wiss.*, 1903, p. 445) he accepted the opinion of Amelung (*Führer durch Florenz*, p. 54; *Ausonia*, III, 1908, pp. 88 f.; he seems less confident in Helbig, *Führer*[3], no. 101) that it is to be attributed to Timotheos. Waldhauer seems to be the only other scholar who has studied the Rospigliosi type carefully, and he (*J.H.S.*, XLIII, 1923, pp. 176-182) would date it about 440; this is incredible. The originality of the conception readily suggests an attribution to Skopas, but the facial type disproves it.

that they are works of Skopas. Indeed they are the fundamental evidence on which our conception of his style is based.

A head of Herakles (Plate 8, B),[44] two helmeted heads (Plate 8, A),[45] and a fourth head[46] are tolerably well preserved. The head is not domed as in Praxitelean sculpture, but is flat on top. The bony structure of the face is emphasized. The head above the ears is broad in proportion to its height, but it narrows rapidly in the lower part of the face; the jaw is not broad, and it again narrows toward the chin. The chin is rectangular rather than curved, but it is not heavy or broad, when considered in comparison with the upper part of the face. The outline of the face is a short oval, which by reason of the slight fleshy padding has almost the appearance of a triangle with a side uppermost and the opposite point somewhat truncated. This relative narrowness of the lower part of the face makes a decided contrast with the broad, fleshy jaw of the apoxyomenos of Lysippos. It ought to be noted that the fourth head from Tegea has a broad and fleshy jaw; but the preponderance of evidence shows that this not the usual Skopaic type.

The eyes were treated in a way altogether unheard of, so far as we can judge, before the time of Skopas,

[44] *B.C.H.*, XXV, 1901, pls. VII-VIII, pp. 258 f.; Gardner, *SGS*, pl. 51; De Ridder and Deonna, *L'Art en Grèce*, pl. 19; Dugas, Berchmans, Clemmensen, *op. cit.*, pls. 99-100, pp. 87 f., no. 7.

[45] One: Dugas, Berchmans, Clemmensen, *op. cit.*, pl. 102, pp. 89 f., no. 9; *Antike Denkmäler*, I, pl. 35; Reinach, *Recueil*, p. 114, pl. 147; Waldmann, *Griechische Originale*, fig. 128; Von Mach, *University Prints*, 469 at right; Collignon, *Scopas et Praxitèle*, fig. 4; Bulle, *Der schöne Mensch²*, pl. 211 at right; Brunn-Bruckmann, 44; Springer-Wolters¹², fig. 610; Neugebauer, *Studien über Skopas*, pls. II and VIII; front view of restored cast in *R. Arch.*, XXXVII, 1900, pl. XVII at left; profile view of restored cast in *Encyclopaedia Britannica*¹¹, article Greek Art, pl. III, fig. 63. The second head: Dugas, Berchmans, Clemmensen, *op. cit.*, pls. 99 and 101, pp. 88 f., no. 8.

[46] Dugas, Berchmans, Clemmensen, *op. cit.*, pl. 102, pp. 91 f., no. 17; *Antike Denkmäler*, I, pl. 35; Collignon, *Scopas et Praxitèle*, fig. 3; Brunn-Bruckmann, 44; Springer-Wolters¹², fig. 609; Neugebauer, *op. cit.*, pl. II; Von Mach, *University Prints*, 469 at left.

and constitute the most conspicuous feature of Skopaic style. They are set far back in their sockets and deeply overshadowed at their outer corners by heavy folds of flesh. The resulting expression is one of passionate intensity. There are few works of art which express, so strongly and so distinctly as these heads, a definite character. They are as far as possible from the serenity and *pondus* of the art of the fifth century. They do not give an impression of intellect, of spiritual dignity, or even of strength; they are the realization in stone of passion in its broadest sense, of the blind will of Schopenhauer.

The style of the Tegea heads has been recognized in a type of Herakles called the Genzano type, which is preserved in many heads.[47] The body that properly belongs with these heads is not definitely determined; but the Skopaic character of the heads is generally, though not quite unanimously, admitted. They differ a good deal among themselves, however; differences in the turn of the head are explained as due to the decorative use in corresponding pairs, but there are differences in style also; and authorities disagree on the boundaries of the list. Ashmole would withdraw from it a head in the Palazzo dei Conservatori, which had been regarded as one of the best examples, but is thought Praxitelean by Ashmole.[48] This appears to be an error: the head does differ somewhat from the others, but many of them show modifications of the Skopaic original in one way or another. On the other hand, it is certainly wrong to regard the Lansdowne Herakles as an example of the Genzano type. The original of the type had a head with good Skopaic eyes and wore an ivy wreath; it is doubtless right to identify it with a standing, beardless Herakles wearing a

[47] Graef, in *Röm. Mitt.*, IV, 1889, pp. 189-216; Preyss, text to Brunn-Bruckmann, 691-692.

[48] *J.H.S.*, XLII, 1922, pp. 242-244; Jones, *Palazzo dei Conservatori*, p. 90, no. 28, pl. 33.

wreath, which appears on Sikyonian coins, and to find
in this figure the Herakles by Skopas which Pausanias
saw in the gymnasium at Sikyon.[49]

A Maenad by Skopas is known from a rhetorical
description by Kallistratos and also from two epigrams.[50] A figure in Dresden[51] was published by
Treu as a copy of the work of Skopas and has been
generally accepted, though classed as Hellenistic by
Loewy[52] and Herrmann. The identification is very
plausible. The Dresden figure corresponds admirably
to the description of Kallistratos and also with our
evidence on the art of Skopas, both in general and in
the morphology of the face. The maddened frenzy of
the Maenad, expressed without restraint in both the
face and the figure, is such as one would expect from
the creator of the Tegea heads. The voluptuous figure
is to be expected from a sculptor who was perhaps the
first to represent Aphrodite nude; and it reminds us
also, in its thorough exposure, of the Amazons on the
frieze of the Mausoleum. The face, with the short,
broad oval of its contour and its heavy brows, is fully
Skopaic. In short, the identification deserves the approval which it has received.

The finds at Tegea include a female torso,[53] which
probably represents Atalanta. In this body the voluptuous type of the Maenad is absent; it is the virgin
huntress who is represented. The drapery shows effective use of light and shade. Unfortunately the head
of Atalanta is lost; it seems certain that the female
head which has been supposed to belong to it[54] does

[49] Imhoof-Blumer and Gardner, *op. cit.*, pl. H, 11; *J.H.S.*, VI, p. 79.

[50] Overbeck, *SQ* 1162-1164.

[51] Treu, in *Mélanges Perrot*, pp. 312-324; Collignon, *Scopas et Praxitèle*, fig. 5; Gardner, *Handbook*, fig. 107; Gardner, *SGS*, pl. 52; Herrmann, *Verzeichnis*, p. 35, no. 133.

[52] *Ausonia*, II, 1907, pp. 84-85.

[53] Dugas, Berchmans, Clemmensen, *op. cit.*, pls. 96, 97, 98, pp. 80-84,
no. 1, with references.

[54] For the head adjusted to the body see Gardner, *Handbook*, fig. 106.
The head was stolen, but has been recovered and is now in the National
Museum at Athens.

not belong to the gable group and is not Skopaic in style.

It will be necessary to refer to Skopas frequently in the course of this book, and here it is intended only to mention a few works whose connection with him is fairly certain. The list which would be accepted by nearly all scholars is perhaps exhausted; but there is one other work which, though accepted as surely Skopaic by nobody, is in my judgment as nearly certain as anything except the temple sculptures at Tegea. This is the Capitoline Aphrodite (Plate 9, C).[55]

We know that Skopas made a nude Aphrodite, that it was brought to Rome, and that some people considered it more beautiful than the Knidian goddess of Praxiteles.[56] This judgment is recorded by Pliny, but it is safe to say that he did not originate it. So far as literature is concerned, the fame of the masterpiece of Praxiteles threw all similar statues into complete obscurity, and we have no other mention of the statue by Skopas, but Pliny's notice is enough to show that it was highly esteemed. In view of the popularity of nude anadoumene. (I omit the Aphrodite standing on there are half a dozen types more frequently copied than the Aphrodite of Knidos—and of the standing of Skopas, it is surely reasonable to expect that examples of the Skopaic type would remain. There are only three completely nude types of which *many* copies are preserved: they are the Capitoline, the Medici, and the nude anadoumene. (I omit the Aphrodite standing on one foot, which is assigned with probability to Polycharmos, and the crouching Aphrodite, certainly by Doidalsas.) The third is usually thought to be later than the other two; besides, it would scarcely be described merely as a nude Aphrodite.

[55] Helbig, *Führer*[3], I, pp. 447 f., no. 803, with citations; Bulle, *Der schöne Mensch*[2], pl. 158; Klein, *Praxiteles,* pp. 276-278; Bernoulli, *Aphrodite,* p. 224; Jones, *Museo Capitolino,* pp. 182 f., pl. 45; Dickins, *Hellenistic Sculpture,* p. 25, fig. 18; Reinach, *Recueil,* pls. 186-187.
[56] Pliny, *N.H.*, XXXVI, 26 (Overbeck, *SQ* 1174).

The Capitoline and Medici types are very similar, but the differences are enough to make it certain that they are derived from two distinct originals. The goddess of the Capitol stands beside a vase on which her garment rests; she is conceived as entering the bath. In the Medici type (Plate 9, A) there is a dolphin and no garment; the goddess has just risen from the sea. The two motives have often been looked on as successive steps away from the Knidian Aphrodite (Plate 9, B); but there is nothing in either type to show that the artist who created it ever saw or heard of the Knidian statue. This can not be stated too strongly. There was an ancient tradition that the goddess in person posed for Praxiteles, and the same belief seems to underlie the modern disposition to assume that all nude Aphrodites are ultimately derived from his work. The statues of Praxiteles are composed in graceful, flowing lines, and the outline of the body is kept unbroken so far as possible; the two other types are as far from Praxiteles as they could be. For the Capitoline type, at least, the dissimilarity is equally great in the head, whether we base our judgment on the head of the Capitoline statue itself or on the much better copy in Munich.[57] The sharp oval of the face is in decided contrast to the long, graceful oval of Praxiteles.

There is another difference between the Medici and Capitol types which goes far to establish the priority of the latter: the Capitol statue represents a mature woman, while the Medici type, as may be seen in the copies good enough to show it, represents a woman distinctly young. This is an innovation as striking as

[57] Wolters, *Führer* (1922), p. 32, no. 479, with plate; published by Sieveking in *Münch. Jahrbuch*, III, 1908, pp. 1-10. He recognizes the non-Praxitelean character of the statute. Pottier (*Mon. Piot*, XXIII, 1918-19, pp. 45-61) believes that there was a statue of the general Capitol-Medici type even in the fifth century, but this seems improbable. Perhaps the most accurate copy of the head is in Geneva: Deonna, *Cat. des Sculptures Antiques*, p. 67, no. 77; *R. Arch.*, XII, 1908, p. 164, fig. 11. A copy found at Leptis Magna, apparently corresponding closely to the Capitol statue: *Illustrated London News*, April 24, 1926, p. 752.

the nudity of the goddess, and suggests a trend of taste which belongs primarily, at least, to the Hellenistic period. The Medici type then is later than Praxiteles, as is universally thought. If the Capitol type were still later, it would be merely a combination of the Knidian and Medici types, lacking the piquant youthfulness of the latter, and would have no element of novelty to attract popular favor. On the other hand, if the Capitoline type were created first, the dolphin and the youthfulness of the figure are just such modifications as would give independent popularity to the original of the Medici type.

Sieveking, guided largely by the character of the head in Munich, has recognized that the Capitol type is derived from an original of the fourth century and has tentatively suggested Leochares and Skopas as possible authors. His chief reason for suggesting Skopas seems to be a slight resemblance to the head of the Aphrodite of Capua, which was ascribed to Skopas by Furtwängler. The resemblance is hardly convincing; and making all allowances for the versatility of Skopas, it is extremely improbable that the Capua and Capitol types are derived from one man. A direct comparison of the Munich head, or the head of the Capitol statue itself, which is too much contemned, with the Skopaic heads found at Tegea reveals as much similarity as could be expected in view of the difference in subject. The Aphrodite of Skopas ought to be preserved; the Capitol type corresponds perfectly, in general character and in details so far as we can judge them, with a natural conception of the Skopaic work; and there is no other existing type in which it can be identified with any plausibility.

CHAPTER III

THE LIFE OF LYSIPPOS

Born in Sikyon, Lysippos naturally fell heir to Sikyonian traditions, but whether he was actually a pupil of any older artist is doubtful. Our only information about his early life is given by Pliny, who tells us, on the authority of Douris of Samos, that Lysippos had no teacher and that he was at first a coppersmith.[1] It is well established that Douris was an extremely unreliable authority;[2] indeed, his inveracity was recognized in antiquity.[3] Nevertheless, he was a younger contemporary of Lysippos, and would hardly invent without reason a story in conflict with facts that would be well known at the time he wrote; so we may safely conclude that Lysippos did not study with any artist of great eminence,[4] and doubtless he did cast bronze for a living till his reputation as sculptor was made. A young man beginning his career in such a way would naturally be less constrained by school traditions than one who had learned his art in the studio of a great master.

There is much disagreement among modern authorities as to the chronology of Lysippos's life. Collignon places his birth in the second quarter of the fourth century, and his period of production between 350 and 300.[5] This is the prevailing opinion among archaeologists; but several respectable authorities be-

[1] *N. H.*, XXXIV 61; Appendix 1, 3.

[2] Sellers, *The Elder Pliny's Chapters on the History of Art*, pp. XLVI ff.

[3] Plutarch, *Perikles*, 28.

[4] Klein (*Gesch. d. griech. Kunst*, II, pp. 346 f.) conjectures that the younger Polykleitos was Lysippos's master. His evidence is the Theban inscription (Loewy, *Insch. griech. Bildh.*, 93) and Cicero, *Brutus*, 86, 296. But the Theban inscriptions do not indicate collaboration and the passage in Cicero means little. Both points are discussed below.

[5] *Lysippe*, p. 8.

lieve that his life was earlier, approximately 390-320.[6]
The argument for this earlier dating is most fully set
forth by Percy Gardner.[7]

Pliny, quoting from Douris in the passage already
cited, mentions the encouragement that Lysippos received from a response of the painter Eupompos.
Pliny does not say that the response was given to
Lysippos, and it is possible that he means that Lysippos
heard of such a saying by Eupompos. More probably,
however, Douris concocted a story to connect the great
sculptor with the great painter of Sikyon; there are
many such stories, of which the tale of Cimabue and
Giotto is perhaps best known.[8] In view of the fami-
liarity of the type and of the unreliability of the authority quoted, it seems hardly worth while to inquire
just how long Eupompos lived;—a point on which
judgment must be formed from various bits of uncertain evidence on his successors.[9] It is not impossible
that he was still alive when Lysippos was some ten
years old, and that a conversation such as Pliny reports
actually occurred.

For his early date of the beginning of Lysippos's
career Gardner relies on the statue of Troilos. It is
mentioned by Pausanias,[10] and the dedicatory inscription, though not the artist's signature, has been preserved.[11] Pausanias clearly says that Troilos won in

[6] Winter, *Jb. Arch. I.*, VII, 1892, p. 169; Milchhöfer, *Arch. Stud. H.
Brunn*, p. 66, note 2; Treu, *Olympia, Ergebnisse*, III, p. 211; Hyde,
A.J.A., XI, 1907, p. 410, and *ÖVM*, pp. 300 f.; Maviglia, *L'Attività
Artistica di Lisippo,* p. 28; E. A. Gardner, *Six Greek Sculptors*, p. 316;
Poulsen, *Delphi*, pp. 291 f.; Robert, Pauly-Wissowa, article on Euty-
chides. Waldhauer (*Lisipp*, p. 9) says that his activity extended over
the whole second half of the century.

[7] *J.H.S.*, XXV, 1905, pp. 243-248.

[8] Sellers, *Pliny*, p. XLVII.

[9] For the chronology of various painters see Pfuhl, *Malerei und
Zeichnung der Griechen*, II, pp. 729 ff.

[10] VI 1, 4 (Appendix 1, 82).

[11] Loewy, *Insch. griech. Bildh.*, no. 94. Discussed by Furtwängler,
Arch. Zeit., XXXVII, 1879, p. 145; Dittenberger and Purgold, *Olympia,
Ergebnisse*, V, p. 290, no. 166.

372, and his words certainly imply that both victories
were won then, though that is not an absolutely necessary conclusion. The inscription has usually been
interpreted to mean that he won victories in successive
Olympiads.[12] Dittenberger and Purgold say that the
use of ἐφεξῆς makes this certain. Percy Gardner thinks
that ἐφεξῆς shows that both victories were won at one
session of the games.[13]

The word seems to be perfectly intelligible, which-
ever interpretation is adopted. He won an Olympic
victory for the second time just after, or he won for
the second time in the session of the Olympic games
just after; ἐφεξῆς fits either interpretation.

Pausanias tells us that Troilos's first victory was
in the biga race and his second in the chariot race for
colts; the inscription has ἵπποις in both cases. This is
surprisingly indefinite; but it becomes explicable if we
assume that the order of the events would make it clear
what two contests were meant. The horse-races were
all held on one day; the quadriga with colts was introduced into the games next after the biga, according to
Pausanias,[14] and it is at least very well possible that
the order of introduction was followed to some extent
in the actual games. If this is so the quadriga with
horses would be followed by the κέλης, which could not
be referred to by ἵπποις; and the biga with colts was
not introduced till later. The biga and the quadriga
with colts would then be the only two successive events
that could be meant by ἵπποις. [15] On the other hand,
if two sessions of the games are referred to, we must

[12] Collignon, *Lysippe*, p. 19; Preuner, *Ein delphisches Weihgeschenk*,
p. 27; Klein, *Gesch. d. griech. Kunst*, II, p. 347; E. A. Gardner, *Six
Greek Sculptors*, p. 216; Lippold, in Pauly-Wissowa, no. 30.

[13] *J.H.S.*, XXV, 1905, p. 245. Winter and Poulsen (*Delphi*, p. 291)
give 372 as the date for both victories.

[14] V 8, 10.

[15] For a discussion of available evidence on the order of events at
Olympia, see Gardner, *Greek Athletic Sports and Festivals*, pp. 195-200;
Klee, *Zur Geschichte der gymnischen Agone*, pp. 22-26.

conclude that Troilos did not care to particularize as to his victories.

The crux of the matter is the interpretation of νικῆσαι 'Ολυμπιάδα. Pausanias quotes an epigram of Simonides, which contains this expression: καὶ νικῶ πὺξ δυ' 'Ολυμπιάδας.[16] Frazer translates: "am victor in two Olympiads." The meaning "Olympic victory" is abundantly attested for 'Ολυμπιάς, however; many examples are cited by Liddell and Scott and Stephanus; so the expression could equally well mean "I win two Olympic victories in boxing." Herodotus has several examples of ἀνελέσθαι 'Ολυμπιάδα,[17] where the verb requires that 'Ολυμπιάδα shall be a direct object. This usage is common, and is apparently closely analogous to νικῆσαι 'Ολυμπιάδα, which ought to mean the same: to win an Olympic victory. Apparently, then, Troilos says "Zeus gave to me to win an Olympic victory the first time with prize-taking horses, and the second time just after with horses;" and both his victories were won in 372, as Pausanias implies.

The date of a victory gives little more than a *terminus post quem* in dating a statue. The most natural course was to erect it at once, but any circumstance might cause a postponement. For an accurate date of the Troilos statue we must consider also the orthography of the inscription. Gardner relates that he consulted Mr. Tod on the epigraphical indications, and that Mr. Tod thought the inscription should be dated between 400 and 360.[18]

The most noticeable feature in it is the use of o for ου. As to this Roberts and Gardner write as follows:[19] "The similar use of o for ου lasted a little longer [than ε for ει]; but it almost disappears about 353 B.C., though also occasionally found in inscriptions of the

[16] VI 9, 9.   [17] VI 103.

[18] *J.H.S.*, XXV, 1905, p. 245.

[19] *Inscriptions of Attica,* preface, p. XIII.

latter part of the fourth century, especially in proper names, in the article, and in the case terminations." Larfeld says substantially the same,[20] and cites examples of such continued use for nearly every year down to 320. Now o for ου occurs only once in our inscription, and that is in a case ending. It follows that this feature does not force us to date the inscription before 360 or even before 353.

Dating it by other characters is made difficult by the facts that the alphabet did not change much during the period in question and that the letters are obviously very carelessly made. Furtwängler[21] places the inscription in the second half of the century and compares it[22] with the inscription of the victor Philip,[23] which is similarly engraved on a bronze plate and does not seem very different epigraphically. Dittenberger and Purgold date Philip's inscription rather after than before 300. On the whole it seems that the most reasonable date for the Troilos inscription is about 350. At any rate it is difficult to place it immediately after 372; and, if the statue was not set up at once, the length of the delay need not surprise us. Perhaps, as Loewy suggests,[24] the wording of the inscription may be taken to indicate a considerable interval between the victory and the dedication: τότε is most naturally so understood.

A block found at Thebes and now in the museum there[25] contains epigrams for two statues of athletes, with the signatures of Polykleitos and Lysippos. The inscription belonging to the statue by Lysippos is fragmentary, but we can discern that it was a statue of

[20] *Handbuch der griechischen Epigraphik*, II, p. 462.
[21] *Ath. Mitt.*, V, 1880, p. 30, note 2.
[22] *Arch. Zeit.*, XXXVII, 1879, p. 145.
[23] *Olympia, Ergebnisse*, V, p. 302, no. 174.
[24] *Insch. griech. Bildh.*, p. 76.
[25] Loewy, *Insch. griech. Bildh.*, no. 93; *I.G.*, VII, 2533; Kaibel, *Epigrammata Graeca*, Praefatio, p. XIV, no. 492 b.

Koreidas, who won the pankration for boys in the Pythian games. Preuner has shown[26] that Koreidas could not have won before 342, since the contest was first held at Delphi in 346 and Koreidas was not the winner then.[27] Thebes was destroyed by Alexander in 335 and restored by Kassander in 316; so no statue was set up there between those dates. The statue of Koreidas, then, was dedicated either between 342 and 335 or after 316. Perhaps we may go still farther: the Pythian festival in 338, within a few days of the battle of Chaironeia, probably had few competitors and especially few from Thebes; and besides it is unlikely that many statues were dedicated in Thebes during the troubled period between 338 and 335. Thus the image of Koreidas, if earlier than 316, is probably to be dated 342 or soon thereafter.

It is agreed that the epigraphical character of the inscription indicates a later date than 335. It may be assumed, however, that the existing inscriptions are renewals, made when the old statues were set up again after the rebuilding of Thebes.[28] This hypothesis is suggested by the fact that the younger Polykleitos, according to the chronology commonly accepted, can not have been working after 316. It may derive some confirmation from the fact that Lysippos calls himself "Sikyonian," as he does in no other signature. This seems more natural in a young artist; but no one will attach great weight to this consideration. It might further be argued that the two statues obviously have no connection with each other, and so could not have been set up together and must have been reërected; but this is not sound, because the block is not an ordinary statue-base, but an architectonic member, on which

---

[26] *Bonner Studien*, p. 219. Cf. Klee, *op. cit.*, p. 85, no. 97; he notes that the word δεύτερον, if restored in the inscription, may refer to the second occurrence of the contest.

[27] Pausanias, X 7, 8; apparently the author was confused in V 8, 11.

[28] So Furtwängler, *Masterpieces*, p. 224, note 2; Preuner, *Ein delphisches Weihgeschenk*, p. 27; Pomtow, *Jb. Arch. I.*, XXXII, 1917, p. 136.

statues of victors may have been set as they were
made.[29] The case for a renewal of the inscriptions,
then, rests wholly on the assumption that no sculptor
named Polykleitos was active after 316. As was seen
in chapter I, this assumption is not quite safe; but
the Koreidas may be provisionally dated 342.

A few years later, probably, Lysippos made a
statue that stood on the parapet around the "Old
Fountain" at Corinth. The base with his signature is
preserved.[30] Very similar epigraphically is the signature found at Thermon.[31] It is engraved on a block
which was the facing for a basis. The width of the
block is 0.745 m., and this was the width of the whole
basis, since the sides of the block are dressed smooth.
I looked without success for the top of the basis. The
dedicatory inscription on the block can not be earlier
than 280, because Herakleia was only then admitted to
the Aitolian League, according to Pausanias,[32] and
Paidias, named in the inscription, is known to belong
to the middle of the third century. The sculptor's
signature, however, shows an earlier style of lettering,
and Pomtow is justified in concluding that the statue
or at least the base was used a second time.

Powell dates the Corinthian signature about 325;
Pomtow thinks that the other is twenty to thirty years
earlier than the Theban inscription discussed above,
which should mean about the same. The similarity of
the Corinthian and Aitolian inscriptions suggests
strongly that they belong to about the same time, but
a date shortly before the death of Philip is more
probable. The forms of the letters are at least as

[29] So Brunn, *Sitzb. Bayer. Akad. Wiss.,* 1880, p. 465.

[30] Powell, in *A.J.A.,* VII, 1903, p. 30.

[31] Sotiriadis, in 'Αρχ. Δελτ., I, 1915, pp. 55 f.; *Rev. Ét. Gr.,* XXI,
1918, pp. 427-428; Pomtow, in *Jb. Arch. I.,* XXXII, 1917, pp. 133-136.
Novello (*Atene e Roma,* V, 1924, p. 263) wrongly denies this signature
to the great Lysippos, thinking it contemporary with the dedicatory
inscription.

[32] X 21, 1.

favorable to this date as to a later one and the statues, apparently of no great importance, seem likely to belong to the youth of the artist.

Fragments of a signature have been found at Pharsalos. They will be discussed at great length in a later chapter; here it will suffice to say that the statue was almost certainly made after 338 and probably not later than 334. It was probably at about the same time that a Thessalian athletic hero, Polydamas of Skotoussa, was portrayed by Lysippos in a statue at Olympia.[33] Polydamas won a victory in 408, certainly before Lysippos was born. If it be assumed that the statue was set up by the people of Skotoussa, there is a *terminus ante quem* in 321, when Skotoussa was destroyed.[34] It is at least as likely, however, that the dedication was made by the same Thessalian prince who set up statues of the heroes of his own house at Pharsalos and at Delphi. At all events it is reasonable to assume that the two Thessalian commissions of Lysippos belong to the same period.

We have a great deal of testimony on Lysippos's connection with Alexander. Pliny says that he made many statues of the conqueror "a pueritia eius orsus."[35] We need not understand from this, however, that the series began earlier than about 340, when Alexander was sixteen. We have no record of any relations between Lysippos and Philip; so it is not probable that Lysippos was especially favored at the Macedonian court until Philip's death, in 336. That monarch apparently preferred Euphranor and Leochares; each of them portrayed him and Alexander together.[36] When Alexander ascended the throne,

[33] Pausanias, VI 5, 1-7 (App. 1, 81); Lippold in Pauly-Wissowa, no. 29.

[34] So Blümner *ad loc.* and Preuner, *Ein delphisches Weihgeschenk,* p. 26.

[35] XXXIV, 63 (App. 1, 3).

[36] Pliny, N. H., XXXIV, 77; Pausanias, V 20, 10.

however, Lysippos assumed the position of court sculptor. It is stated by many authors that no other sculptor
was allowed to portray the king.[37] Perhaps this is not
to be taken too literally, but it is clear that Lysippos
was his chosen sculptor. Unfortunately only one of
his royal commissions can be definitely dated: the great
series of statues set up at Dion, in commemoration of
the battle of the Granikos,[38] must have been made in
334 or shortly thereafter, since this is the date of the
battle.

Among the most famous of Lysippos's works were
a Zeus and a Herakles, both colossal, at Tarentum.[39]
These are the only works in Magna Graecia known.
It is obvious that only an artist who had already
achieved great success would have been summoned to
make such important and expensive statues; besides,
they must have taken a great deal of time, and it is
improbable that Alexander would have released his
favorite for so long a trip while he was himself in
Greece. Now Alexander of Epeiros, uncle of Alexander the Great, went in 332 to assist the Tarentines
against the Lucanians and Messapians. He was successful until his death in 326. It seems very probable
that Lysippos went with him or to him after he finished the Granikos monument.[40] A. Reinach thinks that
Lysippos could hardly have gone to Tarentum during
Alexander's life, and dates the trip 316-306.[41] There
is no particular reason for his going at that time, however; besides, the Tarentines had become estranged
from Alexander before his death, and protégés of his
house were probably not popular there later.

Pausanias mentions a statue of a wrestler Cheilon,
which he saw at Olympia.[42] Cheilon fell in battle; and

[37] App. 1, 55, 58, 61-64, 69-70.   [38] App. 1, 70-73.
[39] App. 1, 18-20, 40-45.
[40] So Bendinelli (*Miscellanea di Studi Sicelioti ed Italioti in onore di
Paolo Orsi*, pp. 303 f.).
[41] *Neapolis*, I, 1913, p. 28.   [42] VI 4, 6 (App. 1, 83).

Pausanias remarks that he might have died either at Chaironeia, in 338, or in the Lamian war, in 322. Later he mentions that the guide at Patrai told him that Cheilon fought at Lamia;[43] that in fact he was the only Achaean to do so. Since the statue was set up after his death it must have been made after 322.

Plutarch speaks of a bronze group, the lion-hunt of Alexander and Krateros, which was made by Lysippos and Leochares and dedicated at Delphi by Krateros.[44] The inscription belonging to the group has been found.[45] From it we learn that the group, though vowed to Apollo by Krateros the general of Alexander, was set up by his son Krateros. Now the elder Krateros fell in 321, fighting as an ally of Antipater against Eumenes and Perdikkas. It is reasonable to assume that the monument was being made at the time of his death, but was not then completed. Apparently a number of years passed before it was actually set up; for the younger Krateros could not have been a year old at his father's death, and the epigraphical character of the inscription seems to indicate a date fairly well along in the third century.[46]

Athenaios relates that Lysippos designed a special kind of jar for Kassander, when that general founded Kassandria.[47] The chief export of the new city was wine, and Kassander realized the value of a container that would attract attention and be recognized everywhere. This story is altogether credible in itself and does not seem reasonably explicable as an invention. Kassandria was established in 316, which is therefore our next date in the career of Lysippos.

A lost inscription, known from a copy by Pietro Sabino,[48] has been taken to indicate that Lysippos

[43] VII 6, 5 (App. 1, 84).   [44] *Alexander*, 40 (App. 1, 74).
[45] B.C.H., XXI, 1897, p. 599.
[46] So Perdrizet, in *J.H.S.*, XIX, 1899, pp. 274 f. (*B.C.H.*, XXII, 1898, pp. 566 ff.) ; Poulsen (*Delphi*, p. 292) would date it about 320.
[47] XI 784 (App. 1, 5).
[48] Loewy, *Insch. griech. Bildh.*, no. 487. No. 477 is the same: see Loewy, in *Jb. Arch. I.*, II, 1887, p. 72.

made a portrait of Seleukos Nikator after 306, when
he took the title of king. The orthography shows that
the inscription was not an original of the time of Lysippos; presumably it was placed on a copy of his portrait. In that case it would be very natural for the
copyist to add the word βασιλεὺς , if it was not present
in the original inscription. This, then, is only another
indication of Lysippos's activity in the circle of Alexander, so far as the inscription is concerned; but we
shall see later that the portrait was probably made soon
after 306.

An inscription found at Delphi contains a reference to a decree to be inscribed on the base of the
chariot of the Rhodian people.[49] A large substructure
was found, well suited to the support of a chariot
group.[50] The inscription on it is fragmentary, but
indication of Lysippos's activity in the circle of Alex-
undoubtedly the chariot referred to in the other inscription.

Pliny mentions as an especially famous work of
Lysippos a "quadriga cum sole Rhodiorum."[51] This
has naturally been understood to mean a quadriga at
Rhodes; but that is perhaps not an absolutely necessary interpretation. Pomtow believes that the chariot
stood on this base at Delphi.[52] The inscription, in his
judgment and that of Hiller von Gaertringen, can be
dated about 300, though it would more naturally be
placed later. Pomtow thinks that the group was dedicated soon after 304, when Demetrios Poliorketes
raised his siege of Rhodes.

That is a possible date for the quadriga of Lysippos, but there is nothing that makes it particularly
probable. The Rhodians were prosperous all through
the third century and may have set up many quad-

[49] B.C.H., XXXV, 1911, p. 462.   [50] B.C.H., XXXV, 1911, p. 457.
[51] N.H., XXXIV, 63 (App. 1, 3) ; Lippold in Pauly-Wissowa, no. 8.
[52] Dittenberger, Sylloge³, I, p. 682, no. 441.

rigas. It is known that there was a famous chariot
with the Sun in Rhodes itself, since Cassius Dio relates
that Cassius, when he captured Rhodes, took away all
the sacred things except the chariot of the Sun.[53]
It is hard to doubt that this was the quadriga of
Lysippos. The base at Delphi supported another
chariot, not necessarily with the Sun, which the
Rhodians dedicated some time in the third century.[54]

An inscription which has not yet been mentioned is
in Megara (Plate 14, C):[55] Θηραμένης Τιμοξένου
ἀνέθηκε. Λύσιππος ἐποίει. This inscription is cut on two
blocks, which apparently formed the top of a large
basis. Pomtow tentatively suggests that it may be a
renewal of about 250. The letters certainly look later
than in any of the other signatures: the bars of the
sigma are parallel and the ends of the strokes show
perceptible thickening. In this respect however there is
only a slight advance on the Leochares-Sthennis inscription,[56] in which, too, there is one sigma with
parallel bars. The general appearance of the Megara
inscription does not suggest a later date than is possible
for Lysippos, but it must be dated very late in his life;
probably after 300. Novello[57] dates it 304, I know not
why.

A fragmentary signature (Λυσιπ)was found at Lindos in Rhodes,[58] but no facsimile or description of
it has been published so far as I know. A study of
the numerous artist's signatures that were found at
Lindos, if it is ever made, will probably make it possible to date the statue of Lysippos with reasonable pre-

[53] XLVII, 33, 4 (App. 1, 30).
[54] So Bourguet, B.C.H., XXXV, 1911, p. 453, and R. Arch., VII, 1918,
pp. 220 f.; Poulsen, Delphi, p. 293.
[55] Loewy, in Ath. Mitt., X, 1885, pp. 145-150, with accurate facsimile;
I.G., VII, no. 38; Michel, Recueil, no. 1063; cf. Pomtow, in Jb. Arch.
I., XXXII, 1917, p. 136.
[56] Loewy, Insch. griech. Bildh., no. 83.
[57] Atene e Roma, V, 1924, p. 263.
[58] Bull. Dan. Acad., 1907, p. 24.

cision. I looked for the inscription at Lindos, but was unable to find it, and a letter of inquiry addressed to Mr. Maiuri went unanswered.

Another signature, found at Corinth,[59] was dated by Powell about 325, though he noted differences from the other Corinthian signature already mentioned, for example that the bars of the sigma are parallel. Kendall K. Smith[60] believes that the inscription is not contemporary with Lysippos, but is a renewal of the late third century, and this is probably right. The stone apparently belonged to the facing of some large basis. The cutting was probably made later when the stone was used for some other purpose.

"Ein reizendes hellenistisches Epigramm der Basis einer Kinderstatue von einem Lysippos (vielleicht nicht dem berühmten)" was found in Kos but has remained unpublished.[61] Through the very kind assistance of Mr. Zarraphtis, the veteran Koan scholar, I found the stone and made a copy and notes, both of which I thereafter lost. From memory and the squeeze, however, I can present the inscription as preserved:

..ΩΝΕΙΜΟΙΜΙΚΟΣΤΙΣ.......
.ΑΙΤΙΝΟΣΕΙΠΑΙΣΑΤΡΕ......
ΣΟΙΓΛΩΣΑΝΕΑΛΕΛΥ....
ΕΠΛΑΣΕΛΥΣΙΠΠΟΣΜΕΟΓΕ...
ΤΙΜΟΞΕΝΟΥΕΙΜΙΥΙΟΣΠΑΤΡ.
...ΛΩΙΤΟΥΝΟΜΑΤΑΥΤΟΝΕΧΩ.

The letters given are all certain. The epsilon at the end of the fourth line is partly gone, but parts of the vertical stroke and the lowest horizontal stroke remain. Since the inscription is not stoichedon, the number of missing letters is not quite definitely determinable, but the apparent number is shown by the

[59] A.J.A., VII, 1903, p. 29, no. 4.   [60] A.J.A., XXIII, 1919, p. 392.
[61] Arch. Anz., XX, 1905, col. 11.

dots. As is indicated above, the letters are closer together in the first two lines than in the last three, while
in the third line they are more widely spaced than elsewhere. The letters have apices; the horizontal stroke
of the alpha is unbroken; the bars of the sigma are
parallel; the xi has no vertical stroke.

Professor David M. Robinson has suggested the
following as a possible reconstruction:

Ἰκ)ὼν εἶ μοι, μικός. Τίς (ὁ γλύπτης
Κ)αὶ τίνος εἶ παῖς ἄτρε(πτος;
Σοὶ γλῶσαν ἔα λέλυ(σθαι.
Ἔπλασε Λύσιππός με ὁ γέ(ρων.
Τιμοξένου εἰμὶ υἱὸς πατρ(ί
Κα)λῶι τοὔνομα ταὐτὸν ἔχω(ν.

"Thou art to me an image, small one. Who the sculptor,
and of whom art thou the immovable child? Allow thy tongue
to be released."—"The old man Lysippos fashioned me. I am
the son of Timoxenos, having the same name as my noble
father."

In the last three lines the restorations are of course
certain except for γέρων, and that is hardly doubtful; the same term is applied to Lysippos in an epigram of the Anthology.[62] These three lines make a
tolerable elegiac distich and Professor Robinson has
restored the first three lines as another. Here the difficulties are greater. It must be assumed that μικός
(for μικρός) is used as a vocative, and one would
naturally assume a loss of more than four letters at
the end of the second line; but the wide spacing in the
third line suggests that the workman may have realized
that he was getting along too fast and have cut the
second line short. At all events, I can not suggest a
better restoration.

The stone on which the inscription is cut is small,
so the statue must have been decidedly smaller than

[62] Anth. Pal., XVI (Plan. App. IV) 332 (App. 1, 77).

life. The inscription apparently belongs to the latter part of the third century, but there should be no doubt that the great Lysippos is meant. If the epigram as we have it was composed when the figure was made, as is probable, this would be a work of the master's later years. One assumes that it belongs to the same general period as his works at Rhodes.

A few other chronological indications may be noted. Lysippos is never mentioned as a contemporary or rival of Skopas or Praxiteles. Pausanias,[63] in speaking of his bronze Eros at Thespiai, says that Praxiteles had made his Eros previously. Thespiai was in a state of ruin from 372 to 338; perhaps not of complete ruin, but the probability is heavily against the dedication of important statues there during this period. The chronology of Praxiteles, as recently examined,[64] indicates that his statue was made after 338 rather than before 372, and Lysippos's Eros was still later, though we can not tell how much later. Lysippos is mentioned as collaborating with only one sculptor, Leochares, whose activity certainly belonged chiefly to the second half of the century. Lysippos's fellow favorite Apelles was certainly late: Pliny mentions him in connection with Ptolemy and Antigonos, after they became kings.[65] The same author gives Lysippos's own "floruit" as 328-325.[66] That is of no great value, as it is probably taken from Alexander's date. Pliny also records a tradition that he made 1500 statues.[67] The number is incredible, but the existence of such a tradition indicates great productiveness and hence a long life. The occurrence in two epigrams of the expression "Old Lysippos" has been noted.

From all this evidence there is no indication of any work before 350; only one has been found that is

[63] IX 27, 3 (App. 1, 32).
[64] Bieber, in Jb. Arch. I., XXXVIII-XXXIX, 1923-24, pp. 272-275.
[65] N.H., XXXV, 89-90.
[66] N.H., XXXIV, 51 (App. 1, 2). [67] N.H., XXXIV, 37 (App. 1, 1).

probably much before 340. On the other hand, one of his signatures seems to be rather after than before 300. Undoubtedly, then, the majority of scholars have been right in placing his birth in 375 at the earliest, and he probably lived nearly till 290.

As to the course of his life in his later years we have little information. After his return from Tarentum, in 326 or somewhat earlier, he may have rejoined Alexander in Asia; the features of a portrait of Alexander, which is attributed to him with great probability, seem to be those of a man of thirty. In 320, however, he was in Greece again: the Krateros group and the statue of Cheilon belong to that period. Since he was associated with Krateros, the ally of Antipater, and with Kassander, the son of Antipater, it may be that he enjoyed special favor with that house. His pupil Chares, if not Lysippos himself, was engaged by the Rhodians to celebrate their victory over Kassander's arch-enemy Demetrios. Apparently no feeling of loyalty to the great Alexander restrained the artist from seeking the favor of his bitterest enemy. There is a considerable time after 316 during which we lose sight of him; perhaps he was in Asia Minor and the islands, where he had hardly spent much time before, though he worked at some time in Rhodes, Myndos, Lampsakos, and Kos. The late signature at Megara indicates that his last years were spent in Greece. Petronius relates that he died of hunger,[88] apparently as a result of his reluctance to leave the figure on which he was working; this probably deserves little credence. From the success of his sons and pupils we may infer that his own prestige did not decline as long as he lived.

[88] *Satirikon*, 88 (App. 1, 10).

CHAPTER IV

LITERARY EVIDENCE ON LYSIPPIAN ART;
THE APOXYOMENOS

Our information on the characteristics of Lysippos's sculpture is not extensive. Even when it is supplemented by detailed descriptions of certain works, the picture remains so incomplete that there exist wide differences of opinion as to the proper application of the term "Lysippian" and as to the extant works that may be accepted as representative of his style. The literary evidence on the sculptor's art may be analyzed in connection with the identification of one of his most famous works, the "apoxyomenos."

Pliny opens his list of Lysippos's works with this statue.[1] That is the only passage of any author in which it is mentioned, and the closest scrutiny will not extract much information from it. Its position at the head of Pliny's list and the space that he devotes to it, as well as his tale of the favor that it enjoyed in Rome, indicate that it was regarded as a masterpiece. The story about Tiberius would suggest that the statue had some flavor of effeminacy or immaturity or both.

A further hint may be drawn from the attribution to Lysippos's son Daippos of a "perixyomenos."[2] An apoxyomenos is one who scrapes himself off; a perixyomenos is one who scrapes himself around. Any perixyomenos could be called an apoxyomenos, but not all apoxyomenoi would be perixyomenoi. περιξύω is a rather rare word, and it appears that no form of it is applied to the use of a strigil except in the cases of Daippos's statue and of another statue by Antignotos,[3] who belongs to the time of Augustus.[4] It seems prob-

[1] *N.H.,* XXXIV 62 (App. 1, 3).   [2] Pliny, *N.H.,* XXXIV 87.
[3] Pliny, *N.H.,* XXXIV 86.
[4] So Robert, in Pauly-Wissowa, *s.v.;* Loewy's doubts (*Insch. griech. Bildh.,* no. 314) seem unnecessary.

able that the term was applied to Daippos's statue especially to distinguish it from the apoxyomenos of his father. The περί-element, then, would have been noticeably more prominent in the one statue than in the other.

Lysippos was not the only Greek sculptor to win fame with an apoxyomenos. In addition to the perixyomenoi of Daippos and Antignotos, Polykleitos made an apoxyomenos[5] and Daidalos of Sikyon made two.[6] Several types to which the name could be applied exist in extant remains of sculpture. An enumeration will be useful.

A grave-relief found at Delphi[7] obviously belongs to a period before 450. Then there are two bronze statuettes, identical in type,[8] which show a man standing stiffly and cleaning the back of his right shoulder with the strigil, which is held in the right hand. Sieveking and Hyde[9] are inclined to identify this type as the creation of Polykleitos; but it seems too archaic. Brueckner has noted that a type of apoxyomenos appears, almost identically, on two grave-steles of the fifth century;[10] he thinks that this may represent the statue of Polykleitos. The theory would not be improbable if it were sure that any statue was imitated; but the steles are alike not only in the principal figure, but also, approximately, in the small attendant. One infers that both are imitated from a painting or— more probably—that one stele is copied from the other.

The type best known by the "Westmacott Athlete" of the British Museum[11] has been interpreted by some

[5] Pliny, N.H., XXXIV 55.   [6] Pliny, N.H., XXXIV 76.
[7] Forschungen in Ephesos, I, p. 197, fig. 146; Bulle, Der schöne Mensch[2], pl. 265, p. 571; Poulsen, Delphi, p. 235, fig. 107; Waldmann, Griechische Originale, pl. 83; Hyde, OVM, p. 138.
[8] Sieveking, Bronzen d. Sammlung Loeb, pl. XI, pp. 27 f.; Babelon-Blanchet, Bronzes Antiques de la bibliothèque Nationale, p. 411, no. 934.
[9] OVM, p. 136.
[10] 77 Programm zum Winckelmannsfeste, Berlin, 1920, pp. 11 f., ills. on pp. 14-15.
[11] Hyde, OVM, pp. 156 ff., with citations; a copy in Baltimore is mentioned by Robinson, Cl. Weekly, XVII, 1923, p. 61.

scholars as a youth scraping his forehead with the
strigil, largely through comparison with a painting
found at Pompeii.[12] If this were really the motive of
the original statue,[13] the search for the apoxyomenos
of Polykleitos might cease; for the Westmacott type
is thoroughly Polykleitan, and its celebrity, as attested
by the large number of copies and imitations, indicates
that it proceeds from the master himself rather than
from a pupil. The assumption of a prototype in sculpture for the Pompeian painting is supported by the
presence, in the same room, of another painted apoxyomenos.[14] The figures in the two paintings differ so
much, in proportion and other respects, as to suggest
that one or both followed an original of some sort.
But the explanation more usually adopted for the
Westmacott type—that the boy is placing a crown on
his head—is supported by more and better analogies.
It may be that a later sculptor used the same position
for an apoxyomenos, or even that Polykleitos made
two statues in which different motives were represented in almost the same way; the lack of variety in
his figures was noted in antiquity.[15]

It is more probable, however, that the apoxyomenos of Polykleitos was correctly identified by Furtwängler, in a type which appears only on gems.[16] It
is said to occur on many gems, with no considerable
variation. It is a reasonable inference that they are
all imitations of a famous statue; and the type is

[12] *Röm. Mitt.*, III, 1888, p. 199, fig. 1; 'Εφ. 'Αρχ., 1890, fig. 4, opposite p. 207.

[13] Cf. Klein, *Jh. Oest. Arch. I.*, XIII, 1910, p. 139.

[14] *Röm. Mitt.*, III, 1888, p. 200, fig. 2.

[15] Cf. Pliny, *N.H.*, XXXIV 56.

[16] Furtwängler, *Masterpieces*, p. 262, fig. 109 (*Meisterwerke*, p. 471,
fig. 79); Furtwängler, *Die Antiken Gemmen*, I, pl. XLIV, 18-19, II, p.
212; Hartwig, in *Jh. Oest. Arch. I.*, IV, 1901, p. 155, figs. 183 f. In *Die
Antiken Gemmen, loc. cit.*, Furtwängler notes that the youth is not
scraping his arm but cleaning the strigil, and Klein (*Jh. Oest. Arch. I.*,
XIII, 1910, p. 139) interprets this as a withdrawal of his identification.
But surely such a figure would be called an apoxyomenos.

exactly what one would expect an apoxyomenos by Polykleitos to be. The posture resembles that of the Doryphoros and the proportions are Polykleitan. This identification is very probable.

A bronze statuette said to have been in Cortona represents a youth holding a strigil in the right hand, at about the level of the waist, while the left hand is placed on the left hip.[17] The feet seem to have approximately the same position as on the base at Corinth. The workmanship of the figure is apparently rude. A bronze statuette in the Bibliothèque Nationale is of Roman manufacture.[18] The legs below the thighs are lost, but it is apparent that the weight rested on the right leg. The head is turned to the right. The two hands are close together, in front of the left breast, and the right hand holds the strigil. In the Boston museum there is a bronze left arm (Plate 14, A), about half life-size, which has not previously been published. It was broken off a little above the elbow, which was bent at an obtuse angle. The hand holds a strigil; the little finger is next the blade. The anatomy is much emphasized, and seems clearly to indicate a Hellenistic origin.

There are many grave-steles showing a youth with a strigil, presumably without any prototype in sculpture: e.g. nos. 829, 881, 888, 912, 2578 in the National Museum at Athens;[19] no. 7 in the Metropolitan Museum in New York;[20] no. 3114 in the Salle Grecque in the Louvre;[21] no. 29 in the museum at Chalkis.[22] No. 1625 in the National Museum at Copenhagen

[17] Micali, *Mon. Ined.*, XVII, 7; Reinach, Répertoire, II, 547, 3. I did not see the statuette in the museum at Cortona.

[18] Babelon-Blanchet, p. 411, no. 933.

[19] Cf. Conze, *Attische Grabreliefs*, II, 2, pl. CCIII.

[20] Richter, *Handbook of the Classical Collection* (1927), pp. 258 f., fig. 181.

[21] Collignon in *Mon. Piot*, XIX, 1911, pp. 151-159, pl. XII; Reinach, *Rép. Rel.*, II, 293, 2.

[22] 'Εφ. 'Αρχ. , 1907, pl. II.

shows the strigil held against the head, by the right
hand. In the smaller museum on the Acropolis there
is a relief,[23] belonging to about 300 B.C., which shows
six apoxyomenoi in various positions. Though vase-
paintings are not included in this enumeration, it
may be worth while to mention one that shows six
apoxyomenoi.[24]

Of another sculptural type[25] the most reliable example, probably, is in the Uffizi.[26] The weight rests
on the right leg; the other foot is equally advanced but
set to the side and the heel is slightly raised. The left
hand was near the left side at the level of the hip; the
right arm crossed the body and the hands were not far
apart. The hands and parts of the forearms, with the
vase held by the hands, are new. The head looks
down and to its left. This figure was discussed by
Bloch in connection with a small statue in the Salle de
Psyché of the Louvre.[27] From the remains of certain
supports in the latter figure and from the position of
its left hand he argues for a restoration as an athlete
pouring oil from a lekythos into an aryballos. Furtwängler denounced such a subject as unparalleled,
unclassical, and absurd;[28] but Bloch's reasoning is
plausible so far as the figure in the Louvre is concerned. He was mistaken however in believing that
it faithfully represented the type known by the Uffizi
figure. In the first place the two statues differ con-

[23] No. 3176; Walter, *Die Reliefs im Kleinen Akropolismuseum*, pp.
195 f., no. 401; Reinach, *Rép. Rel.*, II, 369, 1. There is a cast in the
Dresden Albertinum.

[24] *Mon. Ant.*, XXII, 1913, pl. LXXXI.

[25] Best discussion of the type and its various examples: *Forschungen
in Ephesos*, I, pp. 181-204 (Benndorf); Hyde, *OVM*, pp. 136-138.

[26] *Elenco*, p. 25, no. 100, and ill.; Amelung, *Führer durch Florenz*, no.
25; Furtwängler, *Masterpieces*, pp. 261 ff.; Bulle, *Der schöne Mensch²*,
col. 116; Brunn-Bruckmann, no. 523; Hyde, *OVM*, pl. XII; without
restorations, *Forschungen in Ephesos*, I, p. 193. The head, *Röm. Mitt.*,
VII, 1892, pl. III; Bulle, cols. 473, 476; Brunn-Bruckmann, no. 524.

[27] *Röm. Mitt.*, VII, 1892, pp. 81-105; sketch of the proposed restoration on p. 86.

[28] *Masterpieces*, p. 261.

siderably: for example the free foot of the Louvre figure is set distinctly forward. In the second place, other examples of the Uffizi type show that it was certainly an apoxyomenos. The statue in the Louvre may be regarded as a copyist's variation or, with greater probability, as derived from another work of the sculptor who created the Uffizi type.

A marble statuette in Boston clearly belongs to the Uffizi type,[29] though it differs considerably from the larger statue. The body is boyish and chubby, while the Uffizi statue represents a mature athlete. In the statuette the action is clear: the boy holds the strigil in his left hand and was cleaning it with his right. The same action is shown in a miserable bronze statuette found at Trèves;[30] this probably represents the type under discussion. There is a copy in the Vatican;[31] a poor and fragmentary statue in the Municipal Antiquarium in Rome appears to be another;[32] the same original is represented also on gems;[33] a head in the Hermitage is unmistakably a copy, and a very good one;[34] a head in the Museo Torlonia is said to be a copy, though much worked over.[35] A number of terracotta reliefs show the statue set up along with others between the columns of a gymnasium.[36] In most of the reliefs the figure appears to be cleaning the strigil,

[29] Caskey, *Catalogue of Greek and Roman Sculpture*, pp. 152 f., no. 76; Hartwig, in *Jh. Oest. Arch. I.*, IV, 1901, pp. 151-159, pls. V-VI.

[30] *Forschungen in Ephesos*, I, pp. 200 f.

[31] Braccio Nuovo, 105; Amelung, *Skulpt. d. Vat. Mus.*, I, p. 119, pl. XVII.

[32] *B. Com. Rom.*, XXXIX, 1911, pp. 99 ff.; Maviglia, *L'Attività Artistica di Lisippo*, p. 23.

[33] Furtwängler, *Masterpieces*, pp. 261 f.; *Forschungen in Ephesos*, I, p. 198.

[34] Kieseritzky, *Catalogue of the Hermitage*, p. 26, no. 65; good illustration in *Forschungen in Ephesos*, I, p. 199.

[35] Visconti, *Monumenti del Museo Torlonia*, pl. XXII, no. 86; *Forschungen in Ephesos*, I, p. 199.

[36] Kekulé, *Die antiken Terrakotten*, IV, pl. LXXXII, pp. 280 f., with references.

but in the Ny Carlsberg example[37] he is scraping the left arm.

The most interesting statue in the list is the bronze, slightly larger than life-size, found at Ephesos and now in Vienna (Plates 10 and 11, B).[38] A comparison with the Florence athlete shows various differences: apparently the bronze was a free Hellenistic imitation rather than an exact copy. The action in the statue as restored is different: the athlete is scraping his left forearm instead of cleaning the strigil. This difference affects the appearance very little and is doubtless to be explained as a happy modification by the Hellenistic artist.[39] The face is rounder and softer than in the Uffizi statue, but there can be no doubt that the two represent a common original.

This original is represented by an impressive list of copies, certainly.[40] If a statue's celebrity is to be judged by the imitations of it that remain, this was decidedly the most famous of all apoxyomenoi. To judge from the literary testimony, the most famous of all apoxyomenoi was made by Lysippos. Mme. Ada Maviglia has combined the two lines of evidence and has suggested that the statue in the Uffizi and its fellows represent the true apoxyomenos of Lysippos.[41] Her thesis and arguments deserve careful consideration; but first a later type must be mentioned.

[37] *De antike Kunstvaerker*, p. 328, no. 141.

[38] *Forschungen in Ephesos*, I, pp. 181 ff., frontispiece, pls. VI-IX; Bulle, *Der schöne Mensch*[2], pls. 60 and 208; Brunn-Bruckmann, 682-685 (statue and head in comparison with the Antiquarium diskobolos); Springer-Wolters[12], p. 319, fig. 592. For the position in which it was placed see Heberdey, *Jh. Oest. Arch. I.*, XIX-XX, 1916-1919, pp. 247-252.

[39] The correctness of the restoration has been questioned by Benndorf (*Forschungen in Ephesos*, I, pp. 201 f.) and Sieveking (text to Brunn-Bruckmann, 682-685).

[40] Several doubtful examples are discussed by Benndorf. The head mentioned by him (p. 199, note 3) as for sale in Rome is now in Brussels (Cumont, *Cat. Mus. Royaux*, no. 5). Sieveking (*l.c.*) doubts its genuineness. Mme. Maviglia (*L'Attività Artistica di Lisippo*, pp. 23 f.) includes in her list the gems referred by Furtwängler to a Polykleitan original.

[41] *Op. cit.*

The apoxyomenos long accepted as a copy after
Lysippos is in the Braccio Nuovo of the Vatican (Plates
12 and 13).[42] A somewhat minute description of this
famous statue will be in order. Part of the nose, the left
ear, fingers of the right hand with the die, and parts of
the toes are restored. The weight rests on the left leg,
while the right foot is set back and a considerable distance to the side. The right arm is stretched forward
almost straight from the shoulder; the left elbow is
bent at approximately a right angle and the hand holds
a strigil, scraping the lower side of the right arm just
above the elbow.

The rich musculature of the body is more easily
seen than described; but we may note the triangular
depression between the muscles at the waist and the
distinct division between the muscles in the calf of the
right leg at bottom.[43] The roundness of the shoulders,
the rich modelling of the back, and the very deep
groove along the spine are noticeable. The navel is
shallow, with a crescent-shaped line above it. The
pubic hair occupies a very small area, of roughly

[42] Reinach, *Répertoire*, II, 546, 2; Amelung, *Skulpt. d. Vat. Mus.*, I,
pp. 86 ff., no. 67, pl. XI; Helbig, *Führer²*, no. 23; Brunn-Bruckmann,
281 and (the head) 487; Bulle, *Der schöne Mensch²*, pls. 62 and (the
head) 213; details in pls. 106, 110, 111, 196; bronzed cast on pedestal in
text, col. 117, fig. 22; Von Mach, *University Prints*, 235; *Monuments
Rayet*, IV, pl. 3, with text by Collignon; Collignon, *Lysippe*, figs. 5 and
(the head) 6; Furtwängler-Urlichs³, pl. 34; Friederichs-Wolters, 1264;
Hyde, *OVM*, pl. 29; Waldhauer, *Lisipp*, fig. 1 and (the head) fig. 2.
For the statue's correspondence with literary evidence on Lysippian art,
Braun's article (*Annali dell' Instituto*, XXII, 1850, pp. 223-251) is still
good. Loewy's little book, *Lysipp und seine Stellung in der griechischen
Plastik*, is chiefly valuable for its treatment of the apoxyomenos as
representing a certain stage in the development of art. Schick (*Neue
Jahrbücher*, XXXIII, 1914, pp. 18 ff.) has good notes along the same line,
together with acute morphological observations. Michaelis (*J.H.S.*, IV,
1883, pp. 335 ff.) treats certain proportions as compared with those of
other statues. The principal discussions of the apoxyomenos since the
discovery of the Agias are those of Amelung (*Röm. Mitt.*, XX, 1905,
pp. 136-155), Koepp (*Neue Jahrbücher*, XXIII, 1909, pp. 480-486), and
Percy Gardner (*J.H.S.*, XXV, 1905, pp. 234 ff.). Waldhauer (*Lisipp*,
pp. 17-21) gives a very elaborate and interesting analysis of the figure.

[43] These two points are stressed by Gardner, in *J.H.S.*, XXV, 1905,
p. 238.

semicircular shape. The hands and feet are very carefully made, with much attention to their anatomy. The feet are long and rather flat. The fingers of the antique left hand are rather fleshy. Veins are visible in the backs of the hands and elsewhere. The neck is rather thick than slender; the larynx is marked off by grooves above and below it.

The restless hair, though an important Lysippian characteristic, hardly lends itself to description. The crown of the hair is set low in the back. The unrestored right ear is rather long and narrow; the inner cartilage is broad; the lobe has a distinctly different curve from the rest of the ear. The hair closely approaches the outer corners of the eyes. The face as a whole is broad, almost round. The dolichocephalous form should be noted.

The forehead is divided by a horizontal groove; the part above this groove is set farther back than the part below it, which includes more than half the space above the eyes. The eyes are small, not only in proportion to the face in general but also to the eye-sockets. They are set deep under the brows and are further shaded by the upper lids, which are much thicker than the lower lids. The eyes are not widely opened[44] and the surface of the eyeball shows practically no vertical curvature. The two lids are similarly curved. There is an especially deep hollow outside of and below the outer corner of the eye. The eyes are set in close to the narrow nose, which is very little broader at the base than at the bridge.[45] The upper lip, though not thin, is very little modelled; the central depression and the red border are hardly marked at all. The border of the lower lip is well marked, in a

[44] Waldhauer (*Lisipp,* p. 19) regards the furrowed forehead and "squinting" eye as indicative of muscular tension caused by nervousness and fatigue.

[45] It is somewhat restored, but not enough to invalidate this observation.

roughly rectangular form. There is a deep hollow between the lower lip and the chin, which is broad, solid, and rather long.

Apparently we have no other copy from the original of this type. The announcement that two statuettes of the type were found at Kyme[46] seems to have been a mistake; at all events no such statuettes are now known.[47] A torso in the magazine of the National Museum at Athens (Plate 21, B)[48] had arms starting from the shoulders as in the Vatican statue, and the head was turned to the figure's right; but the weight rested on the right leg, so the general rhythm was altogether different. One can not be sure that it was an apoxyomenos at all. There is no sign of a support for the left arm nor of any other support. The body is slender and the musculature dry and hard, resembling the "Jason" more than the Vatican apoxyomenos. This appearance may be due partly to the poor workmanship of the copy.

We may now consider the theory of Mme. Maviglia.

In the beginning she accepts the views of Percy Gardner in regard to Lysippian chronology.[49] These we have found to be wrong. She observes also that the Vatican apoxyomenos shows a knowledge of anatomy impossible in the time of Lysippos.[50] Here also she follows Gardner,[51] who cites Lange as though Lange were an Alexandrian anatomist; but we have no such exact knowledge of the progress of anatomical science as would justify a positive statement on the matter.

[46] *A.J.A.*, VI, 1890, p. 551, with citations.

[47] See Mendel, *Cat. Imp. Mus. Ottomans*, III, pp. 20-21, no. 818.

[48] Köhler, in *Ath. Mitt.*, II, 1877, pp. 57 f. and pl. IV; *Einzelaufnahmen*, no. 722; Reinach, *Répertoire*, II 819, 1.

[49] *Op. cit.*, p. 28.

[50] *Loc. cit.*

[51] *J.H.S.*, XXV, 1905, pp. 236 ff. So Fowler, *History of Sculpture*, p. 119.

These points are only incidental to Mme. Maviglia, however. She bases her repudiation of the Vatican apoxyomenos on two pieces of literary evidence. Pliny says that Lysippos modified the proportions used by older artists;[52] but the Vatican apoxyomenos shows an entirely new system of proportions; hence it can not reproduce the work of Lysippos. Furthermore, Lysippos is represented as declaring himself the pupil of the Doryphoros of Polykleitos;[53] this shows conclusively that he did not depart radically from Polykleitan usage, and confirms the testimony of Pliny that he only modified the old proportions.

I have not seen much discussion of this thesis,[54] but it does not seem that any one without a theory to prove would interpret the evidence as Mme. Maviglia does. Polykleitos was recognized as a great artist, perhaps particularly as a great formal artist and technician, and the Doryphoros seems to have been made as an example of his methods and principles; it would naturally be studied by all young sculptors, especially by those of the Peloponnesian schools. In exactly the same way young painters of the present day may profitably study the frescoes of the Brancacci chapel, though they do not purpose painting exactly in the manner of Masaccio. There is no reason for supposing that Lysippos meant any more than that, if he called himself a pupil of the Doryphoros.

As for the passage in Pliny, surely the natural and reasonable interpretation is that Lysippos made important changes in the system of proportions. Why would the matter have been mentioned at all, if Lysippos had "adopted the Polykleitan canon in his funda-

[53] *N.H.*, XXXIV 65 (App. 1, 3).
[53] Cicero, *Brutus*, 86, 296 (App. 1, 6). ·
[54] Reinach's review (*R. Arch.*, XXIV, 1914, pp. 157 f.) is non-committal, Urlichs's (*Wo. Kl. Ph.*, XXXIV, 1917, 145-149) unfavorable. The review in *Lit. Zent.*, LXVII, 1916, p. 1023, is only a summary. Philippart (*Rev. belge de phil. et d'hist.*, III, 1924, pp. 3-15) is the only convert known to me.

mental scheme and brought to it only slight modifications"?[55] The successors of Polykleitos were eminent artists; it is highly probable that many of them made slight modifications. Could the chief contribution to art of so eminent a sculptor as Lysippos consist in slight modifications of the old canon? If they were considered so important, we should hear a great deal of the artist that did introduce the new system; but we must assume that he is mentioned only among the many pupils of the great masters. These arguments against the Lysippian character of the Vatican apoxyomenos are not convincing.

Passing then to a consideration of the Uffizi type, Mme. Maviglia observes that according to Pliny the work of Lysippos was famous, and that the Uffizi apoxyomenos is shown by the number of its replicas to have been famous.[56] There can be no doubt of that; and the lack of replicas of the Vatican type is disturbing. The explanation probably is that the statue is very difficult to copy in marble.[57] The sculptor of the copy preserved, who was no mean workman, thought it necessary to use a support for the outstretched arm, which must have marred the effect greatly. Thus, while the abundance of replicas of the Uffizi type proves its celebrity and to that extent supports its claim to Lysippian authorship, the lack of copies of the Vatican type does not indicate the contrary for it.

Mme. Maviglia finds that the Uffizi type represents the canon of Polykleitos with slight modifications.[58] It is certainly much closer to Polykleitos than is the Vatican type;[59] rather too close for a natural

---

[55] Maviglia, op. cit., p. 17. [56] Op. cit., p. 19.

[57] So Von Mach, Handbook of Greek and Roman Sculpture, p. 245. Reinach (R. Arch., XX, 1924, p. 239) ingeniously suggests that during the great popularity of the statue Tiberius may have forbidden the making of copies.

[58] Op. cit., p. 25.

[59] Bloch discusses the proportions, Röm. Mitt., VII, 1892, pp. 102 f.

interpretation of the passage in Pliny. Yet in one respect it differs decidedly from the Doryphoros, where
the Vatican type is in accord with it: that is, in the
shape of the head. Mme. Maviglia explains this[60] by
a passage[61] in which it is implied, as she thinks, that
Lysippos made heads as Myron did. A glance at the
passage in its context shows that the author was dis-
cussing methods of teaching, not art; he says that
Lysippos taught by his own work, not that of others.
Any other three artists would have done as well, for
the author's purpose, as those actually named.

An obvious objection to the attribution of the
Uffizi type to Lysippos is the fact that it has generally
been dated near the beginning of the fourth century.
Bloch,[62] Furtwängler,[63] and Amelung[64] are substantially in agreement on this point, and Kalkmann[65] said
it was much earlier than the Hermes of Praxiteles.
Bulle,[66] however, seems inclined to bring it nearly to
350, and Benndorf[67] places it about 360. Mme.
Maviglia[68] herself brings it down only to 350, which
would be at the very beginning of Lysippos's career.
All the commentators have noted the resemblance between the Uffizi athlete, the Munich oil-pourer and the
diskobolos of Naukydes. Both of these statues have
usually been ascribed to the fifth century. Obviously
the consensus of opinion, founded of course on considerations of style, as to the date of the Uffizi type,
is not favorable to its attribution to Lysippos.

Lysippos seems to have expressed a good deal of
spirit and emotion in his figures. He adequately portrayed the arrogant majesty of Alexander, the pathos
of the weary Herakles, and the fiery spirit of a free
horse. The Vatican apoxyomenos is not lacking in

[60] Op. cit., p. 26.   [61] Auctor ad Herennium, IV 6 (App. 1, 8).
[62] Röm. Mitt., VII, 1892, p. 103. [63] Masterpieces, pp. 260 ff.
[64] Skulpt. d. Vat. Mus., I, p. 120. [65] Arch. Anz., VI, 1891, p. 140.
[66] Der schöne Mensch², col. 113. [67] Forschungen in Ephesos, I, p. 192.
[68] Op. cit., p. 26.

expression. It is not expression of a profound or vigorous sort; but the face does give an impression of gentle meditation, very different from the serenity of the art of the fifth century. It is this earlier manner that appears in the Uffizi athlete, and reenforces the other evidence which indicates that it belongs to a period distinctly earlier than that of Lysippos.

To this course of reasoning some reply can be made. We know nothing of the date at which the apoxyomenos of Lysippos was made, nor is there any reason to think that it was an especially typical or representative work of the master. The distinctive style of Lysippos was not formed at his birth. Daidalos was active after 369; have we any right to assume a great difference between a late work of his and an early one by Lysippos? Daidalos was the leading Sikyonian sculptor of his time, whose influence—even for a time after his death—the young Lysippos could hardly escape.

But if the Uffizi type represents an early work of Lysippos, it ought to be possible to trace a development in style between it and later Lysippian works: the Vatican apoxyomenos, which is unanimously agreed to belong to the school of Lysippos if not to the master himself, and at least two other works which will be mentioned in the next chapter. But such a development can not be traced: at least I have observed nothing, except perhaps a head in Cassel,[69] which could be regarded as illustrating it. The near relatives of the Uffizi type are not later than it, but earlier; it is the work of a sculptor who looked backward.

I said at the beginning that we should expect to find the apoxyomenos of Lysippos effeminate or immature or both. The Boston statuette does look immature, but no other representative of that type does; and the statuette is clearly not an exact copy. The

[69] Bieber, *Die ant. Skulpt. u. Bronzen in Cassel*, no. 27.

Uffizi statue has not the slightest appearance of immaturity or of effeminacy. The body of the Vatican statue, on the other hand, has along with its highly developed muscularity a slenderness and grace that would make the story about Tiberius explicable. The expression also is suitable.

With regard to the Uffizi apoxyomenos a definite conclusion is possible: it is not the work of Lysippos. It is opposed to all the evidence both for Lysippos in general and for his apoxyomenos in particular. Its style is too early for the time of Lysippos; its proportions are not those that can reasonably be attributed to Lysippos; its serenity of countenance is not to be expected from Lysippos. It has not the effeminacy or the immaturity that Lysippos's apoxyomenos must have had.

Hauser attributes this type to Daidalos of Sikyon, and believes that the Ephesos bronze is the original.[70] He notes that Daidalos is credited by Pliny with two apoxyomenoi, that there appear to be two slightly divergent types of this work, and that an inscription of Daidalos was found at Ephesos. It hardly seems probable, however, that an artist would make two statues so nearly alike; it is much more likely that the variation in the Ephesos bronze is due to the Hellenistic adaptor. Furthermore, most commentators had considered the type Attic, and it bears a considerable resemblance to the Hermes of Praxiteles.[71]

To this Hauser replies that we do not know how far the schools kept themselves distinct in the first half of the fourth century. In fact the schools of cities, as distinct from the followers of individual artists, are sufficiently hard to distinguish at any time, and it may be agreed that the Attic affinities of the

---

[70] *Jh. Oest. Arch. I.,* V, 1902, pp. 214-216. Michaelis seems to approve (Springer-Michaelis[8], p. 259). So Fowler (Fowler and Wheeler, p. 267).

[71] See especially *Forschungen in Ephesos,* I, p. 191.

Uffizi type constitute no impediment to an attribution to Daidalos. The type was very probably created in his lifetime and if his work is preserved at all it is certainly in this series of statues. Its resemblance to the diskobolos of Naukydes has been noted (see Plate 11), but it is surely somewhat later; the development from the one statue to the other is just what one would expect between Naukydes and Daidalos. On the whole the attribution to Daidalos seems extremely probable, but the Ephesos bronze can not be accepted as the original: first because it is not good enough for an artist of the standing of Daidalos, and second because its defects—softness, weakness, lack of definition—are those characteristic of the Hellenistic age.[72]

The Vatican type is, or at least in the present state of our knowledge appears to be, the creation of an independent and unconstrained genius. The Uffizi type follows closely the apoxyomenos of Polykleitos, and the Cortona bronze, although its proportions look Lysippian and the position of the feet is the only one known positively to have been used by Lysippos, is apparently derived from an unimpressive and unoriginal work, which would not be notable among the works of Lysippos; that is, if it had any prototype at all. The left arm in Boston clearly belongs to a Hellenistic statue. The great work in the Vatican evidently has a very much better claim to Lysippian authorship than any other statue recognizable as an apoxyomenos.

It has the stage of artistic development, the proportions, and the tinge of effeminacy that are to be expected in the statue by Lysippos. The vivid rendering of the hair, the small head, the extreme delicacy

---

[72] Sieveking (text to Brunn-Bruckmann, 682-685) thinks it an original; Lippold (*Kopien und Umbildungen*, pp. 126 f.) a copy. Dickins (*Hellenistic Sculpture*, p. 34) says that the statue "belongs to a later development of the Scopaic school." Here as elsewhere in his book Dickins evidently set down impressions which would have been completely revised if he had lived to complete his study.

of execution—these characteristics, in addition to those previously mentioned, are ascribed to Lysippos, and all appear in the apoxyomenos of the Vatican as well as could be expected in a copy. There is, however, one adjective in Pliny that seems inappropriate. Lysippos made *corpora graciliora siccioraque*—bodies slimmer and drier. Slimmer and more firm or healthy, it could be translated; but that could hardly mean anything in the field of Greek sculpture. Now the body of the apoxyomenos is slim, but how can it be called dry? It is usual to assume that it was called drier than earlier statues such as the Uffizi apoxyomenos. But even in contrast to them the Vatican statue is not dry; it is anything but dry; with its soft and richly modelled flesh it is dry only in contrast to a body actually fat. The kind of body meant by Pliny is easily recognized once it is seen, in several figures reckoned contemporary with the apoxyomenos or a little later: notably the "Jason" and the seated Hermes at Naples. This discrepancy must be noted, but it is not serious. It is not necessary to assume that Lysippos made all his bodies dry.

There is only one consideration that militates against an unqualified acceptance of the statue as representing the work of Lysippos. That is the attribution of a perixyomenos to Daippos. It can not be denied that the Vatican type, in contrast to statues following the old Polykleitan scheme more or less, might very naturally be called a perixyomenos. Furthermore, we learn that Euthykrates did not imitate the refinement of his father, and that he used "an austere rather than a lighter style of execution."[73] This statement is apparently designed to distinguish Euthykrates from the other sons of Lysippos, whose works then would be characterized by refinement and not by austerity; and certainly the Vatican apoxyom-

[73] Pliny, *N.H.*, XXXIV 66 (App. 1, 3).

enos is neither austere nor lacking in refinement. Daippos's statue was apparently well esteemed, since Pliny selected it as the one work to represent the sculptor in his list.[74]

The confidence with which the apoxyomenos has been assigned to Lysippos is in these circumstances amazing, since there never was any valid reason for choosing the father rather than the son. We shall find such a reason in the close resemblance between the apoxyomenos and a few other works which can not be given to the relatively obscure Daippos, but these works have not hitherto been assigned to Lysippos with anything like unanimity. At this point it can only be said that the attribution to Lysippos would be greatly strengthened by the discovery of some other type for Daippos. Perhaps an imitation of his statue may be recognized in the Pompeii painting which has been mentioned on page 101, note 13. The figure in the painting is slim and rather like the "Jason" than like the Vatican apoxyomenos; its assumed prototype could well belong to the period of Daippos. The youth holds the strigil in his left hand and scrapes his back, drawing the strigil around the right side toward the front. This position is one of the very few that might suggest the name *peri*xyomenos in contrast to the *apo*xyomenos of the Vatican .

[74] *N.H.*, XXXIV 87.

CHAPTER V

THE SIGNED BASES; THE POLYDAMAS BASE; THE
HERAKLES EPITRAPEZIOS; THE EROS

It seemed best to begin the study of works attributed to Lysippos with the apoxyomenos, partly because of the prominence it has always had in the study of Lysippos, partly because of its interest as a work of art, and partly because, being well preserved and easily accessible in reproduction, it offered a good opportunity for the interpretation of the evidence given by ancient authors. There are several extant monuments, however, which can be connected with Lysippos in a more direct and unquestionable way.

I have spoken already of an inscription on a base found at Corinth.[1] The leaded fastenings for the feet of the statue are still in position in their cuttings on the top of the base, and it is possible clearly to understand the position of the feet.[2] The left foot pointed almost straight to the front; the right foot was set at some distance to the side—the cuttings are 33 cm. apart at the point of nearest approach—a little in front, and turned outward; the back end of the cutting is 20 cm. from the side of the base, the front end only 14 cm. The weight evidently rested on the left foot. This position appears in the Cortona bronze mentioned in the preceding chapter and in the Dresden oil-pourer, whose resemblance to the Uffizi apoxyomenos has often been noted, and of course in many other figures. It can not be assumed that Lysippos was especially fond of it.

In Chapter III there was mentioned a base at Thebes which bears the signatures of Lysippos and Polykleitos. This base is now in the museum at

[1] Chapter III.

[2] A drawing of the base: *A.J.A.*, VII, 1903, p. 31.

Thebes, and the cuttings for the fastenings of the feet can be studied. They are shown clearly in the drawing (Plate 14, B), for which I am indebted to the kindness of Miss Dorothy Burr; the drawing itself was made by Mr. R. Stillwell. The Lysippian statue was evidently turned almost straight to the spectator's left. The print of one foot, probably the right, is turned slightly to the front and has the usual form. Farther to the spectator's left is an oval hole with a smaller square hole within it, which must have served for the fastening of some object on which the left foot was placed. The statue evidently did not represent Koreidas actually engaged in the contest, since in the pankration there would be nothing on which a foot could be placed. The motive of the statue is probably to be inferred from the epigram, in which the athlete's washing is mentioned. The left foot was set on a rock or a vase and the athlete was washing his leg. The posture was approximately the same as in the Rondanini Alexander, as restored. The statue by Polykleitos stood at rest, facing the front; the two figures must have been somewhat incongruous, and this increases the probability that they did not stand on this base originally. On the other hand, it should be noted that the figure by Lysippos was well suited to its position at the right end of a row of statues. (The right end of the block is smoothly dressed, while the other end has an anathyrosis.)

A signature in Megara was mentioned in chapter III; the base to which it belongs merits description here. The two inscribed blocks, now in the court of the schoolhouse at Megara, have almost identical dimensions: 1.27 m. long, 0.29 m. high, 0.80 m. deep. The two blocks were fastened together by a hook clamp, for which the cutting is visible in both blocks. The stone with the beginning of the inscription was at the left end of the basis, since the left end of it is smoothly dressed; but the right end of the other block (Plate 14, C) is not so dressed and in it there is a clamp-cutting, so it is evident that at some period, at any rate, there was another block beyond it. The stones are smoothly dressed on the back.

Near the right end of the first block, 0.08 m. from the end and 0.375 m. from the front of the block there is a square hole 0.07 m. deep and 0.285 m. square. Near the right end of the second block there is a similar hole, 0.11 m. from the end and 0.16 m. from the front, 0.32 m. wide and 0.275 m. from front to back. In this instance however the hole is occupied by a marble piece, which is 0.29 m. by 0.253 m. at the bottom and seems to taper slightly; its present height is 0.345 m. There is a small smooth surface on the top, but this is probably due to weathering and not original. Around this inserted piece the hole is filled with lead. On the left vertical face of the piece there is a rectangular vertical cutting, 0.085 m. wide and 0.04 m. deep; its visible height is 0.29 m. and above that the piece is broken. On the surface of the main block a shallow channel, 0.085 m. long, leads to the right to a cutting 0.075 m. wide and 0.045 m. from front to back, which is partly filled with some stony or cement-like substance. This hole is 0.38 m. from the back of the block, and the channel begins 0.44 m. from the left end. There is a smooth border at the right end of the second block and along the front and back for a distance of 0.80 m. from the end, where it becomes imperceptible. At the left of this point the surface of the block is smoother than at the right of it, though the difference is slight and no sharp line of division can be detected. A line drawn across the block from front to back at the place where the border becomes imperceptible, however, would cross the shallow channel which has been mentioned. This suggests that the channel is a pour-channel leading to a dowel hole, and that another block was

above the existing one at this place. The first block
shows a somewhat similar treatment of the surface;
but here it is the right end which is smoother, to a line
0.34 m. from the edge, while the remainder, except for
a smooth border, is rougher than any part of the surface of the second block.

The correct interpretation of all these indications
is far from obvious, but it is clear that no statue,
bronze or marble, stood directly on the surface of these
two blocks. It looks as if two figures stood at a higher
level, separated by a space 0.81 m. wide, in which the
existing blocks were uncovered. At about the middle
of this space was the piece which was inserted in the
large square hole in the first block, perhaps supporting
some object between the two figures. The existing
piece inserted in the second block would serve in some
way for the support of the figure near it or for some
attribute held by that figure. Loewy found a number
of blocks which appeared to belong to the lower courses
of this same basis,[3] and if he had made his examination under more favorable conditions he might have
been able to clear up the matter. These other blocks
are not in the court of the schoolhouse at Megara, but
they may possibly exist.

There is, however, one point about this basis which
we may hope to settle: that is its connection with the
Zeus and Muses by Lysippos which Pausanias saw in
Megara.[4] It was suggested by Loewy and more confidently by Pomtow[5] that our basis belonged to that
group. The study of the base hardly confirms the assumption, but until the base is better understood its
evidence can not be decisive.

Pausanias begins his description of Megara with
the fountain of Theagenes.[6] After mentioning a few

[3] *Ath. Mitt.*, X, 1885, p. 147.   [4] I 43, 6 (App. 1, 23).
[5] *Jb. Arch. I.*, XXXII, 1917, p. 136.
[6] I 40; for its situation see *Ath. Mitt.*, XXV, 1900, pl. VII. On
Megara cf. Highbarger, *The History and Civilization of Ancient Megara*,
1927, especially chapter I.

objects he comes to the Olympieion, of which traces have been found "near the north-west foot of the eastern hill,"[7] and then ascends this hill. Coming down the northern side[8] he first comes to the tomb of Alkmene, "near the Olympieion"; then the local guide led him to "a place which he alleged was named Rhus," where the water from the mountain above the city once flowed; it is evident that Rhus did not immediately adjoin the tomb of Alkmene. Several places in close succession after Rhus are then visited, and from the last of them he "descends" to the shrine of Pandion. Then he ascends the western acropolis Alkathoos.[9] So far he has apparently been in the northern part of the town and has traversed all of it. Rhus must be in the northern region, since the mountains are on the north.

Having reached the summit of Alkathoos[10] he begins the descent[11] and visits the Prytaneion,[12] then a number of sanctuaries including the temple with the statues by Lysippos,[13] then the agora.[14] Thence he "descends"[15] and soon reaches the "old gymnasium near the gate" through which, evidently, the traveller immediately proceeds to Nisaia. This then is at the south edge of town; inscriptions also indicate this as the site of the old gymnasium.[16] The agora from which Pausanias descended would be somewhere on the south slope of the saddle connecting the two hills.

Thus, though only a few of the places mentioned by the periegete can be definitely located, his general route is pretty clear. The statues by Lysippos were certainly in the southern half of the town. But the signed base was found at the northern foot of the eastern hill; it must have been close to the Olympieion and tomb of Alkmene. It is out of the question that the numerous blocks of a large basis should have been

[7] Frazer, *Pausanias,* vol. II, p. 524. [8] I 41.
[9] I 42. [10] I 42, 4. [11] I 42, 6.
[12] I 43, 2. [13] I 43, 6. [14] I 43, 8.
[15] I 44, 2. [16] Frazer, *Pausanias,* vol. II, p. 539.

moved together far from their original situation, so it is certain that the base does not belong to the group described by Pausanias.

There is another base which undoubtedly supported a work of Lysippos: his statue of the famous athlete Polydamas.[17] No evidence remains as to the position of the statue; but the reliefs on the base, described by Pausanias,[18] have been found at Olympia. There is no actual proof that Lysippos had anything to do with these sculptures; but it is eminently probable that he would have charge of everything connected with the statue, and that the sculptures of the base were made by his pupils and under his supervision; probably the master himself modelled the groups in clay.

The sculptures[19] are badly damaged, but we can still determine the subjects and something of the style. Polydamas's struggle with the lion was represented in at least two episodes: in one he is wrestling with the beast, while in the other the struggle is nearly or quite finished. The figures are slender; the postures are free and vigorous.

The best preserved scene shows Polydamas's exploit before Dareios. The king, seated on his throne, looks on while his champions are dispatched by the Greek; the ladies of the harem are also present. It is interesting to compare this relief with the sculpture of the Praxitelean base at Mantineia,[20] which it resembles more or less both in subject and in composition. In the Polydamas relief the figures are perceptibly more slender, as would be expected in a Lysippian work.

[17] See Chapter III for date. Lippold, in Pauly-Wissowa, n.: ?9.

[18] VI 5, 1-7 (App. I, 81).

[19] *Olympia, Ergebnisse*, III, pp. 209-211, pl. LV, 1-3; Frazer, *Pausanias*, vol. IV, p. 18.

[20] For arguments against the connection of this base with the great Praxiteles, see Vollgraff's article (*B.C.H.*, XXXII, 1908, pp. 236-258) and citations there. His conclusions do not seem to me to be substantiated. They are accepted by Dickins (*B.S.A.*, XXI, p. 7). Cf. *Jb. Arch. I.*, XXXVIII-XXXIX, 1923-1924, p. 273 (Bieber).

There is also a notable lack of the charming serenity and repose of the Mantineian group; this is apparent in a comparison of the similarly seated figures of Apollo and Dareios. The ladies of the harem, too, are much livelier than the Muses; though that is hardly a fair comparison. This spirit of unrest is perceptible in the drapery also. In comparison with the garment of Apollo, rendered in broad, harmonious lines reminiscent of the Parthenon frieze, the robe of Dareios appears almost sensational with its many small folds at the top and its large, obtrusive folds at the bottom. It would be most interesting to see how the drapery was arranged on the upper parts of the feminine figures, but unfortunately those parts are almost entirely destroyed. In the lower parts, however, something of the same difference can be seen: the folds are smaller and less regular than in the Mantineia relief, even where the more restless position does not require it.

Of the few works of Lysippos that are described by ancient authors in such detail that copies of them would be easily recognizable, only one seems to exist in extant sculpture: the Herakles Epitrapezios.[21] It is described by Martial[22] and by Statius.[23] It was a small bronze, less than a foot high, in the possession of Novius Vindex. The hero was seated on a rock over which the lion-skin was placed. In his left hand he held a club, in his right hand a cup. His gaze was directed upward. On the base appeared the name of Lysippos. Statius gives a somewhat bizarre history for the statuette, which, to say the least, could hardly have rested on sure evidence.

The line in which Martial mentions the inscription demands some consideration. All manuscripts give

Lysippum lego, Phidiae putavi.

[21] Fullest discussion by Weiszäcker, *Jb. Arch. I.*, IV, 1889, pp. 105-112. Another article by Picard, *R. Arch.*, XVII, 1911, pp. 257-270.

[22] *Epigrammata*, IX, 43 & 44 (App. 1, 45 & 46).

[23] *Silvae*, IV, 6 (App. 1, 47). See Vollmer's *Statius*, pp. 473-483. Cf. Lippold in Pauly-Wissowa, no. 15.

Sometimes the first word appears as "Lisippum," sometimes as "Lysippū," which is "Lysippum" abbreviated in the ordinary way. In this line the metre is satisfactory and so is the sense: 'I read (the name) Lysippus; I thought it was (the work) of Phidias.' But Aldus and apparently all later editors read

Λυσίππου lego, Phidiae putavi.

I have found no discussion of this emendation, but the theory is obvious: Λυσίππου was written "Lysippu" and that was changed to "Lysippum" by a scribe who supposed that the sign of abbreviation had been omitted through negligence. It might have happened so, but a satisfactory reading preserved in all manuscripts is not to be discarded merely because it might have arisen from another reading. This principle applies with special force to Martial, where the manuscripts have been shown to go back to two editions of the classical period. (Unfortunately no manuscripts of the third and best family have this epigram.)

Aldus probably had an idea that in artists' signatures the name usually appeared in the genitive. Modern editors presumably know better. An inscription containing Λυσίππου would not be a signature, but a label; and a statuette bearing such a label would in all probability be a copy, though it is not impossible that an unsigned original might be so inscribed by an owner. Vindex thought that he had the original, and we should not question his belief without a better reason than can be drawn from the possibility of emending Martial.[24]

We are dealing then with a signed work of Lysippos,[25] and with one that enjoyed popular favor, as is

[24] Professor Tenney Frank kindly called my attention to the textual problem.

[25] In spite of the general neglect of the Herakles, few scholars have definitely questioned its connection with Lysippos. Murray (*History of Greek Sculpture*, II, p. 350) rejects the whole story on the ground that Alexander would not ask Lysippos to make an ornament for the table. Lippold, in Pauly-Wissowa, apparently attaches too much importance to the differences between the various copies.

proved by the number of copies that remain. The connection between them and the work of Lysippos, which has recently been questioned,[26] is not open to doubt. The copies represent a statuette of the size required, though they naturally differ somewhat in size among themselves. No other statuette of Herakles was famous. The statuette belonged approximately, at least, to the time of Lysippos; it had a club in the left hand and the head was raised slightly. Martial's description does not require that the Herakles look straight up. The right hand, with the cup, is not preserved in any copy; but the coin of Amastris, to be mentioned presently, is adorned with a figure resembling the copies so closely that it must be reckoned with them, and this figure has a cup in the right hand. The correspondence is therefore complete.

The copies may be enumerated as follows:[27]

1. Marble statuette in Louvre, from Smyrna; height 38 cm.; *Gaz. Arch.*, X, 1885, pl. 8, 1; Reinach, *Répertoire*, II 228, 2.

2. Marble statuette in Louvre, from Gabii; height c. 35 cm.; *Gaz. Arch.*, X, 1885, pl. 8, 2; Reinach, *Répertoire*, II 228, 5; Collignon, *Lysippe*, fig. 13. With restorations: Reinach, *op. cit.*, III 73, 6.

3. Bronze statuette in Constantinople, height 5 cm.; *Olympia, Ergebnisse*, III, p. 236; Reinach, *Répertoire*, III 73, 3.

4. Marble statuette in British Museum, no. 1725, height 50 cm.; *Museum Marbles*, X, pl. 41, 3; Reinach, *Répertoire*, I 466, 3.

5. Cast from a lost statuette in École des Beaux-Arts, height 46 cm.; *Gaz. Arch.*, X, 1885, pl. 7; Reinach, *Répertoire*, I 469, 3; Maviglia, *L'Attività Artistica di Lisippo*, fig. 15; Springer-Wolters[12], p. 364, fig. 684; Collignon, *Sculpture Grecque*, II, p. 425, fig. 221. Drawing perhaps from the original: *Mélanges d'Arch. et d'Hist.*, XV, 1895, pp. 183 ff.

[26] Deonna in *Arethusa*, III, 1926, pp. 107-110. He publishes a bronze statuette of the sixteenth century, which apparently is a free imitation of some copy of the Epitrapezios type.
[27] The list is mostly copied from Weiszäcker.

6. Marble statuette once in Rome, height 40 cm.; *American Art Review*, II, p. 54; Reinach, *Répertoire*, III 73, 1; mentioned in Matz-Duhn, no. 125.
7. Limestone statuette in British Museum, no. 1726, height 50 cm.; *J. H. S.*, III, pl. 25; Reinach, *Répertoire*, II 227, 3. Signed by Diogenes.
8. Bronze statuette in Jagsthausen, height (without lower part) 14 cm.; *Jb. Arch. I.*, IV, 1889, pl. 3; Reinach, *Répertoire*, II 227, 1.
9. Bronze statuette in Museo Archeologico, Florence, height 42 cm.; *Galleria di Firenze*, Ser. IV, vol. III, pl. 107; Reinach, *Répertoire*, I 474, 6.
10. Cast in Dresden from lost original; mentioned by Treu, in *Olympia, Ergebnisse*, III, p. 236. Here plates 15 and 16.
11. Fragmentary marble statuette found at Delos; mentioned by Picard in *R. Arch.*, XVII, 1911, p. 269.
12. Bronze statuette in Vienna, Kunsthistorisches Museum, no. 1205; Von Sacken, *Die antiken Bronzen*, pl. XXXVII, 3 and p. 101; Weiszäcker, p. 110, excludes it from the list.
13. Marble figure in the Hermitage; Waldhauer, *Lisipp*, p. 32, fig. 21.[28]

Coin of Amastris, time of Caracalla; Waddington-Babelon-Reinach, *Recueil des Monnaies Grecques d'Asie Mineure*, p. 53, pl. XXI, 3; Mionnet, *Description de Medailles Antiques*, Supplement IV, 563, 86, pl. XII.

No. 10 is here illustrated for the first time (Plates 15 and 16), by the courtesy of the Director of the Dresden Albertinum. The cast was made by Raphael Mengs. The right hand, which holds apples, was undoubtedly new in the figure from which the cast was made; also, probably, the right arm, the upper part of the long club, and the left forearm. The head shows a groove in the hair where a wreath or fillet must have been worn. A restorer would hardly add such a feature independently; but he might, and probably did, make a small copy of some antique head of Herakles. Apparently some pieces have been found and added to no. 11 since Picard

---

[28] This figure is known to me only from Waldhauer, who does not tell the size or restorations. The head is obviously modern.

wrote. When I saw it in 1923 it lacked the head, both arms, the left foot, and the right leg from the thigh.

Of these copies nos. 1-4, 11, and 10 so far as probably antique have almost exactly the same position, which may be regarded as the original one: the right foot pressed back against the rock, the left foot advanced a little, the club held almost upright at the left. Nos. 5 and 6 deviate from this position only in that the club is more nearly horizontal. It is naturally uncertain how much of the figure from which no. 5 was cast was antique; the arms at least appear to be new, according to Ravaisson. No. 12 resembles nos. 5 and 6 in the position of the club and has the feet reversed. Nos. 7 and 8 are freer imitations; while there is a reasonable doubt whether no. 9, which is much restored, should be included in the list at all.[29] A free imitation was found in Rome.[29a] The marble statuette found at Olympia is of quite distinct type.[30] A bronze statuette found at Pompeii is also of a different type.[31] It corresponds very well to the descriptions of Martial and Statius; but since it has no such array of replicas as the other type, and is considerably larger than the work of Lysippos (height 75 cm.) it need not occupy us in this connection. Among the numerous large seated figures of Herakles there is one that resembles the Epitrapezios so closely that it may have been imitated directly from it.[32]

Numbers 5 and 10 are very similar in the representation of anatomy; the musculature is rich and treated with considerable detail. Nos. 2 and 4 show virtually the same style, and one concludes that it is copied faithfully from the original figure by Lysippos. In no. 1 the flesh is much drier and less anatomical detail is

[29] Weiszäcker, p. 110, argues for its inclusion.
[29a] Not. Sc., 1889, p. 245; Reinach, Répertoire, III 248, 9.
[30] Olympia, Ergebnisse, III, pl. LIX, 1; Reinach, Répertoire, III, 73, 7.
[31] Not. Sc., 1902, p. 573.
[32] Gauckler, Musée de Cherchel, p. 127, no. 4, and pl. XI.

shown. No. 11 is so poor that no evidence can be derived from it, and the testimony of the less exact copies —7, 8, 9, 12—is also valueless for the study of details. I have not examined no. 3 or no. 6; the former is so small that it can hardly be faithful in minutiae. Nos. 2 and 5 show distinctly the triangular opening between the muscles at the waist which has figured in discussions of the apoxyomenos. Nos. 1 and 10 do not have it, while I found it difficult to be sure about no. 4. In small figures the copyists would be especially likely to omit such a detail, and it is altogether probable that it was present in the original. In the feet no. 2 is conspicuously unlike the apoxyomenos; so is no. 10, where, however, the feet may not be original; no. 4 is fairly close to the apoxyomenos in this point.

No. 4 is said to have a head of the same type as the Herakles Farnese, but this is true only in a very general sense: the head of the statuette wore a wreath and fillet. There is a groove in the forehead and the right eye, despite its small scale, can be seen to resemble the eyes of the apoxyomenos. (The left eye is rubbed.) The ear is not like that of the apoxyomenos; the details of the hair can not be made out. The head of no. 5 resembles that of no. 4 pretty closely, and I assume therefore that it was antique in the figure from which the cast was made. This is probably not true of no. 10; at any rate this head bears little resemblance to the other two. The head is unlike the other two, and contrary to our descriptions of the Lysippian original, in its position: it does not look upward. Nos. 1, 2, 6, and 11 are headless.

In the battles among the champions of the Vatican apoxyomenos, the Uffizi apoxyomenos, and the Agias, little attention has been given to the Herakles Epitrapezios; yet it is the only work of Lysippos that can be identified with certainty on external evidence. It is true that statuettes are prone to be carelessly made and

unreliable in details, but it has proved possible to gain
a fairly precise idea of the original by a study of the
various copies. The artist of the Herakles could very
well have made the apoxyomenos of the Braccio
Nuovo, while he could hardly have made the original
of the Uffizi type or an original from which the Agias
was closely copied. Those two works show a different
and earlier conception of the human body.

A word should be said as to the purpose of the
statuette. It has generally been assumed that it was
simply a table-piece: "Herakles on the Table." Picard
cites several passages of Hesychios in which the word
ἐπιτραπέζιος is used in connection with πάταικος ;[33]
and πάταικοι are well accredited Phoenician deities.
Ordinarily, it seems, they were placed in ships for good
luck;[34] a πάταικος ἐπιτραπέζιος would presumably be
placed on the table for a similar reason, and a Herakles
Epitrapezios would be such a figure Hellenized.

All this is plausible. Probably this was the source
of the name for the statue, and probably it was made
in 332, at the time of Alexander's Phoenician campaign.[35] It would be just after the Granikos monument, and just before the trip to Tarentum. We need
not follow Picard, however, in believing that the statuette represented in any definite sense the Tyrian
Herakles or Melkarth.[36]

Of all the works that have been attributed to Lysippos because of their resemblance to the apoxyomenos,
none is more interesting than the Eros with the bow.
This most charming figure was apparently, in antiquity, decidedly the most popular representation of
the adolescent Eros. Thanks to the fact that the bow
serves as a support for the outstretched arms and
makes a copy in marble fairly easy, we have a large
number of replicas. Klein listed twenty-nine examples,

[33] R. Arch., XVII, 1911, p. 261.   [34] Herodotos, III, 37.
[35] So Picard, p. 265.   [36] Picard, p. 261.

including variants, besides six replicas of the head alone and reliefs and gems.[37] As several replicas have been found since Klein wrote, I am presenting a complete list, retaining Klein's numbers for those in his enumeration:

1. Capitoline Museum, Gabinetto di Venere; Jones, *Museo Capitolino*, p. 87, no. 5, pl. 18; Reinach, *Répertoire*, I 352, 7; Helbig³, I, p. 426; Friederichs-Wolters, pp. 635-638, no. 1582; Bocconi, *Musei Capitolini*, fig. 26; Von Mach, *University Prints*, 188.
2. Louvre; Fröhner, no. 329; Reinach, *Répertoire*, I 142, 3.
3. Ny Carlsberg; Arndt, *Glyptothèque*, p. 172; *De Antike Kunstvaerker*, no. 180; Reinach, *Répertoire*, II 427, 5.
4. Brocklesby Park; Michaelis, *Anc. Mar.*, p. 240; *Mus. Wors.*, I, p. 97.
5. Villa Albani; Helbig², II, p. 16; Reinach, *Répertoire*, I 354, 8.
6. Vatican, Museo Chiaramonti, no. 495; Amelung, *Skulpt. d. Vat. Mus.*, I, p. 633, pl. 67; Reinach, *Répertoire*, III 261, 5; Collignon, *Lysippe*, fig. 14.
7. Berlin; *Ant. Skulpt.*, no. 138; Friederichs, *Amor mit dem Bogen des Herkules*, plate; Reinach, *Répertoire*, II 427, 2.
8. Louvre; Fröhner, no. 327; D'Escamps, *Musée Campana*, pl. X; Reinach, *Répertoire*, II 427, 1.
9. Brussels, Musées Royaux; Cumont, *Catalogue*, no. 16; Furtwängler, *Collection Somzée*, no. 39; *Palais de San Donato*, p. 198; Reinach, *Répertoire*, I 357, 7 and II 427, 3.
10. Museo Torlonia; Visconti, no. 171; *Arch. Zeit.*, 1879, p. 76, no. 169; Reinach, *Répertoire*, II 427, 6.
11. Karlsruhe; Von Duhn, *Catalogue of Casts in Heidelberg*⁶, p. 112, no. 305.
12. Despuig collection in Majorca; Hübner, *Ant. Bildw. in Madrid*, no. 702; Reinach, *Répertoire*, II 427, 4.
13. Venice, Museo Archeologico; Dütschke, *Ant. Bildw. in Oberitalien*, V, no. 99; *Arch. Zeit.*, XXX, 1873, p. 84, no. 35; *Einzelaufnahmen*, 2447; Reinach, *Répertoire*, V 175, 7.
14. Louvre; Fröhner, no. 328; Reinach, *Répertoire*, I 142, 7.

[37] *Praxiteles*, p. 230 f.

106   LYSIPPOS

15. Castle Howard; Michaelis, *Anc. Mar.*, p. 326, no. 7; Reinach, *Répertoire*, I 359, 2.
16. Vatican, Galleria dei Candelabri. I did not find it.
17. Lateran; Benndorf-Schöne, *Ant. Bildw. d. Lat. Mus.*, no. 224.
18. Rome, Palazzo Patrizi; Matz-Duhn, *Ant. Bildw. in Rom*, no. 253.
19. Venice, Museo Archeologico; Dütschke, *op. cit.*, V, no. 201; Reinach, *Répertoire*, IV 275, 6, and V 176, 3; *Einzelaufnahmen*, 2533 (cf. *Arch. Anz.*, XXXV, 1920, col. 16).
20. Florence, Giardino Torrigiani; Dütschke, *op. cit.*, II, no. 457.
21. Louvre, no. 1776 (? labeled 450); Reinach, *Répertoire*, II 458, 8.
22. British Museum; Smith, *Catalogue*, III, p. 66, no. 1675; Reinach, *Répertoire*, III 127, 5.
23. British Museum; Smith, *Catalogue*, III, p. 64, no. 1673; *Museum Marbles*, X, pl. 21; Reinach, *Répertoire*, I, 358, 7. Here pl. 17.
24. Hermitage; Kieseritzky, *Hermitage*, no. 342; Reinach, *Répertoire*, III 127, 3; Waldhauer, *Lisipp*, fig. 7.
25. Venice, Museo Archeologico; Dütschke, *op. cit.*, V, no. 166; Reinach, *Répertoire*, I 360, 3; *Arch. Zeit.*, XXX, 1873, p. 86, no. 102. The head is of this type but does not belong to the statue; *Einzelaufnahmen*, 2514 f.
26. Pawlowsk; Stephani, *Antiken zu Pawlowsk* (*Memoires de l'académie impériale de St.-Petersbourg*, Series VII, vol. 18, 1872), no. 5; Reinach, *Répertoire*, I 355, 7.
27. Vatican, Museo Chiaramonti, no. 653; Amelung, *Skulpt. d. Vat. Mus.*, I, p. 755, pl. 81; Reinach, *Répertoire*, III 261, 3.
28. Wilton House; Michaelis, *Anc. Mar.*, p. 695, no. 124; Reinach, *Répertoire*, I 357, 8.
29. British Museum, no. 1674; Smith, *Catalogue*, III, p. 65 f.; Reinach, *Répertoire*, I 357, 6; Bulle, *Der schöne Mensch²*, pls. 63 and 215.
30. Philadelphia, University Museum; *Museum Journal*, V, 1914, p. 117; Reinach, *Répertoire*, V 175, 3 and 4; Luce, *Catalogue of the Mediterranean Section*, p. 173, no. 27.
31. Benghazi; *Gaz. des Beaux-Arts*, XIV, 1918, pp. 1-5; *Cron. B. A.*, V (supplement to *Boll. Arte*, XII), p. 30; *Notiz. Arch.*, II, 1916, p. 43; *R. Arch.*, XII, 1920, p.

141, no. 3; *J.H.S.*, XLI, 1921, pl. XVII, 2 and pp. 242-246; Reinach, *Répertoire*, V 175, 1.
32. Vatican, Sala del Meleagro, no. 15; Amelung, *Skulpt. d. Vat. Mus.*, II, p. 44, pl. IV.
33. Montauban; Reinach, *Répertoire*, II 427, 7.
34. Geneva, Museum; Reinach, *Répertoire*, III 127, 1; *Einzelaufnahmen*, 1914; Deonna, *Catalogue des Sculptures Antiques*, p. 57, no. 62.
35. In possession of Bardini, at Florence, in 1897; mentioned Reinach, *Répertoire*, II, p. 427.
36. Found at Lemnos; *R. Arch.*, III, 1916, p. 157; Reinach, *Répertoire*, V 175, 2.
37. Smith College; *A.J.A.*, XXXVIII, 1923, pp. 369 f.; *Bulletin of Hillyer Art Gallery*, March, 1923, pp. 2-6. Here pl. 9.
38. Athens, National Museum (Magazine), no. 3412; mentioned by Lippold, *Kopien und Umbildungen*, p. 244, note 26.
39. Constantinople; Mendel, *Catalogue des Sculptures*, III, pp. 20-21, no. 818. Unfinished.

HEADS

1. Berlin; *Ant. Skulpt.*, no. 152.
2. Blundell Hall; Michaelis, *Anc. Mar.*, p. 371, no. 193.
3. Ny Carlsberg; Arndt, *La Glyptothèque*, pl. 124, p. 172; *De Antike Kunstvaerker*, no. 181. Here pl. 8.
4. Rome, Barracco Collection; Matz-Duhn, *op. cit.*, no. 298. I did not see it.
5. British Museum, no. 1680; Smith, *Catalogue*, III, pp. 68 f.[38]
6. Dresden; Hettner[4], no. 189. I did not see it.
7. Vatican, Museo Chiaramonti, no. 607 A; Amelung, *Skulpt. d. Vat. Mus.*, I, p. 720, pl. 77.
8. Paris; *Mon. Piot*, XIII, 1906, pp. 137-148, pls. XI-XII and figure on p. 139.
9. Baltimore, Walters Art Gallery; *Art in America*, V, 1917, pp. 192 ff.
10. Museo Torlonia; mentioned *Röm. Mitt.*, I, 1886, p. 114, no. 92; Visconti, no. 92, pl. XXIII.
11. Hermitage; Kieseritzky, *Hermitage*, no. 52.
12. Louvre, no. 447.
13. London, Wallace Collection, no. 7.

[38] I suppose this is the head noted by Klein. It is not recognized in the catalogue as belonging to the type. Sieveking (*B. Ph. Wo.*, XXV, 1905, col. 519) correctly says that it is a replica.

RELIEF

Sarcophagus in Cephisia; Robert, *Die antiken Sarko-phagreliefs,* II, pl. III.

GEMS

1. Berlin; Furtwängler, *Geschnittene Steine,* no. 1603.
2. Berlin; Furtwängler, *Geschnittene Steine,* no. 3701.
3. Leningrad; Furtwängler, *Die Antiken Gemmen,* III, pl. XLIII 60, II, p. 210.
4. Unknown possessor; Furtwängler, *Die Antiken Gemmen,* III, pl. XIV 9, II, p. 67.
5. Cameo in Mainz; *Germania Romana,* pl. 79, no. 4.

No illustration or description of no. 38 has been published; it is small and lacks the head, right arm, left wrist and hand, and legs from thighs. There may be some duplication in the list. I have omitted the statue once in the Giustiniani collection,[39] though it seems certain that Reinach is wrong in identifying it with no. 10. The torso at Naples, which Ruesch calls a copy,[40] does not seem to be one; the legs are in approximately the usual position, but the head and arms are turned in the other direction. A terracotta statuette found at Myrina[41] may show the influence of the type; perhaps also the Eros in a painting found at Pompeii[42] and a coin-type of Kydonia in Crete.[43]

Most of the copies have been badly broken. No. 23, however, is almost perfectly preserved and shows the action clearly. The little god rests his weight on his left foot; the right is set a little distance to the side; the knee is bent and the heel raised slightly from the ground. The left arm passes downward across

[39] Reinach, *Répertoire,* I, 352, 1, reversed? Cf. *op. cit.,* II, p. 427.

[40] *Guida²,* p. 158, no. 495; Reinach, *Répertoire,* II, 608, 7.

[41] Hamdy Bey and Reinach, *La Nécropole de Myrina,* I, pl. VI, pp. 290 ff. A similar terracotta is said (*op. cit.,* p. 291) to exist in Berlin.

[42] *Röm. Mitt.,* XVI, 1901, p. 340; *Jh. Oest. Arch. I.,* XIII, 1910, pp. 138-140.

[43] Wroth, *British Museum Catalogue, Crete,* pl. VII, 1 ff.; Svoronos, *Les Monnaies de la Crète Ancienne,* pl. IX, 2 ff. Wroth (p. 28) dates the coins 400-300.

the body and the hand holds the middle of the bow; the right arm is stretched out almost horizontally from the shoulder and the hand holds the upper end of the bow. The lower end was pressed against the calf of the right leg.

Second in preservation among the copies is probably no. 31. Here, though the positions of the arms and legs is virtually the same as before, the action is entirely different. One end of the bow is pressed against the left thigh, the other held by the right hand, and the middle is pressed back by the right thigh; the left hand evidently held the string, which passed in front of the right leg.

It has usually been assumed that Eros is represented in the act of stringing the bow and that no. 23 represents truly the action of the original. But it has been pointed out that the ordinary way of stringing the bow, as known from many monuments, is that shown in no. 31;[44] while it would be altogether impossible to string a bow of the παλίντονος type in the manner of no. 23, and any sort of bow could be very much better strung in the other way. In no. 23 the right hand must have held the string till the bow was sufficiently bent to allow the attachment of the string to the end of the bow; the bending then must be done by the left hand and the right leg, and it is obvious that virtually no pressure could be exerted in this way. If it were necessary to explain no. 23 as a bow-stringer we should have to say that he bent the upper end of the bow with his right forearm while he held the string with his right hand. But the action of the figure is quite simple and reasonable if it is given another explanation: Eros is *unstringing* the bow. For this purpose very little pressure would be necessary, and it

[44] Bulanda, *Bogen und Pfeil bei den Völkern des Altertums,* pp. 94-95; Bagnani, in *J.H.S.,* XLI, 1921, pp. 242-246. For the Greek bow and methods of stringing it see Bulanda, *op. cit.* and Neuburger, *Technik des Altertums³,* pp. 221-224.

would be supplied chiefly by the right hand, which
would press down the upper end of the bow while the
fingers loosened the string.   The only other possible
explanation is that he is bending or merely playing
with the bow.   This is both improbable in itself and
disproved by the fact that he is not looking at the bow,
but at some distant object;—the object at which he
has shot.

It would be desirable to divide all the statues in the
list between the two types, but it is not easy.   In
stringing the bow the legs would naturally be somewhat
farther apart, and the hands more nearly on a level,
than in unstringing it; but these differences are slight
and hardly perceptible except where the preservation
is unusually good.   In figures like no. 31, however, the
traces of the bow on the thighs ought always to be
visible when the thighs are preserved. Unfortunately
I did not have this matter in mind when I was visiting
museums and must rely on descriptions.   It is certain
that nos. 1, 6, and 25 are like no. 23, and gems 1-4
and the painting in Pompeii show the influence of that
type.   No. 5,[45] on the other hand, is like no. 31.   No.
27, which is a very free imitation, represents the
stringing of the bow, but the bow is in front of the
right leg and the string behind it, instead of the reverse as in no. 31; and the Mainz gem (no. 5) appears
to be like no. 27.   In no. 13, which is purely decorative,
both string and bow are in front of the right leg.   Like
no. 27 and the Mainz gem, it indicates that the artist
knew a statue of the type of no. 31, though he does
not imitate it directly.   Nos. 29 and 37 represent a
variation in which both arms start almost straight
down from the shoulders. No. 29 is restored as stringing the bow in a very inefficient and improbable manner.   Deane[46] is probably right in suggesting that the

---

[45] Described by Reichel, *Homerische Waffen*, pp. 118 f., note 1.
[46] *Bulletin of Hillyer Art Gallery*, March, 1923, pp. 2-6.

lower end of the bow rested on the ground. A straight bow could be strung in this way.

Bulanda gives two lists in which the representatives of the two main types are apparently supposed to be separated. Writing before no. 31 was known, he groups with no. 5: 3, 7, 8, 9, 10, 12, 15, 23, and 33; while he reckons nos. 24 and 28 with the other type. He gives no citations, which ought to mean that his division rests on personal study; but he is certainly wrong about no. 23, and in nos. 7 and 9 it appears to be certain that the parts which would decide the question are lost. One naturally hesitates to trust his grouping in other points. There are several cases in which one may infer, from the silence of the descriptions in regard to traces which figures of the type of no. 31 would show, that the statues belong to the other type. It is apparent that most of the figures in the list are probably like no. 23; a more thorough study at first hand might possibly reverse this conclusion, but would surely establish no very marked preponderance in favor of 31.

There is no question of two distinct originals here, but we have to decide which group of copies more accurately represents the Greek prototype. In making the decision we follow the rule of the *lectio difficilior*. The act of stringing the bow was represented frequently; a statue with that subject would not be modified and changed into something much less familiar, while the reverse might easily and naturally happen. It is significant also that no. 31, the clearest specimen of the bow-stringers, was not intended as a close copy: that is obvious from the omission of the wings.

In the original the lower curve of the bow evidently touched the right thigh, as in nos. 23 and 26, or closely approached it; a dowel-hole in the thigh of the Capitoline example (no. 1) may indicate a short supporting bar. No. 23 is the only copy, I think, in which the

wings are entirely, or even mostly, original; they are
small and elegant in form, but these qualities are to
some extent characteristic of that replica in general.
(In No. 29 the wings are antique, but do not belong to
the figure.) Since the quiver always either forms the
support or hangs on it, we must conclude that there was
no quiver in the bronze original. This adds some probability to Friederichs's hypothesis, founded on the presence of a lion-skin in several replicas (23, 24, 25, 26,
and 12; perhaps restored in the last), that Eros is supposed to have stolen the bow of Herakles.[47] It has generally been recognized, however, that the bow is not dis-
proportionately large, as it surely would be if it were
supposed to belong to Herakles.

In the early days of dilettantism this figure was
frequently identified with the Eros by Praxiteles at
Thespiai, which was so highly regarded. Modern
authorities have generally abandoned this theory,
though it is said that Revaisson-Mollien supported it
in 1908,[48] and Dr. Bates apparently considers Praxiteles the sculptor naturally to be mentioned in connection with the statue.[49] Lysippos also had an Eros
at Thespiai,[50] and Collignon,[51] Klein,[52] Bagnani,[53]
Furtwängler,[54] Studniczka,[55] Loewy,[56] Lippold,[57]
Waldhauer,[58] Arndt,[59] and Cumont[60] confidently find
evidence of his style in the replicas preserved. Mme.
Maviglia[61] thinks the attribution confirmed rather than
weakened by her discovery of the Uffizi apoxyomenos.

[47] *Amor mit dem Bogen des Herkules.*
[48] *Bull. des Antiquaires de France,* 1908, p. 147-8.
[49] *Museum Journal,* I, 1910, p. 31.
[50] Pausanias, IX 27, 3 (App. 1, 32) ; Lippold in Pauly-Wissowa, no. 9.
[51] *Lysippe,* p. 68.   [52] *Gesch. d. griech. Kunst,* II, p. 359.
[53] *J.H.S.,* XLI, 1921, p. 245.   [54] *Masterpieces,* p. 394.
[55] *Neue Jahrbücher,* XLI, 1918, p. 21.
[56] *Griechische Plastik,* p. 104.   [57] In Pauly-Wissowa.
[58] *Lisipp,* p. 24.   [59] *Glyptothèque Ny Carlsberg,* p. 172.
[60] *Cat. des Mus. Royaux,* no. 16.   [61] *Op. cit.,* p. 67 ff.

Michaelis,[62] Helbig,[63] Jones,[64] Edward Robinson,[65] and Bulle[66] are more or less doubtful; while Wolters,[67] Amelung,[68] Smith,[69] Reinach,[70] and Ghizlanzoni[71] regard the statue as Hellenistic. Dickins[72] seems to recognize some type of Eros as Lysippian; I suppose it is this one.

The attribution to Praxiteles seems rightly to have been abandoned. No figure that can be traced with any probability to him shows such lively action, expressed in a momentary posture. On the other hand, the definite arguments against an attribution to Lysippos are not convincing. Wolters[73] once argued that the statues of Praxiteles and Lysippos both were temple-statues; the type in question, he said, certainly does not look like a temple-statue, so it could not be either of them. This must have been a mere slip; there is no reason whatever for supposing that Lysippos's Eros was a temple-statue. He objected also that the childish character of the subject was too well portrayed for any time before the Alexandrian period. That, however, is difficult of demonstration. Smith[74] doubted whether the arrangement of the hair—parted on both sides, with the locks between plaited along the middle line—occurs as early as Lysippos; but it occurs much earlier.[75]

It has very generally been recognized that there is great similarity between the apoxyomenos and the

[62] *Springer-Michaelis*[8], p. 297.   [63] *Führer*[2], no. 437.

[64] *Museo Capitolino*, p. 87.

[65] *Catalogue of Casts in Boston*, 1896, p. 249.

[66] *Der schöne Mensch*[2], col. 122. Apparently he thought better of the hypothesis on further consideration (col. 671).

[67] Friederichs-Wolters, no. 1582.   [68] Helbig, *Führer*[3], no. 776.

[69] *British Museum Catalogue*, III, p. 65.

[70] *Myrina*, II, p. 291. Perhaps he has changed his mind; cf. *R. Arch.*, XII, 1920, p. 140.

[71] *Notiz. Arch.*, II, p. 43.   [72] *Hellenistic Sculpture*, p. 32.

[73] Friederichs-Wolters, p. 637.

[74] *British Museum Catalogue*, III, p. 65.

[75] Steininger, in Pauly-Wissowa, VII, 2125. Cf. *Jb. Arch. I.*, XXX, 1915, pp. 191 f., fig. 15.

Eros in the bodily forms.   The ponderation too is very
similar.   Both figures are represented in unstable positions, which endure but a moment; the weight is
swinging toward the figure's right.   The analogy in
this matter is very striking, and almost proves that the
Eros is not earlier than Lysippos.   Amelung,[76] who
recognizes all this, nevertheless argues that the face is
too unlike that of the apoxyomenos or any other Lysippian figure to allow an attribution to him.

In the Metropolitan Museum casts of the apoxyomenos and the Capitoline Eros are placed near each
other, and I have been able to compare them under
favorable circumstances.   The Eros has no restorations on the head, except the tip of the nose.   The eyes
are not like those of the apoxyomenos: they are larger
in proportion to the size of the face, they are farther
apart, they are wider open, and there are no hollows
at the outer corners.   All these differences, however,
correspond to the differences in subject.   Such deeply
shadowed eyes as those of the apoxyomenos have never
yet occurred in a child.   The hair is in long, straggling
locks, necessarily different from the closely cropped
hair of the athlete.   The general shape of the face is
like that of the apoxyomenos, as are the forehead and
the ears.   The characteristic narrow nose and the still
more characteristic upper lip, as well as the lower lip,
are exactly in the style of the apoxyomenos.   Head no.
3 agrees with no. 1 so closely as to indicate that they
faithfully represent the original.   Head 8 agrees in
general, though the nose is broader and the ears are
not so much like those of the apoxyomenos.   In several heads, e.g. that worn by no. 25, the eyes are more
like those of the apoxyomenos than in the Capitol copy.

[76] Helbig[3], I, p. 426.   He sees a resemblance to the heads of Menander,
which he attributes to the sons of Praxiteles.   The resemblance does
not seem altogether convincing.   Besides, the attribution of these busts
to Kephisodotos and Timarchos rests on the feeblest evidence.   (Most
recent discussions: Studniczka, *Neue Jahrbücher*, XLI, 1918, pp. 1-31;
D. M. Robinson, *Bull. Royal Ontario Museum*, Jan. 1926, pp. 2-6.)

The resemblance between these heads and the head of the apoxyomenos, in the points where similarity could reasonably be expected, seems sufficient, when considered together with the resemblance in body and posture previously mentioned, to remove all reasonable doubt that they represent originals of one artist.

Recently a brilliant suggestion by Frickenhaus has confirmed this conclusion with literary evidence.[77] Kedrenos enumerates the statues that were destroyed in the Lauseion in Constantinople, in 476.[78]   There were the Lindian Athena, by Dipoinos and Skyllis, the Knidian Aphrodite of Praxiteles, the Samian Hera by Boupalos and Lysippos, the winged Eros with a bow, from Myndos, the ivory Zeus of Pheidias, and the image of Time by Lysippos.   The reference to Boupalos and Lysippos as joint authors of the Samian Hera is so patently absurd that students have ignored it.   Frickenhaus observes, however, that while the comments on the other statues show some inaccuracies, they contain no such absurdities as this; and that the name of Lysippos certainly belonged, in the account used by Kedrenos, to the "winged Eros with a bow, from Myndos," which is named just after the Hera and, alone of all the statues, has no sculptor named for it.   A glance at the passage shows the extreme probability of this correction, and one wonders only that it remained for Frickenhaus, in 1915, to suggest it.

Kedrenos is not so good an authority as one could wish; but his testimony, confirming the conclusions reached by many authorities from morphological evidence, leaves no doubt as to the authorship of the Eros. Like the Herakles Epitrapezios, it may be accepted as a work that certainly represents an original from the hand of Lysippos.   Myndos is in Caria, so if we have correctly reconstructed the life of the artist the Eros was made after 316.

[77] *Jb. Arch. I.,* XXX, 1915, pp. 127-9.
[78] 322 B-C (App. 1, 35).   This Eros is no. 10 in Lippold's list.

The evidence derived from the apoxyomenos, the Herakles Epitrapezios, and the Eros, supplemented by the "Old Fountain" base and the Polydamas base, is all perfectly consistent and harmonious. Whatever doubts may be raised as to one part or another are removed by the consensus of the whole. The foundation thus laid for our knowledge of Lysippian art is certain and dependable.

CHAPTER VI

THE DAOCHOS GROUP

On the slope above the east end of the temple of Apollo at Delphi there was an enclosed precinct.[1] Whether it was a roofed building is uncertain.[2] Against the back wall of this precinct is a long base with cuttings for the plinths of nine statues.[3] Dinsmoor[4] has shown conclusively that the base was placed there after the precinct wall had been built. The base is completely preserved except for surface imperfections. It is 11.67 m. long, .98 m. high, and .70 m. thick. On the face of the base, under every cavity except the one at the extreme right, is an inscription naming the man whose statue stood there.[5] I present literal translations of these inscriptions.

Under the second cavity from the right:

"Aknonios son of Aparos, tetrarch of the Thessalians."

The third:

"First from the land of Thessaly, Pharsalian Agias, son of Aknonios, you conquered in the Olympic pankration; five times at Nemea, thrice at Pytho, five times at the Isthmus; and no one ever set up trophies of your hands."

The fourth:

"I was his brother, and I attained the same number of crowns on the same days, conquering in wrestling. I killed the strongest man of the Tyrrhenians, who was helpless. My name was Telemachos."

[1] Photograph: *A.J.A.*, XIII, 1909, p. 448 (Poulsen, *Delphi*, p. 267). For the original ground-plan see Dinsmoor, in *A.J.A.*, XIII, 1909, p. 476 and pl. XIV.

[2] *B. Ph. Wo.*, XXXI, 1911, col. 1550; Bourguet, *Ruines de Delphes*, p. 197. Poulsen thinks it was roofed (*op. cit.*, p. 266).

[3] Photograph: *A.J.A.*, XIII, 1909, p. 447 (Poulsen, *op. cit.*, p. 268).

[4] *A.J.A.*, XIII, 1909, p. 473.

[5] Preuner, *Ein delphisches Weihgeschenk*, pp. 3 f.; Dittenberger, *Sylloge*[3], I, pp. 483-485, no. 274; facsimile, *B.C.H.*, XXI, 1897, pp. 592-594.

The fifth:

"These two had equal shares of prize-winning might, and I, Agelaos, was brother to them. I won the stadium for boys at Pytho, along with them;[6] alone of mortals we hold these crowns."

The sixth:

"Daochos son of Agias am I, of the land of Pharsalos. I ruled all Thessaly, not by force but by law, twenty-seven years; and Thessaly was rich with long and fruitful peace and wealth."

The seventh:

"Pallas did not deceive you in your sleep, Sisyphos son of Daochos, in what she told you clearly and the promise she gave; for since first you put on armor about your body, never did you flee from foes nor receive any wound."

The eighth:

"Increasing the renown of the ancestors of his house, Daochos, set up these gifts to the lord Phoebus, for the honor of his race and fatherland, with eulogy which gives fame. Tetrarch of the Thessalians. Recorder of the Amphiktyons."

The ninth and last to the left:

"Sisyphos son of Daochos."

We learn from these inscriptions that the group was dedicated by Daochos II; that it included his son Sisyphos II, and Sisyphos I, undoubtedly his father; Daochos I, the father of Sisyphos I; Agias, father of Daochos I, and his brothers Telemachos and Agelaos; Aknonios, father of the three brothers; and a ninth figure who had no inscription. Aknonios, Daochos I, and Daochos II were statesmen; Sisyphos I was a warrior; Agias, Telemachos, and Agelaos were athletes. Their inscriptions commemorate them in these rôles

---

[6] That is, at the same session of the games in which Agias and Telemachos won the pankration and the wrestling match respectively. The alleged unique feature doubtless consisted in the winning of victories by three brothers at one session of the games.

and we may expect that the statues will so represent them. Sisyphos II was presumably a mere youth who had not yet distinguished himself in any way.

The cavities in the base vary in shape according to the form of the plinth,[7] and this makes identification of some of the statues easy.[8] The plinths of the statues of Agias (Plate 20) and Daochos II were found in place, so there is no doubt about them. Of Daochos only one foot and a piece of the other remain.[9] We can see that the left leg was the "Standbein," while the right foot was drawn back and rested on the toe only. The sandals, together with the fact that the subject was a statesman and dignitary, indicate that the statue was draped. The plinth of the statue of Aknonios[10] is identified by the fact that it fits the cutting in place II. As Aknonios was a statesman and wears sandals, we expect his statue to be draped. Two draped torsos, apparently belonging to the group, were found. One of them[11] suits the position of the feet of Aknonios very well, while it can not belong to the feet of Daochos II; and the other[12] can not be Aknonios, because part of the left foot is preserved. Undoubtedly, then, the former torso belongs to Aknonios in place II. Sisyphos I[13] is well preserved, and is identified by the adjustment of the plinth to the cutting in place VII. We have left one draped figure, mentioned above, and one cutting

[7] See the drawing, *A.J.A.*, XIII, 1909, pl. XIV.

[8] For the restoration of the group, see Homolle, in *B.C.H.*, XXIII, 1899, pp. 426-438, and chiefly Gardiner and Smith, in *A.J.A.*, XIII, 1909, pp. 447-475. Some comments by Wolters, *Sitzb. Bayer. Akad. Wiss.*, 1913, *Arch. Bemerkungen*, pp. 40-50.

[9] Illustration: *A.J.A.*, XIII, 1909, p. 454; *B.C.H.*, XXIII, 1899, p. 427.

[10] Illustration: *A.J.A.*, XIII, 1909, p. 450; *B.C.H.*, XXIII, 1899, p. 431.

[11] *B.C.H.*, XXIII, 1899, pl. XXV, at right; *Fouilles de Delphes*, pl. LXVI, at left; Poulsen, *op. cit.*, p. 270.

[12] *Fouilles de Delphes*, pl. LXVI, at right; Bourguet, *Ruines de Delphes*, p. 197; *A.J.A.*, XIII, 1909, p. 453; Poulsen, *op. cit.*, p. 274; *B.C.H.*, XXIII, 1899, pl. XXV, at left.

[13] *Fouilles*, pl. LXV; Poulsen, *op. cit.*, p. 277; *B.C.H.*, XXIII, 1899, pl. XXIV.

aside from those probably for nude figures. The figure then is pretty certainly Daochos I, in place VI. These five identifications, made by Homolle, are accepted as certain by Gardiner and Smith. There remain places I, IV, V, and IX.

In place V Homolle placed the figure of a youth leaning on a herm,[14] as Agelaos. Gardiner and Smith present measurements which seem to prove that it could not have rested on a plinth small enough for the cavity.[15] Since its workmanship is in some details very like that of the Agias, they wish to retain it in the group; and as its plinth must have been of a shape unsuited to cavities IX and I, they give it the only remaining place—IV, as Telemachos. Wolters believes that the statue does not belong to the group, because the left leg, to judge from the shape of the cutting, must have been advanced; and the resulting posture must have been awkward and without close parallels.[16] He believes also that the statue is too large for the cutting; but since he spoke from an examination of the casts and Gardiner and Smith had studied the original materials, it is doubtless safe to follow them on this point. Poulsen accepts the identification of Gardiner and Smith. It does seem that the posture would have been awkward; but the similarities to the Agias are considerable, and the identification is probably right.

In place IV Homolle had placed a torso.[17] His chief reason for identifying it as Telemachos was that it so greatly resembled the Agias that it must have been his brother. Gardiner and Smith question this close resemblance,[18] and the illustrations seem to bear them out: the whole torso seems softer than the Agias

[14] *Fouilles*, pl. LXVII; *B.C.H.*, XXIII, 1899, pl. XII; *A.J.A.*, XIII, 1909, p. 452; Poulsen, *op. cit.*, p. 271.

[15] *A.J.A.*, XIII, 1909, pp. 460 ff.

[16] *Sitz. Bayer. Akad. Wiss.*, 1913, *Arch. Bemerkungen*, pp. 42 f.

[17] *B.C.H.*, XXIII, 1899, pl. XXVI; *A.J.A.*, XIII, 1909, p. 451.

[18] *A.J.A.*, XIII, 1909, pp. 459 f.

and wholly different. Furthermore they argue that
the right leg of the figure was advanced, which seems
unquestionably true; hence it could not belong to cavity
IV, where the left leg must have been forward.

After Homolle had written, a torso[19] was found
built into a wall. A head which Homolle had known[20]
and had sought vainly to connect with the group was
found to fit it perfectly. A left leg was found that
fitted perfectly by contact, and a right leg closely resembling it,[21] so that we now have the figure almost
complete.[22] The head resembles the Agias very closely,
the right leg has a support similar to that used for the
Daochos II and for the Agias, and the posture is that
required for the statue of Agelaos.   There can be little
doubt as to this identification.

This statue has recently been put together in the
museum at Delphi.[23]   The right leg illustrated by
Gardiner and Smith is omitted; this is singular, as this
leg should certainly belong to some figure in the group.
In the article cited the figure is called "la statue dite
d'Aparos," though with the comment that it might be
Agelaos or Telemachos.   The identification as Aparos
is very improbable: in the first place the existence of
a statue of Aparos is very doubtful; in the second place
he was apparently known only as the ancestor of the
house of Daochos and would probably not be represented as a young athlete; in the third place the position of the new statue can not easily be reconciled with
the shape of the cutting in place I.   The last objection
applies also against an identification as Telemachos.

Homolle identified as Sisyphos II, in place IX, a

[19] *A.J.A.*, XIII, 1909, pp. 461 and 463; Poulsen, *op. cit.*, p. 272.

[20] *B.C.H.*, XXIII, 1899, pl. XXVI.

[21] *A.J.A.*, XIII, 1909, p. 464.

[22] *A.J.A.*, XIII, 1909, p. 466; Poulsen, *op. cit.*, p. 273.

[23] *B.C.H.*, XLVIII, 1924, pp. 477-479.   An article on the statue by M
P. de la Coste-Messelière, to appear in *Revue de l'art ancien et moderne*,
is promised.

figure decidedly larger than the others.[24] He was confident of the identification, because he thought that the
plinth fitted the cavity exactly.[25] Apparently he was
mistaken in this; Gardiner and Smith show that the
plinth could not possibly have fitted into the cavity.[26]
This figure, then, may be definitely omitted from the
group. According to Poulsen the proper plinth and
feet of Sisyphos were found later in the museum
storehouse.[27] Whether the foot conjecturally assigned
to him by Gardiner and Smith[28] is one of those referred
to by Poulsen I do not know.

For cavity I Homolle had no figure, though he
thought from the size of the cutting for the plinth
that the statue must be draped. Gardiner and Smith
suggest that some divinity, who would need no inscription for identification, stood at the head of the line;
and they suggest Athena, as the patron goddess of
Pharsalos and apparently the special protector of
Sisyphos I. A fragment of a right shoulder is tentatively assigned to this Athena.[29] Keramopoullos,[30]
Wolters,[31] and Poulsen[32] assume a figure of Aparos,
father of Aknonios. This does not explain the size of
the cavity. Perhaps it needs no explanation: a flaw
in the stone of the base or some mistake in cutting
may have made it desirable to cut away a large surface,
or the figure may have held some attribute that required considerable space. Still, it is difficult to understand why Aparos should have no inscription.

It seems necessary to admit that we are entirely in
the dark as to place I. In regard to the remainder of
the group, however, it seems safe to accept the assign-

[24] *Fouilles,* pl. LXVIII; *B.C.H.,* XXIII, 1899, pl. IX; *A.J.A.,* XIII,
1909, p. 455.

[25] *B.C.H.,* XXIII, 1899, p. 427.   [26] *A.J.A.,* XIII, 1909, p. 458.

[27] *Op. cit.,* p. 275.   [28] *A.J.A.,* XIII, 1909, p. 467.

[29] *A.J.A.,* XIII, 1909, p. 468.

[30] Παναθήναια, VIII, 1908, pp. 346 ff.

[31] *Sitzb. Bayer. Akad. Wiss.,* 1913, *Arch. Bemerkungen,* p. 42.

[32] *Op. cit.,* p. 269.

ments of Gardiner and Smith. The date of the monument is determined by the titles given Daochos II in his inscription.[33] He could have held them only between 338 and 334. Of course in such an unofficial dedication he might have used them even if he no longer held the offices; but it is improbable that he relinquished his honors before his death.

In 1811 Otto Magnus von Stackelberg made a trip to Greece, together with P. O. Bröndsted, and kept a journal, which is now preserved at Dorpat. In September they visited Pharsalos and found just one inscription, which Stackelberg copied in his journal.[34] The first three lines are very fragmentary and scarcely permit any observation except that the name Pharsalos, or Pharsalian, occurs. The last four lines, however, are unmistakably parts of an inscription identical with that which appears at Delphi under the statue of Agias. Below them appear the first six letters of a signature of Lysippos. A fragmentary inscription[35] found at Pharsalos in 1895 and later lost again belongs to the same quatrain, which is seen to agree almost exactly with the epigram of Agias at Delphi.

The inscription of Pharsalos is restored by Preuner[36] as follows:

....κ
.....γεσ.......ουσι   [τιμῶν (?)]
[πατ(ϱ)ί]δα Φάϱσ[αλον] (κ)αὶ πατ(έ)[ϱων(?)
                              ἀϱετάς(?)]
[Πϱῶ]τος 'Ολύμπ[ια πα]γκϱάτιο[ν, Φαϱσάλιε,
                              νικᾶις],
['Αγ]ία 'Ακνονίο[υ, γῆς ἀ]πὸ Θεσσ[αλίας],
[πε]ντάκις ἐνΝε[μέοις], (τ)όσα (Π)[ύθια, πεντά-
                              κις 'Ισθμοῖ]·
[κα]ὶ σῶν οὐδείς [πω στῆσ]ε τϱ[όπαια χεϱῶν].
Λύσιππ[ος Σικυώνιος ἐποίησεν (?)].

[33] Pomtow, in Dittenberger, Sylloge³, I, pp. 483-485, no. 274.
[34] Preuner, op. cit., p. 18.
[35] Preuner, op. cit., p. 20; I.G., IX, 2, no. 249.
[36] Op. cit., p. 24; also I.G., IX, 2, no. 249.

At Delphi it appears thus:

Πρῶτος 'Ολύμπια παγκράτιον, Φαρσάλιε,
νικᾶις,
'Αγία 'Ακνονίου, γῆς ἀπὸ Θεσσαλίας,
πεντάκις ἐν Νεμέαι, τρὶς Πύθια, πεντάκις
'Ισθμοῖ·
καὶ σῶν οὐδείς πω στῆσε τρόπαια χερῶν.

Preuner concludes that the inscription and the statue to which it belonged were copied at Delphi from the originals in Pharsalos, and that in the Agias we have an approximately contemporary copy of a statue by Lysippos.

Preuner's brilliant discovery divided the archaeological world into three camps. Percy Gardner,[37] E. A. Gardner,[38] Hyde,[39] and Cultrera[40] accept the Agias as the only reliable example of Lysippian style and see in the apoxyomenos a Hellenistic work of the school of Lysippos; Loewy,[41] Furtwängler,[42] Tarbell,[43] Bieber,[44] Lippold,[45] Wolters,[46] S. Reinach,[47] Klein,[48] Schober,[49] and Urlichs[50] dissociate the Agias from Lysippos and retain the apoxyomenos; while Collignon,[51] Amelung,[52]

[37] J.H.S., XXV, 1905, pp. 234 ff.
[38] Handbook of Greek Sculpture, 1915, p. 443.
[39] A.J.A., XI, 1907, p. 399; OVM, pp. 286 ff.
[40] Memorie dei Lincei, XIV, 1910, p. 188.
[41] Röm. Mitt., XVI, 1901, p. 392; Griechische Plastik, pp. 106 f.
[42] Sitzb. Bayer. Akad. Wiss., 1904, p. 379.
[43] A.J.A., VIII, 1904, pp. 457 f.
[44] Jb. Arch. I., XXV, 1910, p. 172.
[45] Jb. Arch. I., XXVI, 1911, p. 278, note 2. See however note 67 below.
[46] Springer-Wolters[12], p. 360.
[47] R. Arch., XX, 1924, p. 239.
[48] Jh. Oest. Arch. I., XIV, 1911, pp. 108 f.
[49] Jh. Oest. Arch. I., XIX-XX, 1916-1919, pp. 187-188.
[50] Woch. Kl. Ph., XVII, 1900, 541-543, and XXXIV, 1917, 145.
[51] Lysippe, p. 36.
[52] Röm. Mitt., XX, 1905, pp. 144-155.

Lechat,[53] Mariani,[54] Della Seta,[55] Studniczka,[56] Von
Mach,[57] Poulsen,[58] Kekulé,[59] Mahler,[60] Koepp,[61] Michaelis,[62] Walters,[63] and Novello[64] accept both statues as
copied from Lysippian works. Dickins[65] sees in the
Agias an Attic modification of a Lysippian prototype,
if I understand him correctly. Fowler[66] is very non-
committal, and can not be sure whether either work
reliably represents Lysippos. Lippold[67] now accepts the
apoxyomenos and thinks that the Agias may be a free
imitation of the statue by Lysippos. Waldhauer[68]
accepts both.

In view of the considerations brought up in the two
preceding chapters, the Lysippian character of the
apoxyomenos is not open to question. Those authorities who regard the Agias as the only trustworthy example of Lysippos's style and relegate the apoxyomenos to the position of a school work, have not only
failed adequately to consider the evidence in regard to
the apoxyomenos, but have neglected the general circumstances of the case. From all the vague and un-
satisfactory information given in literature about
Lysippos, there is one fact that emerges clearly: he
was a very great and very influential sculptor. In later
ages his name, along with the names of Pheidias and
Polykleitos, represented the greatest heights of Greek
sculpture.[69] More works by him are recorded than by

[53] *Rev. Et. Anc.*, XVI, 1914, pp. 188-191.   [54] *Ausonia*, II, p. 219.
[55] *Vita d'Arte*, V, 1910, p. 53.
[56] *Neue Jahrbücher*, XLI, 1918, p. 20, note 4.
[57] *Handbook of Greek and Roman Sculpture*, pp. 244 f.
[58] *Delphi*, p. 286.   [59] *Sitzb. Preuss. Akad.*, 1909, p. 700.
[60] *Polyklet*, p. 153.   [61] *Neue Jahrbücher*, XXIII, 1909, pp. 480-486.
[62] Springer-Michaelis[8], pp. 291-294.   [63] *Art of the Greeks*, p. 128.
[64] *Atene e Roma*, V, 1924, pp. 261-267. [65] *Hellenistic Sculpture*, p. 56.
[66] *History of Sculpture*, pp. 118 f.
[67] In Pauly-Wissowa, no. 34 and later.
[68] *Lisipp*, p. 22 (for the Agias).   [69] App. 1, 13, 14, 16, 17.

any other sculptor. Pliny devotes more space to him than to any other sculptor except Praxiteles. The Agias can not possibly represent the final achievement of such a man. Moreover, he had an extraordinary number of followers: besides his three sons, Phanis,[70] Eutychides,[71] and Chares[72] are named as his pupils. Teisikrates[73] is said to have been a pupil of Lysippos's son Euthykrates, Xenokrates[74] was a pupil of Teisikrates or of Euthykrates, and Kantharos[75] was taught by Eutychides. We are told that the works of Teisikrates could hardly be distinguished from those of Lysippos; this confirms a natural expectation, that these followers of the great master would preserve, for the most part, the traditions of his style. We should expect, then, to find among extant copies a great number of works which, though not to be attributed to the master himself, show distinctly the influence of his art. This condition exists if the apoxyomenos be taken as the norm of Lysippian style; every catalogue of sculpture makes liberal use of "influence of Lysippos" or some similar term. It does not exist if the Agias be insisted upon as representing the mature style of the master. If Lysippos made the Agias and Daippos made the apoxyomenos, then it was Daippos and not Lysippos who was the great innovator and the dominating personality of the early Hellenistic age. Such a hypothesis does not require extended consideration.

We may reject without hesitation, therefore, the theory that the Agias represents the mature style of Lysippos. Probably a thesis so bristling with im-

---

[70] Pliny, N.H., XXXIV 80. The name was probably Phanias; the signature of a Phanias was found at Lindos (Bull. Dan. Acad., 1907, p. 25).

[71] Pausanias, VI 2, 6.   [72] Pliny, N.H., XXXIV 41.

[73] Pliny, N.H., XXXIV 67 (App. 1, 3).

[74] Pliny, N.H., XXXIV 83.   [75] Pausanias, VI 3, 6.

probabilities would never have been suggested if its distinguished authors had not fallen into two errors in regard to chronology. If, as Gardner believed,[76] Lysippos's artistic activity extended from 372 to 320 and the Agias represented his style in the period 338-334, then the Agias might fairly be considered representative of his final style. But 350-290 more accurately defines the sculptor's period of production; and there is not a shadow of evidence to indicate that the Agias shows his style in the period 338-334. If the Agias at Delphi is accurately copied from the Lysippian Agias at Pharsalos, it represents his style of the time when the statue at Pharsalos was made: a time to which there is no clue.[77] The evidence from the inscriptions, which establishes the date of the group at Delphi, obviously does not apply to the Pharsalian work unless the same inscription—that of Daochos II—existed there in identical form. The fragmentary inscription which preceded the Agias quatrain at Pharsalos proves that the whole body of inscriptions was not the same in both places; and it is the purest assumption that the epigram of Daochos II, as it is found at Delphi, ever existed on the base at Pharsalos, —even if it be taken for granted that there was a statue of Daochos there. There is in fact a sound argument against that assumption: the epigram of Daochos contains a dedication to Apollo, and seems clearly to have been written for Delphi.[78]

But did any statue of Daochos II exist at Pharsalos? It seems natural to assume that a group of some sort existed there, since there is no obvious reason for

[76] *J.H.S.*, XXV, 1905, p. 247.

[77] Klein (*Gesch. d. griech. Kunst*, II, p. 351) thought it was about 350; Poulsen (*Delphi*, p. 291) 350-345; Koepp (*Neue Jahrbücher*, XXIII, 1909, p. 484) recognizes the importance of this point.

[78] So Wolters, *Sitzb. Bayer. Akad. Wiss.*, 1913, *Arch. Bemerkungen*, p. 47.

setting up a statue of Agias alone, some 120 years after his victory.[79] Furthermore, if the Agias was copied from Lysippos the "Agelaos" must have been also; for the two are so similar that their genesis must have been the same. Now in reading in order the inscriptions at Delphi, it is noticeable that those of Agias, Telemachos, and Agelaos are bound together much more closely than the others. The Telemachos epigram would be unintelligible unless preceded by that of Agias, and the reader must know both of those in order to understand the Agelaos inscription. On the other hand, Agias's epigram does not presuppose any knowledge of Aknonios; Agias is introduced as Pharsalian, son of Aknonios, from the Thessalian land, as though the reader were expected to know nothing about his house. Daochos II, too, is carefully called a Pharsalian, and Agias is named simply as his father, as he would be under any circumstances. This survey may suggest that the original group consisted of three figures, the great athletic heroes of the Thessalian house. The draped figures, which complete the group at Delphi, differ considerably in style;[80] besides, they appear to be slightly larger;[81] and the inscriptions add their indications that these statues are additions to the original group in Pharsalos.

A comparison of the Agias and the apoxyomenos is interesting.[82] The proportions are approximately

[79] Agias probably won at Olympia in 460 (K. K. Smith in *Classical Philology*, V, 1910, pp. 169-174) or 444 (Klee, *Zur Gesch. d. gymnischen Agone*, pp. 74 f.).

[80] So Gardiner and Smith, *A.J.A.*, XIII, 1909, p. 475, note 1; Klein, *Jh. Oest. Arch. I.*, XIV, 1911, pp. 107-8; see Poulsen's valuable comments on the various figures.

[81] See the sketches, *A.J.A.*, XIII, 1909, p. 471.

[82] Best illustrations of the Agias: *Fouilles de Delphes*, IV, pl. LXIII and Hyde, *OVM*, pl. 28 (front view); *A.J.A.*, XIII, 1909, p. 465 (side and back); *Fouilles*, IV, pl. LXIV and Hyde, *OVM*, p. 287, fig. 68 (the head, side view); *B.C.H.*, XXIII, 1899, pl. X and Deonna and De Ridder, *L'Art en Grèce*, pl. 20 (the head, front view); *J.H.S.*, XXV, 1905, p. 239 (the waist) and p. 237 (the left foot); *A.J.A.*, XIII, 1909, p. 468 (the right foot).

the same. The treatment of the body is very different; very much less anatomical knowledge is shown in the Agias. This is evident in every part, but especially in the feet and in the waist. The feet of the Agias, though by no means badly made, seem formless in comparison with those of the apoxyomenos, with their display of scientific knowledge. At the waist of the Agias the triangular depression between the muscles, which appears in the apoxyomenos and is guaranteed as a genuine Lysippian feature by the Herakles Epitrapezios, does not occur. The division between the muscles in the calf of the leg, at bottom, is also absent from the Agias. The pubes in the Agias is triangular in form, differing wholly from that of the apoxyomenos. The navel, which in the apoxyomenos is a shallow depression with a crescent-shaped groove above it, seems in the Agias to have a raised surface inside the depression and certainly has no wrinkle above it. The roundness of the shoulders, so noticeable in the apoxyomenos and in many works ascribed to the followers of Lysippos, is totally absent from the Agias. In short there is no detail of the treatment of the body in which the two statues do not differ widely. In the posture of the figures as wholes, however, there is no such great difference; neither figure shows an altogether stable posture, but in both the weight seems about to swing to the leg that is at present the "Spielbein." This momentary posture has always been thought to be a notable feature of the apoxyomenos, and its occurrence in the Agias is important.

The shapes of the heads are as different as they could well be. If the Agias is copied from a bronze original, it is certain that the hair was not accurately copied, since it shows no trace of bronze technique. One may conjecture, however, that the hair of its original did not differ greatly from that of the apoxyomenos. The ears are of totally different form. The

shape of the face is very different: it is longer and narrower than in the apoxyomenos, and the bony structure is much more emphasized. There is no groove in
the forehead. The nose is rather broad, and apparently a good deal broader at the base than at the
bridge. The lips do not resemble the lips of the
apoxyomenos. The chin is narrower and rounder in
the Agias. The eyes are close-set and in general are
very like those of the apoxyomenos, with the exception
that the lower lid is noticeably thick;—a feature in
remarkable contrast with the eye of the apoxyomenos.

In the foregoing pages I considered the conclusions
to be drawn from the assumption that the Agias of
Delphi was copied from a statue by Lysippos. In view
of these very great morphological differences, in spite
of the proto-Lysippian posture and eyes, it is necessary
to examine very carefully the evidence on which the
assumption is based. It is true that the somewhat
careless execution of the statue at Delphi suggests that
it may be a copy; but certainly it does not prove it, and
exact copies of statues in good Greek times are not to
be expected.[83] It is true that the close similarity of the
inscriptions suggests some kind of relation between
the statues, and that Lysippos assuredly did not copy
the Agias at Delphi; but identity or similarity of subject might have suggested to the dedicator a repetition
of the epigram, whoever the sculptor was. It is true
that the Agias has some distinction, especially in the
face, and that in some important features of style it
seems to be a forerunner of the apoxyomenos; but the
influence of Skopas on Lysippos was recognized before
the discovery of the Agias, and the qualities that suggest Lysippos may only be those of the Skopaic school.
It is true that the statues of Agias, Telemachos, and
Agelaos are bound together both by their style and by

---

[83] Furtwängler, *Ueber Statuenkopieen in Alterthum,* p. 8 (*Abh. Bayer.
Akad. Wiss.,* XX, 1896-7, p. 532) ; Hyde, *OVM,* p. 304, note 1.

the inscriptions in a way that suggests that they may have been copied from a group complete in itself; but the closely related epigrams may be explained by their similar achievements and by the fact that they were brothers, and the resemblance in style by the hypothesis that one sculptor made all the nude figures in the Delphi group. It may be noted that the foot[84] tentatively attributed to Sisyphos II shows close stylistic relations with the Agias; yet the Sisyphos II could hardly have formed part of any group that did not include all the rest of the statues at Delphi.[85]

Clearly the connection between the Agias and Lysippos does not rest on irrefragable evidence. Several definite arguments against it have been adduced by Wolters.[86] He observes that the group at Delphi was placed in a building that already existed and fitted it admirably; hence it was probably designed for it. The force of this argument is undeniable, as against those who regard the whole group at Delphi as copied from Lysippos; but it offers no objection to the theory that an original group of three was repeated with additions. Wolters also thinks that the mention of Pharsalos in the inscriptions of Agias and Daochos I would be unnatural if the inscriptions were written for Pharsalos. This objection appears to be without force, especially as "Pharsalos" or "Pharsalian" appears in the fragmentary inscription which precedes the Agias epigram in Pharsalos.

He argues also that the difference between the two inscriptions shows that the monument in Pharsalos was the later one. The Pythian victories, three at Delphi, are five at Pharsalos, and the expression in the Pharsalian inscription is singularly awkward. As far as

---

[84] *A.J.A.*, XIII, 1909, p. 467.

[85] Gardiner and Smith make the Sisyphos II the only addition to the Pharsalian group (*A.J.A.*, XIII, 1909, p. 474).

[86] *Sitzb. Bayer. Akad. Wiss.*, 1913, *Arch. Bemerkungen*, pp. 40-50.

the difference in number is concerned, the most plausible explanation is that given long ago by Preuner,[87] that the number had to be reduced to accord with the official records at Delphi. The language of the Pharsalian inscription, however, is indeed very strained. It is not that it lacks literary grace—none of the epigrams are masterpieces—but that the expression is unnatural and such as would never occur to any man if he were writing independently. It is difficult to resist Wolters's conclusion that the epigram at Pharsalos is the result of a mechanical change in the epigram at Delphi; hence, that the latter was earlier; hence, that the work of Lysippos at Pharsalos was later than the statues at Delphi and that they have no connection with Lysippos. We need not concern ourselves unduly with the motives that led to the change in the epigram. Probably the Pharsalian version represents a family tradition that was denied utterance at Delphi; conceivably the researches of Aristotle had shown that Agias had won more victories than had been remembered.[88]

Wolters notes also that there is a difficulty about the epigram of Telemachos. He claims the same number of victories as Agias; now the number of Agias's victories was not the same at Delphi as at Pharsalos; hence the Telemachos inscription, which is more spirited than most of them and shows no sign of alteration, was written for the group at Delphi. Yet there could hardly have been any group at Pharsalos without Telemachos, and his epigram, as has been noted, fits very naturally into the series. The dedicator would surely not have allowed Telemachos to be deprived of any of his victories simply because he had been forced to acquiesce in a reduction in the case of Agias. Nevertheless, this consideration can not be

---

[87] *Ein Delphisches Weihgeschenk*, p. 36.

[88] So Pomtow, in Dittenberger, *Sylloge*[3], I, p. 483.

given great weight.   The fact that two brothers won the same number of victories is one in which tradition would probably not err; and the same records which, according to Preuner's theory, caused a reduction in the number of Agias's victories would have a similar effect in the case of Telemachos.

I have attempted to present fairly all the arguments for and against the connection of the Agias with Lysippos.   The arguments for it are weak; at best they justify a presumption, which hardly withstands the test of a comparison between the Agias and certified Lysippian works.   The definite arguments against it are also weak, except that drawn from the statement of the number of victories in the inscription at Pharsalos.   This objection has not equally impressed all students, but to me it is convincing.   I conclude, therefore, that the statue at Pharsalos was set up after the one at Delphi, and that we have no reason for associating the latter with Lysippos in any way.   Probably when Alexander saw it he felt sorry for Daochos, who was a friend and partisan of Macedon, and asked Lysippos to make a good statue to be set up at Pharsalos.

CHAPTER VII

STATUES OF DEITIES

In the preceding chapters consideration has been given to the works that might be expected to furnish the most reliable evidence no Lysippian style. It has proved possible to gain an idea, reliable so far as it goes, of his manner, by which the attribution to him of other statues may be tested. From now on it seems better to discuss his works in order according to their subject, beginning with his representations of Zeus.

Among the works of Lysippos at Sikyon was a statue of Zeus.[1] Pausanias gives no description of the statue, though he says that it was placed in the open agora. A Sikyonian coin of the time of Caracalla shows a figure of Zeus that may well be imitated from this statue.[2] The god is nude; he holds a long scepter in his left hand, and a thunderbolt in his right. The weight rests on the right leg; the left leg is drawn back, apparently into about the same position as the right leg of the apoxyomenos. It is apparently impossible to tell, in the present condition of the coin, the direction in which the head was turned. The proportions are Lysippian; the posture appears to be Lysippian; and the outstretched right arm would suggest that the statue copied, if any statue was copied, was of bronze.

Except for the position of the legs, this type of Zeus was familiar before the time of Lysippos, as was seen in chapter I. Numerous existing figures follow the type in a general way;[3] some of them clearly illustrate pre-Lysippian style, but some may well have been influenced by the statue in Sikyon. The best of

---

[1] Pausanias, II 9, 6 (App. 1, 21); Lippold in Pauly-Wissowa, no. 2.
[2] Imhoof-Blumer and Gardner, *Num. Comm. on Pau.*, pl. H, 10; *J.H.S.*, VI, 1885, p. 78.
[3] See Bulle, in Roscher, *Lexikon*, III, 2, 2884 ff.

these is a bronze found at Paramythia and now in the British Museum (Plate 21, A).[4] The body is not so slender as might be expected from Lysippos, but the head is small. The musculature in general is less rich than in the apoxyomenos and the triangular opening between the muscles at the waist does not appear; but an early work of the master might well have this appearance. The bronze shows a somewhat singular treatment of the hair: there is a distinct "mane," but it is not formed, as in most heads of Zeus, by the ends of long locks confined by a fillet; on the contrary the hair behind the "mane" consists of short wisps, like the hair of the apoxyomenos. In the Alexander Azara a sort of "mane" is formed by brushing back locks of the same length as those on the back of the head, but in the Zeus it seems that the locks in the "mane" must be longer than the others. This is evident only on close inspection; at a casual glance the individual locks are not seen at all and the hair has the appearance of a richly curling mass. We are reminded that Lysippos was a specialist in the treatment of the hair; and considering also that his fabulous productiveness might be explained on the assumption that he made many small figures, one is inclined to suggest that this splendid little figure may be a production of the master's own hand. In so small a statuette a comparison of details with other Lysippian works is impossible; hence the hypothesis can not be proved and, in recompense, can not be disproved either. At any rate the bronze will aid us in visualizing the Zeus of Lysippos.

Two other bronzes, one in Vienna[5] and one in Naples[6] may be mentioned also as corresponding closely to the coin-type and suggesting in proportions and style the influence of Lysippos. The bronze Zeus

[4] No. 275; Walters, *Catalogue of Bronzes,* pl. VII; *Select Bronzes,* pl. XX; Cook, *Zeus,* II, 1, pp. 74 f., fig. 685.

[5] Von Sacken, pl. II, 3 and p. 9; Reinach, *Répertoire,* II 3, 5.

[6] Inv. no. 5036.

in Evreux,[7] almost half life-size, has much less swing
and life than the bronze in the British Museum. If it
accurately reproduces any original, that original was
hardly earlier than Lysippos; as tangible evidence we
may note the presence of the triangular opening between the muscles at the waist. Yet the general treatment of anatomy does not suggest any strong influence
of Lysippos.

A small bronze in Copenhagen[8] corresponds to the
coin-type in position and may be termed Lysippian in
general style, though details are not now discernible;
there is a garment around the shoulders and the left
arm. A small bronze in the museum at Catania may
be described in the same way, but the garment is on
the left shoulder only, the left foot is set back only
slightly; the left arm below the elbow is lacking. In
the museum at Syracuse there is a similar figure, which
lacks the hands and parts of the feet. Bronze no. 1 in
the Bibliothèque Nationale, reversed throughout as
compared with the coin-type, is quite Lysippian in style.
A bronze in Frankfurt (Plate 21, C),[9] lacking the left
arm and left foot, has the weight resting on the left leg
instead of the right as in the coin-type, but the arms
were in the position shown on the coin. Though the
workmanship of the bronze is not good, it shows Lysippian style in its slenderness, elasticity, and treatment of
anatomy. No. 5 in the Bibliothèque Nationale is
similar.

The cult-statue in the temple of Zeus Nemeios at
Argos, near the northwest corner of the agora,[10] was
also a work of Lysippos.[11] In this case Pausanias tells

[7] *Album des Musées de Province*, pl. 2; Reinach, *Musée de St. Ger-
main*, frontispiece; *Catalogo della Mostra archeologica nelle Terme di
Diocleziano*, p. 89; Reinach, *Répertoire*, I 194, 5. Cf. Klein, *Gesch. d.
griech. Kunst*, II, pp. 356 f.

[8] Thorwaldsen Museum, no. 37.

[9] *Kurzes Verzeichnis*[3], p. 35, no. 169. Height 11 cm.

[10] Boethius, in *Strena Philologica Upsaliensis*, p. 269.

[11] Pausanias, II 20, 3 (App. 1, 22); Lippold in Pauly-Wissowa, no. 3.

us that the statue was standing. Certain Argive coins of imperial times show a figure of Zeus which is perhaps imitated from this work.[12]   The type persists through several reigns, so it very probably reproduces some statue.   The figure has been described as nude, but in the Hunterian example of the coin a garment, flung over the left shoulder, is perceptible.   The god's left hand rests on his hip, while his right holds the long scepter.   The position of the feet appears to be much the same as in the apoxyomenos, but reversed: the right leg is the "Standbein."   If at Sikyon Lysippos followed a standard type in his statue of Zeus, at Argos he introduced a novelty in the hand placed on the hip.   Apparently it won little favor: I have not observed any work in the round which reproduces exactly, or even reversed, the coin-type.   A relief at a fortress near Alyzia,[13] where Lysippos worked, differs only in that the right hand grasps the spear or scepter at a higher point.   Some resemblance to the coin-type may be seen in the Hellenistic portrait statue in the Museo Nazionale at Rome[14] and in a marble statuette of Poseidon in the British Museum,[15] which has a similar position.   Both show a general influence of Lysippos, but both have the scepter on the same side as the "Spielbein."

This latter position appears also in a bronze statuette found at Dodona and now in Berlin.[16]   It is quite uncertain whether it is a Zeus or a Poseidon.   The

[12] Imhoof-Blumer and Gardner, op. cit., pl. K, no. 28; J.H.S., VI, p. 85; Macdonald, Hunterian Collection, II, pl. XXXIX, no. 13, p. 154; Frazer, Pausanias, vol. III, p. 194.

[13] Heuzey, Le Mont Olympe et l'Acarnanie, pl. XII. I am told that a good photograph will soon be published in a book by Noack, which will deal with Akarnanian sites.

[14] Hyde, OVM, p. 73, with references; Paribeni, Mus. Naz. Rom.⁴, p. 195, no. 474. For its Lysippian character see Schick, in Neue Jahrbücher, XXXIII, 1914, pp. 18-29.

[15] Smith, Catalogue of Sculpture, III, no. 1540.

[16] Kekulé and Winnefeld, Bronzen aus Dodona, pp. 24-27, pls. IV-V; Reinach, Répertoire, IV 20, 3; discussed briefly by Sieveking, Sammlung Loeb, pp. 46 f. Kekulé emphasizes its Lysippian character.

anatomy is represented with much naturalistic detail
in some places, including the feet and hands, and is
somewhat stylized elsewhere, for example in the folds
below the breasts; but in general it suggests the influence of Lysippos, as do the proportions. The treatment
of the hair resembles that seen in the Azara Alexander.
The details of the countenance do not bear the Lysippian impress; and it is not to be supposed that the early
Hellenistic artist who made this beautiful figure intended it as a copy from anybody. But we can gain
from it a fairly good general idea of the appearance of
some of Lysippos's statues of the greater deities.

A third statue of Zeus was at Megara.[17] In the
same temple were muses, also by Lysippos; and it is
usually assumed that the muses and the Zeus belonged
to a group. The language of Pausanias, however, by
no means requires this; indeed in his expression
"muses and a bronze Zeus" the mention of the material indicates either that the muses were not bronze or
that it was necessary to specify the "bronze Zeus" in
order to distinguish it from some other Zeus in the
temple. The first would prove, and the second would
strongly indicate, that the Zeus and the muses did not
belong together. There is a type of Zeus on Megarian
coins[18] that seems to reproduce a statue, since it occurs
frequently and seems sometimes to stand on a base.
He is nude and striding to the right; the left hand is
stretched out in front and holds an eagle, according
to the commentators, while the right is drawn back
and hurls the thunderbolt. The figure is slender and
might be considered Lysippian. It appears in the illustration, however, that the hair is long and flowing,
which should indicate a much older statue; but Pausanias, who usually mentions "ancient" things, does not
speak of any such figure in Megara. If Lysippos made

[17] Pausanias, I 43, 6 (App. 1, 23); Lippold in Pauly-Wissowa, no. 4.
[18] Imhoof-Blumer and Gardner, op. cit., pl. A4; J.H.S., VI, 1885,
p. 54; Cook, Zeus, II, 2, p. 1139, fig. 960.

a figure of this kind he was following a type which had come down from the geometric age.[19]

Much the most famous of the statues of Zeus by Lysippos was the colossus at Tarentum.[20] We are told that it was placed in the agora, that it was bronze, and that it was second only to the Colossus of Rhodes in size, being forty cubits, 58 feet, in height. Pliny relates that it could be moved by the hand. Jex-Blake's translation, "turned round," is not in the Latin, and the meaning seems clearly to be that the statue could be slightly rocked. This is not wholly incredible, if it was a seated statue. The Colossus of Rhodes, to be sure, was a standing figure,[21] and an author desiring to emphasize the magnitude of the statue at Tarentum might well have stated that the difference in height between the two was due partly to a difference in posture, if this was the fact; but the notices of the Tarentine statue are so casual that little weight can be attached to this consideration.

This statue was second in fame, though a very poor second, among the representations of Zeus known through literature, and we should expect to find some imitations of it, though of course a true copy of so large a statue is out of the question. Our clue by which to identify such imitations is found in the column mentioned by Pliny; however mistaken his belief as to the purpose of the column, that belief could hardly have arisen unless a column had been there. Now we

[19] See Casson, in *J.H.S.*, XLII, 1922, pp. 211-212; Cook, *Zeus*, II, 2, pp. 1222-1224.

[20] App. 1, 18-20 a; Lippold in Pauly-Wissowa, no. 1. The statue is doubtless included among those referred to by Livy (XXVII 16, 8; App. 1, 20 a), but no sound inferences as to its appearance can be drawn from Livy's vague remark.

[21] Since this is generally agreed and rests on irrefragable evidence it seems unnecessary to discuss it, though F. Préchac (*R. Arch.*, IX, 1919, pp. 64-76) has tried to show that the Colossus belonged to a chariot group. He has suggested the same erroneous hypothesis for the colossus of Nero (*C. R. Acad. Insc.*, 1914, pp. 231-242), which displaced the Tarentine Zeus as second in size.

find representations of Zeus in a Pompeii painting
and a relief in Naples which evidently reflect one
original, and in both cases a column is present.[22] The
god is seated on an elaborate throne, over which a robe
is placed. Zeus himself is entirely nude above the
waist. His right elbow is placed on the back of the
throne, and his chin rests on the right hand. This, the
striking feature of the representation, lends an air of
human weariness to the ever-watchful Zeus; a suggestion unusual and somewhat startling, like the weariness of Herakles. From the two imitations we can
gain little idea of the details of the original, but it appears in the relief that there is an effective mass of
hair above the forehead. The identification is very
probable, and we are thereby enabled to gain a good
general idea of one of the sculptor's greatest masterpieces.

We have, however, no accurate copy of any of Lysippos's statues of Zeus, and the bronzes that have been
mentioned, though they suggest to us the appearance
of the Lysippian statues, give little idea of his treatment of the head. Next to Pheidias, Lysippos was
the leading maker of statues of Zeus among all the
Greek sculptors, and it is certain that his influence
would be felt in later representations of the god. The
famous mask found at Otricoli (Plate 22)[23] is the best
representative of an ideal of Zeus which appears, with
various modifications, in a great number of monuments.
In spite of the overwhelming prestige of the Zeus of

[22] Cook, Zeus, I, pp. 34-36, frontispiece and pls. 1 and 2. On the
painting cf. Overbeck, KM, Atlas, pl. 1, 39; Helbig, Wandgemälde, pp.
30 f., no. 101. On the relief: Overbeck, op. cit., Atlas, pl. 3, 16; Ruesch,
Guida², pp. 94 f., no. 289.

[23] For its Lysippian character see Klein, Gesch. d. griech. Kunst, II,
p. 357. Recent discussion: Poulsen, Collection Ustinow, pp. 15-17, with
citations; Dickins, Hellenistic Sculpture, pp. 23 f.; Helbig, Führer³, I,
pp. 188-191, no. 288, with bibliography. A new example found at
Sabrata in Tripoli: Gnomon, I, 1925, pp. 178 f. De Bosis, in a lecture
at the University of Illinois in 1925, showed a picture of an example
recently found near Praeneste and said that it was better than the
Otricoli mask.

Pheidias, it was the Otricoli type which became the canonical one for later antiquity. Undoubtedly it was created in the later fourth century or early Hellenistic period, and it is highly probable *a priori* that the creator was Lysippos. This is confirmed by a consideration of the morphology. The eyes are in every detail amazingly like those of the apoxyomenos; the forehead, though high, the nose, and the open mouth are also Lysippian. The impressive "mane," which contributes so largely to the majesty of the head, is a feature that would be expected from an artist who was noted for his treatment of the hair.

It would be risky to say that the Otricoli mask itself and the other heads that correspond to it closely were copied directly from Lysippos. Technical peculiarities seem to indicate an original which was not bronze, and the bronze statuette[24] of which the head corresponds most closely to the mask shows little Lysippian character in body. Amelung may therefore be right in naming Bryaxis as the author of the immediate prototype of the mask; but if so, it was Bryaxis under the strong influence of some creation of his greater contemporary.[25]

There are instances, however, in which a head which may be included in the Otricoli type, if that term is understood in a somewhat broad sense, is united with a Lysippian body. A figure in Dresden (Plate 23) is an example.[26] The weight rested on the right leg; the left leg was advanced. The left arm held the long scepter, while the right, now lost, apparently came almost straight down from the shoulder; a mark on the outside of the thigh probably indicates a supporting bar for the hand. In a figure in the British Museum the left leg is the "Standbein" and the scepter

[24] In Constantinople; *B.C.H.,* IX, 1885, pl. XIV.
[25] So Waldhauer (*Lisipp,* pp. 26 f. and fig. 11).
[26] Herrmann, *Verzeichnis,* no. 158.

is held on that side;[27] some object, probably the thunderbolt, was held in the lowered right hand. A garment passes from the left shoulder behind the back and over the right forearm. A fine seated figure of Zeus found at Khamissa[28] has a noble head resembling the Otricoli mask in a general way.

Other Lysippian heads which represent or may represent Zeus may be mentioned. One is a head in Naples,[29] called Asklepios. The eyes and lips resemble those of the apoxyomenos, and the beard is somewhat like that worn by Socrates in certain portraits which we shall refer to Lysippos. There is a fillet and "mane." A head in the Palazzo dei Conservatori[30] resembles the apoxyomenos closely in the forehead and eyes and has the usual "mane." A head called Asklepios (probably rightly) in the Salle de la Pallas de Velletri in the Louvre[31] resembles the apoxyomenos considerably in the mouth, eyes, and forehead.

We are told by Lucian[32] that Lysippos made for the Corinthians a bronze statue of Poseidon. It was suggested by Lange[33] and has been accepted by many later investigators that the statue mentioned was the cult statue of the temple of Poseidon in the Isthmian sanctuary. The only foundation for this belief is the fact that Lucian groups Lysippos's statue with the Parthenos and Olympian Zeus of Pheidias. These statues are mentioned because they were famous masterpieces, however, not because they were temple statues; and the only inference that can be drawn as to Lysippos's Poseidon is that it was highly esteemed.

[27] Walters, *Catalogue of Bronzes*, no. 786.
[28] Known to me by the cast in Algiers; I think the statue is in Guelma.
[29] Ruesch, *Guida*², p. 95, no. 292.
[30] Sala degli Orti Lamiani, no. 9; Jones, p. 132, pl. 47.
[31] Fröhner, *Notice*, no. 37; present number 626.
[32] *Zeus Tragoedus* 9 (App. 1, 24); Lippold in Pauly-Wissowa, no. 6.
[33] *Das Motiv des aufgestützten Fusses*, pp. 31 ff.

The temple in the Isthmian sanctuary was small,[34] and it would have been absurd to compare its statue with the Athena or the Zeus. Furthermore the temple was built, as is shown by the scanty remains[35] (if they are correctly referred to the temple), about the middle of the sixth century; whence it is highly probable that the cult-statue was made long before the time of Lysippos. It is probably to be recognized in the seated figure which appears on several coins.[36] On one of the coins a victorious athlete faces the god. On another Athena approaches him; perhaps there is an allusion here to the special position of the Athenians at the Isthmian games.[37]

Many authorities have seen a copy of the Lysippian Poseidon in the colossal statue in the Lateran (Plate 24). Lange, one of the early protagonists of this view, relied on certain evidence which will be discussed later;[38] it may suffice here to say that recent students have placed little confidence in it. For other reasons, however, the type has been attributed to Lysippos by Collignon,[39] Von Mach,[40] Michaelis,[41] Klein,[42] Overbeck,[43] Percy Gardner,[44] and Waldhauer.[45] Loewy,[46] Richardson,[47] and Cultrera[48] are also inclined to this opinion. Bulle,[49] however, denies that there is any Ly-

[34] Pausanias, II 1, 7 (App. 1, 25). Numismatic evidence indicates that it was tetrastyle prostyle or amphiprostyle; Imhoof-Blumer and Gardner, *op. cit.*, pl. D, 49-50; *J.H.S.*, VI, 1885, p. 65.

[35] *Gaz. Arch.*, IX, 1884, pp. 358 f.; Frazer, *Pausanias*, vol. III, p. 11. For later researches see Πρακτικά, 1903, pp. 14-17.

[36] Imhoof-Blumer and Gardner, *op. cit.*, pl. D, 54-56; *J.H.S.*, VI, 1885, pp. 65-66.

[37] Plutarch, *Theseus*, 25.

[38] In connection with the Medici Aphrodite, in chapter VIII.

[39] *Lysippe*, pp. 70 f.   [40] *Handbook*, p. 252.

[41] Springer-Michaelis[8], p. 297. [42] *Gesch. d. griech. Kunst*, II, pp. 366 f.

[43] *Griechische Plastik*[4], II, p. 151.

[44] *J.H.S.*, XXV, 1905, p. 255. [45] *Lisipp*, p. 25.

[46] *Griechische Plastik*, p. 105. [47] *Greek Sculpture*, p. 233.

[48] *Memorie dei Lincei*, XIV, 1910, pp. 239 ff.

[49] Roscher, *Lexikon*, III, 2, cols. 2890 ff.

sippian character in the Lateran type, and his conclusions are accepted by Amelung,[50] who suggests Bryaxis as the author, and by Lippold.[51] Six[52] would attribute it to the shadowy Euphranor.

The representations of Poseidon in the general scheme of the Lateran statue—that is, with one foot placed on some elevation—are very numerous. The following list is founded on that given by Bulle.[53]

1. Rome, Lateran Museum. Benndorf-Schöne, *D. ant. Bildw. d. Lat. Mus.,* no. 287; Waldhauer, *Lisipp,* fig. 9; Reinach, *Répertoire,* II 27, 1; without restorations, I 428, 5; Helbig, *Führer³,* II, p. 25, no. 1188, with bibliography; Brunn-Bruckmann, 243; Bulle, *Der schöne Mensch²,* pl. 73; Von Mach, *University Prints,* no. 239. The head: Overbeck, *KM,* Atlas, XI, 1-2. Principal restorations: r. hand, l. arm, both legs below knees, ship's prow, dolphin.

2. Tunis, Musée Alaoui, C 949. *Musée Alaoui* (1907), p. 31; Reinach, *op. cit.,* IV 19, 6. R. foot raised, head looks down; feet lost.

3. Dresden, Albertinum. Herrmann, *Verzeichnis d. ant. Original-Bildwerke,* p. 42, no. 157; Reinach, *op. cit.,* I 428, 2; Becker, *Augusteum,* II, pl. 47; Overbeck, *KM,* Atlas, pl. XII, 31. The head: Overbeck, *l.c.,* pl. XI, 6. R. foot raised, on dolphin; otherwise close to no. 1. Half life size.

4. British Museum. Smith, *Catalogue of Sculpture,* II, p. 186, no. 1242; Reinach, *op. cit.,* III 10, 9. R. foot raised; head and feet lost. Half life size.

5. Vienna, Kunsthistorisches Museum; room IX, case 9, no. 69. Marble statuette; right foot raised.

6. Zurich, bronze statuette. Reinach, *op. cit.,* II 27, 2. R. foot raised, on rock.

7. Cologne, bronze statuette. Reinach, *op. cit.,* III 10, 5. R. foot raised.

8. Louvre, bronze statuette. No. 514; De Ridder, *Les bronzes antiques du Louvre,* I, p. 76, pl. 38. R. foot raised.

9. Louvre, bronze statuette. No. 515; De Ridder, *op. cit.,* I, p. 76, pl. 38. Reinach, *op. cit.,* V 13, 4. R. foot raised; more erect than no. 1.

[50] Helbig, *Führer³,* II, pp. 25 f. [51] In Pauly-Wissowa.
[52] *Jb. Arch. I.,* XXIV, 1909, p. 25.
[53] Roscher, *Lexikon,* III, 2, cols. 2888 ff.

10. British Museum, bronze statuette. Walters, *Catalogue of Bronzes*, p. 176, no. 961. R. foot raised, on prow.

11. British Museum, bronze statuette. Walters, *op. cit.*, p. 176, no. 962. R. foot raised, on rock.

12. Vevey, bronze statuette. Reinach, *op. cit.*, V 12, 3. R. foot raised, on rock.

13. Louvre, bronze statuette. No. 248. Reinach, *op. cit.*, II 27, 6. R. foot raised, on *low* rock.

14. Paris, Bibliothèque Nationale, bronze statuette. Reinach, *op. cit.*, II 27, 5; Babelon-Blanchet, no. 830. R. foot raised, on globe. Inexact.

15. Constantinople. Mendel, *Catalogue des Sculptures*, III, p. 17, no. 814; Reinach, *op. cit.*, V 13, 5. L. foot raised; more slender than no. 1.

16. Zagreb. Reinach, *op. cit.*, IV 19, 5. L. foot raised.

17. Rome. Villa Albani, marble statuette. Reinach, *op. cit.*, II 27, 3; Helbig, *Führer²*, no. 880; Overbeck, *KM*, Atlas, XII, 30. L. foot raised, on prow which is new.

18. Eleusis, marble statuette. Reinach, *op. cit.*, II 27, 4; *Memorie dei Lincei*, XIV, 1910, p. 241; *Ath. Mitt.*, XXXII, 1907, p. 389; Roscher, *Lexikon*, III, 2, col. 2890, fig. 19. L. foot raised, on dolphin.

19. Candia, marble statuette. No. 250. L. foot raised. Here pl. 25.

20. Pergamon, marble statuette. Reinach, *op. cit.*, IV 20, 7; *Ath. Mitt.*, XXXII, 1907, p. 389. Only legs and l. arm. L. foot raised, on dolphin.

Coins

1. Demetrios Poliorketes. Gardner, *Types of Greek Coins*, pl. XII, 2; Helbig, *Führer³*, II, p. 26; Ἐφ. Ἀρχ., 1903, pl. 7. R. foot raised, on rock.

2. Bruttium. Gardner, *op. cit.*, pl. XI, 37. R. foot raised, on Ionic capital.

3. Corinth, Roman period. Imhoof-Blumer and Gardner, *Numismatic Commentary on Pausanias*, pl. D, 53. R. foot raised, on rock. In the text (*J.H.S.*, VI, 1885, p. 65) the authors describe other similar coins of Corinth.

4. Argos. Svoronos, Τὸ Ἐθνικὸν Μουσεῖον, I, p. 86, figs. 74-75. Left foot raised, on rock; fig. 75 shows the statue in a building. Fig. 76 is a third coin, which seems to be an inexact repetition of the design in fig. 75.

5. Hermione, Roman period. Imhoof-Blumer and Gardner, *op. cit.*, pl. GG 17; *J.H.S.*, VIII, p. 58. L. foot raised, on rock.

6. Phokaia, Roman period. Poseidon and Athena, facing. Imhoof-Blumer, *Kleinasiatische Münzen*, pl. III, 18. L. foot raised, on rock.

7. Patrai, Roman period. Overbeck, *KM*, II, 2, Münztafel VI, 3.

Other coins with designs more or less similar are shown in Overbeck, *l.c.*, and discussed by him, *op. cit.*, pp. 293-298.

GEMS

1. Cameo in Cabinet des Medailles. Reinach, *Répertoire de Reliefs*, II 236, 1. Poseidon and Athena; l. foot raised.

2. Cameo in Vienna, Kunsthistorisches Museum. Overbeck, *KM*, II, 2, Gemmentafel II, 8; Baumeister, *Denkmäler*, II, col. 1390; Arneth, *Antike Cameen d. k. k. Münz- u. Antiken-Cab.*, pl. 11. L. foot raised, on rock; l. arm rests on leg but does not cross it; l. hand holds *mappa*, as signal which started the games. Around the figure, symbolic representations of the Isthmus and the games.

Intaglios:

3. Overbeck, *op. cit.*, Gemmentafel, II, 3. R. foot raised, on rock.

4. Overbeck, *l.c.*, II, 6. R. foot raised, on prow.

5. Overbeck, *l.c.*, II, 7. R. foot raised.

Bulle names also others which reproduce the type more or less exactly: Furtwängler, *Die Ant. Gemmen*, I, pl. XXX, 17 and 19; Furtwängler, *Geschnittene Steine in Berlin*, 3452-3463; three unpublished gems in Arndt Collection, Munich. Of all the gems, including the five enumerated above, he says that the left foot is raised in only two cases and that in twelve instances the raised foot rests on a prow.

PAINTINGS

Pompeii. Helbig, *Wandgemälde*, no. 171; Overbeck, *KM*, Atlas, XII, 22. R. foot raised.

Pompeii. Helbig, *l.c.*, no. 172. R. foot raised.

MOSAIC

Pompeii. Overbeck, *KM*, II, 2, p. 313, fig. 10.

RELIEF

Trajan column. Reinach, *Répertoire de Reliefs*, I 351; cf. Strong, *Roman Sculpture*, p. 187. One of three statues on an arch; l. foot raised.

Puteal in Cordova. Reinach, *op. cit.*, II 191, 1. Close to Eleusis type.

Smyrna. Reinach, *op. cit.*, II 110, 7. L. foot raised.

Overbeck, *KM*, II, 2, p. 304, 1-5, enumerates other reliefs which are more or less closely related to the type in question.

GLASS

Berlin, Antiquarium. Bowl, no. 2129. Poseidon with sea-beasts. R. foot raised.

OTHER POSEIDONS WITH RAISED FOOT

Dresden. Herrmann, *Verzeichnis d. ant. Original-Bild-werke*, p. 42, no. 160; Reinach, *Répertoire de la Statuaire*, I 428, 1; Becker, *Augusteum*, II, pl. 40; Overbeck, *KM*, Atlas, pl. XII, 32. The head: *l.c.*, pl. XI, 10. L. foot on dolphin, only slightly raised; garment around back and legs.

Vienna, Kunsthistorisches Museum, bronze statuette; room XV, case 13, no. 1109. Reinach, *op. cit.*, II 28, 4; Von Sacken, *Die ant. Bronzen des k. k. Münz- u. Antiken-Cabinets*, pl. VI, 1; Roscher, *Lexikon*, III, 2, col. 2895, fig. 24. L. foot on prow, slightly raised; l. hand holds trident; r. hand holds dolphin, to front and side at level of waist; hair in impressive mane.

Budapest, National Museum. Same type, less well preserved; l. foot on low rock.

Nos. 1-12 contain no significant difference from the Lateran statue except that in some cases, notably nos. 3 and 11, the head clearly does not look down. Coins 1 and 2, gem 3, and the mosaic also correspond closely. Nos. 18-20, corresponding closely to one another, evidently are copied from a different original: the left foot is raised instead of the right, the left forearm lies along the thigh and does not cross it, and there is a garment on the thigh. The cameo representing the Isthmian festival (no. 2) and the relief in Cordova are certainly derived from this type, which may be called the Eleusis type. Nos. 13-14, with the right foot raised, and nos. 15-17, with the left foot raised, do not follow closely either original or any third original, so far as can be judged. The coin of Hermione (no. 5) probably reproduces the statue of Poseidon which Pausanias saw there,[54] though the statue had its foot

[54] Pausanias, II 35, 1 (App. 1, 26).

on a dolphin instead of a rock. The Argive coins
(no. 4), showing the figure within a building, are quite
certainly copied from a statue. The type is the same
as in the Hermione coins, and the statue reproduced
might possibly be the same, since Hermione belonged
to Argos in part of its history; but Pausanias implies
that the statue at Hermione was in the open. It is
singular that these statues, whose location is known to
us, are not represented by any copies in sculpture.

The only clue to the original home of the Eleusis
type is found in its occurrence on the Vienna cameo;
and that is no clue at all, because it is the god himself
who is represented there and no statue. The persistent
occurrence of Poseidon in the general scheme under
discussion on coins of Corinth does suggest strongly
that some such statue stood there; but it was probably
the original of the Lateran type. To judge from the
number of its copies, it was much more highly esteemed
than the Eleusis type. Its occurrence on the coin of
Demetrios Poliorketes is significant: it was at Corinth
that the title of commander-in-chief was conferred on
Demetrios in 303, and he might very naturally place a
Corinthian statue on his coin.

Cultrera believes that the Eleusis type is the one
which closely copies an original by Lysippos.[55] In this
opinion he is influenced chiefly by the Agias and the
"Jason," both of which are very unreliable guides to
Lysippian style. It is probable *a priori* that if Lysippos made any statue in this general scheme it was the
one which proved most influential in later times, and
that was not the original of the Eleusis type. Furthermore the head of this type, especially as seen in the
Candia copy, suggests strongly that the original was
made some years before Lysippos was born. If that is
true the man who made it introduced an admirable and
profoundly appropriate motive into the representation

[55] *Memorie dei Lincei*, XIV, 1910, pp. 239 ff.

of Poseidon; but it was the later artist of the Lateran type who won the flattering imitation of antiquity.

The Lateran type must be judged primarily by the Lateran statue, and it is difficult to find in it any evidence for the attribution to Lysippos. Richardson says that it has "Lysippian eyes,"[56] but they are Lysippian only in a very general sense. The head is large in proportion to the body. Little anatomical detail is shown, and the musculature is flabby and lifeless. The figure on the coin of Demetrios is slimmer and more powerful, and if our impression of the original were based on the coin we could ascribe it to Lysippos reasonably enough. There is a difference also in the head, which in the coin-type does not look down but straight ahead; and it may be that more than one original are represented in the "Lateran type." It seems on the whole probable, however, that there was only one and that the Lateran statue represents it with reasonable fidelity. If this is true the attribution to Lysippos is not plausible.

Willers[57] would combine the Poseidon with the Praying Boy of Berlin[58] in a group made by Boedas and originally in Tarentum. His arguments are ingenious but not convincing, and the group as reconstructed[59] will not commend itself to connoisseurs of art. If it be thought necessary to name the Adorans Taras and to place him in any group, surely it should be in the group shown on Tarentine coins,[60] as suggested by Svoronos;[61] Willers's reasons for rejecting this [62] are inadequate. The true conclusions about the Praying Boy, however, seem to be those reached by

[56] *Greek Sculpture,* p. 233.
[57] *Stud. zur griech. Kunst,* pp. 127-159.
[58] Hyde, *OVM,* pp. 130 ff., with citations; no. 2 in the museum.
[59] Willers, *op. cit.,* pl. XIII.   [60] *Op. cit.,* pl. XII, 12-16.
[61] *J. Int. Arch. Num.,* IV, 1901, pp. 94 f.   [62] *Op. cit.,* pp. 142 f.

Lucas,[63] anticipated partly by Sauer:[64] that the statue is an original[65] by Boedas son of Lysippos, which stood originally in Byzantium.

Amelung and apparently Waldhauer[66] follow Bulle in ascribing to Lysippos the original of a head of Poseidon in the Vatican,[67] which was perhaps found at Porcigliano. The Lysippian character of the forehead, eyes, and nose is unmistakable, and the hair, with its locks wet with sea-water, reminds us of Pliny's statement that Lysippos excelled "capillum exprimendo."[68] This head bears a close resemblance to the head of a bronze statuette in the Loeb collection,[69] which may, therefore, be accepted as reproducing the position of the original. The proportions of the statuette are as slender as in the apoxyomenos, if not more so. The musculature, though it seems somewhat soft, may be considered Lysippian.

The head, in spite of its undeniably Lysippian characteristics, lacks dignity and nobility to an extent very surprising in a statue of so mighty a god, by a sculptor whose fame was based largely on portrayals of Zeus and Alexander. The statuette similarly shows sensationalism in the exaggerated swing of the figure and in the swaggering protrusion of the right arm. On the whole it is probable that the original was made not by Lysippos himself, but by a later artist who studied his manner closely but lacked his ability and his taste and exaggerated his mannerisms. A head of Zeus in Berlin (no. 291) has a similar character.

[63] *Neue Jahrbücher,* XXIX, 1912, pp. 112-123.

[64] *Philologus,* LXVII, 1908, pp. 304-310.

[65] On this point see Willers, *op. cit.,* pp. 150-157.

[66] *Lisipp,* p. 26 and fig. 10.

[67] Roscher, *Lexikon,* III 2, cols. 2892 ff.; Amelung, *Skulpt. d. Vat. Mus.,* I, p. 719, pl. 77; Bulle, *Der schöne Mensch²,* pl. 232; Brunn-Bruckmann, no. 140; Helbig, *Führer³,* I, p. 62, no. 106.

[68] *N.H.,* XXXIV 65 (App. 1, 3).

[69] Roscher, *Lexikon,* III, 2, col. 2892; Reinach *Répertoire,* IV 19, 2; Cecil Smith, *Forman Collection,* pl. VI; Sieveking, *Sammlung Loeb,* pp. 41 ff., pls. 17-18; Neugebauer, *Antike Bronzestattuetten,* pl. 44. Sieveking is very confident of the Lysippian origin.

Mme. Maviglia believes that the Poseidon of Melos represents the Poseidon of Lysippos.[70] This figure has always been regarded as a Hellenistic work. Dickins sees in it primarily the influence of the second Pergamene school, with influence also from other sources, including Lysippos.[71] It is a melodramatic rendering of the sea-god, and seems certainly later than Lysippos, to say nothing of the sculptor of the Uffizi apoxyomenos.

Pausanias[72] and Lucian[73] mention a Dionysos of Lysippos. The statue mentioned by the former was in the sanctuary of the muses on Mt. Helikon; whether Lucian was speaking of the same work is uncertain. Pausanias implies, by immediately afterward speaking of another image of Dionysos as "the upright one," that the statue by Lysippos had some other position; presumably it was seated. Further than that we have no indication of his mode of treatment. So far as I know no scholar has identified any figure of Dionysos as copied from Lysippos, though Farnell[74] mentions two heads of Dionysos that show somewhat Lysippian style.[75]

A group representing Apollo and Hermes in dispute for the possession of the lyre is mentioned by Pausanias in the same sentence with the Dionysos. Some critics, emending the text slightly, have assumed that the group was made by Lysippos, instead of, or as well as, the Dionysos.[76] Jamot found in the sanctuary some fragments of bronze figures and suggested that they

---

[70] *L'Attività artistica di Lisippo*, pp. 86 ff.

[71] *Hellenistic Sculpture*, p. 63.   [72] IX 30, 1 (App. 1, 28).

[73] *Zeus Tragoedus*, 12 (App. 1, 29). Cf. Lippold in Pauly-Wissowa, no. 7.   [74] *Cults of the Greek States*, V, p. 278.

[75] One in the Lateran (Benndorf-Schöne, *D. ant. Bildw. d. Lat. Mus.*, no. 236); another was in the Palazzo dei Conservatori.

[76] So Waldhauer (*Lisipp*, p. 13).

might belong to the Lysippian group.[77]   It appears,
however, that the fragments belong to Roman work[78]
and that the group mentioned by Pausanias did not
belong to Lysippos.[79]

The satyr in Athens was doubtless a work of some
celebrity, since it found a place in Pliny's list,[80] but we
have no description of it.   It is the only work in Athens
of which we hear, though one would suppose that
Lysippos would have preferred to make a Zeus or a
Herakles for the city of Praxiteles.   It is not wholly
impossible that Pliny's brief phrase refers to the
Seilenos-Dionysos group, to be discussed in the next
chapter; but this is improbable, and no other satyr of
distinct Lysippian character has been pointed out.   A
bronze statuette in Naples,[81] representing a flute-playing satyr, is thought by Bulle to be copied from an
original made in the circle of Lysippos; the well-known
figure in the Villa Borghese would be a Hellenistic
modification of this original.   It is risky to assume the
existence of a Greek statue on the evidence of one
Roman bronze.   Mme. Maviglia[82] would recognize the
work of Lysippos in the satyr playing with his tail;
but that is probably later than Lysippos.   Waldhauer
tentatively ascribes the Borghese satyr itself to Lysippos; but it seems to represent a Hellenistic development
of his style.[83]

A particularly esteemed work of Lysippos, according to Pliny,[84] was his statue of Helios in a chariot, at

[77] B.C.H., XV, 1891, pp. 381-401.

[78] This is indicated especially by the type of shoe; cf. Stais, Marbres
et Bronzes au Musée National², p. 33.

[79] On the textual point see Hitzig's note ad loc.

[80] N.H., XXXIV 64 (App. 1, 3) ; Lippold in Pauly-Wissowa, no. 12.

[81] Einzelaufnahmen, 504; Bulle, Der schöne Mensch², fig. 30.

[82] L'Attività Artistica, pp. 104 ff.

[83] Lisipp, p. 25 and fig. 8.   For the figure see also Von Mach, University Prints, no. 282; Helbig, Führer³, II, p. 252, no. 1564; Reinach,
Répertoire, II 50, 8.

[84] N. H., XXXIV 63 (App. 1, 3).

Rhodes.[85]   We could hardly expect any exact copies of
such a group, and no detailed description of it is given.
Certain amphora stamps found at Rhodes contain a
representation of Helios in a quadriga, and it has been
suggested that they are derived from Lysippos's
work,[86] since it was doubtless the most famous such
group in Rhodes.[87]   This connection, if it were proved,
would convey the very interesting information that
all four horses were represented as rearing;—or,
as it would doubtless be in the mind of the artist, as
ascending the sky.   But a definite connection between
the quadriga of Lysippos and the amphora stamps is, to
say the least, uncertain.   Of the various representations of Helios in sculpture the head found at Trianda
and now in Copenhagen[88] shows most Lysippian influence.   The eyes and nose are quite in his style.   The
face is longer than in the apoxyomenos, however, and
in some respects the head distinctly suggests the
Agias.[89]   It is almost the only piece of sculpture I
know that can reasonably be regarded as marking a
transition from the style of the Agias to that of the
apoxyomenos.   No distinct traces of Lysippian style
can be traced in any other Helios that I have seen.[90]

It has been thought that Lysippos's Zeus in Megara
formed a group with muses;[91] at any rate he had a
group of muses in the same temple.   The muses, like
the Zeus, are not described; but it can safely be assumed
that they were fully clad figures, and if grouped with

[85] See chapter III for its location and probable date.

[86] A. Maiuri, in *Atene e Rome*, I, 1920, pp. 133-137.

[87] I disregard Préchac's theory (*supra*, p. 139) that the Colossus of
Chares was such a group (*R. Arch.*, IX, 1919, pp. 64-76).

[88] Hartwig, in *Röm. Mitt.*, II, 1887, pp. 159-166; Arndt, *Glyptothèque
Ny Carlsberg*, pl. 118, p. 166. Arndt thinks it possible that the holes for
the rays are modern and that the head is a portrait.

[89] So Arndt and, according to him, Lechat.

[90] For a discussion of various types see Shear, in *A.J.A.*, XX, 1916,
pp. 283-298.

[91] Pausanias, I 43, 6 (App. 1, 23).

Zeus they would probably be standing. Mnemosyne, their mother, as Zeus was their father, might very naturally form part of the group.

There are of course a great many types preserved which correspond in general to a reasonable conception of these statues, without having any peculiarities that permit a definite attribution to any artist.[92] Among the most admirable of these extant works are three statues found at Herculaneum and now at Dresden. Two of them are examples of one type, which closely resembles, in general style, the third statue. It is this work, primarily, which has been connected with Lysippos by Salomon Reinach,[93] who sees in it a copy of the Mnemosyne of Lysippos's group. His conclusion has been accepted without qualification only by Sieveking,[94] so far as I know, though Bulle[95] and E. A. Gardner[96] seem inclined to view it with some favor; Klein[97] says the figure is more Lysippian than any other feminine statue. Amelung,[98] Dickins[99] and Arndt[100] are determined champions of an attribution to the school of Praxiteles, or to Praxiteles himself. Michaelis[101] believes that a Lysippian head has been placed on a Praxitelean body. Hekler[102] emphatically rejects the attribution to Lysippos.

The Dresden lady, usually known as the "Grande Herculanaise," is the best of a considerable series of

[92] For various figures of muses see Lippold, in *Röm. Mitt.*, XXXIII, 1918, pp. 64-102.

[93] *R. Arch.*, XXXVII, 1900, pp. 380-403.

[94] *Einzelaufnahmen*, no. 1292.

[95] Bulle, *Der schöne Mensch*², col. 280.

[96] *J.H.S.*, XXVIII, 1908, p. 145.

[97] *Gesch. d. griech. Kunst*, II, pp. 372 f.

[98] *Einzelaufnahmen*, no. 1292, p. 39, note.

[99] *Hellenistic Sculpture*, p. 38.

[100] Brunn-Bruckmann, text to pl. 558. So also Della Seta, *Cron. B.A.*, 1920, p. 54.

[101] Springer-Michaelis⁸, p. 297.

[102] *Römische weibliche Gewandstatuen*, in *Münch. arch. Stud. d. Andenken Furtwänglers gewidmet*, p. 127.

replicas. Miss Van Deman enumerated twenty-six.[103] Hekler's brief list,[104] obviously made without knowledge of Miss Van Deman's work and presumably not intended to be complete, nevertheless adds three examples, and others have been published recently. As Miss Van Deman's citations are not very full, it may be worth while to set down the whole list, retaining Miss Van Deman's numbers for those known to her.

1. Dresden, Albertinum: Herrmann, *Verzeichnis*, p. 71, no. 326; Brunn-Bruckmann no. 310; Bulle, *Der schöne Mensch*², pl. 132; Furtwängler-Urlichs³, no. 59; Von Mach, *University Prints*, no. 208; Baumeister, *Denkmäler*, III, p. 1846, fig. 1937; Hekler, *op. cit.*, pp. 127 ff. The head: Reinach, *Recueil*, pls. 216 f. Here pl. 26.
2. Syracuse, no. 697: Reinach, *Répertoire*, II 665, 7; Hekler, *op. cit.*, p. 248; Poulsen, *Greek and Roman Portraits in English Country Houses*, fig. 42 opposite p. 72.
3. Olympia: *Ergebnisse*, III, pl. 67, 1; Reinach, *Répertoire*, II 669, 13.
4. Museo dei Conservatori: Jones, *Palazzo dei Conservatori*, p. 109, no. 57, pl. 38; Hekler, *op. cit.*, p. 192.
5. Louvre, Salle de Sevère, 1130: Reinach, *Répertoire*, I 158, 3; *Marbres Antiques*, pl. 47.
6. Wilton House: Michaelis, *Anc. Mar.*, pp. 671 f.; Reinach, *Répertoire*, I 585, 3; Hekler, *op. cit.*, p. 192; Poulsen, *op. cit.*, p. 91, no. 76.
7. Louvre, Salle de l'Afrique, 1780: Reinach, *Répertoire*, II 666, 10.
8. Once in Rome: *Museo Naniano*, 189; Matz-Duhn, no. 1477; Reinach, *Répertoire*, II 668, 1.
9. Ny Carlsberg Glyptotek, from Palazzo del Drago: Poulsen, *Tillaeg til Katalog*, no. 552 b., pl. X; Matz-Duhn, I, no. 613; Reinach, *Répertoire*, III 75, 4, V 373, 9, and II 244, 7; Overbeck, *KM*, Atlas, pl. XIV, 12 and II, III, p. 465, no. 18.
10. Constantinople: Reinach, *Répertoire*, II 665, 4 (?); Mendel, *Catalogue*, III, no. 1125.
11. Hermitage: Reinach, *Antiq. du Bosph. Cim.*, p. 39; Reinach, *Répertoire*, II 666, 8.

[103] *A.J.A.*, XII, 1908, pp. 331 f.   [104] *Op. cit.*, p. 226.

12. Torlonia Collection: Reinach, *Répertoire,* I 207, 7.
13. Constantinople: Mendel, *Catalogue,* III, no. 1126.
14. Athens, National Museum, no. 219, from Andros:
    Amelung, *Basis des Praxiteles,* p. 26; Collignon, *Statues Funéraires,* p. 168; Reinach, *Répertoire,* II 671, 4;
    R. Arch., III, 1846, pl. 53, 1.
15. Olympia: *Ergebnisse,* III, pl. 62, 6; Reinach, *Répertoire,* II 671, 9; Hekler, *op. cit.,* p. 175.
16. Olympia: *Ergebnisse,* III, pl. 67, 2; Reinach, *Répertoire,* II 670, 6; Hekler, *op. cit.,* pp. 201 f.
17. Olympia: *Ergebnisse,* III, pl. 67, 3; Reinach, *Répertoire,* II 671, 8; Hekler, *op. cit.,* pp. 201 f.
18. Louvre, Salle des Saisons, 1049: Reinach, *Répertoire,* I 150, 4.
19. Vatican, Braccio Nuovo, 80: Amelung, *Skulpt. d. Vat. Mus.,* I, pp. 96 f., pl. 13; Reinach, *Répertoire,* I 583, 4; Hekler, *op. cit.,* p. 167.
20. Cherchell: Gauckler, *Musée de Cherchel,* pp. 58, 59; Reinach, *Répertoire,* II 671, 6.
21. Phillipeville: Delamarre, *Exploration scientifique de l'Algérie,* pl. 48, 2; Reinach, *Répertoire,* II 677, 6.
22. Sparta, no. 616; Tod and Wace, *Catalogue,* p. 197.
23. Lillebonne: *Annali dell' Inst.,* 1829, pp. 147 ff.; Reinach, *Répertoire,* II 670, 5.
24. Uffizi, West Corridor, no. 197; Dütschke, *Die ant. Bildw. in Oberit.,* III, no. 221.
25. Villa Borghese, Portico. Torso.
26. Rome, Atrium Vestae: Jordan, *Der Tempel der Vesta,* VIII, 4; Reinach, *Répertoire,* II 661, 2; *A.J.A.,* XII, 1908, p. 330; Hekler, *op. cit.,* p. 211, fig. 26.
27. Ny Carlsberg: *De Antike Kunstvaerker,* pl. 22, no. 310; Reinach, *Répertoire,* IV 410, 3.
28. Timgad, no. 9474: Hekler, *op. cit.,* p. 206.
29. Lateran, now no. 976: Benndorf-Schöne, *Ant. Bildw. d. Lat. Mus.,* no. 523; Hekler, op. cit., p. 205.
30. Found at Carmona: Reinach, *Répertoire,* IV 420, 8.
31. Found at Tomi: *Arch. Anz.,* 1914, col. 435.
32. Leptis Magna: *Notiz. Arch.,* III, p. 87; Reinach, *Répertoire,* V 538, 10.
33. Philippeville: Court of the museum. Headless; original surface destroyed.
34. Merida, Sta. Clara: Reinach, *Répertoire,* V 520, 3.
35. Villa Borghese: *Einzelaufnahmen,* 2772. Inexact; head new.

36. Vienna, Estensische Sammlung. Portrait in high relief.
37. Athens, Asklepieion. Four fragments put together, others lying about.
38. Silistria (Rumania) : *Aboba-Pliska*, pl. CIII, no. 7.

Recently a well-preserved example of either this type or the following one has been found in Athens (*R. Arch.*, XXIV, 1926, p. 275).

As showing clearly the influence of this type may be mentioned: an alabaster statuette in church of S. Agnese Fuori in Rome;[105] a statue in the museum at Susa, with a portrait head; a fragmentary portrait statue, only head and right arm and shoulder, found in the Cyrenaica and now in the Louvre;[106] two small grave-reliefs in Thebes; a figure on a sarcophagus in the Musée Alaoui at Tunis (C 1475) ; and a figure on a sarcophagus in the Villa Colonna.[107]

Of the thirty-eight fairly close copies, fourteen have their original heads,[108] and all save no. 1 are portraits. We have then only one copy of the original head. In seven cases[109] the left hand holds poppies or wheat-heads, the attributes of Demeter. At least three of the eight (nos. 6, 9, 12) are portraits. Such attributes would naturally be lost in many instances, when the type was used for portraits; their survival in nearly one fifth of the total number of copies justifies a strong presumption that the original statue represented Demeter. Reinach's identification, based on the slight resemblance between the "Herculanaise" and a figure in the relief representing the apotheosis of Homer,[110]

[105] Mentioned by Amelung, *Röm. Mitt.*, XII, 1897, p. 73.

[106] Salle de la Paix, no. 3130; Reinach, *Répertoire*, III 185, 11.

[107] Wulff, *Altchrist. u. Byz. Kunst*, p. 170, fig. 164.

[108] Nos. 1-13 and 36. For several of these I rely on Miss Van Deman's statement.

[109] Nos. 6, 9, 12, 20, 22, 25, 26. Miss Van Deman gives 21, but I saw no trace of such attributes; probably 21 was substituted for 22 by a typographical error.

[110] British Museum; Smith, *Catalogue of Sculpture*, III, no. 2191.

which he identified with great probability as Mnemosyne, must be discarded.

Miss Van Deman[111] enumerated forty-one copies of the "Petite Herculanaise." Her no. 6, however, belongs to the other type; I have numbered it 29 in the list above. Her no. 23 is the same as no. 14 in the foregoing list. Her no. 22 is the fragmentary portrait statue from the Cyrenaica, mentioned above as showing the influence of the other type. Her no. 37 is a figure in high relief[112] which can hardly be reckoned a derivative from either type. I have replaced these by statues which were not included in her list, retaining for the other figures the numbers used by Miss Van Deman. Hekler's brief list[113] supplies one addition.

1. Dresden, Albertinum: Herrmann, *Verzeichnis,* p. 72, no. 327; Brunn-Bruckmann, no. 558; Von Mach, *University Prints,* no. 208; Baumeister, *Denkmäler,* III, p. 1845, fig. 1935; Reinach, *Répertoire,* I 256, 4 and II 665, 1; Hekler, *op. cit.,* pp. 127 ff. Here pl. 27.
2. Athens, National Museum, no. 242, from Aigion: *Ath. Mitt.,* III, 1878, pl. VI; Brunn-Bruckmann, text to pl. 558, fig. 2; Collignon, *Statues Funéraires,* p. 170; Bulle, *Der schöne Mensch²,* cols. 279 ff.; Reinach, *Répertoire,* II 665, 2.
3. Athens, National Museum, no. 1827, from Delos: *B.C.H.,* XIX, 1895, pl. VII, pp. 482 ff.; *R. Arch.,* XXXI, 1897, pl. XIII (the head) and pp. 23-27; Collignon, *Statues Funéraires,* p. 171; Reinach, *Répertoire,* II 665, 11; Hekler, *op. cit.,* p. 129.
4. Dresden, Albertinum: Herrmann, *Verzeichnis,* p. 72, no. 328; Brunn-Bruckmann, text to pl. 558, fig. 1; Reinach, *Répertoire,* II 666, 2. Head new.
5. Torlonia Collection: Reinach, *Répertoire,* II 665, 3; Visconti, *Museo Torlonia,* no. 35, pl. IX.
6. Ny Carlsberg: *De Antike Kunstvaerker,* no. 311, pl. XXII; Hekler, *op. cit.,* p. 129. Head new.
7. Rouen: Reinach, *Répertoire,* III 192, 3.

[111] *A.J.A.,* XII, 1908, pp. 333 ff.
[112] Athens, National Museum, no. 1005; Conze, *Att. Grabr.,* no. 807.
[113] *Op. cit.,* p. 227.

8. Vatican, Galleria degli Candelabri, no. 168: Reinach, *Répertoire,* I 256, 8; Hekler, *op. cit.,* pp. 180 f., fig. 21.
9. Naples, Museo Nazionale: Ruesch, *Guida²,* no. 988; Reinach, *Répertoire,* I 569, 6.
10. Naples, Museo Nazionale: Ruesch, *Guida²,* no. 22; Reinach, *Répertoire,* I 566, 1.
11. Naples, Museo Nazionale: Reinach, *Répertoire,* I 567, 3; Ruesch, *Guida,²* no. 63.
12. Constantinople, from Crete: *Gaz. Arch.,* II, 1876, pl. XII; Reinach, *Répertoire,* II 666, 4; Hekler, *op. cit.,* p. 171; Mendel, *Catalogue,* II, pp. 340 f., no. 604.
13. Olympia: *Ergebnisse,* III, pl. 68, 1; Reinach, *Répertoire,* II 665, 8; Hekler, *op. cit.,* p. 202 (no. 3).
14. Florence, Uffizi, no. 149; Dütschke, *Ant. Bildw. in Oberit.,* III, 110.
15. Venice, Museo Archeologico: Dütschke, *op. cit.,* V, 105; Reinach, *Répertoire,* I 585, 2 and V 374, 1; *Einzelaufnahmen,* 2449.
16. British Museum, no. 1415: Smith, *Catalogue,* II, p. 235; Reinach, *Répertoire,* II 665, 12; Hekler, *op. cit.,* p. 192.
17. Constantine: Doublet-Gauckler, *Musée de Constantine,* pp. 89 f., pl. V; *Gaz. Arch.,* V, 1879, pl. 32; Reinach, *Répertoire,* II 666, 5 and 12; Hekler, *op. cit.,* p. 192.
18. Lambèse: Cagnat, *Musée de Lambèse,* pp. 46 f., pl. III, 3; Reinach, *Répertoire,* II 666, 9; Hekler, *op. cit.,* p. 180.
19. Louvre, Salle des Saisons, 1043: Reinach, *Répertoire,* I, 150, 5.
20. Cairo: Mariette, *Alb. du Mus. du Cairo,* pl. 38; Edgar, *Greek Sculpture,* pl. XII, no. 27477, p. 22; Reinach, *Répertoire,* II 665, 5.
21. Rome, Pacetti Collection: Reinach, *Répertoire,* I 275, 6.
22. Ostia: *Not. Scav.,* 1913, pp. 178 f. and fig. 5; *B. Com. Rom.,* XLI, 1913, pp. 193 f., fig. 11; *Art and Archaeology,* VIII, 1919, p. 346; Reinach, *Répertoire,* V 374, 2.
23. Sold at the Anderson Galleries, New York, in 1921: Riefstahl, *Introductory Notice* (of the sale), frontispiece and p. 9. Trajanic portrait head, which had been broken off but seemed likely to belong.
24. Athens, National Museum, from Karystos: Stephani, in *Bull. Acad. St. Petersbourg,* X, 1855, p. 250; Heydemann, *Die antiken Marmor-Bildwerke,* no. 206; Sybel,

Katalog der Sculpturen zu Athen, no. 275. I did not see it.

25. Delos: *B.C.H.,* III, 1879, pl. IX; IV, 1880, pp. 41 ff.; Reinach, *Répertoire,* II 670, 1; Hekler, *op. cit.,* p. 129.

26. Corinth: *A.J.A.,* VI, 1902, p. 424; Hekler, *op. cit.,* p. 167; Reinach, *Répertoire,* III 192, 11 (not 7).

27. Olympia: *Ergebnisse,* III, pl. 68, 3; Reinach, *Répertoire,* II 670, 9; Hekler, *op. cit.,* p. 202, no. 5.

28. Sparta, museum, no. 443; Tod and Wace, *Catalogue,* p. 178.

29. Thebes, from Thespiai: Reinach, *Répertoire,* II 677, 1; *B.C.H.,* XLVI, 1922, pp. 242-244.

30. Louvre, Salle de l'Afrique, 1779; Reinach, *Répertoire,* II 670, 4. From Cyrene.

31. Bordeaux: Reinach, *Répertoire,* II 667, 1. Head does not belong.

32. British Museum, no. 1688: Smith, *Catalogue,* III, p. 72; *Ancient Marbles in B.M.,* IX, pl. IV; Reinach, *Répertoire,* II 670, 3.

33. Vicenza: Dütschke, *Ant. Bildw, in Oberit.,* V, p. 5, no. 19; Reinach, *Répertoire,* II 665, 6. Head new.

34. Rome, Museo dei Conservatori: Jones, *Palazzo dei Conservatori,* p. 87, no. 21, pl. 32. Head new.

35. Naples, Museo Nazionale: Ruesch, *Guida²,* no. 228; Reinach, *Répertoire,* I 275, 3. Head new.

36. Ostia, Terme.

37. Athens, National Museum, no. 707 from Thera (?). Veiled portrait.

38. Munich, Glytothek, no. 249: Furtwängler-Wolters, *Beschr. d. Glypt.,* p. 258. High relief.

39. Rome, Magazzino Archeologico, in the garden. Chest and part of head.

40. Rome, Colosseum. I did not see it.

41. Rome, Atrium Vestae: Jordan, *Der Tempel der Vesta,* pl. IX, 8; *A.J.A.,* XII, 1908, p. 332; Reinach, *Répertoire,* II 670, 2; Hekler, *op. cit.,* p. 211.

42. Rome, Villa Borghese, garden: *Einzelaufnahmen,* no. 2975. Head new.

43. Tunis, Musée Alaoui, no. 1023: *Direction des Antiq. de Tunisie, Notes et Documents,* I, pl. VI, no. 1; *R. Arch.* XVIII, 1911, p. 399, no. 7.

44. Gortyna: *Ann. Scuol. It. At.,* I, p. 140, fig. 3; Reinach, *Répertoire,* V 383, 3.

45. Corfu, museum. Shoulders to knees.

46. Tigani, Samos, museum. Shoulders to knees. Somewhat elaborated.
47. Carthage, museum. Shoulders to thighs.
48. Leningrad, Hermitage: Kieseritzky, no. 312; D'Escamps, *Musée Campana*, pl. 17; Reinach, *Répertoire*, II 665, 10. Head new.
49. Stockholm: Guattani, *Monumenti Antichi*, 1784, opposite p. 100; Reinach, *Répertoire*, I 275, 4.
50-51. Two headless figures in the church of St. George at Saloniki. Here pl. 48, B.

Miss Van Deman names five cases in which she considers that the type has been modified into a Polyhymnia.[114] Two of these are nos. 48 and 49 in the list above. The head, on which the identification as Polyhymnia is based, is restored in no. 48, according to Kieseritzky; the figure seems otherwise to be among the better replicas. I do not know whether the head of the figure in Stockholm is original or not; in any case the close correspondence of the body with the type entitles it to a place in the list. Miss Van Deman was undoubtedly right in regarding the statues in the Vatican,[115] in the Louvre,[116] and in the Prado[117] as modifications of the original type.

Of the fifty-one examples of this type twenty-one (1-3, 5, 7-18, 20-23, 37) seem to have their original heads. Sixteen of these are portraits; the remaining five (nos. 1-3, 5, 7) apparently are not. Of these three (nos. 1-3) are in close agreement with one another, and may be accepted as reproducing the original with approximate accuracy. The heads of these statues resemble considerably the head of the "Grande Herculanaise" and show the same coiffure. The general resemblance of the two types[118] makes it very probable that they are to be attributed to one artist. The fact that the Dresden figures were found together suggests

[114] *A.J.A.*, XII, 1908, p. 335.   [115] Reinach, *Répertoire*, I 275, 1.
[116] Reinach, *Répertoire*, I 166, 5-6. [117] *Einzelaufnahmen*, no. 1532.
[118] See especially Collignon, *Statues Funéraires*, p. 171.

that the originals may have formed a group; this is confirmed by a relief which shows free but unmistakable imitations of the two figures together.[119] Such a group, a mature woman and a maiden, could hardly be anything but Demeter and Persephone. An example of each type has been found on a grave along with a statue of Hermes.[120] Hermes of course is Hermes Chthonios, and the persons most naturally associated with him are Demeter and Persephone. Both types occur alone as grave statues. Figures of Demeter and Persephone would more naturally be so used than statues of any other kind, though of course any statue might occasionally be used in that way. When to these considerations is added the fact previously noted, that nearly a fifth of the existing replicas of the "Grande Herculanaise" are clearly characterized as Demeter, there seems to remain no doubt at all that the originals really represented Demeter and Persephone.[121]

We are not informed that Lysippos made a group representing these goddesses. There is no reason, however, for believing that he did not, if stylistic evidence justifies an attribution to him.

Reinach shows the face of the "Grande Herculanaise" side by side with the face of the apoxyomenos,[122] and the similarity is indeed striking. The shape of the forehead, the treatment of the eyes, and the heaviness of the lower part of the face are justly emphasized by Reinach. Yet there are differences: the eyes are farther apart than in the apoxyomenos, the nose expands more from the bridge to the base, the upper lip is richly modelled, and the face as a whole

[119] *Ath. Mitt.*, XXXI, 1906, Beilage to p. 308, fig. 24, p. 331; *Cron. B.A.*, 1920, p. 52.

[120] "Grande," no. 14; "petite," no. 2.

[121] Hekler notes all these facts and brushes them aside, concluding that the originals were grave-statues. Collignon (*Statues Funéraires*, p. 172) also thinks that they were, at any rate, iconic. The conclusion given above is that of Della Seta (*Cron. B.A.*, 1920, p. 54).

[122] *R. Arch.*, XXXVII, 1900, pl. XVIII.

is not so round. Some of these differences may be explained by the differences in sex.

In the fifth chapter we spoke of the reliefs on the Polydamas base, and noted the increase in number and irregularity of folds and in general sensationalism in the drapery of the feminine figures, as compared with the Muses of the Praxitelean base at Mantineia. The Dresden ladies show further development in the same direction. In the case of the Polydamas base we could compare only the lower parts of the figures; but the dramatic cross-folds of the garments of the Dresden figures clearly belong to the same manner. The advanced "Spielbein" of the Demeter suggests the Corinth base and the Farnese Herakles, while no statue commonly ascribed to Praxiteles has this position.

On the whole it seems that a draped feminine figure by Lysippos must have looked very like the "Herculanaises." The attribution to him, though not proved, is very plausible. Certainly they are later than Praxiteles: the facial type is unlike his in both figures, though much less so in the Persephone than in the Demeter, and the restless elaboration of the drapery is not to be expected from him. There is a suggestion of arrogance in the figures which is very unlike the graceful languor of Praxiteles.

Hekler[123] would connect more or less closely with Lysippos another type, represented by a statue found at Pozzuoli,[124] the Fortuna of the Vatican,[125] and others. The drapery of this type bears little resemblance to that which appears on the Polydamas base; the "Herculanaises" are much more likely to be derived from Lysippos.

"Lysippos enrolled Kairos among the gods," says Himerios,[126] and we may consider the work by which

[123] *Op. cit.*, pp. 179 f. and 196 f.
[124] *Not. Sc.*, 1902, p. 58.
[125] Amelung, *Skulpt. d. Vat. Mus.*, I, p. 101, pl. XIII.
[126] *Eclogae*, XIV, 1 (App. 1, 36).

he did so along with the other statues of deities. Several vivid descriptions of the Kairos are extant,[127] some of which are apparently intended rather as rhetorical displays than as accurate descriptions. Poseidippos gives a relatively simple and probably reliable description. A young man was represented: he was long-haired in front and bald on the back of his head. He stood on tiptoe, and his feet were winged. In his right hand he carried a razor.

We are not surprised that the statue was more esteemed among rhetoricians than among artists. In fact no reproduction of it has been identified, though certain gems and reliefs show its influence or the influence of the rhetoricians' descriptions.[128] Bulle has suggested that a bronze statue in the Prado[129] may be derived from the work of Lysippos, and it is not impossible; but the connection is at best too remote to have much interest.

In Olympia there was found a base in the form of an astragal or knucklebone.[130] The position of the feet of the statue that stood on it is still determinable, and it was the same as in the apoxyomenos. Now the Greeks used knucklebones somewhat as we use dice; and it seems highly probable that a statue of Kairos stood on this base, especially as it was found near

[127] App. 1, 33-39 and 67; cf. Lippold in Pauly-Wissowa, no. 11, and Waldhauer, *Lisipp*, pp. 13 and 23 f. Both authors discuss the Kairos at relatively great length. Also Cook, *Zeus*, II, 2, pp. 859-868: here the author observes that Kairos was a singular subject for Lysippos and suggests that the statue really represented the Age of Puberty—a much more singular subject.

[128] Daremberg-Saglio, III, 1, p. 787, figs. 4251 f.; Springer-Wolters", p. 575; Baumeister, *Denkmäler*, II, pp. 771 f., figs. 823 f.; Roscher, *Lexikon*, II, 1, p. 899; Kieseritzky, *Hermitage*, p. 35, no. 87 d.; Waldhauer, *Lisipp*, fig. 6; Furtwängler, *D. ant. Gemmen*, I, pls. XXX, 38 and XLIII, 49-51; cf. Lamer in Pauly-Wissowa, article Kairos, cols. 1512-1521. In col. 1511 he mentions a few ancient passages which I have omitted; they are of doubtful relevancy.

[129] Bulle, *Der schöne Mensch²*, pl. 101; Brunn-Bruckmann, pl. 514; Ricard, *Marbres antiques du Musée du Prado*, p. 121, no. 210, pl. LXXIV.

[130] *Ergebnisse*, III, pl. LV, 4-5, p. 212.

the location of the altar of Kairos described by Pausanias.[131]

Mahler[132] and Klein[133] are convinced that this statue was the Kairos of Lysippos. Kallistratos, indeed, says that the statue stood in Sikyon,[134] but his account does not inspire confidence. A fatal objection to the theory, however, is that so notable a feature as the astragal would surely not have been omitted from any description of the statue.

[131] V 14, 9. Bulle (*op. cit.*, col. 679) and Lamer (*op. cit.*, col. 1510) reject this explanation of the basis, on grounds that seem too logical for the problem.

[132] *Polyklet*, p. 52.   [133] *Gesch. d. griech. Kunst*, II, p. 362.

[134] *Descriptiones*, VI (App. 1, 34).

CHAPTER VIII

STATUES OF DEITIES ASCRIBED TO LYSIPPOS BY MODERN SCHOLARS

We have now considered all the statues of gods by Lysippos that are mentioned by classical authors. Certainly, however, the prolific sculptor made other such statues, and modern scholars have felt no hesitancy in attributing to him, from considerations of style, images of other gods. Among the most notable of such statues is the Ares Ludovisi, in the Museo Nazionale at Rome.[1] It appears to be a faithful copy from a noble original. Another copy of the head, in Munich,[2] has less of the moody expression which is so noteworthy in the face of the Ludovisi statue, though this difference seems in some way to be exaggerated in pictures of the Munich head; this is partly because they do not show the head tilted forward. Since a copyist would probably not contribute such expression, we judge that the Ludovisi head (Plate 28) is the more trustworthy, though it is the inferior in quality. Another copy of the head, of Hellenistic workmanship, has been found in Albania.[3] The torso of another copy (Plate 29),[4] in Naples, is superior in quality to the Ludovisi statue.

[1] Paribeni, *Mus. Naz. Rom.*[4], p. 95, no. 72; Reinach, *Répertoire,* I 349, 2; Von Mach, *University Prints,* 213; Helbig, *Führer*[3], II, pp. 91 ff; Brunn-Bruckmann, pl. 388; Bulle, *Der schöne Mensch*[2], pl. 165; Furtwängler-Urlichs[3], pl. 23 and fig. 20; Loewy, *Griechische Plastik,* fig. 217 a-d; Gardner, *Six Greek Sculptors,* pls. LIV-LV; *Jh. Oest. Arch. I.,* XXI-XXII, 1924, pp. 203 and 208, figs. 73, 76, 77 (latter two the head). *Einzelaufnahmen,* 254-255 (the head).

[2] Furtwängler-Wolters, *Besch. d. Glypt.,* p. 296, no. 272; *Einzelaufnahmen,* 832-833; *Jb. Arch. I.,* XXVI, 1911, p. 277; *Jh. Oest. Arch. I.,* XXI-XXII, 1924, p. 209, fig. 78; *Jb. Arch. I.,* XXVII, 1912, Beilage 5-8, d. Cf. the accompanying article by Dehn, pp. 203 f.; I judge that neither the Nelson head nor the head in Athens (on which cf. Lippold, *Kopien u. Umbildungen,* p. 197) has any connection with the Ludovisi type.

[3] *Jh. Oest. Arch. I.,* XXI-XXII, 1924, pp. 203-221.

[4] Reinach, *Répertoire,* II 192, 5; Ruesch, *Guida*[2], p. 95, no. 293; *Einzelaufnahmen,* 534-535; *Jh. Oest. Arch. I.,* XXI-XXII, 1924, p. 212, fig. 79.

Certain remains on the left side of the Ludovisi figure have given rise to the opinion that a spear rested there; that a second Eros placed his hand on the god's left shoulder; and that Aphrodite stood beside him. It seems that the evidence favors the third hypothesis. The question is of little interest, however, since the Naples torso shows none of these marks and the addition, whatever it was, was doubtless due to the copyist. The same is true of the Eros seated at the feet of Ares; such a conception of Eros belongs to the late Hellenistic age, and the figure introduces a discordant element into the composition. Eliminating these accessories we have left a self-sufficient and admirably expressive representation of the restless god of war.

It is known that there was in Rome a colossal seated statue of Ares by Skopas,[5] and many authorities consider the Ludovisi statue a reduced copy of it: E. A. Gardner,[6] Bulle,[7] Klein,[8] Richardson,[9] Collignon,[10] and Von Mach[11] are more or less confident advocates of this view. Others think it a copy of an unmentioned statue by Lysippos: Amelung,[12] Michaelis,[13] Loewy,[14] and formerly Wolters.[15] Others, recognizing Lysippian influence but seeing also something of Hellenistic art in the work, have ascribed the original to the later Lysippian school: Robinson,[16] Murray,[17] Overbeck,[18] Mayer,[19] and Paribeni.[20]

[5] Pliny, *N.H.*, XXXVI 26.

[6] *Handbook* (1915), p. 422.   [7] *Der schöne Mensch*[2], cols. 359 ff.

[8] *Gesch. d. griech. Kunst*, II, p. 278. [9] *Greek Sculpture*, p. 215.

[10] *Scopas et Praxitèle*, p. 42.   [11] *Handbook*, pp. 211 ff.

[12] Helbig, *Führer*[3], II, p. 91.   [13] Springer-Michaelis[8], p. 294.

[14] *Griechische Plastik*, p. 104.

[15] Friederichs-Wolters, no. 1268. Now (Springer-Wolters[12], p. 360) he suggests Leochares.

[16] *Catalogue of Casts in Boston*, p. 235.

[17] *History of Greek Sculpture*, II, p. 308.

[18] *Gesch. d. griech. Plastik*[4], II, p. 17.

[19] *Arch. Anz.*, IV, 1889, p. 41.

[20] *Mus. Naz. Rom.*[4], p. 95. He regards the Eros as part of the original composition.

Mayer suggests that it may be the work of Piston
mentioned by Pliny,[21] who makes Piston a collaborator
with Teisikrates,[22] who was a pupil of Lysippos or
Euthykrates. The epigraphical character of Piston's
surviving signature[23] would indicate that he was active
in the later years of Lysippos or soon thereafter.
Percy Gardner[24] also regards the statue as a product
of the later Lysippian school, but that for him means a
work contemporary with the apoxyomenos. Furtwängler[25] was inclined toward Skopas, though much
less confident than formerly.[26]

Praschniker, in publishing the head found in Albania, discusses the type at considerable length. According to him, the left ear and the hair above it were
never fully worked out; he infers from this that this
part of the head was not visible, and hence that another
figure was at the side of the Ares as in the Ludovisi
group. The original, then, is represented by the Munich head and the Naples torso, while the Ludovisi
group and the Albanian head are two copies of an
adaptation, in which the Ares was embellished by two
or perhaps three Erotes. Piston, who made a Hermes
as well as a seated Ares, is the author of the original
Ares, and his Hermes is the bronze statue in Naples.
The group with the Erotes was only slightly later.

The Albanian head is certainly derived from the
original of the Ares Ludovisi, as the correspondence in
the hair shows; but the moodiness of the Ludovisi figure is exaggerated into weakness and pathos. The patch
of apparently unfinished surface is very uncertain evidence on which to conclude that the figure corre-
sponded in design to the Ares Ludovisi, which has no
such lack of finish on its head. I should regard the

---

[21] *N.H.*, XXXIV 89.

[22] For a signature of Teisikrates recently published, see *B.C.H.*,
XLIV, 1920, p. 242.

[23] Loewy, *Insch. griech. Bildh.*, no. 107.   [24] *J.H.S.*, XXV, 1905, p. 257.

[25] *Besch. d. Glypt.* (1900), no. 272.   [26] *Masterpieces*, p. 304.

Albanian head as a free copy of the usual Hellenistic sort, to be used with great caution in reconstructing a predecessor, either immediate or remote. Neither it nor either of the other heads bears any resemblance to the head of the bronze Hermes; it seems to me very improbable that the Hermes and the Ares are works of one sculptor.

Considering the head of the Ludovisi statue we may note that the shape of the face is a rather sharp oval, as in the Tegean heads; the lower part of the face is decidedly narrower than in the apoxyomenos. The eyes are farther apart than in that statue; and the hair is more confused, resembling that of the Meleager. The ears are quite unlike those of the apoxyomenos. The groove in the forehead, which is so notable in the apoxyomenos, is not present in the Ares. The Munich head differs in several features: the lips are swelling and richly modelled, while in the Ludovisi head they are like the lips of the apoxyomenos; and the ears in the Munich head resemble those of the apoxyomenos.

The proportions of the body are approximately those of the apoxyomenos. Much less anatomical knowledge is shown in the Ares, however; and the excellent Naples torso shows this early style more clearly than the Ludovisi statue. This almost excludes the possibility of Hellenistic origin. Indeed, once the Eros is recognized as a copyist's addition, there is nothing in the statue which in any way suggests a late date. It is certainly a creation of the fourth century, earlier than the apoxyomenos, and either a late work of Skopas or an early one by Lysippos.

All three copies are made on the same scale, which may therefore be accepted as the scale of the original; the immediate source was not then the colossal Ares of Skopas. Yet having made one such statue, Skopas was more likely than another man to receive a commission for a smaller seated Ares; or the existing copies may all be derived from one early copy of the colossal Ares. The morphological evidence on the whole favors Skopas: the head in profile greatly resembles the apoxyomenos, but when seen from the front it has a very Skopaic look. The effective and unexaggerated expression of the god's moody nature is to be expected from Skopas rather than from Lysippos, one would think, though one could not easily demonstrate it. On the whole the attribution to Skopas is clearly the more probable.

Another very interesting work that is frequently attributed to Lysippos is the "Jason." The best copy of the entire statue is in Lansdowne House (Plates 30-31).[27] It is much restored. "New: r. forearm, r. foot, rock, sandal, ploughshare, the support, the greater part of the plinth, l. arm from shoulder to elbow, the l. hand, parts of chlamys, l. half of nates, lower part of l. leg between knee and ankle; the l. foot with a portion of the plinth is antique. The head is connected with the body by a narrow modern strip but is antique (restored: nose and part of the back of the head), and to judge by the quality of the marble and the workmanship obviously belongs to the statue."[28] Another copy is in the Louvre.[29] It also is very extensively restored; the head is antique, but does not belong to the statue. A third copy, in Munich,[30] is likewise restored in large part; its importance lies largely in the fact that the

[27] Michaelis, *Ancient Marbles*, pp. 464-466, with illustration; Michaelis-Springer[8], p. 293; Reinach, *Répertoire*, I 487, 6. Cast with Fagan head: Springer-Wolters[12], p. 361, fig. 676. Head of the Lansdowne statue: Arndt, *Glypt. Ny Carlsberg*, p. 178, figs. 96-98.

[28] Michaelis, *Ancient Marbles*, pp. 465 f.

[29] Brunn-Bruckmann, pl. 67; Hyde, *OVM*, p. 86, fig. 8; Collignon, *Lysippe*, fig. 16; Waldhauer, *Lisipp*, fig. 13; Dickins, *Hellenistic Sculpture*, fig. 30; Von Mach, *University Prints*, no. 238 b.; Fröhner, *Notice*, no. 183; Reinach, *Répertoire*, I 157, 1-4. The head: Arndt, *Glypt. Ny Carlsberg*, pp. 180 f., figs. 108-110.

[30] Furtwängler-Wolters, *Besch. d. Glypt.*, no. 287; Von Mach, *University Prints*, no. 238a; Reinach, *Répertoire*, I 487, 7.

right hand, lost in the other copies, is preserved. The head is antique, but does not belong to the statue. An unfinished copy was found in Athens.[31] The head (Plate 32, A) is sufficiently near completion to allow comparison with the head of the Lansdowne statue, which is thus proved to belong to the figure. A badly mutilated copy is in Perinthus.[32] A statuette in the Galleria dei Candelabri of the Vatican[33] is a fairly accurate copy so far as preserved, except that it is reversed. Both arms and the right leg from the middle of the thigh are new, and apparently most of the left leg. The head appears to be antique and if so certainly belongs to the figure, though it was broken off. Christodoros,[34] in describing a number of statues in the Lauseion at Constantinople, mentions a statue of Hermes which corresponds precisely with the Lansdowne figure; it was either the original or a copy. The figure as seen in the Lansdowne replica occurs on coins of Marcianapolis in Moesia,[35] Amastris in Paphlagonia,[36] and Trapezus.[37] The best copy of the head is usually thought to be the Fagan head in the British Museum (Plate 32, B).[38] Another is in Ny Carlsberg, placed on a bust that does not belong to it.[39]

Several paintings in Pompeii and Rome, apparently derived from a single Greek prototype, represent Io

---

[31] *Ath. Mitt.*, XI, 1886, pl. IX, pp. 362 ff.; *Einzelaufnahmen*, 733-734; Reinach, *Répertoire*, II 153, 10.

[32] *Jh. Oest. Arch. I.*, I, 1898, *Beiblatt*, cols. 119-120; Reinach, *Répertoire*, III 53, 1.

[33] Reinach, *Répertoire*, I 487, 5; *Mus. Pio-Clementino*, III, pl. 43.

[34] *Ecphrasis* (*Anth. Pal.* II) 297-302 (App. 1, 87).

[35] Pick, *Münzen Nordgriechenlands*, I, pl. XVI, 25 and p. 340.

[36] Waddington-Babelon-Reinach, *Monnaies grecques d'Asie Mineure*, I, pl. XIX, 25, p. 144.

[37] Waddington-Babelon-Reinach, *op. cit.*, pl. XV, 25, p. 111.

[38] No. 1785; Smith, *Catalogue*, III, p. 119; Gardner, *Six Greek Sculptors*, pl. 76; *Marbles and Bronzes in B.M.*, pl. 25; Arndt, *Glyptothèque*, p. 178, figs. 99-100.

[39] Arndt, *Glyptothèque*, pl. 128-129, pp. 177-181; *De Antike Kunstvaerker*, no. 273.

watched by Argos.[40] The figure of Argos is much
like the "Jason," though he looks straight ahead and
his right arm is raised and placed on a rock. The
original painting was probably influenced by the original statue, unless the influence was exerted in the other
direction. A connection between the sculptural type
and the Pylades in another painting[41] seems much less
likely. A remarkable silver dish in Bari is decorated
with a group consisting of a man and a woman.[42] The
man has his left foot set up on a rock; the left arm,
with drapery, is placed across the thigh. The right
arm is stretched forward toward a dog and the head
looks down. The interpretation of the group is uncertain; perhaps it had no definite meaning even in the
mind of the artist. In proportions and modelling the
male figure resembles the "Jason," and it is highly
probable that the silversmith knew the statue, but he
imitated it so freely that no inferences about the statue
can be based on the dish.

A coin of Sybrita in Crete shows a figure of
Hermes somewhat resembling the "Jason."[43] There are
however considerable differences: the rock is decidedly
lower, so the figure is bent farther forward; the
chlamys is on the shoulder; the left hand as well as the
right is engaged with the sandal-straps; and the head
looks down. The total effect of these differences is so
great that one can assume no connection between the
coin-type and the "Jason."

The statues in Munich and in the Louvre are restored with the arms in the position seen on the coin

[40] Herrmann, *Denkmäler der Malerei*, pl. 53, with text; cf. Klein, in
Jh. Oest. Arch. I., XIII, 1910, p. 142.
[41] Herrmann, *op. cit.*, pl. 20, 3; the connection suggested by Klein, *l.c.*
[42] Nachod, in *Röm. Mitt.*, XXXIII, 1918, pp. 103-124, with citations;
Antike Denkmäler, III, pls. 25-26; Reinach, *Répertoire de Reliefs*, III,
5; cf. Klein, *Gesch. d. griech. Kunst*, II, p. 364.
[43] British Museum Catalogue, *Crete*, p. 79, pl. XIX, 12; Svoronos,
Num. de la Crète Anc., pl. XXX, 18, p. 315; Macdonald, *Hunterian Collection*, II, p. 199; Gardner, *Types of Greek Coins*, pl. IX, no. 13.

of Sybrita. Klein once argued that in the Munich copy the restoration was correct, since he thought that if the left arm had been bent as in the Lansdowne copy, either both shoulder and arm would have been lost, or part of the arm would have been preserved with the shoulder.[44] This reasoning is not unplausible, so far as the Munich statue is concerned; but as regards the original some other support was necessary, and Klein could find it only in the coin of Sybrita and in an erroneous translation of Christodoros. His conclusion was accepted by nobody except Von Mach,[45] so far as I have observed, and Klein himself later[46] abandoned it and agreed that all copies went back to an original which is represented with approximate correctness by the statue in Lansdowne House.

Klein formerly believed that the Lansdowne type, which he regarded as the original one, represented an athlete removing his clothing as he prepared to enter the contests of the palaestra, and that this type was later modified to make a Hermes. When he abandoned his belief in two types, he held that the original statue was an athlete. In this opinion he was followed by Wolters[47] and Studniczka,[48] but most scholars have held to the opinion that Hermes was represented. The figure described by Christodoros was a Hermes, and two of the three coin-types derived from the statue clearly represent Hermes; the figure on the Amastris coin also is described as Hermes, but I can discern no attributes in the illustration. Furthermore, the antique right hand of the Munich example shows that the man was not removing, but fastening the sandal,[49] and

[44] *Praxitelische Studien*, p. 8.
[45] *Handbook*, pp. 250 ff.
[46] *Gesch. d. griech. Kunst*, II, pp. 364-365.
[47] *Führer* (1922), p. 43, no. 287.
[48] *Neue Jahrbücher*, XLI, 1918, p. 21.
[49] So Arndt, *Glyptothèque Ny Carlsberg*, pp. 178 ff., and I convinced myself by my examination that he is certainly right, though Wolters (*l.c.*) disagrees.

this is strong evidence against the interpretation as an athlete. On the other hand it is noteworthy that no sculptured copy has any attribute of Hermes preserved;[50] and Klein's observation that the head does not look like the head of a god, though necessarily subjective, will probably find general acceptance. The preponderance of evidence favors the interpretation as Hermes, but since the true name is uncertain it is better to keep the conventional name "Jason."

Collignon,[51] Furtwängler,[52] Wolters,[53] Klein,[54] Studniczka,[55] Loewy,[56] Arndt,[57] Lippold,[58] and Waldhauer[59] attribute this work to Lysippos. Arndt is particularly confident; speaking of the head of the Lansdowne replica, which he thinks gives the purest impression of Lysippian work, he says: "Ce n'est que par une observation plus minutieuse qu'il [the writer] a constaté que ce n'était point une tête de l'Apoxyomène." Percy Gardner,[60] E. A. Gardner,[61] Michaelis,[62] Wace,[63] and Dickins[64] regard it as a Hellenistic work of the Lysippian school; though Arndt and Waldhauer think it earlier than the apoxyomenos, and Cultrera,[65] who insists on the Agias as the sole norm for Lysippian art, accepts the Jason as a work of his. Mme. Maviglia[66] rejects it.

[50] Hyde explains this by the hypothesis that the existing copies are athletes assimilated to the type of Hermes (*OVM*, pp. 86 f.); this may well be right.

[51] *Lysippe*, p. 71.   [52] *Beschreibung der Glyptothek*, no. 287.
[53] *Führer* (1922), p. 43, no. 287.
[54] *Gesch. d. griech. Kunst*, II, p. 364.
[55] *Ath. Mitt.*, XI, 1886, pp. 362-364.   [56] *Griechische Plastik*, p. 104.
[57] *Glyptothèque Ny Carlsberg*, pp. 177-181.   [58] In Pauly-Wissowa.
[59] *Lisipp*, pp. 28 f. and 47.   [60] *J.H.S.*, XXV, 1905, p. 257.
[61] *Six Greek Sculptors*, p. 232.
[62] *Ancient Marbles*, p. 466. I am not sure whether he modified this opinion (compare Springer-Michaelis[8], p. 294).
[63] *J.H.S.*, XXVI, 1906, pp. 239 f.   [64] *Hellenistic Sculpture*, p. 40.
[65] *Memorie dei Lincei*, XIV, 1910, pp. 238 ff.
[66] *L'Attività Artistica di Lisippo*, p. 109.

Casts of the Lansdowne "Jason" and of the apoxyomenos were placed close together in the Metropolitan
Museum, where I was enabled to make a comparative
study under favorable conditions. The general proportions are approximately similar. The musculature
is much less emphasized than in the apoxyomenos, and
fundamentally different: it is drier and harder, and
gives the figure an appearance of wiry toughness and
agility. The back and the antique left foot are especially notable in their difference from the corresponding
parts of the apoxyomenos. The triangular depression
between the muscles at the waist does not appear. The
shoulders are not rounded as in the apoxyomenos.
The pubes apparently is about the same. The bodies
of the copies in Munich and the Louvre differ in no
important particular from the Lansdowne copy.

The face is a narrower and sharper oval than in
the apoxyomenos. The hair is more or less similar,
though much flatter. The ears are narrower, and have
the inner cartilage more prominent in comparison with
the rim; they lie closer to the head, so that the hair
almost covers them. The forehead has the same shape
as in the apoxyomenos, though the horizontal furrow
is missing. The eyes are larger, not only in proportion
to the size of the face, but more noticeably in proportion to the size of the socket; hence there are no hollows at the outer corners. The lachrymal sacs are
much larger than in the apoxyomenos. There is no
such decided difference in thickness between the two
eyelids. The lower eyelid is almost straight and the
upper almost semicircular; the shape is thus very different from that in the apoxyomenos. The upper lip
is richly modelled in a Cupid's bow, and the central
depression is strongly marked. If an artist had carefully studied the lip of the apoxyomenos and designed
a lip that would be as different as possible from it, he

would have reached such a result as this. The lower lip is thicker than in the apoxyomenos and the red part is curved instead of nearly rectangular.

In the Fagan head the eyes have not a semicircular form as in the Lansdowne figure, but are rather shaped as in the apoxyomenos. In other respects, however, they resemble the eyes of the Lansdowne "Jason." The lower lip, in the Fagan head, is like that of the apoxyomenos. The hair also approaches the style of the apoxyomenos more closely. The ears are restored. In other respects the head shows the same qualities as the Lansdowne head. In the Ny Carlsberg head the hair is very elaborately treated; Arndt is doubtless right in attributing this to the copyist. The upper lip is restored; the lower lip is like that of the apoxyomenos. The eyes in general are more like the apoxyomenos than in either of the other two heads; but the lachrymal sacs are large, and there are no depressions at the outer corners. In most points the head is in accord with the Lansdowne head, though on the whole considerably closer to the apoxyomenos. The head in Athens is so far from finished that it is not possible to say anything of its style in details.

The comparison of the heads affords convincing evidence that the "Jason" and the apoxyomenos are not copied from works of the same sculptor, and the difference in the treatment of anatomy is still more thoroughgoing. The difference seems to be primarily in method, not in knowledge. If either statue shows an advance in scientific knowledge of anatomy, it is probably the "Jason" and not the apoxyomenos. Dickins classes the "Jason" with the warrior of Agasias in this respect:[67] both statues "reveal new details in abdomen, groin, and the inner side of the thighs, unknown to the earlier sculptor" (Lysippos). But the

[67] *Hellenistic Sculpture,* p. 41.

principal difference is in the appearance which the artist sought to represent. As we saw in the fourth chapter, Pliny's description of the body as represented by Lysippos is eminently applicable to the style of the "Jason," but not well to the style of the apoxyomenos. Furthermore the "Jason" is apparently the earliest and most important work in which this manner can be found. This consideration makes the attribution to Lysippos obvious, and perhaps it will at some time prove to be right; but I find it incredible, because the morphological differences between the "Jason" and the apoxyomenos—and all other sure Lysippian works are on the side of the apoxyomenos—are too great. If the two were made by one sculptor there must have been a great interval between them; and neither can be ascribed to the youth of Lysippos. One might intrepidly suggest Euthykrates as the most probable author of the "Jason."

A head in Turin,[68] apparently a portrait, resembles the "Jason" heads, but has more Lysippian character. If the "Jason" were copied from Lysippos, this head would be ascribed to him *a fortiori*. It should be contemporary with the "Jason" or slightly earlier. An identification of this portrait might throw much light on the problem of the "Jason." It is probable that the warrior of Agasias[69] is a copy, translated into late Hellenistic style, from an original by the sculptor of the "Jason"; there is a great similarity in facial type.

The bronze seated Hermes (Plate 35), found at Herculaneum, has been brought into connection with Lysippos by various scholars. The type represented by it was popular: several statuettes reproduce it, and it appears also on gems. The complete list, as known to me, is as follows:

[68] *J.H.S.*, XXVI, 1906, pp. 239 f. and pl. 16 (Wace); Hyde, *OVM*, p. 87.

[69] Hyde, *OVM*, pp. 208 f., with citations.

1. Life-size bronze in Museo Nazionale, Naples: Ruesch, *Guida*², p. 208, no. 841; Brunn-Bruckmann, pl. 282; Waldhauer, *Lisipp*, fig. 12; Bulle, *Der schöne Mensch*², pl. 166; Von Mach, *University Prints*, no. 237; *Monuments Rayet*, VI, pl. 6; Collignon, *Lysippe*, fig. 24; Reinach, *Répertoire*, I 367, 1 and 3; Lippold, *Kopien und Umbildungen*, p. 129. The head: Reinach, *Recueil*, pl. 219; Gardner, *SGS*, pl. 77. Cast, from the front: Farnell, *Cults of the Greek States*, V, pl. 29.
2. Small bronze in Berlin: Reinach, *Répertoire*, II 168, 3; Friederichs, *Berlins antike Bildwerke*, II, no. 1833. Cast in British Museum.
3. Small bronze in Bibliothèque Nationale: Babelon-Blanchet, *Catalogue des bronzes*, no. 347.
4. Small bronze in British Museum: Michaelis, *Ancient Marbles*, p. 213; Reinach, *Répertoire*, I 368, 6; Farnell, *Cults of the Greek States*, V, pl. 28; Walters, *Select Bronzes*, pl. XXVI; *Burl. Mag.*, VI, 1904, p. 219.
5. Le Chatelet: Reinach, *Répertoire*, III 243, 7.
6. Small bronze in Rouen: Reinach, *Répertoire*, III 52, 7.
7. Small silver statuette in Boston Museum.
8. Small bronze in Berlin Antiquarium, room IV, case 5. Garment on left shoulder.
9. Small bronze in Metropolitan Museum: Reinach, *Répertoire*, V 480, 7.

GEMS

Berlin: Furtwängler, *Die Antiken Gemmen*, I, pl. XLIV, 64; Furtwängler, *Geschnittene Steine*, no. 2718; Schadow, *Eine attische Grablekythos*, pl. III, 11.

Berlin: Furtwängler, *Geschnittene Steine*, no. 2719; Schadow, *Eine attische Grablekythos*, pl. III, 12.

New York, Metropolitan Museum: Richter, *Catalogue of Gems*, no. 156.

All these works are clearly characterized as Hermes, and all are certainly representatives of the type of the Herculaneum bronze. That this type was highly esteemed and widely known is further attested by a large number of figures which, while hardly to be termed replicas, unquestionably show the influence of the original. Some of these represent, or may represent, Hermes;[70] one found at Merida is interesting because it is life size, but for no other reason.[71] Many of them differ from the nine listed above in that the head is turned to the figure's left and the right foot placed at a considerably higher level than the left. It is possible that these features belong to the original.[72] Others have been adapted to other uses. A bronze described, without obvious reason, as Herakles,[73] represents the type fairly accurately. A cast in Roanne,[74] 15 cm. in height, is identified as Herakles by a lion-skin on the rock, and corresponds closely to our type. Reinach says that the profile and proportions and structure of the body are Lysippian. A bronze statuette of Herakles in the Loeb Collection[75] is almost identical with the cast for the most part, yet the cast can not have been made from it unless it has been damaged and newly restored since that time. The sleeping satyr found at Herculaneum[76] is apparently influenced by the Hermes type, and in turn was modified by the much greater artist of the Barberini Faun in Munich.[77]

[70] Reinach, *Repértoire*, II 169, 5; 168, 2; 168, 1; III 52, 4; IV 96, 9; I 370, 7. Furtwängler, *Geschnittene Steine*, 2720-26, Schadow, *Eine attische Grablekythos*, pls. II and III.

[71] *Arch. Anz.*, XXIX, 1914, col. 377; Reinach, *Répertoire*, V 76, 2.

[72] A figure of this kind in the National Museum at Copenhagen is perhaps the original of the cast in Boston (Robinson, *Catalogue of Casts*, no. 332). The left hand, as well as the right arm and left foot, is lacking in the bronze, and Mr. Caskey kindly informs me that this is true also of the cast. I could find no small bronze in Naples that accurately represented the type (cf. Robinson, *op. cit.*, no. 331 and Ruesch, *Guida²*, p. 207, no. 837).

[73] Reinach, *Répertoire*, V 94, 8.

[74] Reinach, in *R. Arch.*, XXXV, 1899, pp. 58 ff.; *Répertoire*, III 249, 4.

[75] Mr. Francis Bacon has kindly shown me the photograph, which was sent to him by Mr. Loeb. The bronze was published by Sieveking in the *Münchener Jahrbuch* in July, 1925, but I have not seen this publication.

[76] Ruesch, *Guida²*, p. 209, no. 842; Brunn-Bruckmann, 594; Von Mach, *University Prints*, no. 281.

[77] Furtwängler-Wolters, *Beschreibung der Glyptothek*, no. 218; Von Mach, *University Prints*, no. 280.

It is unmistakable, however, that the original or at least the most highly esteemed use of this type was as Hermes. Certainly the Naples bronze is by far the finest example extant. The extraordinary alertness and life of the body have been accorded admiration by all critics; no other figure expresses so well the nature of Hermes as the celestial messenger. Several scholars have felt that so fine a work must have proceeded from a great master. Richardson,[78] Bulle,[79] and Reinach[80] are strongly tempted to pronounce it an original work of Lysippos, though none of them quite yields to the temptation. Benndorf,[81] Collignon,[82] and E. A. Gardner[83] consider it an original work of the Lysippian school.—It will be remembered that Gardner believes that the apoxyomenos is copied from a work of that kind.—Loewy,[84] Michaelis,[85] Edward Robinson,[86] Mariani,[87] and Waldhauer[88] see in it a copy from Lysippos or a pupil. Mme. Maviglia[89] finds it in accordance with her idea of Lysippos. Cultrera,[90] the arch-Agiast, finds no Lysippian character at all in the Hermes. Klein[91] considers it a school work, like the "Praying Boy," but he does not make it clear whether as an original or as a copy. Walters[92] strangely terms it "Pheidian in treatment."

[78] *Greek Sculpture,* p. 234.
[79] Bulle, *Der schöne Mensch²*, col. 361.   [80] *Recueil,* pl. 219.
[81] *Jh. Oest. Arch. I.,* IV, 1901, p. 186.   [82] *Lysippe,* p. 112.
[83] *Six Greek Sculptors,* p. 243. For Praschniker's view, see p. 168.
[84] *Griechische Plastik,* p. 104.   [85] *Springer-Michaelis⁸,* p. 294.
[86] *Catalogue of Casts in Boston,* p. 236.
[87] Ruesch, *Guida²,* p. 208.   [88] *Lisipp,* p. 27.
[89] *L'Attività Artistica di Lisippo,* p. 109.
[90] *Memorie dei Lincei,* XIV, 1910, p. 240.
[91] *Gesch. d. griech. Kunst,* II, pp. 406 f.
[92] *Select Bronzes,* text to pl. XXVI.

External evidence proves definitely that it is neither altogether copy nor original. Of the twelve imitations I have listed, all save the Naples statue show the posture reversed as compared with the large statue: the right arm and left leg are advanced, and the left arm and right leg are drawn back. Such an overwhelming preponderance of evidence compels the conclusion that this was the position of the original. All the figures that were mentioned as free imitations of the type support this conclusion. The artist of the Naples figure, then, reversed the posture of his original. In the position of the arms he may have been influenced by another type of seated Hermes, of which we have the original, as it seems, as well as two copies.[93] In this, however, the legs are crossed and the posture indolent; the later artist owed little to it.

He made another and more important change. The appearance of alertness so notable in the Naples bronze arises, in large part, from the forward inclination of the body: it is this, more than any other one detail, that conveys the impression that the god is ready to leap up in a fraction of a second. Now this forward inclination does not appear to any such extent in any other representation of the type: it is necessary therefore to ascribe it to the artist of the Naples figure. It is clear that he followed closely an earlier and very celebrated figure, but modified it and, in one important detail at least, distinctly improved it. It is altogether probable that the morphological details are his own.

An examination of the Hermes makes it quite clear why scholars have been so hesitant in connecting the work closely with Lysippos, in spite of its remarkable excellence. The musculature is treated more in the manner of the "Jason" than of the apoxyomenos. The

[93] The original is in the Acropolis Museum (Casson, *Catalogue*, p. 250, no. 1346; Reinach, *Répertoire*, V 76, 6); the copies in the Corsini Garden in Florence (Reinach, *Répertoire*, II 169, 4) and in the Hermitage (Reinach, *Répertoire*, III 52, 1).

figure is lithe and wiry rather than muscular. The triangular depression at the waist does not occur. The feet are broader and show less anatomical detail.

The head is more or less restored; the exact extent of the restoration is uncertain, but the face at least is nearly all original. The hair may be called Lysippian, though the closest analogy is the Fagan head. The ears resemble those of the apoxyomenos in shape; their protrusion is noticeable. The eyes, nose, and lips are wholly un-Lysippian. The general construction of the face is entirely different from that used by Lysippos: the surface of the face slopes back rapidly from the nose, so that the eyes, instead of being deeply shadowed, seem to lie along the surface.

The sculptor of the Naples Hermes, then, was certainly not Lysippos. As to his time there is little evidence, but the third century seems more probable. Dickins finds great similarity between the Hermes and the Praying Boy,[94] attributed with virtual certainty to Boedas. I can not agree with him; it seems to me that the only difference between the Praying Boy and the apoxyomenos is that one represents a more mature figure than the other.

There is no evidence as to the original author of the Hermes type, but he was probably considerably earlier than Lysippos. The bronzes that are sufficiently large and well preserved to allow observation of their style seem to belong to the early fourth if not the fifth century. Indeed, the figure from Paramythia (no. 4) is probably itself earlier than Lysippos.

Another type sometimes used to represent Hermes is known in a number of examples,[95] of which the best known is the "Mercure Richelieu" in the Louvre. Formerly Furtwängler and Amelung separated the

[94] *Hellenistic Sculpture*, p. 38.
[95] Listed by Lippold in *Jb. Arch. I.*, XXVI, 1911, pp. 279 f.; cf. Jones, *Palazzo dei Conservatori*, p. 160, no. 11; Furtwängler, *Masterpieces*, pp. 289 ff.; Amelung, in *Röm. Mitt.*, XX, 1905, pp. 146 f.

Hermes of Atalanti from the Richelieu type chiefly because of the difference in the heads: it was not believed
that the head of the Richelieu statue itself was original, but the copy in Ny Carlsberg[96] was thought to
show the original type. Lippold has shown, however,
that the head of the Hermes of Atalanti is only a rude
variant of that of the Ares Ludovisi;[97] so that statue
is to be regarded as a Hellenistic combination of diverse elements. Furthermore, it has been established
that the head of the Ny Carlsberg statue does not
belong to it;[98] and the head of the Lecca-Ducagini
replica seems rightly explained by Lippold as a portrait type.[99] Finally, one of the marble statues from
the Cerigotto wreck[100] is an example of the type and
is sufficiently preserved to establish the original type of
head, of which several copies are identifiable.

Amelung, believing in the existence of two closely
related originals, ascribed both to Lysippos. Since it
now appears that neither of the heads on which that
opinion was based belonged originally to the type, and
since the true head had generally been considered
Attic,[101] Amelung now agrees that the statue is
Attic,[102] and that is doubtless right. It might well be
attributed to Lysippos if the Agias were his.[103] Lippold[104] has suggested that it may be the Theseus of
Seilanion.

The head now worn by the Copenhagen replica,[105]

[96] *De Antike Kunstvaerker*, no. 272.

[97] *Jb. Arch. I.*, XXVI, 1911, p. 277.

[98] *Ausonia*, II, 1907, p. 216 (Mariani).

[99] *Jb. Arch. I.*, XXVI, 1911, p. 274.

[100] *Jb. Arch. I.*, XXVI, 1911, p. 272; 'Εφ. 'Αρχ., 1902, pl. E, 2;
Svoronos, Τὸ 'Εθνικὸν Μουσεῖον, pl. XV, 1.

[101] Furtwängler-Wolters, *Beschreibung der Glyptothek*, no. 289.

[102] Helbig, *Führer³*, I, p. 625.

[103] The body was declared Lysippian through comparison with the
Agias by Mahler (*Polyklet*, p. 153, note 1) and Klein (*Gesch. d. griech.
Kunst*, II, p. 352).

[104] *Röm. Mitt.*, XXXIII, 1918, p. 93; *Kopien und Umbildungen*, p. 197.

[105] Good illustration: *Ausonia*, II, 1907, p. 216.

though pronounced by Klein[106] "rein lysippisch," can not be confidently attributed to Lysippos.

Furtwängler[107] mentioned a bronze Hermes in Berlin as an original from the school of Lysippos. The bronze has since been published by Mariani,[108] who describes it as a translation of the Palatine Hermes into Lysippian style. This may well be a true account of its origin; but the style is Lysippian only in general character. A bronze statuette in the museum at Geneva (Plate 53, B),[109] belonging in a general way to the Richelieu type, is more likely to represent the immediate following of the master.

The group representing Seilenos with the infant Dionysos exists in several copies. As Klein's citations[110] are now antiquated I repeat his list, with three additions:

1. Louvre: Fröhner, *Notice,* no. 250; Brunn-Bruckmann, no. 64; Friederichs-Wolters, no. 1430; Klein, *Praxiteles,* p. 397, fig. 80; Von Mach, *University Prints,* no. 245; Reinach, *Répertoire,* I 169, 1-3; *Marbres Antiques,* pl. XVIII; Waldhauer, *Lisipp,* fig. 22. Here pl. 33.

2. Munich, Glyptothek: Furtwängler-Wolters, p. 244 ff., no. 238; *Hundert Tafeln,* no. 39; Reinach, *Répertoire,* I 375, 6; Von Mach, *University Prints,* no. 245; Wolters, *Führer* (1922), p. 27 and plate.

3. Vatican: Amelung, *Skulpt. d. Vat. Mus.,* I, pp. 16 f., pl. II; Helbig, *Führer*[3], I, p. 3, no. 4; Bulle, *Der schöne Mensch*[2], no. 71; Von Mach, *University Prints,* no. 245; Reinach, *Répertoire,* II 64, 7.

4. Wilton House: Michaelis, *Ancient Marbles,* p. 687, no. 70; Reinach, *Répertoire,* I 411, 7.

[106] *Gesch. d. griech. Kunst,* II, p. 352.

[107] *Masterpieces,* pp. 300 and 338 (*Meisterwerke,* pp. 520 and 572). He gives two inventory numbers; 6305 is correct.

[108] *Ausonia,* II, 1907, pp. 226 ff. and fig. 9; details about the bronze by Zahn.

[109] Reinach, *Répertoire,* II, 786, 4; *Einzelaufnahmen,* 1883; Deonna, *Cat. des bronzes figurés antiques,* p. 16, no. 27, pl. II; De Ridder and Deonna, *L'art en Grèce,* pl. 9.

[110] *Praxiteles,* pp. 395 ff.

5. Palazzo Massimi: Matz-Duhn, *Ant. Bildw. in Rom.*, I, no. 471. "Unglaublich schlecte, vermuthlich moderne Arbeit."
6. Stud. Carimini: Matz-Duhn, *op. cit.*, I, no. 472. Unfinished.
7. "Fragment in V Saale des Orto botanico."
8. Hermitage: Kieseritzky, no. 291; Reinach, *Répertoire*, III 19, 8. "Suspect."

HEADS OF SEILENOS

1. Berlin: *Ant. Skulpt.*, no. 279.
2. Palazzo Rospigliosi: Matz-Duhn, *op. cit.*, no. 482.
3. Museo Capitolino: Jones, *Sculpt. of the Mus. Cap.*, p. 110, no. 35, pl. 30.
4. Naples, Museo Nazionale; Ruesch, *Guida²*, p. 79, no. 254.
5. Madrid: Hübner, *Die antiken Bildwerke in Madrid*, no. 119; *Einzelaufnahmen*, 1637.
6. Rome, Museo Nazionale: Paribeni, *Mus. Naz. Rom.⁴*, p. 154, no. 346. Here pl. 34.
7. Vatican, Magazine: *Illustrated London News*, September 9, 1922, p. 380 and fig. 19.

Klein wishes to see in this group the "symplegma" of Kephisodotos, the son of Praxiteles.[111] This suggestion has not found favor; the word "symplegma" can not naturally be interpreted to mean simply "group." Besides, it is difficult to see Praxitelean influence in the statue. The kinship in subject with the Hermes serves to emphasize the complete difference in style. The Hermes is a figure of youthful beauty; the Dionysos, incidentally added, is not allowed to obscure the graceful lines of the young god. In the Seilenos group, on the contrary, the child is used especially, it seems, to make a transverse line across the chest, such as exists in the apoxyomenos and the Medici Aphrodite. The "Spielbein," set forward and resting on its outer side, reminds one of the Farnese Herakles; indeed the whole posture suggests that statue.

[111] *Praxiteles*, pp. 395 ff.; *Gesch. d. griech. Kunst*, II, pp. 398 f.

Accordingly Loeschcke,[112] Furtwängler,[113] Bulle,[114] Amelung,[115] Lippold,[116] and Waldhauer[117] are inclined to ascribe this type to Lysippos.

A study of details, as seen in the three good copies and in several of the heads, furnishes strong support for the attribution. Similarities to the apoxyomenos are discernible not only in the general proportions and the treatment of anatomy, but in the forehead, the eyes, the navel, the long, flat feet, and indeed in every feature except the pubes. The hair on the head of the child and on the back of the head of Seilenos is also like that of the apoxyomenos. There is no other work which can be so certainly assigned, solely on stylistic grounds, to Lysippos. As has been noted, this may be the work which appears in Pliny's list as a "satyr in Athens." At any rate the number of copies indicates that it was more popular in antiquity than the Praxitelean Hermes which fortune has preserved; and it deserved its popularity, for it was finely conceived and finely designed.

Lorenzo Ghiberti records[118] the discovery of three antique statues in Italy. One found at Rome represented a hermaphrodite the size of a girl thirteen years old. Another, found in Florence, seems to have been an Aphrodite. The third was found in Siena. It is said to be like ("simile") the other two. It had a dolphin against the leg on which the weight rested; at least that seems to be the most natural interpretation of Ghiberti's words: "et aveva in sulla gamba in sulla quale ella si posava, uno delfino."[119] On the base

---

[112] *Arch. Anz.*, X, 1895, p. 217.

[113] *Beschreibung der Glyptothek*, no. 238.

[114] *Der schöne Mensch*[2], col. 136.   [115] Helbig, *Führer*[3], I, pp. 3 ff.

[116] In Pauly-Wissowa.   [117] *Lisipp*, p. 33.

[118] The passage in full in *Bull. dell' Inst.*, 1837, pp. 68-70; the part dealing directly with the Lysippian figure in Loewy, *Insch. griech. Bildh.*, no. 476.

[119] The manuscript has "alfino," which might mean a bishop in chess. The emendation, however, is probably right.

appeared the name of the sculptor, who was Lysippos. The statue excited general and enthusiastic admiration, and was set up over a public fountain of the city. The Sienese encountered bad fortune in war with Florence, however; and it was suggested that the honor paid the statue was the cause of it. It was denounced in the consistory as indecent (disonesta),[120] and was finally broken to pieces and buried in Florentine soil. Its discovery was prior to 1348, since Ambrogio Lorenzetti, who is mentioned as having made a drawing of it, died in that year.

Lange identified this statue as a Poseidon of the Lateran type.[121] In the first place, however, Ghiberti's description can hardly be interpreted to correspond with that figure. Then it is not easy to understand why a great wave of popular enthusiam should surge about the Poseidon, even if a fine replica of it were discovered; it is not unduly cynical to suggest that a feminine figure of seductive beauty would be much more likely to appeal to the populace. Finally, what would the term "disonesta" mean, if applied to the Poseidon? General recognition of these objections has led to a loss of interest in the incident in Siena, so far as the Poseidon is concerned.

More recently two writers[122] have independently suggested that the statue was a replica of the Medici Aphrodite (Plate 9, A).[123] It might very naturally arouse unbounded enthusiasm, and very naturally be

[120] This detail is not derived from Ghiberti, but from the consistory records; see Loewy, l.c..

[121] Das Motiv des aufgestützten Fusses, p. 47.

[122] Mahler, in R. Arch., I., 1903, pp. 33-38, and C. R. Acad. Insc., 1905, pp. 623-628; Julius von Schlosser, in Jb. Kunsth. Samm., 1904, pp. 141-150.

[123] Amelung, Führer durch Florenz, no. 67; Bulle, Der schöne Mensch², no. 156; Von Mach, University Prints, no. 202; Friederichs-Wolters, no. 1460. Head of the Dresden replica: Reinach, Recueil, pls. 184-185. List of replicas: Bernoulli, Aphrodite, pp. 229-233. The history of the Medici statue: Mélanges Perrot, pp. 285-290 (S. Reinach) and Röm. Mitt., XIX, 1904, pp. 267-275 (Correra).

condemned as "disonesta"; and the dolphin corresponds well to Ghiberti's description. Furthermore, a rough but quite unmistakable adaptation of the Aphrodite appears in a group in Pisa,[124] which certainly belongs to the fourteenth century; it is tentatively attributed to Tino di Camaino, a Sienese sculptor. Here the Aphrodite has become a figure of Prudence! This shows clearly that an example of the type was known in Tuscany during the period of the Sienese statue's popularity; probably it was very well known, since the adaptation is a rather surprising one unless the statue imitated was especially esteemed.

Mahler, in his first article, noted several points of stylistic resemblance between the Aphrodite and the apoxyomenos. The arms cross the body similarly, giving a broken rhythm in the lines very different from that in such statues as the Knidian Aphrodite, where the torso is kept as clear of obstruction as possible. The hair in each case has a restless character, with a tuft almost upright on the middle of the head. The face, as seen in the Dresden replica (Plate 36), also shows decided resemblances to the apoxyomenos: the shape is somewhat Lysippian, and the eyes, lips, and chin are noticeably like those of the apoxyomenos. The back, with its deep groove along the spine resembles that of the apoxyomenos; it is very unlike the back of the Capitoline Aphrodite, for example.

This hypothesis has been accepted by Reinach and, if hearsay evidence is reliable, by Furtwängler.[125] The prevailing opinion among scholars, however, remains what it was before: that the Aphrodite is a Hellenistic work of the Praxitelean school. Von Schlosser was so reluctant to attribute the statue to Lysippos that he declared the inscription worthless. Few scholars would follow him in that: an antique label is not

[124] Von Schlosser's figs. 4, 5, 10.
[125] R. Arch., XXIV, 1914, p. 158.

lightly to be disregarded, though the Dioskouroi of Monte Cavallo warn against too implicit faith.

We may deplore the absence of divine character in the statue, but its significance as a work of art is not to be denied. The sculptor deliberately chose to depict the goddess simply as a petite, chic, seductively beautiful young woman. His taste in so doing may not command approval; but it must be admitted that it required an original and intellectually vigorous artist to take such a step. That is the sort of artist Lysippos was. We find no evidence anywhere of lofty idealism or of profound spiritual expression in his work. It seems to me quite likely that he did make the original of the Medici Aphrodite. Neither the internal nor the external evidence alone would carry conviction; but together they make the attribution plausible.

Mme. Maviglia,[126] though somewhat impressed by Mahler's arguments, finally rejects the attribution because of the absence of literary evidence—"inesplicabile in tal caso." But the argument from silence is exceedingly feeble. Pliny was an ignorant and uncritical compiler from sources of undeterminable value, so that no omission from his account is significant. In other classic authors, works of art are, with the exception of a comparatively small number of especially esteemed works, mentioned only when they accidentally become necessary to the writer's theme. The numerous replicas of the Aphrodite prove that it was popular with the people; the judgment of the connoisseurs, which is reflected in literature, may reasonably have been less favorable.

[126] *L'Attività Artistica di Lisippo,* pp. 76 ff. Lippold, in Pauly-Wissowa, also rejects the hypothesis, and Waldhauer does not mention it.

CHAPTER IX

THE REPRESENTATIONS OF HERAKLES

Among Lysippos's favorite subjects was Herakles; his recorded works include several images of this hero. We have already spoken of the Herakles Epitrapezios. In a sanctuary near Alyzia there was a whole series of groups representing the labors of Herakles;[1] later they were taken to Rome. Excavation has yielded fragments that perhaps belonged to the original bases,[2] but Mr. Rhomaios tells me that they are too much broken to afford any sort of evidence on the statues. It is highly probable that these works are to be placed fairly early in the life of the sculptor: it is not likely that the Akarnanian town could have commanded the services of Lysippos for so large a series of sculptures after he had reached the position of court sculptor to Alexander. It may well be that the activities of Lysippos in Akarnania and in Aitolia belonged to about the same time. Cultrera[3] and Mme. Maviglia[4] have considered the problem of identifying copies of these groups.

A group of Herakles and the lion exists in several examples, differing somewhat from one another.[5] In its general scheme the type is a very old one;[6] but the representations on vases and in early sculpture differ in essential particulars from these groups,

[1] Strabo, *Geographica*, X, 459 (App. 1, 48) ; Lippold in Pauly-Wissowa, no. 17.

[2] Πρακτικά, 1919, pp. 47-49.

[3] *Memorie dei Lincei*, XIV, 1910, pp. 244-256.

[4] *L'Attività*, pp. 70-75.

[5] Reinach, *Répertoire,* I 463, 1 and 3 (Florence) ; 467, 5 (Oxford); II 237, 4 (Bibliothèque Nationale) ; 797, 2 = III 249, 7 (Cologne) ; III 73, 4 = Waldhauer, *Lisipp,* fig. 18 (Hermitage) ; Maviglia, *op. cit.,* fig. 16 (Florence).

[6] For a tabulation of its occurrence on vases see Luce, in *A.J.A.,* XX, 1916, pp. 460 ff. Cf. Roscher, *Lexikon,* I, 2, 2223-4, 2243.

which must be referred to a sculptured original of considerable celebrity. The details of form do not suggest Lysippian authorship, but small copies are rarely dependable for such details. The group was designed for observation from more than one point of view, since the lion's head was presumably not intended to be invisible; and Waldhauer justly notes that the composition, if correctly represented in the groups in Florence and the Hermitage, was truly pyramidal.[7] Derivation from Lysippos, then, is probable.

A group of Herakles and the hind is best represented in a beautiful little bronze in Palermo.[8] At least one other group, formerly in the Museo Campana, is evidently inspired by the same original,[9] and its celebrity is further attested by an epigram in the Anthology,[10] and the design on a Pergamene coin.[11] The maker of the Palermo bronze has changed the sex of the deer, however, and has made a fountain decoration of the group, so it is evidently not a dependable copy. It is scarcely possible that the originals of both this and the lion group were parts of the series at Alyzia, since the hero is bearded in one case and not in the other. It may be assumed, however, that Lysippos's treatment of the themes was not very different from that in these groups.

There is a possibility of something better in a statue in the Palazzo dei Conservatori.[12] It is hardly

[7] *Lisipp*, pp. 30 f.

[8] Collignon, *Lysippe*, fig. 17; Maviglia, *op. cit.*, fig. 18; Reinach, *Répertoire*, I 468, 4; Waldhauer, *Lisipp.* fig. 20 and pp. 31 f.

[9] Reinach, *Répertoire*, I 476, 5. Restorations, if any, are unknown to me. The two groups are discussed somewhat by Keil, in *Annali dell' Inst.*, XVI, 1844, pp. 175-186.

[10] *Anth. Pal.*, XVI (*Plan. App.*, IV) 96 (App. 1, 49).

[11] Von Fritze, pl. VI, no. 7, pp. 69 f.

[12] *B. Com. Rom.*, VIII, 1880, pls. IX-X, pp. 153-161; Brunn-Bruckmann, no. 352; Bulle, *Der schöne Mensch²*, no. 87; Reinach, *Répertoire*, II 540, 2; Helbig, *Führer³*, I, p. 538, no. 948; Maviglia, *op. cit.*, fig. 17; Jones, *Palazzo dei Conservatori*, p. 158, no. 7, pl. 58; Bocconi, *Musei Capitolini*, fig. 25.

to be doubted that Herakles is represented, though it is difficult to decide in what contest he is engaged. The statue has usually been considered earlier than Lysippos, but I believe that it is possible to agree with Mme. Maviglia[13] that it is copied from an early work of Lysippos. The musculature seems to be about such as would be expected from the artist of the apoxyomenos, near the beginning of his career. It is very unlike that of the Agias: Cultrera, as a champion of the Agias, has reason to declare this Heracles non-Lysippian. The free and vigorous posture, with the twist of the body, warrants the belief that the original was not earlier than the middle of the fourth century. The hair, the grooved forehead, the eyes, the ears, the navel, and the long flat feet bear considerable resemblances to the corresponding features of the apoxyomenos. It ought to be noted that the pubes, which would reasonably be expected to be a fairly constant feature in an artist's style, is more or less triangular and unlike that of the apoxyomenos.

Certain other groups, chiefly on sarcophagi, are suggested by Cultrera as derived from the cycle at Alyzia; but their connection with Lysippos, if any, is indirect and vague. The Constantinople bronze,[14] which Mme. Maviglia[15] would consider copied from the Lysippian group of Herakles and the Erymanthian boar, has generally and rightly been dated much earlier. A statuette in the Hermitage[16] might be derived from Lysippos, but hardly from the series at Alyzia, since no labor is represented.

It is improbable that many such complete cycles

[13] *Op. cit.,* p. 75.

[14] *Gaz. Arch.,* VIII, 1883, pl. I; Collignon, *Histoire,* I, p. 479, fig. 246; *R. Arch.,* XXXV, 1899, pp. 19-33 (Joubin); Maviglia, *op. cit.,* fig. 19; Reinach, *Répertoire,* II 548, 3.

[15] *Op. cit.,* pp. 78-84.

[16] Waldhauer, *Lisipp,* p. 31 and fig. 19; Reinach, *Répertoire,* III 73, 2; Kieseritzky, Catalogue, no. 269A.

in the round were ever made, and any existing series
would have a strong claim to consideration as possibly copied from Lysippos. There are four groups
in the Vatican,[17] all found together at Ostia; but
Amelung seems undoubtedly right in explaining them
as creations of the second century after Christ, in
which various Greek statues are freely imitated. A
figure of Herakles drawing the bow,[18] in the Lateran,
resembles the Vatican series in size and style and
probably had the same origin, though it was found
in Rome. The museum at Lambèse in Algeria contains five fragmentary groups representing Herakles
in various labors. They are mostly unpublished, so
far as I know, though there is a drawing of the Hydra
group in the Répertoire,[19] and I think a torso in
Cagnat's catalogue of the museum[20] is another member of the series. These groups are approximately
the same size as those in the Vatican and Lateran:
they are about two thirds life size. The workmanship is so poor that few inferences about the style of
of the originals can be drawn; but the figures are
rather slender and the treatment of anatomy offers
no evidence against an attribution to the young Lysippos. It is by no means improbable *a priori* that the
groups in Alyzia were smaller than the life-size; if
so the statue in the Palazzo dei Conservatori would
not be copied from any group there.

The most famous of Lysippos's statues of Herakles, like his most famous statue of Zeus, was at
Tarentum.[21] We have a good deal of information
about it.[22] Fabius Maximus took it to Rome when

[17] Amelung, *Skulpt. d. Vat. Mus.*, II, nos. 137, 141, 208, 213.
[18] Benndorf-Schöne, *D. ant. Bildw. d. Lat. Mus.*, no. 285; present
number 238.
[19] V 96, 6, with citation: *Rec. de Constantine*, 1914, pl. 1.
[20] P. 29; Reinach, *Répertoire*, II 148, 3.
[21] See chapter III for date.
[22] App. 1, 19-20, 40-43.

he captured Tarentum in 209 B.C., and set it up on the
Capitol. There it remained probably till 325 A.D.,
when it was transferred to Constantinople. It perished in 1204, when the city was captured by the
Latins. Meanwhile, however, Niketas Choniates had
seen it, and he gives a gratifyingly detailed description.
The hero had no weapon. He sat on a basket, over
which the lion's skin was spread. His right leg and
right arm were extended; his left leg was bent at the
knee, and he rested his head on his left hand, which
was supported at the elbow. The shin of its leg was as
tall as a man. Niketas calls the artist Lysimachos,
but that is undoubtedly a mistake.

Clearly the pathetic element was stressed in this
work. The basket, as is shown by other monuments,
indicates a connection with the cleaning of the Augean
stables.[23] Herakles bows his head beneath a burden
not only of toil but of humiliation. His mighty
strength, which was surely adequately rendered by
Lysippos, would emphasize by contrast the despondency in which the hero was sunk.

Klein[24] says that the well-known boxer in the
Museo Nazionale at Rome (now known to be a signed
work of Apollonios, son of Nestor, the sculptor of
the Belvedere torso)[25] "stammt unverkennbar von
diesem Werke ab." The resemblance between them
seems to be limited to the fact that both represent
men sitting down. He also says that Mahler found in
Tarentum a life-size head of Herakles of Lysippian
character, but closely resembling the boxer's head;
this would be a copy of the original by Lysippos.
This head seems never to have been published, and I
have tried in vain to secure a photograph.

[23] So Furtwängler, *Sitzb. Bayer. Akad. Wiss.,* 1902, p. 441.

[24] *Gesch. d. griech. Kunst,* II, p. 371; cf. III, pp. 45 f.

[25] Paribeni, *Museo Nazionale Romano*[4], p. 197, no. 480; Hyde, *OVM,*
pp. 145-147, with references. For Carpenter's discovery of the signature
see *Gnomon,* III, 1927, p. 190.

The head was broken from a statue. Originally it looked up to the left of the figure, as in the Terme boxer, but apparently the head was thrown back more than in that figure; at all events the resemblance between them is not such as to prove any connection. The hair of the head in Tarentum resembles that of the Meleager or Farnese Herakles. There are several horizontal lines in the forehead. The eyes are widely opened; the balls show little curvature; the upper lid is thicker than the lower. The ears resemble those of the apoxyomenos, the mouth that of the Farnese Herakles. The base of the nose is broad. On the whole it seems altogether possible that this head is copied from an original by Lysippos or one of his followers; in the latter case the original might have been influenced by the famous Herakles. It is very doubtful whether the head represents Herakles: it is a rather thin and old face and should not belong to a strong man. The expression may indicate either weariness or sadness. Herakles or Herakleitos?

Furtwängler has recognized in a carving on an ivory chest, made probably in the tenth or eleventh century, an imitation of the Herakles of Lysippos. The chest is now in Xanten, in Germany.[26] With similar works, it had previously been regarded as made in Constantinople. The carving corresponds so perfectly with the description of Niketas that it seems certain that it is derived from the Lysippian statue. Yet one hesitates to trust it on one point, where Niketas is silent: Herakles is shown as beardless. Certainly the pathos of the design would have been more effective if the hero were older.

Two epigrams describe a statue of Herakles, expressly ascribed by one of them to Lysippos.[27] In this

[26] *Sitzb. Bayer. Akad. Wiss.*, 1902, pp. 435-442. The carving on p. 439. Cf. Dalton, *Byzantine Archaeology*, p. 122; Schlumberger, *L'Épopée Byzantine*, II, p. 271, illustration.

[27] *Anth. Pal.*, XVI (*Plan. App.*, IV) 103-104 (App. 1, 50-51) ; Lippold in Pauly-Wissowa, no. 16.

case Herakles was not only unarmed, but lacked his
usual attribute, the lion-skin. The interpretation of
the poets was that he had been overcome and stripped
of his arms by Love. It has been thought that these
epigrams referred to the famous work at Tarentum.[28]
But why should there be solicitous inquiries about the
lion-skin, if Herakles was sitting on it? Of course it
is conceivable that the poets were celebrating a work
that they knew by reputation only. Geminus and
Philip, however, lived during the period when the
Tarentine colossus was at Rome, and they would surely
have had no difficulty in learning the details of its
treatment, even if they never visited Rome themselves.
It seems unlikely that they would have emphasized the
absence of the lion-skin unless they were sure it was
absent. Jahn suggests that the poet Geminus is identical with the consul Geminus, 18 A. D.[29] If this is
true he could hardly fail to be acquainted with the
Tarentine work.

The poets, then, describe a different statue. It appears that it was seated, though the epigrams do not
say so directly. Geminus's epigram was cut on a
block of marble formerly in Venice,[30] which may have
been the base for a copy of the statue; but the block
is now lost. So far as can be inferred, the original
was quite without attributes by which it could be
identified as Herakles; it may be that copies have escaped notice because of that.

At Sikyon Pausanias saw a bronze Herakles by
Lysippos.[31] He gives no description whatever of it.
Whether the Herakles mentioned by Lucian[32] is iden-

[28] So Furtwängler, *Sitzb. Bayer. Akad. Wiss.*, 1902, p. 436.
[29] *Rh. Mus.*, X, 1856, p. 626.
[30] Loewy, *Insch. griech. Bildh.*, no. 534.
[31] II 9, 8 (App. 1, 44) ; Lippold in Pauly-Wissowa, no. 13.
[32] *Zeus Tragoedus*, 12 (App. 1, 29).

tical with any of those mentioned, it is impossible to say; perhaps the author had no particular statue in mind.

Of the various standing types of Herakles that have been associated with Lysippos, much the most interesting is that which represents the hero leaning wearily on his club.[33] A great number of copies are known. Unfortunately they vary a good deal among themselves, so some caution is necessary in determining the style of the original.

1. "Herakles Farnese" in the Museo Nazionale at Naples: Ruesch, *Guida*[2], p. 90, no. 280; Bulle, *Der schöne Mensch*[2], no. 72; Von Mach, *University Prints*, no. 236; Collignon, *Lysippe*, fig. 18; Brunn-Bruckmann, no. 285; Friederichs-Wolters, no. 1265; Reinach, *Répertoire*, I 465, 1-3; Waldhauer, *Lisipp*, fig. 14; Stephani, no. 10. Here pl. 37. The head: *Mon. Ined.*, VIII, 1868, pls. 54-55, 2.

2. Florence, Palazzo Pitti: Amelung, *Führer durch Florenz*, no. 186; Brunn-Bruckmann, no. 284; Springer-Wolters[12], p. 364, fig. 683; Reinach, *Répertoire*, II 210, 5; Dütschke, *Ant. Bildw. in Oberit.*, II, no. 36. The head is a portrait of Commodus.[34]

3. Florence, Uffizi: Amelung, *op. cit.*, no. 40; *Einzelaufnahmen*, no. 346; Ruesch, *Guida*[2], p. 91, fig. 32; Reinach, *Répertoire*, I 474, 1; *Elenco*, no. 138, with ill.; Dütschke, *op. cit.*, II, no. 95; Stephani, no. 21. Here pl. 38, A.

4. Athens, from the Cerigotto wreck: 'Εφ. 'Αϱχ., 1902, supplementary plate B, 1, col. 158; Svoronos, Τò 'Εθνικὸν Μουσεῖον, pl. XI, 1; Reinach, *Répertoire*, III 248, 1. Head modern.

[33] Valuable discussions of the type: Furtwängler, in Roscher, *Lexikon*, I, 2, cols. 2172 ff.; Amelung, *Führer durch Florenz*, no. 44; Svoronos, Τò 'Εθνικὸν Μουσεῖον, pp. 55-65; Lippold, *Kopien und Umbildungen*, pp. 56-58; a few remarks in Pauly-Wissowa, Supplementband III, col. 1112 (Gruppe). List of copies: Stephani, *Der ausruhende Herakles*, pp. 161 ff. I have not been able in all cases to identify the statues listed by him.

[34] Arndt (text to *Einzelaufnahmen*, no. 231) thought that the head must be modern, but this is contrary to the records of the discovery of the statue. Lippold (*Kopien und Umbildungen*, pp. 247 f., note 19) suggests that the existing head replaced the original one in antiquity.

5. Villa Borghese: *Einzelaufnahmen*, nos. 2775-2777; cf. no. 1489; *Memorie dei Lincei*, XIV, 1910, p. 235, fig. 12; Reinach, *Répertoire*, I 467, 1; mentioned by Amelung, *op. cit.*, no. 40. Here pl. 38, B. The head: text to Brunn-Bruckmann, 609, figs. 4-5. Here pl. 39.

6. Louvre: Reinach, *Répertoire*, I 152, 6. Head does not belong.

7. Rome, Torlonia collection: Reinach, *Répertoire*, I 467, 3; II 215, 2; Visconti, *Museo Torlonia*, pl. LIV, no. 214; Stephani, no. 17.

8. Once in Rome, Mattei collection: Reinach, *Répertoire*, I 473, 4; Stephani, no. 16. Perhaps identical with the following.

9. Rome, Torlonia collection: Reinach, *Répertoire*, II 215, 1; Visconti, *Museo Torlonia*, pl. CXVIII, no. 462.

10. Compiègne: Reinach, *Répertoire*, II 795, 4; Espérandieu, *Recueil général des bas-reliefs, statues et bustes de la Gaule romaine*, V, p. 153, no. 3918. Statuette.

11. Dijon: Reinach, *Répertoire*, IV 127, 2.

12. Leyden: Reinach, *Répertoire*, IV 127, 4.

13. Milan, Museo Archeologico: Dütschke, *op. cit.*, V, p. 412, no. 999; *R. Arch.*, III, 1916, p. 45, fig. 16. Fragmentary.

14. Toulouse: Reinach, *Répertoire*, II 210, 7; Espérandieu, *op. cit.*, II, p. 33, no. 893. Fragmentary.

15. Toulouse: Reinach, *Répertoire*, I 476, 2 and III 174, 1; Espérandieu, *loc. cit.*, no. 894; Stephani, no. 33.

16. Saloniki, church of St. George. Small. Possibly identical with a headless statuette at the "Villa Bitzos, au faubourg de Pyrgos" (*B.C.H.*, XXIII, 1899, p. 342). Here pl. 48.

17. Geneva, torso: *Einzelaufnahmen*, 1886; *R. Arch.*, IV, 12, 1908, p. 161, no. 5, fig. 7; Deonna, *Cat. des sculpt. ant.*, p. 51, no. 63.

18. Vienna, Estensische Sammlung, no. 28; torso: Reinach, *Répertoire*, II 226, 7; *Einzelaufnahmen*, 64; Dütschke, V, no. 796.

19. Louvre, Salle de Clarac: Reinach, *Répertoire*, II 210, 8. Fragmentary.

20. Sparta: Tod and Wace, *Catalogue*, p. 151, no. 115.

21. Florence: Reinach, *Répertoire*, II 210, 6. Partly modern.

22. Marble statuette in Vienna, Kunsthistorisches Museum, room X, no. 69.

23. Marble statuette in Rome, Palazzo Spada: Matz-Duhn, *Ant. Bildw. in Rom,* I, no. 121; Stephani, no. 15.

24. Marble statuette in the Hermitage: Kieseritzky, *Catalogue of the Hermitage,* p. 4, no. 3; Reinach, *Répertoire,* III 65, 5. Head does not belong.

25. Fragmentary marble statuette in Karlsruhe: Friederichs-Wolters, no. 1267.

26. Marble statuette in Baltimore, Walters Gallery: unpublished.

27. Bronze in Vienna, no. 1208: Von Sacken, *Die ant. Bronzen des k. k. Münz und Antiken-Cabinets in Wien,* pl. XXXVIII, 3, pp. 97 f.; Reinach, *Répertoire,* II 214, 8.

28. Bronze in Louvre: Collignon, *Histoire,* II, pl. IX; Collignon, *Lysippe,* fig. 19; Reinach, *Répertoire,* II 211, 5; *R. Arch.,* XXVII, 1895, pp. 278-281 and pl. XIII; De Ridder, *Les bronzes antiques,* p. 91, no. 652, pl. 46; Waldhauer, *Lisipp,* fig. 15.

29. Bronze in Avignon: Reinach, *Répertoire,* III 248, 4.

30. Bronze in Florence: Zannoni, *Galleria Reale,* IV, 3, 111; Reinach, *Répertoire,* II 211, 3.

31. Bronze in Florence: Zannoni, *op. cit.,* IV, 3, 110; Reinach, *Répertoire,* II 211, 4.

32. Bronze in Berlin: *Arch. Anz.,* IX, 1894, p. 121, fig. 20; Reinach, *Répertoire,* II 215, 6.

33. Bronze in Collection Gréau: Reinach, *Répertoire,* II 209, 7.

34. Bronze in Depoletti Collection: *Mon. Ined.,* VIII, 12, 9; *Annali dell' Inst.,* XXXVI, 1864, p. 388; Reinach, *Répertoire,* II 210, 1.

35. Bronze in Rennes: *Gaz. Arch.,* I, 1875, pp. 133 f., pl. 36; Reinach, *Répertoire,* II 215, 3.

36. Bronze in Naples: First room of small bronzes, no. 5185; Stephani, no. 2?

37. Bronze in Bologna, Museo Civico: Room IX, case H.

38. Bronze in Budapest, National Museum. Club and skin lost.

39. Bronze in Turin, museum. Ca. 10 inches tall; lacks left arm, club, right foot and ankle.

40. Bronze in Villa Albani: Morcelli, Fea, Visconti, *Description de la Villa Albani,* no. 933.

41. Bronze in Cambridge, Fitzwilliam Museum. Lacks left foot.

42. Terracotta statuette in Patras? Πρακτικά, 1911, p. 246.
43. Terracotta statuette in Loeb Collection: Sieveking, *Sammlung Loeb, Terrakotten*, II, pl. 107, pp. 46-49.
44. Terracotta statuette in Berlin: Weber, *Die ägyptisch-griechischen Terrakotten*, p. 181, no. 301, pl. 29.

HEADS

1. British Museum: Smith, *Catalogue*, III, no. 1736; Collignon, *Lysippe*, fig. 20; Reinach, *Recueil de Têtes Antiques*, pl. 236; Waldhauer, *Lisipp*, fig. 17.
2. Basle: *Mon. Ined.*, VIII, pls. 54-55, 1; *Annali dell' Inst.*, XL, 1868, pp. 336-350; Friederichs-Wolters, no. 1266; *Arch. Anz.*, 1925, cols. 22-25 (with illustration made after the removal of restored parts).
3. Metropolitan Museum, New York: *Bulletin*, XVI, 1921, pp. 13 f.
4. Small terracotta head in Ashmolean Museum, Oxford; from Smyrna.
5. Bronze head in the Hermitage.[35]

To the list should probably be added two torsos in the Palazzo dei Conservatori (Jones, *Palazzo dei Conservatori*, pp. 234 and 235, nos. 21 and 25, Plate 92), though it is not clear from either the illustrations or the descriptions how closely the torsos correspond to the type. A decorative figure of this type appears on one of the capitals in the Baths of Caracalla.[36] There are many other statues extant which clearly show the influence of this original, though not to be classified as copies: Reinach, *Répertoire*, I 466, 4; I 466, 6 (perhaps the same; cf. Michaelis, *Anc. Mar.*, p. 286, no. 18); I 476, 1; II 209, 6; IV 129, 1, 2, and 5; British Museum, bronzes 1292 and 1293. *Répertoire*, II 209, 3; II 210, 4; III 65, 1, and Matz-Duhn, no. 122 are thought to be modern.

There are several statues which are derived from an earlier type, in which the body is more erect, the head does not look down, the right hand grasps the

[35] This is known to me only from Waldhauer's illustration (*Lisipp*, fig. 16) and I hesitate to use it as a basis for any inferences.
[36] Reinach, *Répertoire de Reliefs*, III, p. 325, 2.

hip, and the left foot is set back instead of forward.[37] This type probably originated in the following of Polykleitos. The artist of the Farnese type set the "Spielbein" in front; it rests on the side of the foot. This was a new position; with the bowed head and the other changes introduced in the Farnese type, it entirely transforms both the design and the spirit of the statue. A statue in Dresden,[38] if accurately copied from any original, represents a true and immediate precursor of the Farnese type; but the workmanship of the statue is poor, and it is probably a derivative of the Farnese type itself.

No. 1, bearing the signature of Glykon of Athens,[39] is of course the best known. It is a Neo-Attic production of great technical excellence and probably was famous on its own account. A papyrus in Geneva, which contains a list of works of art in Rome in the third century after Christ, includes this work of Glykon.[40] The mountainous flesh and exaggerated musculature of this statue are doubtless due in part to the copyist, and the same may be assumed in regard to the colossal scale of the figure. If this is true we should have to regard nos. 4 and 13, as well as the colossal heads in Basle and the British Museum, as copied directly from Glykon's work. It is more probable, however, that the original was colossal; many of the copies would naturally be reduced. No. 3 is usually thought to be the best of all. Here the musculature is much

---

[37] One in the Villa Borghese: *Einzelaufnahmen*, 132; Reinach, *Répertoire*, II 209, 9. One in Dresden: Mahler, *Polyklet*, p. 147, fig. 48; Reinach, *Répertoire*, II 210, 3; Herrmann, *Verzeichnis*, no. 92(?). One in Museo Torlonia: *Museo Torlonia*, pl. XIV, no. 56; Schreiber, *Arch. Anz.*, 1879, p. 68, no. 54. Cf. also a relief in Athens: Reinach, *Répertoire de Reliefs*, II 352, 1; Svoronos, Τὸ 'Εθνικὸν Μουσεῖον, pl. LX, no. 1404, pp. 352 f. It is possible that one or two of the statues listed as examples of the Farnese type, *e.g.* no. 18, really belong to the earlier type.

[38] Reinach, *Répertoire* I 463, 5; Herrmann, *Verzeichnis*, no. 161.

[39] Loewy, *Insch. griech. Bildh.*, no. 345.

[40] Nicole, *Un catalogue d'oeuvres d'art conservées à Rome à l'époque impériale.*

more moderate; still this copy does not suggest that no.
1 is very inaccurate; the differences between them are
largely explained by the difference in scale. No. 5 is
not good, though it offers better analogies to the
apoxyomenos, in details, than most of them. The
small bronze in Vienna, no. 27, probably gives as good
an idea of the original as any of the marbles. The best
evidence for the head is found in the colossal head of
the British Museum, though Waldhauer regards it as
a development from, rather than an example of, the
type.[41]

In some copies the right hand holds some apples,
which are obviously the apples of the Hesperides. It
is singular that the apples should be held where the
spectator would not ordinarily see them; perhaps the
artist was given a commission for a statue of Herakles
with the apples, and followed his own taste in making
them inconspicuous. The addition of the apples by a
number of copyists working independently seems impossible. The presence of the apples, together with
the occurrence of a somewhat similar figure in relief
beside the gate at a fortress near Alyzia,[42] may suggest
that the original of the Farnese type belonged to the
cycle there; but if one member of that cycle were so
widely copied, we should certainly find abundant copies
of the others also.

In some cases adaptations of the same type are
used with the infant Telephos.[43] It has been thought
that Telephos was present in the original;[44] but in none
of these cases is the Herakles exactly reproduced, and

---

[41] *Lisipp*, p. 30.

[42] Heuzey, *Le Mont Olympe et l'Acarnanie*, pl. XI, p. 413.

[43] Statue in the British Museum, no. 1728 (Reinach, *Répertoire*, III
65, 3); inner frieze at Pergamon (Pontremoli-Collignon, *Pergame*, p.
94; *Altertümer von Pergamon*, III, 2, pl. XXXI, 6); painting at Herculaneum (*Ath. Mitt.*, XXXIX, 1914, p. 66; Helbig, *Wandgemälde der
versch. Städte Campaniens*, no. 1143; Herrmann-Bruckmann, *Denkm. d.
Malerei*, pls. 78-79).

[44] So Weiszäcker, *Arch. Zeit.*, XL, 1882, pp. 255-264.

the presence of Telephos is usually recognized as a modification. Svoronos[45] has suggested that the rock on which Herakles's cluþ rests is the ἀγέλαστος πέτρα that stood at the entrance to the lower world. He explains in the same way the rocks employed as accessories with the Lateran Poseidon, the "Jason," the Herculaneum Hermes, and other figures. This hypothesis would be rather tempting if the Herakles alone were concerned, but when the whole series of statues with rocks is considered, the explanation lacks probability. The original of the Farnese type, then, simply portrayed the mighty hero weary and despondent, as in the case of the seated colossus at Tarentum.

The copy in the Pitti palace, no. 2 in our list, has on the base an inscription: ΕΡΓΟΝ ΛΥΣΙΠΠΟΥ. [46] The genuineness of the inscription was formerly disputed, but is now generally acknowledged. This antique label is evidence of the greatest importance, and I do not know of any scholar who altogether rejects the attribution of the type to Lysippos, though Mme. Maviglia[47] and the champions of the Agias[48] naturally do not give it a prominent place in their treatment of the artist. Perhaps it should have been discussed along with the Eros and the Herakles Epitrapezios; but there are cases in which antique labels are deceptive, and the general acceptance of the evidence of the label in this instance is due to the satisfactory correspondence between this type and other Lysippian works. In general conception the Farnese type resembles the colossal statue at Tarentum, and the elongated figure and small head are familiar characteristics of Lysippos. As has been seen, the treatment of anatomy varies

[45] Svoronos, Τὸ ᾿Εθνικὸν Μουσεῖον, pp. 55-65. See also Journ. Int. Arch. Num., IV, 1901, pp. 237-254.

[46] Loewy, Insch. griech. Bildh., no. 506.

[47] L'Attività Artistica di Lisippo, pp. 68 f.

[48] P. Gardner, in J.H.S., XXV, 1905, p. 240; Cultrera, in Memorie dei Lincei, XIV, 1910, pp. 233 f; Hyde, OVM, pp. 253 f.

a great deal in the different copies; but if one looks through the whole list one finds the anatomy consistent with a conception of Lysippos based on the apoxyomenos and the Herakles Epitrapezios. The list contains no encouragement for the Agiasts, to say nothing of Mme. Maviglia. It must be noted that no head known to me, except that of no. 5, resembles the head of the apoxyomenos in details. But copies of a colossal statue are likely to be inaccurate in small details, particularly if the copies are much reduced.

The head in the British Museum and the Zeus of Otricoli, whose Lysippian character has been noted, offer a study in comparison and contrast. In both the hair is effectively treated and enhances the character of the face. Instead of the rich, orderly hair and the leonine mane, the Herakles has bushy, unkempt hair and beard. The groove in the forehead of the Zeus is short, rather shallow, and turns up slightly at the end; in the Herakles it is deep, runs almost entirely across the forehead, and the ends turn down slightly. The greatest difference is in the eyes: in both cases they are heavily shadowed and have depressions at the outer corners, but in the Herakles these hollows continue all around the lower part of the eyes, and the eyes are widely opened: the effect is one of sad despondency, in striking contrast to the serene majesty of the Zeus.

The statue appears on various coins, of which one[49] is certainly not later than 300. The way in which the statue is added to the design would indicate that it had some special importance, and very probably it stood in the city to which the coin belonged. Unfortunately this city has not been determined. Sikyon and Argos have been suggested; if Sikyon is right, it is highly probable that the statue mentioned by Pausa-

[49] *Numismat. Chron.*, 1883, p. 9, pl. I 5; Svoronos, Tὸ 'Εθνικὸν Μουσεῖον, p. 58, fig. 44.

nias is the original of this type.[50] Probably no one will agree with Miss McDowall[51] that the occasional occurrence of the statue on Corinthian coins[52] proves that it stood in Corinth.

Furtwängler[53] rightly observed that the figure by the gate at the Alyzian fortress is not so close to the Farnese type as to a little bronze in the Louvre.[54] This figure is quite different from the Farnese type, not only in position, which suggests that of the apoxyomenos, but in spirit: the Herakles of the Louvre bronze is alert and unwearied. It differs from the Alyzia figure, which is nude, in that the lion-skin is knotted about the neck and hangs down like a cloak. It is not impossible that this little figure may reproduce the general lines of one of Lysippos's statues of Herakles, though it is more likely to be an independent and original work by a good artist of his school.

A statue in the Ny Carlsberg Glyptotek,[55] representing Herakles youthful and beardless, resembles the Louvre bronze in the posture and in the arrangement of the lion-skin. Arndt assumes that the right hand was raised and held a cup, but this is not certain. It may be that the young Herakles is copied from a work of Lysippos, which was freely imitated by the artist of the Louvre bronze. The musculature is early for Lysippos, however, and the head is distinctly Skopaic. It may possibly be copied from an early work of Lysippos, but this is not probable.[56]

[50] So Friederichs-Wolters, no. 1265; Lippold, *Kopien u. Umbildungen*, p. 57.

[51] *J.H.S.*, XXV, 1905, p. 157.

[52] B.M. Catalogue, Corinth, pl. XXII 5; Imhoof-Blumer and Gardner, *Num. Comm. on Pausanias*, pl. F, CIII.

[53] Roscher's *Lexikon*, I, 2, col. 2173.

[54] *Mon. grecs*, 1880, pl. 1; Reinach, *Répertoire*, II 209, 2; De Ridder, *Les bronzes antiques*, p. 34, no. 186, pl. 19.

[55] *De Antike Kunstvaerker*, no. 253; Arndt, *Glyptothèque Ny Carlsberg*, pls. 102-103, p. 149; Mahler, *Polyklet*, pp. 142 f.; Reinach, *Répertoire*, II 222, 9.

[56] Furtwängler (*Masterpieces*, p. 341, note 1 = *Meisterwerke*, p. 576, note) says: "One hesitates whether to call Lysippos or Skopas the author."

A bronze statuette in the Villa Albani[57] reproduces the Farnese type in general. The position of the feet is not quite the same, however; the musculature is simpler, the left hand holds forth some object, and the right hand grasps the hip instead of resting behind the back. The result of these differences is that the impression of weariness disappears altogether. A marble statuette privately owned in Rome resembles the Albani bronze somewhat;[58] its preservation is so poor that it is difficult to determine how close the resemblance is. The head is lost, as are most of both arms, the right leg below the knee, and the left foot. The anatomy is richer than in the Albani bronze; the right hand did not rest on the hip; there are considerable differences in the lion-skin; and the Malatesta statuette, unlike the bronze, has something on the shoulders.

Della Seta believes that these two figures are derived from one original and that this original was the work of Lysippos.[59] So close a relation between the two statuettes seems uncertain, however. The Albani bronze was very reasonably explained by Furtwängler as a variation of the Farnese type.[60] For the Malatesta statuette an attribution to Lysippos is by no means absurd, but it is far from certain.

Another type that has been attributed to Lysippos is represented by the Herakles Albertini in the Museo Nazionale at Rome.[61] The feet are in the position used by Lysippos on the signed base at Corinth except that they are reversed. The right arm, which is lost, ap-

[57] Brunn-Bruckmann, no. 554; Reinach, *Répertoire,* II 209, 4, and I 472, 5; *Vita d'Arte,* V, 1910, p. 50; Helbig, *Führer*[3], II, pp. 414 f., no. 1858; Cultrera, *Memorie dei Lincei,* XIV, 1910, p. 235.

[58] *Vita d'Arte,* V, 1910, pls. I-II.

[59] *Vita d'Arte,* V, 1910, pp. 47-54.

[60] Roscher's *Lexikon,* I, 2, col. 2173; Amelung would attribute its original to Bryaxis (*Ausonia,* III, p. 127).

[61] Reinach, *Répertoire,* V 84, 1; Cultrera, *Memorie dei Lincei,* XIV, 1910, pls. I-IV; *Jh. Oest. Arch. I.,* XIV, 1911, p. 95; Paribeni, *Mus. Naz. Rom.*[4], p. 209, no. 509.

parently hung straight down and held a club upright; the left arm was bent at the elbow and extended straight toward the front; over the forearm the lion-skin was flung. A statue in the Palazzo Pitti (Plate 40, A), appears to have the same posture.[62] In this case the head, neck, shoulders, right arm, left hand, and other parts are restored; a part of the club, however, is antique. In this example the left leg is not advanced beyond the other, but is placed at the side, as in the Lansdowne Herakles. Another statue in the Palazzo Pitti (Plate 40, B)[63] has the same position for the feet as the Herakles Albertini, though there are consider-able differences in other particulars. The head is an-tique. A bronze in Ny Carlsberg[64] is very similar; but it can hardly be considered a trustworthy replica, since there is a quiverband on its back. The left hand seems to have held a bow;[65] it may be that the other statues did also, since in all of the other three the left hand is lost. The feet of the bronze have approximately the same relative position as in the Lansdowne Herakles.

Cultrera believes that the original of the Albertini type was a statue by Lysippos,[66] but the style of the Albertini statue is very old for that artist. Cultrera erroneously regards the Agias as the true norm of Lysippian style; but even in comparison with that work, the Herakles seems stiff and lifeless. Mac-chioro, indeed, has contributed to the gaiety of the dis-

[62] *Einzelaufnahmen*, 231; Reinach, *Répertoire*, II 214, 2; Dütschke, *Ant. Bildw. in Oberit.*, II, no. 35; Furtwängler, *Masterpieces*, p. 296, note 3; no. 28 in the list given by Preyss, in text to Brunn-Bruckmann, 691-692.

[63] *Einzelaufnahmen*, 228-230; Reinach, *Répertoire*, II 211, 2; Dütschke, *Ant. Bildw. in Oberit.*, II, no. 33; Preyss, *l.c.*, no. 26.

[64] Arndt, *Glyptothèque Ny Carlsberg*, pp. 136-137, pls. 89-92; *De Antike Kunstvaerker*, no. 261; Lippold, *Antike Skulpturen der Glyptothek Ny Carlsberg*, pl. 18; *Ny Carlsberg Glyptotek, Antik Sculptur* (a series of 30 plates), pl. 22; Preyss, *l.c.*, no. 39.

[65] These observations are made by Miss Bieber (*Jb. Arch I.*, XXV, 1910, p. 168). She would attribute both the Albertini statue and the bronze, which she regards as a distinct type, to Euphranor.

[66] *Memorie dei Lincei*, XIV, 1910, pp. 179-192.

cussion by dubbing the Albertini statue "arcaico."[67] Its feet are more Lysippian than those of the Agias, and the same may be said of the treatment of the torso, in spite of its early character. But these observations have little value, because the workmanship of the Albertini statue is so miserable that no conclusions at all can be based on it. The attribution gains nothing from a consideration of the bronze in the Glyptotek, which is a solid figure resembling the Lansdowne Herakles, nor from the two figures in the Pitti.

Cultrera thinks that a Herakles of this type was the statue by Lysippos which Pausanias saw in Sikyon, and finds an imitation of it in the design on a Sikyonian coin of Geta.[68] It is quite possible that the Albertini Herakles and the numerous other figures that show a more or less distinct relationship to it[69] are ultimately derived from the same statue that gave inspiration to the artist of the coin-type; but the head was rightly identified long ago in the Genzano Herakles,[70] and the author of the head as Skopas.

Cultrera remarks that if the Lansdowne Herakles were derived from Skopas, the Albertini type also would be Skopaic.[71] The Lansdowne Herakles (Plate 41)[72] is a beautiful statue, with no restorations of importance, and is certainly the best existing representation of the young Herakles. Preyss has listed 21 heads and 15 statues and torsos as "Wiederholungen und Um-

[67] *Jh. Oest. Arch. I.,* XIV, 1911, p. 94.

[68] Imhoof-Blumer and Gardner, *Num. Comm. on Pau.,* pl. H, 11; *British Museum Catalogue, Peloponnesos,* no. 247, pl. IX, 22.

[69] Cf. Cultrera, pp. 181-184.

[70] Graef, in *Röm. Mitt.,* IV, 1889, pp. 189-226; cf. the second chapter of this book.

[71] *L.c.,* p. 187.

[72] Hyde, *OVM,* pl. 30 and p. 298, fig. 71; Brunn-Bruckmann, 691-692, with text by Preyss; Jones, *Palazzo dei Conservatori,* p. 91; Gardner, *Six Greek Sculptors,* pls. 56-58; Furtwängler, *Masterpieces,* p. 297; Kalkmann, *Prop. des Gesichts* (53rd Berlin Winckelmann Programm), p. 61; Springer-Wolters[12], p. 329, fig. 611; Michaelis, *Ancient Marbles,* pp. 451 f.

bildungen" of the type, but this list is perhaps the most uncritical ever published. The list of heads includes all the examples of the Genzano type; all but three of the 21 wear garlands instead of plain bands. An examination of the illustrations cited by him shows that in only three cases (his nos. 1, 4, 15) do the heads resemble the head of the Lansdowne statue closely enough to indicate direct derivation from a common original. In his no. 1[73] a band is worn as in the Lansdowne figure; in his no. 4[74] and no. 15[75] the wreath is narrow and differs very little in appearance from a simple fillet. All other heads listed by Preyss differ in the eyes from the Lansdowne statue, being decidedly more Skopaic in this important feature, and none of them shows such correspondence in the hair as may be expected in copies from one original. The three heads which may be regarded as real copies are all much inferior to the Lansdowne Herakles and throw little or no light on the original. Of the fifteen statues and torsos it need only be remarked that only one of them has the club on the shoulder, and that it is reversed throughout as compared with the Lansdowne statue, and wears a lion-skin. (Cultrera mentions a statuette in Mykonos which apparently had the club on the shoulder.)[76] Most of the others[77] belong more or less clearly to the Albertini type, though Preyss does not list the Albertini statue itself. In his text he acknowledges that the Lansdowne Herakles is probably derived from an original different from that represented

[73] In the Uffizi; *Einzelaufnahmen*, 85-86; Graef's no. 14; *R. Arch.*, XXXVII, 1900, pl. XVII, right.

[74] In Naples; Ruesch, *Guida²*, no. 848; Brunn-Bruckmann, 365.

[75] In Dresden; *Einzelaufnahmen*, 164-165; here in text Arndt says that it is not an example of the Lansdowne type, though closely related to it; Herrmann, *Verzeichnis*, no. 105?

[76] *L.c.*, p. 184, note 1, no. 2.

[77] For a profile illustration of the Hope statue (Preyss no. 35), see *Bull. de la Soc. Arch. d'Alex.* 17, 1919-1920, p. 228.

by most of the entries in the list, but thinks it a closely related work by the same master. This can not be assumed.

Michaelis[78] long ago declared that the Lansdowne Herakles was copied from Lysippos, and since the discovery of the Agias that opinion has been accepted by those who attach great importance to the Agias.[79] Most scholars, however, considered and still consider the Herakles derived from Skopas.[80]

Michaelis justified his original attribution as follows: "In spite of the powerful square-built frame, which befits a Herakles, the statue is unmistakably in the spirit of Lysippos. The head . . . is of characteristic smallness. . . . The legs are long in proportion to the thick-set torso, the feet somewhat flat, as in all statues of the school of Lysippos. The style of this master is especially evinced in the noble unconstrained freedom of the whole movement, the freshness and elasticity of the slightly twisted pose. The *argutiae operum custoditae in minimis quoque rebus* (Pliny 34, 65) show themselves, for example, in the naturalistic rendering of the soft folds of skin between thumb and finger of the right hand." The discovery of the Agias seemed to confirm this attribution: the statues are very similar in posture.[81]

Amelung[82] explains this resemblance by the assumption that Lysippos, in making the Agias, imitated a Herakles already created by Skopas. E. A. Gardner,[83] one of the leading champions of the Agias, finds

[78] *Ancient Marbles,* pp. 451 f.

[79] Percy Gardner, *J.H.S.,* XXV, 1905, p. 256; Hyde, *OVM,* p. 298; Cultrera, *Memorie dei Lincei,* XIV, 1910, p. 187.

[80] Furtwängler, *Masterpieces,* p. 296; Collignon, *Scopas et Praxitèle,* p. 34; Klein, *Gesch. d. griech. Kunst,* II, p. 275; Loewy, *Griechische Plastik,* pp. 69; Mahler, *Polyklet,* p. 140; Amelung, *Röm. Mitt.,* XX, 1905, p. 151.

[81] Comparative illustrations: *J.H.S.,* XXIII, 1903, p. 129.

[82] *Röm. Mitt.,* XX, 1905, pp. 150 f.

[83] *Six Greek Sculptors,* p. 199.

in the Herakles "all the characteristics that we have learned to look for in the work of Scopas. . . . It is in the proportions of body and limbs, as well as of the head, that we see the contrast with the lighter and more agile Lysippian type which we see in the Agias—-a contrast too essential to be explained by the fact that heavier proportions are suitable to the type of Heracles, and emphasized the more by the similarity in position of the two statues."

This appears to be a just statement of the case. The modelling of the muscles of the trunk and the treatment of the knees, for example, are quite different in the two statues. There is little similarity in the heads. It does not seem, then, that the attribution of the Agias to Lysippos lends substantial support to a similar attribution for the Herakles. This, however, is a matter of small importance. In comparison with the apoxyomenos the Herakles is not only much earlier in appearance, but differs entirely in many details: the nose and the upper lip are very different; the face is not so heavy in its lower part, though one would expect it to be in a Herakles; the hair, though it clearly indicates bronze technique, does not resemble the hair of the apoxyomenos. A comparison with the Herakles Epitrapezios is equally decisive.

In the few features where comparison is possible, the Herakles greatly resembles the Demeter of Knidos. It seems that in the general method and design of these two works there is something of the same spirit, so far as the very diverse subjects permit, and it may well be that the Herakles was copied from a work by the sculptor of the Demeter. It is not obvious nor indubitable that this sculptor was Skopas, but he certainly was not Lysippos.

Furtwängler has tentatively assigned two other types of Herakles to Lysippos. One of them is represented by a statue in the Museo Chiaramonti.[84] This is probably, as Amelung had suggested, the work of a sculptor who grafted certain Lysippian details on to a Polykleitan figure. The other type[85] has been fully discussed by Schick,[86] who has shown that it is a Hellenistic work, made under the influence of Lysippian tradition.

We may find the style of Lysippos, though probably in a later stage than it ever reached in the work of the master himself, in a marble statuette in the Louvre (Plate 42).[87] The large neck, the small head, the feet, the back, the forehead, and the position show the manner of Lysippos. The hair is sketchy. The eyes and the face in general seem Skopaic rather than Lysippian. The treatment of anatomy suggests a date in the third century. The action of the right arm, which is lost, is not clear, but the hand was lowered. The left hand held the club by the handle, the head of the club being raised; the lion-skin hangs from the club. The workmanship is good and the figure has a great deal of vigor and life.

[84] Furtwängler, *Masterpieces*, p. 363, note 5 (*Meisterwerke*, p. 597, note 1) ; Mahler, *Polyklet*, p. 144 ff., fig. 47; Hartwig, *Jh. Oest. Arch. I.*, VI, 1903, p. 23, fig. 13; Amelung, *Die Skulp. d. Vat. Mus.*, I, p. 506, no. 294, pl. 52; Reinach, *Répertoire*, I 467, 4; cf. Jones, *Sculptures of the Museo Capitolino*, pp. 328 f.

[85] *Masterpieces*, p. 301, note 1; Roscher's *Lexikon*, I, 2, col. 2172; Reinach, *Répertoire*, I 463, 2; II 209, 1; Springer-Wolters[12], p. 423, fig. 807.

[86] *Neue Jahrbucher*, XXXIII, 1914, pp. 29-40; cf. Jones, *Palazzo dei Conservatori*, pp. 282-284, no. 5, pl. 113.

[87] No. 3083; *Marbres antiques*, pl. XVII, center, at right.

CHAPTER X

LYSIPPOS, COURT SCULPTOR

The Azara herm in the Louvre (Plates 43-44),[1] identified as it is by an inscription, has generally been regarded as our most trustworthy portrait of Alexander. A violent attack on its value by Hauser[2] has been fully refuted by Michon,[3] who discusses fully the history of the bust. He concludes, however, that its artistic worth has been overestimated, so far at least as its present condition is concerned; and certainly where the nose, lips, and part of the eyebrows are restored,[4] and the surface of the whole is badly corroded, it is difficult to form an opinion as to the quality of the original work. One must beware also of relying on the restored parts for the attribution of the original.

The Louvre contains a second copy from the same original, which formerly belonged to the Campana collection.[5] This is in worse state than the Azara head, since the face is entirely new; only the treatment of the hair shows the relation between this head and the Azara herm. There is another copy in the British Museum.[6] This head has suffered no

---

[1] No. 436; *Marbres antiques*, pl. IX; Springer-Wolters[12], p. 362, fig. 678; Collignon, *Lysippe*, fig. 9; Koepp, *Ueber das Bildniss Alexanders des Grossen*, pp. 8-9 and pl. I; Schreiber, *Studien über das Bildniss Alexanders des Grossen*, pl. I, A; Bernoulli, *Die erhaltenen Darstellungen des Alexanders*, pl. I and fig. 1; Arndt-Bruckmann, nos. 181-182; Von Mach, *University Prints*, no. 398; Hekler, *Greek and Roman Portraits*, pl. 62, B; Ujfalvy, *Le type physique d'Alexandre le Grand*, pls. II, VIII, IX; Friederichs-Wolters, no. 1318.

[2] *B. Ph. Wo.*, XXV, 1905, pp. 483 ff.

[3] *R. Arch.*, VII, 1906, pp. 79-110. Cf. Blum, in *R. Arch.*, XXIV, 1914, p. 97.

[4] Article cited, p. 82.

[5] No. 234; Ujfalvy, *op. cit.*, p. 53, fig. 16; Bernoulli, *op. cit.*, p. 26, fig. 2; Springer-Michaelis[8], p. 295, fig. 539.

[6] Smith, *Catalogue of Sculpture*, III, no. 1859, pl. XII; *Berichte über die Verhandlungen der König. Sächs. Gesells. der Wissensch. zu Leipzig*, LXIV, 1912, pp. 197 f. and plate I (Studniczka)

injury except through corrosion, but it has small artistic value and apparently was not intended as a close copy. According to Lippold there is a copy in the Palazzo del Drago at Rome.[7] Schreiber names two other "Repliken und nächstverwandten Nachbildungen" of the Azara head:[8] a head in Berlin[9] and another head there, which belongs to a statuette.[10] Neither of these feeble works can give any information on the style of the original, and it seems that the head first mentioned, at least, is influenced rather by the Chatsworth type. A rude head in Bologna[11] is clearly influenced by either the Chatsworth or the Azara type.

In the museum at Geneva there is a head (frontispiece and Plate 45),[12] broken from a statue or bust, which appears to be good Hellenistic work. The greater part of the nose and parts of the upper lip and chin are new. The resemblance to the Alexander Azara is obvious: while the influence of bronze technique is much less apparent in the Geneva head, and locks of the hair are not similar in detail, the general likeness is so great as to leave little doubt that the two are derived from one original. The head in Geneva, through its better preservation and superior workmanship, undoubtedly gives a vastly better idea of the general character of that original, and hence may confidently be regarded as the best portrait of Alexander known to exist.

Here may be mentioned also an alabaster head in Frankfurt (Plate 46),[13] of poor workmanship but good

[7] In Pauly-Wissowa.

[8] *Op. cit.,* pp. 19 ff.

[9] *Beschr. d. ant. Skulpt.,* no. 305; Arndt-Bruckmann, pl. 190.

[10] *Beschr. d. ant. Skulpt.,* no. 304; Reinach, *Répertoire,* II 567, 8. The head illustrated: Schreiber, *op. cit.,* p. 22, fig. 2.

[11] *Gaz. Arch.,* X, 1885, pl. 15.

[12] Deonna, *Cat. des sculpt. ant.,* pp. 80-86, no. 120; *Mon. Piot,* XXVII, 1924, pp. 87-92 (Deonna).

[13] *Kurzes Verzeichnis,* p. 33, no. 153.

preservation. The hair, with its exceedingly large locks around the face, suggests the Chatsworth portrait rather than the Azara type; but the face has none of the androgynous character of the Chatsworth head, and appears to be derived more or less directly from the original of the Azara type; at any rate it reflects a similar conception of Alexander. The Frankfurt head was fitted into a statue, and the muscles of the neck indicate that the head looked straight forward.

The attribution of the original of the Azara type to Lysippos has been widely accepted. Koepp,[14] Helbig,[15] Winter,[16] Furtwängler, [17] Wulff,[18] Kekulé,[19] Collignon,[20] Schreiber,[21] Reinach,[22] Klein,[23] Lechat,[24] and Studniczka[25] favor it. Hauser,[26] P. Gardner,[27] Mme. Maviglia,[28] Hekler,[29] Arndt,[30] Blümner,[31] and Bernoulli[32] dispute or doubt Lysippos's authorship.

Koepp's chief ground for assigning the type to Lysippos was its resemblance to the apoxyomenos. A comparison of the two heads, which are placed side by side on Koepp's plate I, rather supports than weakens the attribution, though it scarcely proves it.

[14] Op. cit., p. 10; Neue Jahrbücher, XXIII, 1909, p. 485.
[15] Mon. Ant., VI, 1897, p. 79.
[16] Gercke-Norden, Einleitung in die Altertumswissenschaft, II², p. 178.
[17] J.H.S., XXI, 1901, p. 214.   [18] Alexander mit der Lanze, p. 46.
[19] Sitzb. Preuss. Akad. Wiss., 1899, p. 287; Griechische Skulptur, p. 242.   [20] Lysippe, p. 43.   [21] Op. cit., p. 20.
[22] R. Arch., V, 1905, p. 34.
[23] Gesch. d. griech. Kunst, II, p. 354.
[24] Collection de Moulages² (Museum at Lyons), no. 854.
[25] Neue Jahrbücher, XLI, 1918, p. 2.
[26] B. Ph. Wo., XXV, 1905, col. 484.
[27] J.H.S., XXV, 1905, p. 251.
[28] Op. cit., p. 58.   [29] Op. cit., p. XVI.
[30] Griech. u. röm. Porträts, text to pls. 186-187.
[31] Führer durch . . . Universität Zürich, no. 666.
[32] Op. cit., pp. 25 f.

It is always difficult to use morphological evidence in the case of a portrait. The hair on the back of the Azara head, however, is much like that of the apoxyomenos, and the open mouth, proved by the antique parts of the lips, is favorable to the attribution to Lysippos. The left ear has some similarity to the ear of the apoxyomenos; the right one is different, but it has been injured. The eyes, with the hollows at their outer corners and the thick upper lids, suggest those of the apoxyomenos. The head in Geneva, in spite of its excellence, can not be used to recover the details of form in the original. It is evident that the original was a work possessing both spirit and noble simplicity; it was well worthy of Lysippos and was certainly far more Lysippian in style than any other original that was widely copied. The attribution, though not definitely demonstrable, is beyond reasonable doubt. It has been objected by Bernoulli that this type represents Alexander as a man of thirty or thereabouts and that Lysippos was probably not with him so late.[33] Pursued to its logical conclusion, this argument would compel us to believe that the original of the herm was made by a Persian or Babylonian artist. We are told by Plutarch that Alexander summoned many artists from Greece to Ekbatana,[34] and certainly his favorite was among them if he was not already with the king.

Winter[35] advanced a hypothesis that a small bronze in the Louvre (Plate 47)[36] was copied from the same original as the herm. Schreiber,[37] who was able care-

[33] Op. cit., p. 26.   [34] Alexander, LXXII, 1.

[35] Arch. Anz., X, 1895, p. 162.

[36] Reinach, Répertoire, II 567, 1; Neue Jahrbücher, XXXIII, 1914, pl. III opposite p. 48, 3; De Ridder, Les bronzes antiques, p. 58, no. 370, pl. 31; Collignon, Lysippe, fig. 10; Bernoulli, op. cit., p. 102, fig. 31; Schreiber, op. cit., pl. VI, L; Ujfalvy, op. cit., p. 65, fig. 22.

[37] Op. cit., p. 103.

fully to compare the two works in the Louvre, considered their common origin unquestionable; while Bernoulli[38] and Gardner,[39] without making such an examination, doubted the connection. Through the great and
in the circumstances truly extraordinary courtesy of M.
Merlin, I also was permitted to have the bronze removed from the case and to examine it minutely, and
was forced to the conclusion that derivation from a
common original could not be proved, though it may
have been a fact. The bronze is much corroded and
few details can be made out. The head is turned to
the side much more sharply than in the bust. The general shape of the face is the same. The projection of
the lower part of the forehead is not perceptible in the
bronze. The eyes were deep-set; nothing else can be
said of them with certainty now, though they may well
have been directed upward originally. There are considerable similarities in the hair, even to the arrangement of some of the locks at the side of the forehead;
yet in the present condition of the bronze it is impossible to tell just how close the resemblance is. One
can hardly doubt, however, that the bronze represents
Alexander; and the style of Lysippos is very clear
in the proportions, the general character of the modelling, the swing of the body, and the treatment of the
waist and feet. Without doubt it represents one of
Lysippos's statues of Alexander.[40]

Another bronze, formerly in the Nelidow collection,[41] has been proposed as a copy of Lysippos's

[38] *Op. cit.*, p. 25.
[39] *J.H.S.*, XXV, 1905, p. 252.
[40] So Collignon (*Lysippe*, p. 52), Klein (*Gesch. d. griech. Kunst*, II,
p. 355), and, hesitantly, Bernoulli (*op. cit.*, pp. 144 f). Also Bieber (*Jb.
Arch. I.*, XL, 1925, p. 182).
[41] The identification by Wulff (*Alexander mit der Lanze*, with plates
I-II) ; illustrations also in Pollak, *Klassisch-antike Goldschmiedearbeiten
im Besitze Sr. Exc. des Herrn von Nelidow*, pp. 3, 139, 184; Ujfalvy, *op.
cit.*, pls. XV-XVI; Reinach, *Répertoire*, III 159, 1 and 4; *Neue Jahrbücher*, XXXIII, 1914, pl. III opposite p. 48, 1 and 2. Wulff is followed

"Alexander with the lance."[42]   As Bernoulli has noted in an excellent criticism of this hypothesis,[43] it is doubtful whether the original held a lance at all; it appears from the position of the upraised hand that a lance would have obscured the view of the face. Furthermore, the rendering of the torso seems not only naturalistic, but taken from a model who did not lead the active life of Alexander.   The posture is, as has been seen, one that was probably used by Lysippos; and it does not appear impossible that the Nelidow bronze is imitated from one of his portraits of Alexander or of some one else.   However, it is more probably Hellenistic.   In any case the attribution to Lysippos of the Louvre bronze is in no way affected by any opinion that may be held as to the Nelidow figure; Lysippos made many portraits of Alexander and doubtless most of them were standing nude figures.

There is in the Louvre a figure of a youth wearing a helmet.[44]   The slightly twisted neck indicates that the subject is Alexander, and an examination of the features confirms this impression. There are few figures extant that so clearly show evidence of Lysippian style, whether we consider the general posture, with its complex and vigorous swing, or the treatment of the body; one would place it fairly early in the career of Lysippos.   The intense upward gaze reminds one of the description of the "Alexander with the Lance," and it

by Helbig (*Führer²*, II, p. 231, with illustration), Furtwängler (*J.H.S.*, XXI, 1901, p. 213, note 1), Sauer (*W. kl. Phil.*, XVIII, 1901, p. 265), Schick (*Neue Jahrbücher*, XXXIII, 1914, pp. 24 f.), Lippold, in Pauly-Wissowa, and Waldhauer (*Lisipp*, p. 34).   Waldhauer mentions two statuettes of the type, of which one is in the Hermitage; I do not know whether this is the Nelidow figure or another.

[42] Plutarch, *De Iside et Osiride*, 24 (App. 1, 65), *De Alex. Fort. aut Vir.*, II, 2 (App. 1, 64).   Various other passages may be taken as referring to this statue.

[43] *Op. cit.*, pp. 141 ff.   Schreiber also rejects the hypothesis (*op. cit.*, p. 104, note 8).

[44] No. 2301; Schreiber, *op. cit.*, pp. 111 ff. and 287, pl. VII, where the restorations are indicated; Bernoulli, *op. cit.*, pp. 84 and 145 f., fig. 25 on p. 83; Reinach, *Répertoire*, I 133, 8; *Jb. Arch. I.*, XL, 1925, p. 177, fig. 9.

has been suggested by Overbeck[45] and, tentatively, by Bernoulli[46] that the right arm, which is restored, originally extended upward and held a lance. The existing restoration was indicated, however, by a puntello on the thigh. Besides, certain coins of Ilium,[47] of imperial date, show a figure that seems certainly derived from the original of this statue, and they indicate that the restoration is correct in its general lines. The right hand, as appears from the coins, did hold a lance, though it was lowered as in the statuette; but since the figure also had a sword and a helmet, the lance was not nearly so prominent a feature as it would have been if held by a nude figure like the original of the Louvre bronze. It seems that this bronze is more likely than any other work to represent the "Alexander with the Lance." The Lysippian character of the marble figure remains beyond doubt. The figure on the coins is labeled Hector; but this is clearly not the original name. Alexander's interest in Troy[48] would make readily intelligible such an adaptation of his statue.

The three works in the Louvre seem fairly certainly to represent two or three of Lysippos's representations of Alexander. It is probable *a priori* that more or less close imitations of others of his portraits of the king are extant; but it is impossible to identify them with even approximate certainty, in some cases because of the poor quality of the extant works, in other cases because of the difficulty of distinguishing between Alexander and Lysippos on the one hand, and their influence on the other hand. It may be more

---

[45] *Gesch. d. griech. Plastik*[4], II, p. 148.

[46] *Op. cit.*, p. 84 and pp. 143 f.

[47] Dörpfeld, *Troja und Ilion*, II, Beilage 62, 32-34; Beilage 65, no. 108. Mentioned by Schreiber, *op. cit.*, p. 287. Bernoulli apparently does not think there is any connection between the statue and the coins, as he does not mention the latter. I feel little doubt about it.

[48] Plutarch, *Alexander*, XV 4; Arrian, *Anabasis*, I, 11, 7-8; 12, 1.

worth while to mention a few of which it can confidently be said that they are not derived directly from Lysippos.

One of these is a fine head in the British Museum.[49] Wolters,[50] Wulff,[51] and Bulle[52] have expressed doubts as to whether the head represents Alexander at all. Alexander would doubtless have felt similar uncertainty if he had seen the head, but it is probable that the sculptor called it Alexander. Percy Gardner,[53] E. A. Gardner,[54] Richardson,[55] and apparently Hyde[56] regard it as copied from Lysippos. It is a highly idealized portrait, however, such as is made under the influence of a tradition rather than that of a living man, and the consensus of scholarly opinion has undoubtedly been correct in referring it to a Hellenistic sculptor, probably living in Alexandria. The style has no affinities with that of Lysippos, and the broad masses of hair seem clearly to indicate marble technique.

The fragmentary statue found at Priene[57] and now in Berlin bears a considerable resemblance to the head just mentioned, both in general conception and in detail. If one of these were attributed to Lysippos, the other should be so attributed also; and in fact Kekulé has sought to connect the Priene statue with Lysippos. Like the head in the British Museum, it seems to be an original work of early Hellenistic time, made under the influence of idealizing tradition such as usually arises soon after the death of a celebrated man. No

[49] Smith, *Catalogue of Sculpture*, III, no. 1857; *Marbles and Bronzes*, pl. 26; Bulle, *Der schöne Mensch*[2], pl. 218; E. A. Gardner, *Six Greek Sculptors*, pl. LXIX; Koepp, *op. cit.*, p. 19, fig.; Schreiber, *op. cit.*, pl. II, D, 1; Bernoulli, *op. cit.*, pl. VI; Ujfalvy, *op. cit.*, pl. XIV.

[50] Friederichs-Wolters, no. 1602.   [51] *Op. cit.*, p. 59.

[52] *Der schöne Mensch*[2], col. 483 f.   [53] *J.H.S.*, XXV, 1905, p. 253.

[54] *Six Greek Sculptors*, p. 227.   [55] *Greek Sculpture*, p. 232.

[56] *A.J.A.*, XVIII, 1914, p. 470 f.

[57] Wiegand-Schrader, *Priene*, p. 181, fig. 176; Ujfalvy, *op. cit.*, pls. 12-13; *Sitzb. Preuss. Akad. Wiss.*, 1899, pp. 280-288 with figs.; Kekulé, *Griechische Skulptur*, p. 255, fig.; Bernoulli, *op. cit.*, p. 59, fig. 15; Schreiber, *op. cit.*, p. 84.

example closely resembling the British Museum head has been found far from Alexandria,[58] with the exception of the Priene statue; when the Romans wanted portraits of Alexander they had recourse to more authentic types.

A head very different from the sculptures just mentioned was found at Pergamon, and is in Constantinople.[59] Hauser[60] earnestly advocated it as Lysippian, and the hypothesis has found surprising acceptance: Michaelis,[61] Kekulé,[62] Hekler,[63] Lippold,[64] and Waldhauer[65] all favor it. Schreiber[66] and Bernoulli[67] doubt whether it is a portrait of Alexander at all, and indeed it is difficult to see why any one should so regard it. The hair, though unlike the hair in any work that can be connected with Lysippos, is expressive and Lysippian to that extent; but the Pergamenes were well acquainted with the art of heightening an emotional effect through the hair. There is nothing else about the head that suggests Lysippos; his authorship is still less probable than Alexander as the subject. Simple addition of these improbabilities, however, lacks much of equalling the improbability that the head is an Alexander by Lysippos; for we know something of the way he represented the monarch. The expression in this head indicates actual suffering; if Alexander had died in battle, some such portrait as this might have been set up by his enemies. There is another head of similar style.[68]

[58] Several such examples are mentioned by Schreiber (op. cit., pp. 45 ff.).

[59] Antike Denkmäler, II, pl. 48; Hekler, op. cit., pl. 59; Ujfalvy, op. cit., pl. 22, figs. 77, 81, 82; Bernoulli, op. cit., figs. 23-24; Waldhauer, Lisipp, fig. 26; Mendel, Catalogue des sculptures, II, p. 254, no. 538; Altertümer von Pergamon, VIII, 2, pp. 147-149, pl. XXXIII; Springer-Wolters[12], p. 363, fig. 680.

[60] B. Ph. Wo., XXV, 1905, cols. 479 ff.

[61] Springer-Michaelis[8], pp. 294 f., fig. 540.

[62] Griech. Skulpt., p. 242.   [63] Op. cit., p. XVI.

[64] In Pauly-Wissowa.   [65] Lisipp, p. 36.

[66] Op. cit., pp. 85 f.   [67] Op. cit., pp. 81 f.

[68] Arndt-Bruckmann, 921. Several other possible portraits of Alexander: op. cit., 922-928.

Another type is represented by a famous head in the Museo Capitolino,[69] by a head in Boston,[70] by a head in Holkham Hall,[71] and, according to Schreiber, by a head in Philippeville.[72] The genuineness of the head in Boston was questioned by Furtwängler[73] and, according to Bernoulli,[74] by Hauser and Waldhauer, and Caskey has omitted it from the recent Boston catalogue as probably modern. Bernoulli has reason also to observe that the Holkham head "could easily be a modern copy,"[75] and he rightly doubts whether the head in Philippeville is connected with the type. Thus the Capitoline head is left alone. In the fillet about the hair there are seven holes, which can hardly have served any purpose except that of containing rays; this shows that in some sense it represented Helios. Yet the individuality of the features makes plausible the identification as Alexander.[76]

I mention this head because Furtwängler once ascribed it to Lysippos. There is, however, no evidence of Lysippian style in minutiae, though the impressive treatment of the hair shows his influence. The original seems to have been a head of Helios influenced somewhat by the physical type of Alexander.[77] Helbig conjecturally attributes it to Chares,

[69] Jones, *Sculpt. of the Mus. Cap.*, pp. 341 f., pl. 85; Ujfalvy, *op. cit.*, pl. III; Collignon, *Lysippe*, fig. 8; Hekler, *op. cit.*, pl. 62a; Arndt-Bruckmann, pls. 186-187; Helbig, *Führer*[3], I, pp. 496 f., no. 882; Koepp, *op. cit.*, p. 21; Schreiber, *op. cit.*, pp. 68 ff., pl. V; Bernoulli, *op. cit.*, pp. 65 ff., pl. VII; Von Mach, *University Prints*, no. 397; *Mon. Ant.*, VI, 1895, pp. 73 ff., pl. II.

[70] *Mon. Ant.*, VI, 1895, pl. I; Arndt-Bruckmann, pls. 481-482; Ujfalvy, *op. cit.*, pl. IV; Bernoulli, *op. cit.*, pp. 70 f., figs. 16-17; Von Mach, *University Prints*, no. 396; Reinach, *Recueil*, pl. 250.

[71] Schreiber, *op. cit.*, p. 72, fig. 10; not mentioned by Poulsen, *Greek and Roman Portraits in English Country Houses*.

[72] Gsell, *Musée de Philippeville*, pl. VII, no. 3.

[73] *J.H.S.*, XXI, 1901, p. 213, note 2.

[74] *Op. cit.*, p. 73.   [75] *Op. cit.*, p. 74.

[76] *J.H.S.*, XXI, 1901, p. 213.

[77] Six (*Röm. Mitt.*, X, 1895, pp. 179 ff.) would consider it a portrait of Mithradates Eupator. The feebleness of his position is exposed by Bernoulli (*op. cit.*, p. 67).

pupil of Lysippos and sculptor of the Colossus of Rhodes;[78] this may well be right. Mme. Maviglia thinks that the figure found at Cyrene may be copied from a portrait of Alexander as Helios, by Lysippos;[79] but this is probably erroneous.[80]

Some of the famous or notorious medallions said to have been found at Aboukir bear representations of Alexander.[81] Professor D. M. Robinson doubts the genuineness of these medallions, and I am told that many numismatists question it. So far as tangible evidence is concerned, Dressel makes out a good case for the medallions. They are accepted as probably genuine by Svoronos,[82] who was formerly so thoroughly convinced of the opposite opinion that he wrote an exhaustive exposition of it; when he changed his mind he suppressed the article. Thiersch,[83] Six,[84] Sauer,[85] Delbrück,[86] and Wolters[87] seem to regard them as certainly genuine, and I have not observed any recent writer who questions them.

Assuming the genuineness of the medallions, consideration must be given to Thiersch's hypothesis; that they represent the Alexander with the Lance of Lysippos.[88] The fiery expression does in fact seem to accord better with the literary descriptions of Lysippos's portraits than in any other monument extant;

[78] *Mon. Ant.*, VI, 1895, pp. 73 ff. Amelung's objections (*B. Com. Rom.*, XXV, 1897, 140, note 1) are adequately answered by Reinach (*Recueil*, pp. 203 f.).

[79] *R. Arch.*, III, 1916, pp. 169-183.

[80] See S. Reinach, in *R. Arch.*, I, 1915, p. 181.

[81] Fullest discussion with good illustrations: Dressel, *Fünf Goldmedaillons aus dem Funde von Abukir* (*Abh. d. könig. preuss. Akad. d. Wissenschaften*, 1906) ; *J. Int. Arch. Num.*, X, 1907, pl. XI; *A. J. Num.*, XLIV, 1910, pp. 128-130. One is in the Walters Gallery in Baltimore.

[82] *J. Int. Arch. Num.*, X, 1907, pp. 369 ff.

[83] *Jb. Arch. I.*, XXIII, 1908, pp. 162 ff.

[84] *Jb. Arch. I.*, XXV, 1910, pp. 147 ff.

[85] *Neue Jahrbücher*, XLI, 1918, p. 380.

[86] *Jb. Arch. I.*, XL, 1925, pp. 10-12.

[87] Springer-Wolters[12], pp. 363 f.

[88] *Jb. Arch. I.*, XXIII, 1908, pp. 162 ff.

and the arrangement of the hair is very similar to
that of the Azara herm. It is most improbable, however, that a figure in full armor should be called
"Alexander with the Lance." That of course is no
argument against a derivation from some other statue
by Lysippos. It seems more probable, however, as
Six suggests,[89] that the prototype was a painting. Lippold (in Pauly-Wissowa) plausibly suggests that it
may have been a gem by Pyrgoteles. It is not to be
be assumed, however, that the artist of the medallions
imitated closely any work of art: the admirable adaptation of the portrait to the circular field can hardly
be due to any one except him. In any case the medallions may doubtless enable us to appreciate the vigor
and expression that appeared in Lysippos's portraits
of the king.

Lysippos's most important work for Alexander
was apparently the monument erected after the battle
of the Granikos.[90] According to Arrian it consisted of
statues of twenty-five of the king's companions, who
fell at the first onset.[91] Plutarch says that thirty-four
fell, of whom nine were foot-soldiers.[92] He under-
stands that Lysippos made statues of the whole thirty-
four; but we are doubtless safe in following Arrian,
and considering that only the twenty-five horsemen
were portrayed. Justin represents that statues were
made—he does not expressly say by Lysippos—to one
hundred twenty-nine men, who, according to him,
were all that the Macedonians lost in the entire battle.[93] This probably rests on a misunderstanding; at
any rate, it does not affect the number of statues to
be ascribed to Lysippos. Velleius Paterculus tells us
that Alexander himself was among those portrayed,[94]

[89] *Jb. Arch. I.,* XXV, 1910, pp. 147 ff.
[90] Lippold in Pauly-Wissowa, no. 22.
[91] *Anabasis,* I, 16, 4 (App. 1, 70).
[92] *Alexander,* 16, 7-8 (App. 1, 72).
[93] *Historiae,* XI, 6, 12-13 (App. 1, 71).
[94] I, 11, 3-4 (App. 1, 73).

and both he and Pliny[95] add the information that
Metellus transferred the statues to Rome (c. 146
B.C.). Pliny says that all the men were portrayed
very exactly. This sounds like the usual enthusiast's
exaggeration, but it is altogether possible: Lysippos
was probably personally acquainted with the Companions, or there may have been portraits of them made
previously.[96] It is clear that the monument consisted
simply of a number of equestrian statues; none of the
enemy was represented, so it could hardly be called a
battle-group. The sculptor must have found full ex-
ercise for his ingenuity in avoiding monotony in the
series.

There is a bronze statuette in Naples (Plate 48,
A),[97] representing an armed horseman, which has been
conjecturally identified as a reduced copy of the figure
of Alexander in the Granikos monument.[98] Arndt[99]
and Schreiber[100] find no evidence in the features of the
man that he is Alexander, and Pottier, in a very acute
study of the matter, has shown that a similar figure
occurs in several representations of Alexander in battle,
but always as a subordinate figure;—never as Alexander himself.[101] From this he infers that the statuette
represents one of the Companions; but this inference is
valid only on the assumption that the other monuments
are derived from the Granikos monument:—an assumption impossible in the case of the Alexander
mosaic and improbable in the cases of the others. The

[95] N.H., XXXIV 64 (App. 1, 3).

[96] So Sellers, note ad loc.

[97] Ruesch, Guida², p. 353, no. 1487, with fig.; Brunn-Bruckmann, no.
355 b; Arndt-Bruckmann, nos. 479-480; Koepp, op. cit., figs. on pp. 15
and 29; Bernoulli, op. cit., figs. 29-30; Ujfalvy, op. cit., pl. XVII;
Collignon, Lysippe, fig. 11.

[98] So Koepp, op. cit., pp. 15 f.; Collignon, Lysippe, pp. 55 f.; Bernoulli
thinks it is Alexander, but not from the Granikos group (op. cit., pp.
98 ff.).

[99] Arndt-Bruckmann, text to plates 479-480.

[100] Op. cit., pp. 95 f. and 282.

[101] Mélanges Nicole, pp. 427-443.

argument that Alexander would be represented as forging forward and not as fighting a foe at his side is ingenious, but not wholly convincing. We are unable then to determine whether the bronze represents Alexander or not.

Pottier observes also that the horse in the Naples group, as well as the riderless horse found with it,[102] is supported by a rudder.[103] This seems a most singular object for such a purpose; it is scarcely explicable except on the assumption that the statue was connected in some way with the sea or with a river. Now cavalry forces very rarely win glory on the sea; and the Granikos monument is the only one recorded which was erected in commemoration of the exploits of cavalry in a battle fought over a river. This circumstance establishes a strong probability that the statuettes are imitated from the work of Lysippos.[104] Such reduced copies are of course not dependable for the study of niceties in style; still we can see and admire something of the splendid vigor that appeared in the original.

Another great work, resulting indirectly from Lysippos's association with Alexander, was the Krateros group.[105] It was placed in a building at Delphi, just above the west end of the temple of Apollo and below the theatre. The building is mostly destroyed, but seems to have been about fifteen meters long and six deep.[106] The inscription, cut on the wall, clearly indicates that the chamber was designed for the sole purpose of providing a proper setting for the group. Of the sculpture itself no vestige has been found, nor

[102] Ruesch, *Guida²*, p. 354, no. 1488; Pottier, fig. 2.

[103] His citations prove this beyond dispute; Daremberg-Saglio, IV, I, p. 28, figs. 5273-5274; Baumeister, *Denkmäler*, III, figs. 1684, 1691, 1696, 1697.

[104] I suspect that this is the mysterious observation of L. Curtius (Bernoulli, *op. cit.*, p. 101, note 1).

[105] Kluge, *Die Darstellungen der Löwenjagd*, p. 45, no. 178; Lippold in Pauly-Wissowa, no. 21. See chapter III for date.

[106] See Pomtow's restoration (*B. Ph. Wo.*, XXXII, 1912, col. 1014).

even of the base that supported it; but it is safe to conclude, from the dimensions of the room, that the figures were above life size.

It is very probable that we may recognize the general character of the group in a relief found at Messene and now in the Louvre.[107] It corresponds well to the description given by Plutarch:[108] "the lion, the dogs, the king in combat with the lion, and Krateros coming to the rescue" are all present, and the group is harmonious and complete, though we may conjecture that the figures were more closely placed and overlapped more than in the relief, where they are spread for the sake of clarity.[109] The connection of the relief with the Krateros group is confirmed by the hat worn by Krateros: it is a "causia," an especially Macedonian type of headgear.

The same kind of hat is worn by the rider on an intaglio owned by Sir Arthur Evans; and M. Perdrizet has argued that the gem more accurately represents the group.[110] Here, however, the other figure is shown beaten to his knees by the onslaught of the lion, which fixes its teeth in the man's body. It does not seem probable that the conqueror would have been so represented. Furthermore, there are no dogs on the gem; and though this is easily explicable by the smallness of the available space, the omission indicates a lack of regard for accuracy in the reproduction. The gem-cutter apparently received only a general suggestion from the work of Leochares and Lysippos. The two medallions from Tarsus[111] seem to have no definite connection with the group.

[107] No. 858; Loeschcke, in *Jb. Arch. I.*, III, 1888, pp. 189-193 and pl. VII; Kluge, *Die Darstellungen der Löwenjagd*, p. 46, no. 179; Collignon, *Lysippe*, fig. 12.

[108] *Alexander*, 40, 4 (App. 1, 74).

[109] So Pomtow (*B. Ph. Wo.*, XXXII, 1912, col. 1016).

[110] *J.H.S.*, XIX, 1899, pp. 273-279, and pl. XI, 3 (also *B.C.H.*, XXII, 1898, pp. 566 ff.).

[111] *Revue Numismatique*, XIII, 1868, pls. X and XII; *J.H.S.*, XIX, 1899, pl. XI, 2 & 4; Collignon, *Histoire*, II, p. 442, fig. 229; Koepp, *op. cit.*, p. 3, fig.

Homolle suggested that the hunting scene on the
Alexander Sarcophagus might have been influenced by
the Krateros group.[112] It seems, however, to be composed in essentially the same way as the other scenes
on the sarcophagus. It is occasionally suggested that
all the sculptures of the sarcophagus show the influence
of Lysippos. This is perhaps a natural hypothesis, in
view of the position of Lysippos as the favored sculptor of Alexander; but there is grave doubt whether
the figures of Alexander on the sarcophagus indicate a
personal knowledge, on the part of the sculptor, of the
king. At all events, a study of the sculptures discloses
not a trace of Lysippian style in detail. There is a
good deal of affinity with the style of Skopas.

The collaboration of Lysippos and Leochares on
the Krateros group offers an interesting but wholly
insoluble problem, as to the share taken by each sculptor. Probably we can safely conjecture that the figure
of Alexander, at least, was made by Lysippos. Possibly the whole group was ordered from Leochares, and
work on it interrupted by his death; Leochares was
probably older than Lysippos, since he worked on the
Mausoleum, and we have little idea how long he lived.

Statius[113] mentions a horse in Rome, which, according to hearsay, was originally made by Lysippos
for Alexander, but in the poet's time bore a statue of
Caesar. Pliny and Suetonius[114] speak of this same
horse in connection with Caesar, but know nothing of
any earlier connection with Alexander or Lysippos;
and they add that its hoofs were abnormal, as they
were in a horse actually owned by Caesar. It seems
clear that the story reported by Statius deserves no
credit, though Lippold[115] believes it and suggests that
Caesar may have had the the hoofs changed.

[112] B.C.H., XXI, 1897, pp. 599 f.
[113] Silvae, I, 1, 84-87 (App. 1, 94).
[114] App. 1, 93 and 95.
[115] In Pauly-Wissowa, no. 20

A number of figures derived from one original have been published by Perdrizet.[116] In this type Alexander is represented clothed in an unmistakable aegis; an aegis of unusual form, however, which seems to be derived from the Macedonian chlamys. Apparently the original was a figure of a type invented especially for Alexander, and Perdrizet did not fail to note that Lysippos was much more likely than anyone else to originate it. The figures as preserved offer little opportunity for the study of style, but it is established that they were all found in Egypt. This is unfavorable to the proposed attribution, since we have no reason to believe that Lysippos ever went to Egypt. The use of the aegis also, though it may have some meaning not exactly known to us, certainly implies a conception of Alexander as in some sense deified, and indicates that the original was made after the death of the king. Of course it is altogether possible that Lysippos made portraits of Alexander after his death, but he had then no advantage over other sculptors; and it is more plausible to ascribe the Alexander with the aegis to some sculptor who worked in Alexandria.

Since there has been occasion, in this chapter, to mention most of the interesting portraits of Alexander, it will not be out of place to note that a crystal head in the Museo Archeologico at Florence has been published[117] by Delbrück as an Alexander, which seems certainly right, and conjecturally ascribed to Pyrgoteles.

[116] *Mon. Piot*, XXI, 1913, pp. 59-72; Reinach, *Répertoire*, V 311, 7 and 312, 1 and 3-6.

[117] *Jb. Arch. I.*, XL, 1925, pp. 8-13.

CHAPTER XI

MISCELLANEOUS WORKS

Alexander was not alone in his esteem for Lysippos's talent in portraiture. The attribution to Lysippos of a portrait of Hephaistion is, as was seen in chapter III, probably true, but the portrait can not be identified. Inscriptional evidence, also previously mentioned, shows that he made a portrait of Seleukos Nikator. There is in Naples a very fine bronze bust (Plate 49) certainly identified as Seleukos by its resemblance to his numismatic portraits.[1] Wolters has suggested that this bust is probably copied from Lysippos's portrait.[2] This view is more or less definitely accepted by Winter[3] and Studniczka;[4] Wace seems to view it with some favor;[5] Lippold doubts it.[6]

As Wolters observed, several portraits of Seleukos are recorded, including two by Bryaxis and Aristodemos. We know nothing of the style of Aristodemos and little of that of Bryaxis, so we are hardly in a position to refute an attribution to either of those artists. With full justification, however, Wolters emphasizes the analogy between this portrait and the apoxyomenos in the carriage of the head, the treatment of the eyes, and the rendering of the hair. This last point is particularly important, since it is one of the few points in which correspondence between an ideal head and a portrait may be demanded. The neck, with the small folds above and below the larynx, re-

[1] Ruesch, *Guida²*, p. 221, no. 890; Arndt-Bruckmann, pls. 101-102; *Röm. Mitt.*, IV, 1889, pl. II; Hekler, *Greek and Roman Portraits*, pl. 68; Delbrück, *Antike Porträts*, pl. 22; *J.H.S.*, XXV, 1905, pl. VIII, 2.

[2] *Röm. Mitt.*, IV, 1889, pp. 39 f.

[3] Gercke-Norden, *Einleit. in d. Altertumswissenschaft²*, II, p. 178.

[4] *Neue Jahrbücher*, XLI, 1918, p. 21.

[5] *J.H.S.*, XXV, 1905, p. 94.

[6] In Pauly-Wissowa, no. 24 and thereafter.

sembles the neck of the apoxyomenos. In addition to these points we should consider the extraordinary vigor and vividness of the portrait, which is one of the finest left to us. There is nothing to indicate that Aristodemos was capable of such work. As for Bryaxis, no other portrait by him is recorded; and a consideration of the Sarapis, the only extant work attributable to him with even approximate certainty, does not suggest that portraiture would have been a field especially suited to his talents.

Certainty in the attribution of a portrait is very difficult of attainment, in the sculpture or painting of any age. There is however a very strong probability that the Naples bust is an excellent copy of the portrait by Lysippos. If this is true, it affords an additional indication as to the length of the sculptor's life: the band around the hair shows that the portrait was made after Seleukos became king;—that is, after 306. The evident age of the man also points to a late date.

We are told by Diogenes Laertius that Lysippos made a portrait of Socrates shortly after his death.[7] There is a manifest inaccuracy in the story, since if the statue was set up soon after Socrates's death it must have been some twenty-five years before Lysippos was born. It remains probable, however, that Lysippos made a portrait of Socrates; Diogenes apparently confused two pieces of information.

It appears that the existing portraits of Socrates are referable to three types:[8] One is best represented by the Munich bronze,[9] one by a head in the Museo

[7] *De Vitis Philosophorum*, II, 5, 43 (App. 1, 75).

[8] Hekler, *Greek and Roman Portraits*, pp. XI f.; Loeschcke, in *Arch. Anz.*, XXIX, 1914, cols. 515-517. On the portraits of Socrates in general see Bernoulli, *Griechische Ikonographie*, I, pp. 184-205; Lippold, *Griechische Porträtstatuen*, pp. 53 f.; Arndt-Bruckmann, 1031-1050; Kekulé, *Die Bildnisse des Sokrates* (*Abh. d. König. preuss. Akad. d. Wissenschaften*, 1908); Bieber, in *Röm. Mitt.*, XXXII, 1917, pp. 118-122 (here a good brief characterization of the three types).

[9] No. 448; Arndt-Bruckmann, pls. 1031-1032; Kekulé, *op. cit.*, fig. 38; Loeschcke, *loc. cit.*, fig. 1; Hekler, *op. cit.*, p. XI, fig. 2; Wolters, *Führer*, p. 52, with ill.; Bieber, *loc. cit.*, p. 121, fig. 2.

Nazionale at Rome,[10] and one by a head in the Villa Albani.[11] If any of these types is derived from Lysippos, it is certainly the second. An attribution to him has frequently been suggested for it,[12] but rarely with great confidence. It is very probably true. The type was almost certainly created during Lysippos's life-time, if we may judge from its style, and we are not told of any other sculptor who made such a portrait. Portraits of Socrates were in demand in later times, as the number of them in existence proves; but the subject was not one that would appeal much to Greek sculptors, and it is improbable that many portraits of the philosopher were made during the fourth century. The type of the Museo Nazionale recalls the style of Lysippos in its treatment of the eyes and forehead, and there is nothing about it that is in any way opposed to our expectations as to the Lysippian portrait. If, on the other hand, there is no evidence that would justify the attribution on stylistic grounds alone, that is probably because there is no accredited work of Lysippos of similar nature.

A marble statuette which represents Socrates has recently been acquired by the British Museum. It is published by Walters in a brief article,[13] in which he deals to some extent with other portraits of Socrates

---

[10] Hekler, *op. cit.*, pl. 20; Kekulé, *op. cit.*, figs. 26-27; Helbig, *Führer*[3], II, p. 170, no. 1396. The well known bust in the Louvre, which we illustrate (pl. 50), belongs to this type.

[11] Hekler, *op. cit.*, pl. 21; Bernoulli, *op. cit.*, I, pl. 23; Helbig, *Führer*[3], II, p. 434, no. 1884; Furtwängler-Urlichs, *Denkmäler*[3], no. 53; Arndt-Bruckmann, pls. 1045-1046.

[12] Bernoulli, *op. cit.*, I, p. 202; Hekler, *op. cit.*, p. XII; Lippold, *op. cit.*, p. 53; Loeschcke, *loc. cit.*, col. 517; Wolters, *Führer*, p. 44, no. 291; Bieber, *loc. cit.;* Waldhauer, *Lisipp*, p. 37 and fig. 27.

[13] *J.H.S.*, XLV, 1925, pls. X-XIII, pp. 255-261. Now in Arndt-Bruckmann, 1049-1050; and studied by Studniczka (*Ein neues Bildnis des Sokrates*), who thinks it is a work of the second century after Christ and represents the Lysippian version. Miss Richter (*A.J.A.*, XXXI, 1927, pp. 136 f.) evidently thinks that the statuette is probably modern. I have not seen it, but see little reason for suspicion.

but makes little use of discussions later than Bernoulli. Walters follows Bernoulli in regarding the Munich type as later than the type of the Museo Nazionale, and differs with him in assigning the former rather than the latter to Lysippos.   In both cases he appears to be wrong.   He considers that the new statuette is to be asociated with the Munich type rather than with the Museo Nazionale type, "though the facial resemblance is not so close."   I see no evidence of any relation between the statuette and the Munich type, while there is certainly a connection of some sort with the Lysippian type of the Museo Nazionale.   Perhaps the statuette is simply a free adaptation of that type; or it may be that both Lysippos and the artist of the statuette were influenced by an earlier portrait which is not otherwise known to us.

In a Gnomologium in the Vatican[14] there is mention of a statue of Demos (the People) by Lysippos, with the curious detail that the statue had no ears. This is suggestive of the rhetorician rather than of the artist and inspires no faith in the accuracy of the writer.   Pausanias[15] mentions a Demos by a sculptor named Lyson; and there is little doubt that it is this work which is credited to the more celebrated Lysippos.

We learn also, though not on the best authority,[16] that Lysippos made a portrait of the Theban poetess Praxilla.   Praxilla lived about 450, so the portrait could not have been made from life.   It has been suggested that a copy of this portrait is preserved in the celebrated maiden of Anzio,[17] but I can see nothing Lysippian in that statue.[18]   If the Agias were by Ly-

[14] *Wiener Studien*, XI, 1889, p. 62, no. 399 (App. 1, 96).

[15] I 3, 5.

[16] Tatian, *Contra Graecos* 52 (App. 1, 76).   On the unreliability of Tatian see Kalkmann, in *Rh. Mus.*, XLII, 1887, pp. 489-524.

[17] Arvanitopoullos, in Παναθήναια, X, 1909, p. 58.

[18] Amelung (*Ausonia*, III, p. 133) remarks on its resemblance to the Eros, which is slight.   On the statue in general add to Amelung's bibliography (Helbig, *Führer*³, II, p. 146); Preyss, *Röm. Mitt.*, XXIX,

sippos, a head in the Palazzo Pitti might be conjectured
to represent his Praxilla.[19] Förster once made the
unfortunate suggestion that the drunken flute-girl
mentioned by Pliny was this portrait of Praxilla.[20]

A portrait of Aesop by Lysippos is mentioned in
an epigram of Agathias,[21] who appears to imply,
though he does not clearly say,[22] that it made a group
with the "Seven Sages" by the same master. We have
it on the uncertain authority of Tatian that Aristodemos made an Aesop,[23] and he is one of several sculptors to whom "philosophers" are ascribed by Pliny.[24]
It is possible that this is one of the instances in which
a work by a relatively obscure artist is ascribed to a
greater contemporary, but this is far from certain.
At all events, the remarkable bust of Aesop in the Villa
Albani[25] is probably copied from an original later than
Lysippos, and shows no marks of his style.

It is highly probable *a priori* that Lysippos made
a portrait of Aristotle, the philosopher and tutor of
Alexander. Studniczka has very plausibly identified
as Aristotle a type which could very well be a creation

1914, pp. 12-37; Anti, *Boll. Arte,* XIII, 1919, pp. 102-106, and Paribeni,
Mus. Naz. Rom.[4], pp. 202-204, no. 488. The copy published by Anti is
characterized as Hygieia. This of course does not prove that the original represented Hygieia, but may serve to settle any question that may
have existed as to the sex of the figure.

[19] Arndt-Bruckmann, pls. 149-150; Bernoulli, *op. cit.,* I, p. 69, fig. 12.
Percy Gardner (*J.H.S.,* XXXVIII, 1918, p. 15, with fig. 6) speaks of its
Skopaic and Lysippian style.

[20] *Rh. Mus.,* XL, 1885, p. 637. Lippold in Pauly-Wissowa, no. 27,
seems to think this possible.

[21] *Anth. Pal.* XVI (*Plan. App.* IV), 332 (App. 1, 77); Lippold, *l.c.,*
no. 28.

[22] On this point see Förster, *l.c.;* he thinks that Agathias means that
Lysippos chose to portray Aesop rather than the Seven Sages. So also
Lippold, *l.c.*

[23] *Contra Graecos,* 55 (App. 1, 79).

[24] *N.H.,* XXXIV 86 (App. 1, 78).

[25] Helbig, *Führer*[3], II, p. 415, no. 1859, with references; Von Mach,
University Prints, no. 387; Arndt-Bruckmann, 787-790. The traditional
identification is questionable; the figure is sometimes thought of as an
Antonine portrait.

of Lysippos,[26] though on grounds of style alone it could not confidently be assigned to him.

Pausanias saw at Olympia several statues of athletes by Lysippos. We have already discussed the sculptures on the base of the statue of Polydamas.[27] We know nothing of the statue itself, or of the statues of Troilos,[28] Kallikrates[29] or Koreidas[30] at Thebes. Cheilon[31] was both an athlete and a warrior. As to Pythes,[32] Pausanias apparently knew little, but judged from the epigram or from the statues that he was a warrior. There were two statues of him by Lysippos, but Pausanias gives no description of either. The statue of Polydamas was certainly made long after his death. The statues of Cheilon and of Pythes were apparently made after the deaths of the men; in these cases, however, it is possible that Lysippos knew them in life and that his statues were real portraits. The statue of Troilos was probably made many years after his victory, and must have been an idealized figure, even if Troilos was still living. There is no reason to doubt that the statues of Kallikrates and Koreidas were accurate portraits made from life.[33]

The remaining victor-statue at Olympia is mentioned in a passage of Pausanias that appears to be corrupt.[34] He was a pankratiast from Stratos in Akarnania, but it is uncertain whether his name was Xenarches or Philandridas or a name that has

[26] *Das Bildnis des Aristoteles;* cf. Bernoulli, *Griechische Ikonographie,* II, pp. 94-98.

[27] Chapter V. The date is discussed in Chapter III.

[28] See Chapter III for date.

[29] Pausanias, VI 17, 3 (App. 1, 85).

[30] See Chapter III for date, and Chapter V for the base.

[31] See Chapter III for date.

[32] Pausanias, VI 14, 12 (App. 1, 80).

[33] On the idea that portraits could be set up only by those who had won three times see Kekulé, *Sitzb. Preuss. Akad. Wiss.,* 1909, pp. 701 ff., and Hyde, *OVM,* pp. 54-58.

[34] VI 2, 1 (App. 1, 86).

dropped out of the text altogether. Furtwängler[35] tentatively identified the famous bronze head of a boxer or pankratiast found at Olympia (Plate 51)[36] as a part of this statue, and Waldhauer[37] regards it as quite possibly an original work of Lysippos. In it the hair is very unlike any Lysippian hair that we know, and none of the morphological details which have been found elsewhere are perceptible here. Yet the identification may be correct: the treatment of the hair is very effective, which is all that can be expected, since we have no sure Lysippian head in which the same style of wearing the hair occurs; and it is obvious that in this head the morphological details were taken from life. The head is a first-rate piece of sculpture—contrast it with the Agias!—in which the battered features and uninspired countenance of the bruiser are rendered with fine realism and consummate technical skill. It is easily possible to overemphasize the naturalism of the head and hence to assign to it a date too late: we do not find in it the repulsive brutishness of the bronze boxer in the Terme museum.[38] Kekulé was wrong, but not wholly without justification, when he assigned the Olympia head to the end of the fifth century.

Hyde has suggested that a marble head found at Olympia (Plate 52, A-B) belonged to the statue of the Akarnanian pankratiast.[39] He is certainly right in his

[35] *Olympia, Ergebnisse,* IV, pp. 10 f.

[36] *Olympia, Ergebnisse,* IV, pl. 2; Von Mach, *University Prints,* no. 482; Stais, *Marbres et Bronzes*², p. 299, no. 6439; Bulle, *Der schöne Mensch*², pl. 235; Hekler, *op. cit.,* p. XIX, pl. 79; Springer-Wolters¹², p. 365, fig. 686; Kekulé, in *Sitzb. Preuss. Akad. Wiss.,* 1909, pp. 694 ff.; Hyde, *OVM,* pp. 254-255. Hyde assigns the head to the statue of Kapros, who won in 212.

[37] *Lisipp,* pp. 38 f. and fig. 30.

[38] Paribeni, *Mus. Naz. Rom.*⁴, p. 197, no. 480. See note 25 in chapter IX.

[39] *Olympia, Ergebnisse,* III, pl. LIV, 3-4, pp. 208 f.; Hyde, *OVM,* pp. 293 ff.; cf. *A.J.A.,* XXVI, 1922, pp. 426-429, and *A.J.A.,* XI, 1907, pp. 396-416; Gardiner, *History and Remains of Olympia,* fig. 33, opposite p. 98; Bieber in *Jb. Arch. I.,* XXV, 1910, pp. 172 f. (between Euphranor and Skopas).

contention that the head represents some mortal, not
Herakles as was thought by some authorities. The attribution to Lysippos is based on the resemblance of the
head to the Agias, and falls automatically when the
Agias is seen to have no connection with Lysippos. The
resemblance lies chiefly in the shape of the skull and has
been well set forth by Hyde.   The hair in the two
heads is altogether different, however, and there are
considerable dissimilarities in the eyes.   It is somewhat disconcerting to find that the ears of the "Philandridas"—that name may serve in the absence of a
better one—are unlike each other; the left one, though
injured, apparently was like the ears of the Agias.

There is a well-known grave-stele in Athens[40] containing a youth whose head, according to Hyde, resembles the Agias markedly.   But this head and the
"Philandridas" resemble each other decidedly more
than either resembles the Agias; this was the unani-
mous and unprompted opinion of five members of the
American School at Athens who looked at good illustrations of the "Philandridas" and the Agias in the
presence of the stele.   The resemblance is so close as
almost to prove that the stele and the "Philandridas"
are made by one artist, or at the very least that there
is no difference of school or tendency between them.
The resemblance between these two works and the
Agias is enough to suggest, though not to prove, that
it also is an Attic work.   If it be accepted that the
Agias and the "Philandridas" are by the same artist,
that is a strong argument against the attribution of
the Agias to Lysippos. Hyde rightly maintains,
against the apparent assumption of some scholars, that
Lysippos was not incapable of making a marble statue;
but it is clear that he made few, and it would be remarkable if one of them should survive.

[40] Hyde, *OVM*, p. 312, with citations; the head: *Einzelaufnahmen*,
698-699; here pl. 52, C-D.

A statue in Berlin (Plates 54 and 53, C),[41] representing a nude youth, has been ascribed to Lysippos, because of its style, by Furtwängler[42] and Amelung;[43] Lippold[44] seems to agree; Schober[45] questions it. A head in the Museo Nazionale at Rome[46] is said to be another copy, though I doubted it when I saw the head; another is said by Arndt[47] to have been placed on a statue once in the possession of Bardini in Florence; two others are in the Museo Torlonia.[48] The subject apparently is a boy victor.

The nose and the upper lip are mostly new. The face is a rather sharp oval and thinner than the face of the apoxyomenos, and the ears are unlike those of that statue. In the hair, the eyes, the lower lip, and the neck the two statues are quite similar. The body does not show very much muscular detail, but this may be due partly to the copyist. The elastic movement of the waist is Lysippian, though the triangular opening between the muscles does not appear. The feet are slender and flat. The abdominal muscles are differently represented, and the whole figure shows a style considerably earlier than that of the apoxyomenos. On the whole this statue corresponds well to a reasonable conception of the early style of Lysippos. I can not see, with Amelung, a development in style from this figure through the Agias to the apoxyomenos; one can easily assume a progress from the Berlin

[41] Kurzes Beschreibung³, p. 40, no. 471, with ill.; Röm. Mitt., XX, 1905, pp. 147 ff., figs. 5-7.

[42] Masterpieces, p. 364.

[43] Röm. Mitt., XX, 1905, pp. 147 ff.

[44] Jb. Arch. I., XXVI, 1911, p. 278.

[45] Jh. Oest. Arch. I., XIX-XX, 1916-1919, p. 188.

[46] Paribeni, Mus. Naz. Rom.⁴, p. 211, no. 517; phot. of German Institute, no. 212; Helbig, Führer³, II, p. 163, no. 1380.

[47] La Glyptothèque Ny Carlsberg, p. 181, note 10.

[48] Mentioned in Helbig, l.c.; Visconti, Museo Torlonia, pl. XIV, 53 and XV, 57. Lippold, in Pauly-Wissowa, says that they are copied from another Lysippian original.

statue to the apoxyomenos, but the Agias is not in line with them.

There are in Dresden two copies from an original representing a bearded athlete[49] and two from another type representing a beardless man in a similar posture.[50] Furtwängler[51] ascribed both types to Lysippos; Klein[52] and apparently Arndt[53] only the beardless one; Herrmann thinks the beardless type earlier than Lysippos, the bearded type later than our sculptor. This is certainly right for the bearded type. The two copies differ somewhat, and the Hellenistic character is more evident in no. 236 than in 235; but it is sufficiently clear in both the face and the treatment of the body in both figures.

The beardless type is obviously earlier. In the hair, the ear, the shape of the head, and the pubes there is considerable similarity to the apoxyomenos. There is a striking difference in the shape of the face: in the Dresden athlete it is a long oval. There is no groove in the forehead. The treatment of anatomy suggests the "Jason" rather than the apoxyomenos, but seems distinctly earlier than either. The head and the legs (the legs are new except for the right leg above the knee) are large in relation to the body, so the proportions are those ascribed to Euphranor. It is not likely that the original was made by Euphranor, who was no sculptor of athletes; but it could be an early work of Lysippos, made when he was feeling his way toward his own system of proportions.

[49] Herrmann, *Verzeichnis*, nos. 235 and 236. Our pl. 56 is 236. Head of no. 235: Hekler, *Greek and Roman Portraits*, pl. 48; Reinach, *Répertoire*, I 529, 2-3.

[50] Herrmann, *op. cit.*, nos. 233 and 234, with illustration of no. 233 (here pl. 55); Reinach, *Répertoire*, I 528, 3 and 529, 1. Head of no. 233: Arndt, *La Glyptothèque Ny Carlsberg*, p. 179, figs. 101-103. No. 234 has been reduced to a torso by the removal of restorations and antique parts that did not belong to the statue.

[51] *Masterpieces*, p. 364, note 2.

[52] *Gesch. d. griech. Kunst*, II, p. 363.

[53] *Op. cit.*, p. 181.

Furtwängler and Arndt note a resemblance between the head of the bearded athlete in Dresden and
a bearded head in Ny Carlsberg (Plate 57).[54] This
Furtwängler calls "one of the finest and most purely
Lysippian works in existence," and he is certainly right.
The nose and part of the upper lip are new. The forehead with its furrow, the eyes, close together and with
depressions at the outer corners, the lower lip, the chin,
the shape of the face and of the head all resemble the
corresponding features of the apoxyomenos very
closely. The ears are mostly lost. The identity of
style between this head and the head of the apoxyomenos is so perfect that it is quite certain, in my judgment, that they proceed from one sculptor. Klein[55]
strangely ascribes the head to Skopas.

Arndt notes that Sieveking has suggested that a
portrait head in the Uffizi[56] is a replica of the Ny
Carlsberg head. Miss McDowall once suggested that
this head was a portrait of Demetrios Phalereus,[57] and
it now bears (or recently bore) that name in the museum; but more recently she, now Mrs. Esdaile, has
identified it, with much probability, as Aristippos.[58]
It is not quite clear whether she considers it copied
from the same original as the other portraits of Aristippos, but this appears to be the fact. An attribution
to the school of Lysippos, if not to the master himself,
is suggested, and justly. Arndt was assuredly right in
rejecting the hypothesis that this head and that in Ny
Carlsberg were derived from one original.

While visiting the Ny Carlsberg Glyptotek I was
much impressed by the close similarity between a head

[54] Arndt, *Glyptothèque Ny Carlsberg*, pls. 130-131, pp. 182-183; *De Antike Kunstvaerker*, no. 118; Lippold, *Antike Skulpturen der Glypto-thek Ny Carlsberg*, pl. 34.

[55] *Gesch. d. griech. Kunst*, II, p. 279.

[56] Amelung, *Führer durch Florenz*, no. 118; no. 370 in the museum; Arndt-Bruckmann, 341-342; Hekler, pl. 91 b.

[57] *J.H.S.*, XXIV, 1904, pp. 93 ff. and pl. IV.

[58] *J.H.S.*, XXXIV, 1914, p. 53.

which I noticed there and the apoxyomenos of the Vatican. This resemblance was great in many points: the shape of face, the profile, hair, eyes, ears, lips, and chin; I concluded that the head was certainly copied from Lysippos or from his immediate following,—and presently I found that it was an example of the Meleager type. I had the same experience with a head in the Museo Nazionale at Rome.

The Meleager was most thoroughly studied by Graef,[59] who drew up a list of copies from which the following list is chiefly taken. The statues 15-17 are mentioned by Furtwängler[60] and none of them is known to me otherwise.

1. Vatican, Belvedere. Amelung, *D. Skulpt. d. Vat. Mus.*, II, p. 33, no. 10, pls. 3 and 12; Reinach, *Répertoire*, I 479, 2; Helbig, *Führer*[3], I, p. 79, no. 128; Bulle, *Der schöne Mensch*[2], fig. 145; Brunn-Bruckmann, 386; Chase, *Greek and Roman Sculpture in American Collections*, fig. 98; Von Mach, *University Prints*, 216. Here pl. 58. The head: *Ant. Denk.*, I, 1889, pl. 40, 1; Gardner, *SGS*, pl. 1.

2. Holkham Hall. Michaelis, *Ancient Marbles*, p. 306, no. 20; Reinach, *op. cit.*, I 480, 1. Much restored.

3. Vatican. Reinach, *op. cit.*, I 479, 1. Doubtful; known to Graef (and to me) only from Clarac's drawing.

4. Rome, Palazzo Barberini. Matz-Duhn, no. 1104. Head new.

5. Versailles. Reinach, *op. cit.*, I 479, 7.

6. Naples, Museo Nazionale. No. 6077. Ruesch, *Guida*[2], p. 250, no. 1036; Bernoulli, *Römische Ikonographie*, II, 2, p. 61; Reinach, *Répertoire*, I 580, 2. Restored as Domitian.

7. Rome, Villa Borghese. Reinach, *op. cit.*, II 555, 1; Helbig, *Führer*[3], II, p. 233, no. 1532; *Einzelaufnahmen*, 2714. Head new.

8. Rome, Palazzo Corsini. Matz-Duhn, 1048. Only torso antique.

---

[59] *Röm. Mitt.*, IV, 1889, pp. 218 ff.

[60] *Meisterwerke*, p. 526, note 2; *Masterpieces*, pp. 304 and 184.

9. Berlin, no. 215. Conze, *Beschreibung d. ant. Skulpt.*, p. 93; *Kurze Beschreibung*[3], p. 26, pl. 41; Reinach, *op. cit.*, I 484, 1; Von Mach, *University Prints,* 214; Chase, *op. cit.,* fig. 99. Head new.
10. Rome, Lateran. Benndorf-Schöne, p. 32, no. 49. Torso.
11. Verona, Museo Lapidario. Torso.
12. Rome, Palazzo Barberini. Reinach, *op. cit.,* I 486, 1.
13. Copenhagen, Ny Carlsberg Glyptotek. No. 387. *De Antike Kunstvaerker,* p. 139, *Tillaeg,* p. 149; Furt-wängler-Urlichs[3], pl. XXXII; Reinach, *op. cit.,* IV 349, 1. Head new.
14. Cambridge, Massachusetts, Fogg Museum. Reinach, *op. cit.,* II 555, 6; Von Mach, *University Prints,* 215, and *Handbook,* p. 214 ff. (good description); Hyde, *OVM,* p. 315, fig. 77; Chase, *op. cit.,* fig. 97. The head: Chase, fig. 101.
15. Museo Torlonia. Torso restored as Hermes.
16. Louvre. Torso.
17. Rome, Palazzo Doria. Small.

HEADS

1. Rome, Villa Medici, on a statue to which it does not belong. *Ant. Denk.,* I, 1889, pl. 40, 2; Gardner, *Handbook,* p. 422; Gardner, *SGS,* pl. 1; Hyde, *OVM,* p. 314; Chase, *op. cit.,* fig. 101; Bulle, *Der schöne Mensch*[2], fig. 144; Matz-Duhn, no. 215.
2. Rome, Museo Nazionale. Paribeni, *Museo Nazionale Romano*[4], p. 212, no. 523; *B. Com. Rom.,* XLVII, 1921, pp. 51-53 and fig. 3; *Memorie dei Lincei,* XIV, 1910, p. 269, fig. 21; Helbig, *Führer*[3], II, p. 164, no. 1383.
3. Naples, Museo Nazionale, on a statue of Aristogeiton. Ruesch, *Guida*[2], p. 28, no. 104; *Einzelaufnahmen,* 518-519.
4. Rome, Vatican. Amelung, *D. Skulpt. d. Vat. Mus.,* I, p. 645, no. 509, pl. 69.
5. Rome, Museo Nazionale, on a seated figure. Paribeni, *op. cit.,* p. 84, no. 52; *Einzelaufnahmen,* 277-278.
6. Rome, Villa Albani. No. 57.
7. Rome, Museo Torlonia, on statue no. 473. Visconti, *Museo Torlonia,* pl. CXXII.
8. British Museum, from Castle Howard. *Marbles and Bronzes,* pl. 38; *Catalogue of Burlington Fine Arts Club,* 1904, pl. XIV, no. 14; *J.H.S.,* VI, 1885, p. 38, no. 27 (Michaelis).

9. Copenhagen, Ny Carlsberg Glyptotek, no. 362. *De Antike Kunstvaerker,* p. 132, *Tillaeg,* p. 148; Arndt, *La Glyptothèque Ny Carlsberg,* pl. 100. Here pl. 59.
10. Rome, Vatican. Amelung, *op. cit.,* I, p. 609, no. 453, pl. 64. On a statue to which it does not belong.
11. Venice, Museo Archeologico. Dütschke, *Ant. Bildw. in Oberit.,* V, no. 148; *Einzelaufnahmen,* 2499-2502.
12. Vienna, from Catajo. *Einzelaufnahmen,* 48.
13. Leningrad, Hermitage. Kieseritzky, *Catalogue,* no. 355b.

A youth stands with the weight on his right leg and his right hand behind him and resting on the hip. A hunting spear is held loosely in the left hand and arm. So far all copies agree,[61] but in other details they vary considerably. In statue no. 1, which is probably the best known, the youth wears a chlamys, a dog sits at his right, and there is a boar's head on the support at his left. All three, in the opinion of Amelung,[62] are additions of the copyist.

The original was undoubtedly of bronze; this is evident from the treatment of the hair and from the variety of supports which were employed by the copyists. In a bronze statue the chlamys would present no difficulties, while in the marble copies it is brittle; one concludes then that it was present in the original, as in eight copies, while in six it was omitted.[63] The dog is present in five cases, while there is no case in which it is sure that there was no dog;[64] hence the presumption is that it too was present in the original. The boar's head is present in three copies, while in three

[61] It has been stated that in the Fogg copy (no. 14) it is not a spear but a stick. This seems to be an error.

[62] Helbig, *Führer³,* I, p. 80.

[63] Present in nos. 1, 5, 6, 7, 8, 10, 11, 13; absent in 2, 4, 9, 12, 14, 17. 3 is omitted as doubtful; 15 and 16 are unknown to me. The chlamydes differ in the various copies, but not more than would be expected.

[64] Present in nos. 1, 4, 7, 9, 13; the part is lacking or modern in 2, 6, 8, 10, 11, 14, 15, 16; in 5, 12 and 17 I do not know the restorations. Winter (*Jb. Arch. I.,* XXXII, 1917, pp. 226-229) believes that the dog stood at the figure's left in the original, as in no. 9.

others it certainly was absent;[65] here a conclusion is difficult, but the probability is perhaps against the boar, since its position varies in its three occurrences. It is on the boar's head that the identification as Meleager, hero of the Calydonian hunt, rests, and one can say only that three of the copies were called Meleager. The original may have been Meleager or it may have been a votive offering or a grave statue for a young hunter.

Graef referred the Meleager to Skopas and this opinion has been adopted almost unanimously, though the scholars who refer the Lansdowne Herakles to Lysippos are inclined to dispose of the Meleager in the same way.[66] This is singular, because the two statues can hardly belong to any one artist; the treatment of anatomy in the Meleager looks thirty years later than in the Herakles, the hair is very different, and there is no significant resemblance anywhere. The attribution of the Meleager to Skopas is largely due to an exaggerated importance which has been ascribed to the Medici head (no. 1) and recently to the Fogg copy (no. 14). These are certainly better, as works of art, than the other copies; they were made in the third century or thereabouts, when fine workmanship was common but nobody tried to make exact copies. Naturally they are unlike the other copies and equally unlike each other, and deserve little attention in speculations about the original.

The other heads agree fairly well among themselves, though no. 8 (of the heads) has a somewhat Skopaic look. The resemblance to the apoxyomenos has already been stated. The lower part of the face is not so heavy as in the apoxyomenos, but on the other hand it does not approach the triangular form of the

---

[65] Present in nos. 1, 4, 17; absent in 7, 9, 13; original condition unknown to me in the others.

[66] P. Gardner, in *J.H.S.*, XXIII, 1903, pp. 128 f.; Hyde, *OVM*, pp. 312-315; Cultrera, *Memorie dei Lincei*, XIV, 1910, pp. 266 ff.

Tegea heads. In other respects, with the exception of the bearded head in Ny Carlsberg, there are no closer analogies for the head of the apoxyomenos. The bodies of nos. 1, 9, and 12, which I have been able to examine carefully, also show great resemblance to the apoxyomenos. In the long, flat feet, the scant pubes, the navel with a crescent above it, the back, the knees, and the general musculature the two statues are very similar. The triangular opening between the muscles at the waist is not present in the Meleager, and in other places a knowledge of anatomy is less evident, but this difference is not very great. The Meleager is not so slender as the apoxyomenos, but we can not assume that all of Lysippos's statues were; compare the Herakles Epitrapezios. The position of the right arm is reminiscent of the Farnese Herakles.

The Meleager then is essentially a Lysippian work. There would be no great violation of probability, perhaps, in ascribing it to a son of Lysippos if there were reason to do so; and reason used to be found in Pliny, who says of Euthykrates:[67] *Itaque optume expressit Herculem Delphis et Alexandrum Thespiis venatorem et proelium equestre. . . .* It is possible that the "venator" is a separate work, and if so it might easily be the Meleager. More probably however "venatorem" is descriptive of "Alexandrum," and the Meleager is an unmentioned work of Lysippos himself.

Two bronze statues found at Herculaneum (Plate 60)[68] are now generally interpreted as wrestlers. They have been regarded also as runners, and this can not be altogether disproved, so far at least as 5627 is concerned; but in runners the advanced arm ought to be

[67] *N.H.,* XXXIV 66 (*SQ* 1522).

[68] Ruesch, *Guida²,* p. 214, no. 861 (5626) and 862 (5627); Brunn-Bruckmann, 354; Bulle, *Der schöne Mensch²,* pls. 91 and (head of 5627) 214; Von Mach, *University Prints,* no. 289. In each plate, as in ours, 5626 is at the left. Reinach, *Répertoire,* I 527, 3 and II 541, 1; Reinach, *Recueil,* pl. 70; Comparetti and De Petra, *La Villa Ercolanese,* pp. 269 f., nos. 42 f.; Hyde, *OVM,* pp. 230 f.; Lippold, *Kopien und Umbildungen,* p. 129.

on the same side as the advanced foot, since it is both
natural and usual in vase-paintings to bring the right
or left arm and leg forward together. For a wrestler
the position is quite satisfactory. For the two statues
as a group of wrestlers there are numerous fairly close
analogies in mosaic,[69] vase-paintings,[70] and coins;[71]
but the statues do not make a good group, because 5626
is set diagonally on its plinth, so that neither its action
nor its gaze is directed toward the other statue. It is
just possible that the sculptor intended to represent a
wrestler about to secure some side-grip on a lunging
opponent; but if so the design is not altogether satisfactory, and the statues make a better appearance when
set in corresponding positions at some distance from
each other, as for example reproductions are placed in
Constitution Square at Athens, than when seen together as a group.

Hauser was the first to observe that one model
(hardly one mould) had served for large parts of both
statues.[72] The differences are in the head, the arms,
and the advanced foot. Benndorf indeed said that the
advanced foot of 5626 was restored,[73] and this has
been repeated by later writers; but an examination of
the original statue shows that no part of either leg of
5626 is restored. In all the points where differences
exist, they are in favor of 5627. One concludes that it
is an accurate copy from an original that represented a
victorious wrestler, and that the copyist, desiring another figure as a pendant, introduced some unfortunate
modifications into his second copy.

[69] Ruesch, *Guida²*, p. 215, fig. 55.

[70] E.g., Hoppin, *A Handbook of Attic Red-figured Vases*, I, p. 426,
no. 54.

[71] E.g., *Num. Chron.*, 1921, p. 175, no. 26, pl. V.

[72] *Jb. Arch. I.*, IV, 1889, p. 116, note 8; so also Benndorf, *Jh. Oest.
Arch. I.*, IV, 1901, p. 172 and Pernice, *Jh. Oest. Arch. I.*, VII, 1904, pp.
174 f.

[73] *L.c.*

The priority of 5627 was suggested by Mahler,[74] who believed that it was a free imitation of the Ladas of Myron; Reinach[75] seems inclined to accept this hypothesis. It has not found general favor, however, and I see nothing in the head which suggests an original of the fifth century. The general style indicates a date at about the end of the fourth century. In their proportions and freedom of posture the statues show obvious Lysippian influence, and Richardson[76] and Bulle are strongly impressed by their Lysippian character. The hair and ears are indeed very like those features in the apoxyomenos. The treatment of the body, however, resembles that of the sitting Hermes, which, as has been seen, is very different from that of the apoxyomenos. The faces are totally unlike the face of the Hermes, but are almost equally un-Lysippian. The eyes, nose, and lips are so definitely distinct from his manner that, when considered together with the treatment of the body, they entirely preclude the possibility of his authorship.

Miss Richter[77] includes in "sculptures illustrating the style of Lysippos" a seated figure in the Museo Nazionale at Rome.[78] The head does not belong to the figure; it is no. 5 in our list of Meleager heads. The torso is somewhat in the style of the "Jason"; the limbs, so far as original, are rather large for the body. No close connection with Lysippos can be assumed.

There is in the Ny Carlsberg Glyptotek a seated statue of a poet, perhaps Alkaios,[79] which is confidently

[74] *Polyklet,* p. 18.

[75] *Recueil,* p. 56.

[76] *Greek Sculpture,* p. 235. Cf. also Waldhauer, *Lisipp,* p. 33 and fig. 23.

[77] *Catalogue of Casts in the Metropolitan Museum,* no. 733.

[78] Helbig, *Führer²,* II, p. 90, no. 1296; Reinach, *Répertoire,* II 193, 1; Paribeni, *Mus. Naz. Rom.⁴,* p. 84, no. 52.

[79] *De Antike Kunstvaerker,* p. 154, no. 430; *Tillaeg,* p. 152; Brunn-Bruckmann, 477; Lippold, *Griech. Porträtstatuen,* pp. 68-70, and *Antike Skulpturen der Glyptothek Ny Carlsberg,* pl. 32; also in Pauly-Wissowa; Hekler, *Greek and Roman Portraits,* pl. 109 a; Reinach, *Répertoire,* II, 568, 3.

ascribed to Lysippos by Lippold. The position of the
body and the treatment of the face make an attribution
to Lysippos possible, but the same might be said of a
great many portraits commonly assigned to the fourth
century or the early Hellenistic age. The resemblance
to the Seilenos, which Lippold emphasizes, is not very
tangible, and the attribution is only fairly probable.

Waldhauer ascribes portraits of Bias[80] and Euripides[81] to Lysippos. Both attributions are possible,
neither very convincing. The Bias would belong early
in the artist's career, the Euripides in his latest days.

A statue of Ganymede in Florence[82] is confidently
ascribed to Lysippos by Amelung, because of its resemblance to the apoxyomenos. He names the left
lower leg and foot and the left hand as the only large
restorations; from this list the head, which is given by
Dütschke among the new parts, is apparently omitted
through oversight. The general design of this composition suggests Praxiteles rather than Lysippos, but
the proportions and the treatment of anatomy are in
the manner of our artist. The photograph, from which
alone I know the statue, does not permit a careful
study of details; but one may safely accept Amelung's
testimony that the resemblance to the apoxyomenos is
great.

The support on which the eagle rests, having the
appearance of rough natural rock, is intended to represent the mountain from which Ganymede was taken.
Amelung is therefore justified in concluding that it
was present in the original, and with it the dog which
is visible at the left. The landscape element is more
distinct than in the Niobid group or in any other
sculpture in the round, so far as I know, before the

[80] In the Vatican; *Lisipp,* p. 38, fig. 28; Hekler, *77*; Arndt-Bruckmann, 371-372; Helbig, *Führer³,* I, p. 181, no. 275.

[81] In Copenhagen; *Lisipp,* p. 38, fig. 29; Hekler, 89; *De Antike
Kunstvaerker,* p. 150, no. 414 b.

[82] *Einzelaufnahmen,* 323, with text by Amelung; Dütschke, *Ant.
Bildw. in Oberitalien,* II, no. 250; Reinach, *Répertoire,* II 475, I.

Farnese Bull. If the original was really made by Lysippos, we have in this group one example of his representation of dogs.

One of Lysippos's feminine figures remains to be mentioned: it is described as a "drunken flute-player" (feminine).[83] "Sans doute une Ménade," says M. Collignon.[84] But *tibicina* should be a translation of αὐλητρίς, a word of perfectly definite meaning: the statue represented one of the girls who enlivened Greek banquets with music and otherwise. If Klein[85] and others refuse to believe that Lysippos would make such a statue, that is their affair; it is by no means incredible that the flute-girl or a patron might desire a statue of her and be able to pay for it. In forming an idea of the figure it is necessary to remember that there are various degrees of drunkenness. The famous old woman ascribed to Myron of Thebes would have excited some astonishment at the end of the fourth century; but not a beautiful girl represented in that state of good cheer where one is brilliant, convivial, and only beginning to find the kylix a trifle topheavy.

Studniczka,[86] Arndt,[87] S. Reinach,[88] and Waldhauer[89] are inclined to regard a charming statue in Berlin[90] as copied from Lysippos's flute-girl. There is another copy in Frankfurt (Plate 61)[91] and a third in the Bibliothèque Nationale.[92] The figure in Berlin has usually been termed a Maenad, but Bulle calls it a

[83] Pliny, *N.H.*, XXXIV, 63 (App. 1, 3) ; Lippold in Pauly-Wissowa, no. 27.

[84] *Lysippe*, p. 87.

[85] *Gesch. d. griech. Kunst*, II, p. 361.

[86] *Die Siegesgöttin*, p. 24, note 2.

[87] *La Glyptothèque Ny Carlsberg*, p. 188.

[88] Quoted by Six, in *Jb. Arch. I.*, XXXIII, 1918, p. 48.

[89] *Lisipp*, p. 34 and fig. 25.

[90] *Kurze Beschreibung*[3], p. 25, no. 208; Reinach, *Répertoire*, II 398, 1; Bulle, *Der schöne Mensch*[2], pl. 138; Neugebauer, *Studien über Skopas*, p. 54; Klein, *Gesch. d. griech. Kunst*, III, p. 241.

[91] *Kurzes Verzeichnis der Bildwerke* (1915), p. 30, no. 129.

[92] Reinach, *Répertoire*, II 809, 2.

dancer. It is certainly dancing and not rushing along in
frenzy as is the Maenad of Skopas. The castanets which
appear on the support would not prove that the figure
was a Maenad, if they were known to be present in the
original. Of course in the original there was no support,
and the addition of the castanets in the copy merely
shows that there were no castanets in the hands of the
figure, since if there were it would be absurd to add a
second set on the support. In no copy is there any
trace of a fawn-skin or any other attribute that would
identify a Maenad. In all probability, then, it is simply a dancer. The twist of the body suggests the
influence of Lysippos, and nothing in the figure offers
evidence against the attribution; but the corpus of certain Lysippian works contains no analogous figure, so
the conjecture can not be confirmed. If the Medici
Aphrodite be admitted as a work of Lysippos, the identification of the flute-girl becomes more probable: both
statues show a taste for the representation of the
youthful, yet voluptuous, female body.

The figure in the Villa Albani,[93] which Mme.
Maviglia suggests in this connection, is a real Maenad,
as the presence of the skin of an animal shows, and
hence can not be copied from the statue of Lysippos.

Waldhauer has ascribed a female head in Munich
to Lysippos.[94] The rather heavy, round face and the
small eyes do suggest the Lysippian type, especially
when contrasted with Praxitelean heads; but an attribution to the master himself is bold. A girl satyr in
the Lateran[94a] is quite possibly copied from a piquant
work of Lysippos. It suggests the Eros considerably,

[93] Reinach, *Répertoire*, I 389, 8; Helbig, *Führer²*, II, p. 435, no. 1886;
Maviglia, *op. cit.*, pp. 98-104 and fig. 29.

[94] Waldhauer, *Lisipp*, p. 34 and fig. 24; Brunn-Bruckmann, pl. 125.
A replica in the Hermitage is described by Kieseritzky as Greek work
of the fourth century (Kieseritzky, *Catalogue*, p. 137, no. 292 B).

[94a] Benndorf-Schöne, no. 273; Helbig, *Führer²*, II, no. 1185; *Einzelaufnahmen*, no. 2145.

and its hair, eyes, lips, and shape of face have some resemblance to the corresponding features of the apoxyomenos.

The majesty of Zeus and the gayety of an exhilarated flute-girl did not mark the limits of Lysippos's versatility; he also achieved distinction as a sculptor of animals. Pliny mentions dogs as especially notable among his works,[95] and it is not probable that the author had in mind only the dogs in the Krateros group or in similar groups. In another passage the same writer describes a celebrated bronze statue of a dog (male or female) which was in Rome: the animal was licking a wound.[96] Pliny names no artist for this dog; but statues of dogs that were famous must have been few, and one naturally thinks of an artist who was particularly celebrated for his figures of dogs. A bitch in the Museo Barracco[97] is, without much doubt, copied from the statue mentioned by Pliny, and in the museum it is boldly labeled "di Lisippo." It may well be true; but it can hardly be proved, even if we accept the dog in the Corsini Ganymede group as certainly Lysippian. The Barracco dog seems somewhat more likely to belong to Lysippos than another type of which several examples are known[98] and which is suggested by Collignon as Lysippian.

His skill in the representation of horses must have been remarkable. The effect of his great quadriga at Rhodes, which Pliny apparently thought the finest of all his works, must have depended largely on the spirited portrayal of the horses. We are told also that he made quadrigas "of many kinds."[99] He must have found abundant opportunity for his skill in the series

[95] *N.H.*, XXXIV 63 (App. 1, 3).   [96] *N.H.*, XXXIV 38.

[97] Reinach, *Répertoire*, II 762, 4; *Collection Barracco*, pl. 58, p. 45; Helbig, *Führer*³, I, p. 628, no. 1140.

[98] Amelung, *Skulpt. d. Vat. Mus.*, II, pp. 162 ff., nos. 64-65; Collignon, *Lysippe*, pp. 94 f., fig. 23.

[99] Pliny, *N.H.*, XXXIV, 64 (App. 1, 3).

of equestrian statues at Dion and also in the Krateros
group, if he made the horse in it. In the Palazzo dei
Conservatori there is a bronze horse, evidently of
Greek workmanship, which once bore a rider.[100] The
form of the horse is slender and elegant, and the ner-
vous vivacity of the high-bred steed is rendered with
extraordinary success. It is safe to say that if the
rider had been as well preserved as the horse, the work
would have been reckoned far superior to any antique
equestrian statue that now exists. The statuettes in
Naples, which appear to be traceable to the Granikos
monument, are of no extraordinary merit in themselves, but one may divine something of the fire and
spirit of the originals. The most famous of Lysippos's horses, apparently, belonged neither to a chariot
nor to an equestrian statue: it was a free horse, which
later stood in Constantinople.[101] The authors are enthusiastic in speaking of the exultant and spirited pride
of the steed.

At Lampsakos there was a slain lion by Lysippos,
which Agrippa took to Rome.[102] Lippold suggests
that it may have marked the tomb of soldiers killed in
a battle,[103] and this may be right; but it is not known
that a *slain* lion was used in this way in antiquity, and
no battle in the lifetime of Lysippos, for which such a
monument would naturally be placed at Lampsakos, is
known. It will be remembered that there was a lion
also in the Krateros group, though we can not be sure
whether it was made by Lysippos. It seems that Lysippos might without much trouble improve on the

[100] Collignon, *Lysippe,* fig. 22; Helbig, *Führer³,* I, p. 543, no. 955;
Jones, *Palazzo dei Conservatori,* p. 171, no. 4, pl. 61 (where the horse
is underestimated and called Roman); Reinach, *Répertoire,* II 739, 5.

[101] App. 1, 89-91; Lippold in Pauly-Wissowa, no. 40.

[102] Strabo, XIII, 590 (App. 1, 88).

[103] In Pauly-Wissowa, no. 39. On the general subject see Rambo,
The Lion in Greek Art.

usual treatment of lions in Greek art, but one can not tell whether he did so.

Prokopios[104] mentions Lysippos as a possible author of a bronze bull that stood in Rome.   He also suggests Pheidias; from which it is evident that he knew nothing about the fact in the case.

[104] *De Bello Gothico*, IV, 21, 12-13 (App. 1, 92).

CHAPTER XII

CONCLUSIONS

The survey of the evidence on Lysippos is completed. It has been the plan to consider everything from which information on the life and work of the artist may reasonably be expected, and everything from which serious attempts have been made, whether reasonably or not, to derive such information. It remains now to summarize the results and to draw such general conclusions as are possible on the style of the sculptor and the general aesthetic attitude which found expression in his work.

In the Thebes base, the "Old Fountain" base, and the base for the statue of Polydamas we have three pieces of sure, but all too slight, evidence. There are good copies of two of his statues of Herakles, of his Eros, and of his apoxyomenos. Three of his portraits of Alexander are clearly represented by existing sculptures: one of them by a copy which, though inexact in details, gives a satisfactory idea of the noble, yet realistic, portraits that delighted the monarch. By comparative study alone, three and only three works can be ascribed to him with certainty: the bearded head in Ny Carlsberg, the Seilenos with the Infant Dionysos, and the Meleager. Perhaps it is justifiable to add the Ganymede, relying on the confidence with which so good a judge as Amelung announced the attribution on the evidence of morphology. The Lysippian origin of the originals of the Seleukos bust, the Socrates, and the bronzes in Naples supported by rudders, though not definitely demonstrable, is virtually certain. The Medici Aphrodite is ascribed to him with great probability. The Demeter and Kore are attributed to him more reasonably than to any other artist, far more reasonably than to Praxiteles; but certainty can not be claimed. For the rest we must rely on the descriptions of ancient authors and on inexact imitations; but these suffice, in a number of instances, to give a good general idea of the original work: thus we feel sure of the Lysippian ideal of Zeus, though we have nothing that can be proved to be copied directly from any of his representations of the god.

Perhaps one would expect, *a priori*, that many of his works would be preserved in copies. It may well be that we have more than we can identify. For Lysippos as for all other Greek sculptors—perhaps Praxiteles should be excepted—our sure evidence is scanty: we know only a few works, we know little of their chronology, and we know them only through copies. On this basis we can identify other works that belong to the same period or periods of the master's career and are of somewhat the same kind as those known to us; but the limits of a versatile artist's style can not be defined without more evidence than we possess for any of the Greeks. The attribution of portraits is always difficult in the most favorable circumstances, and it is probable that portraits made up a considerable proportion of Lysippos's production.

Even with this clearly in mind, one can not suggest many types that, in the present state of our knowledge, can reasonably be assigned to Lysippos. Before this condition excites distrust of the methods used, there are other considerations to be noted. The scarcity of copies of the apoxyomenos is plausibly explained by the difficulty of making an effective copy in marble, and the same would probably apply to other works of the master: when an artist utilizes to the utmost the possibilities of one material, his work is not likely to be susceptible of satisfactory translation into another. Then, too, several of his most famous works could hardly be copied in any material: accurate copies of colossal statues, such as his Zeus and Herakles at

Tarentum, were rare, and I suppose that nobody ever made an accurate copy of a quadriga. Great groups such as the lion-hunt of Krateros and the Granikos group certainly would not be copied. It is therefore no cause for surprise that the works on which the artist's fame primarily rested are known to us only through literature.

Judging from the hints of ancient authors, one might expect to find in Lysippos's work the influence of Polykleitos and of Euphranor. In the fourth chapter the influence of Polykleitos was considered: Lysippos doubtless studied the old master's system of proportion and admired the care and consistency with which the system was followed, and surely he studied the Doryphoros as a masterpiece of craftsmanship; but he could not, in his time, show a direct and strong Polykleitan influence unless he was a deliberate archaizer, and that he certainly was not. But was there a gradual development from Polykleitos through his pupils to Lysippos? Mahler, in his book on Polykleitos, attempted to trace such a development, but not with complete success. Considering the works which can be ascribed, with some confidence, to the successors of Polykleitos, it is difficult to find the smallest trace of any debt owed to them by Lysippos. It is true that Herakles was represented with a club under his left arm by one of those artists; but Lysippos transformed the figure so thoroughly, in making the Farnese type, that there is hardly question of real indebtedness. Since Euphranor made a special study of proportion, his work must have been of interest to Lysippos; but the degree of his influence can hardly be determined at present. The praying woman, which is very plausibly ascribed to Euphranor, has an expressive and elastic posture which suggests that the elder artist was in some respects a true precursor of Lysippos.

The one artist whose influence is obvious and cer-

.tain is Skopas. This is strikingly evident in the statues that have been ascribed to both sculptors. The similarities in style are notable: the overshadowed eyes, which so materially affect the appearance of statues of the fourth century, were introduced by Skopas and adopted by Lysippos. In his use of slender proportions, also, Lysippos was probably influenced by the Attic school, which had previously adopted proportions much slighter than those of Polykleitos or (apparently) his successors. It is not alone nor primarily in such matters as these that Lysippos shows the influence of Skopas. A consideration of the Dresden Maenad, of the Tegean gable-figures, and of the Mausoleum frieze discloses the partial source, at least, of the freedom of posture and the vigorous expression that appeared in the art of Lysippos.

Lysippos rendered the hair more vividly than his predecessors, and he was remarkable for "extreme delicacy of execution even in the smallest details." These features are of course not perfectly discernible in copies. His innovations in proportion, however, are clear enough in the apoxyomenos, the Farnese Herakles, and the Seilenos. In the ponderation of his figures he seems to have used the advanced "Spielbein" more than any earlier artist.

In his style of design, as indeed in many respects, Lysippos appears to have been the antithesis of his older contemporary Praxiteles. Praxiteles liked to leave the torsos of his figures as free as possible of obstruction: the arms are so placed as to harmonize with, but not to cross, the long and rhythmical lines of the body. We find this sort of design in Lysippos also, in the Farnese Herakles and the Meleager; but we also find another kind, in which the arms cross the body and give a very different effect: contrast the Hermes of Praxiteles with the Seilenos. The apoxyomenos also is a clear example; and the Medici Aphrodite is another, though there the artist was probably imitating an earlier work by Skopas.

When the arms cross the body, the spectator is invited to note the dimension of depth, the difference in plane between the parts of the body; and this is greatly emphasized when the arms project forward toward the spectator and define a plane perpendicular to the plane of the body, as in the apoxyomenos. Here we touch on one of the most noteworthy characteristics of Lysippos, and one in respect to which he most distinctly affected the course of Hellenistic art. It has long been recognized that Greek statues in general were designed to be seen from one point of view: however perfectly rounded the figure, its essential design, like that of a picture, was in one plane, and the spectator's gaze ought to be perpendicular to this plane. But Lysippos, with the arms crossing the body and extending to the front—straight out of the picture— and the body twisted forward or back, makes it impossible to gain a satisfying view from any one point, and compels the observer to take his view from several angles. A statue of this kind must present beauty of mass and line from any point of view. In this way Lysippos looks forward to groups such as the Uffizi pankratiasts and the Farnese Bull, which can not even be understood until examined from all sides. Lysippos may be regarded as the representative of a conception in which the difference between sculpture in the round and painting or bas-relief is for the first time fully recognized and frankly utilized as the basic consideration in design.

Pliny records a statement that purports to come from the master himself:[1] he said that whereas the older artists had represented men as they were, he represented them as they appeared to be. Much ingenuity has been expended on the interpretation of this

[1] N.H., XXXIV 65 (App. 1, 3).

passage,[2] but with no perfectly satisfactory result. Perhaps it is hardly worth while: Socrates and many after him have noted the peculiar inanity that frequently appears in the comments of artists on their own works. Certainly the statement can not be brought into relation with the three-dimensional character which was really, so far as we can judge, the principal innovation of Lysippos. The context in Pliny suggests that the "appearing" had something to do with proportion; and it has been suggested that Lysippos gave special attention to effective proportion in colossal statues, which, as is well known, can not be made simply by enlarging statues of ordinary size. But this is by no means convincing, and in Pliny the juxtaposition of two clauses is always likely to be accidental.

There is one explanation that is surely to be rejected: that Pliny mistranslated his original, which had "ought to be" instead of "appeared to be."[3] This makes Lysippos class himself as an idealist in contrast to "the older sculptors," who are Polykleitos and his followers; and this is absurd. If Lysippos "certainly disclaims realism"[4] he certainly attributes realism to Polykleitos; and if he does that, no statement of his deserves any consideration.

It is probable that Lysippos's remark had no technical or specific meaning. "Quales viderentur esse" may well refer to the appearance of reality in a general sense; to expressiveness, vividness, the quality of being "animosa," which was added to (not substituted for) the accurate physical representation of the older artists. To this effect various factors would con-

[2] *Jb. Arch. I.,* VIII, 1893, pp. 39-51 (Kekulé) ; *Arch. Anz.,* VIII, 1893, pp. 11 f. (Diels, Trendelenburg, Kalkmann, and Conze) ; *Arch. Anz.,* XIII, 1898, pp. 181 ff. (Schöne and Kekulé) ; Collignon, *Lysippe,* pp. 107 f.; *C. R. Acad. Insc.,* 1921, pp. 262-269 (Homolle).

[3] So first K. O. Müller (*Kunstarchaeologische Werke,* II, pp. 165 ff.). Percy Gardner (*J.H.S.,* XXV, 1905, p. 250) thinks that "the suggestion is at all events ingenious."

[4] Gardner, *l.c.*

tribute: a free and elastic posture, treatment of the arms and legs which makes their action conspicuous, and expression of emotion in the face or position. In these respects Lysippos did, unless our scanty evidence misleads us, make a decided advance beyond the older Peloponnesians, and some advance beyond any earlier sculptor. The Hermes of Praxiteles is simply a beautiful god, though as it chances a child is attached to his arm: the Seilenos of Lysippos is interested in the child which he holds. The Lansdowne Herakles is Herakles the hero: the Lysippian figures of Herakles express pathos or the joy of wine. The Doryphoros is an athlete: the apoxyomenos is a pensive athlete.

In all this there is a dangerous possibility of sentimentality, sensationalism, and affectation. The third danger Lysippos escaped, but it is doubtful whether he entirely avoided either of the other two. The type of the Loeb bronze Poseidon is probably a little later than Lysippos, but the beginning, at least, of a swagger is perceptible in some of the similar figures that seem to be more closely connected with him. And the deliberate introduction of pathos into a figure that does not call for it, such as Herakles, is a distinct step toward sentimentality.

If Lysippos was not essentially an idealist, it is equally true that nothing authorizes us to believe that he was particularly given to realism. Quintilian[5] indeed names him with Praxiteles as having been "most successful in adhering to nature"; but he goes on to say that Demetrios was "censured for too much exactness in that respect," so he evidently does not mean that Lysippos and Praxiteles were the most realistic of Greek sculptors;—a statement that would be obviously absurd as applied to Praxiteles. The meaning apparently is that these two artists made the most effective use, in the judgment of the critic, of their obser-

[5] *De Institutione Oratoria*, XII, 10, 9 (App. 1, 12).

vation of nature. Demetrios was much earlier than Lysippos, so it is clear that the latter made no advance in the direction of realism in style. He may, however, have introduced improvements in the technique of naturalistic representation in works which demanded naturalism; this is indicated by the fact that his brother Lysistratos was said to be the first to take a mould from the face.

In his portraits we may safely assume that Lysippos was as realistic as seemed to him advisable in each case. Let us consider in comparison the work of Tintoretto or Titian. It includes no such portraits as the head of Alexander in the British Museum; none of their portraits would have required identification for the subject or his acquaintances. Yet it is hardly possible that all their sitters possessed in reality the nobility with which the Venetians endow them: in some cases the nobility was doubtless contributed largely by the artist, in others almost entirely by the sitters. Various wrinkles are undoubtedly omitted in many portraits; but it is agreed that there have been no greater portrait-painters and few as great. We may conceive that Lysippos portrayed his patrons in the same general manner, when they were kings or generals; such realism as we see in the bearded bronze head from Olympia would be employed for other subjects.

Between Lysippos and Tintoretto an analogy of a more general sort may be found. Tintoretto is said to have boasted that he combined the line of Michelangelo with the color of Titian. He made the combination very successfully, not borrowing slavishly from either, and added extraordinary physical and mental vigor and virtuosity in technique greater than that possessed by either of the others; this made possible productiveness and rapidity of execution that astonished his contemporaries. But it is usually recognized that his figures are not, after all, so mighty as those of Michelangelo, nor his color in sum so beautiful as that of Titian, nor his conceptions equal to those of either of them: intellectual vigor and technical expertness could not atone for the lack of creative genius and the highest perfection of taste.   Now Skopas, if magnified several times, would not be unlike the titanic Florentine, and Titian and Polykleitos are both characterized by dignified and somewhat impassive formal beauty. The analogy can not be pressed too far; but it does seem that Lysippos sought to combine the technical and theoretical expertness of the Peloponnesians (considerably changed by his own contributions) with the expression and life of Skopas (made somewhat superficial, and applied without perfect discrimination). Though our conclusion must be based on scanty evidence, it appears that Lysippos was a smaller man than either of his predecessors.

One frequently finds, more or less clearly expressed, the feeling that Lysippos ushered in the decline; that he was the first of Hellenistic sculptors rather than the last of the great masters.   This is most definitely set forth in the opinion of the late Jay Hambidge,[6] that Lysippos introduced static symmetry into the place of the dynamic symmetry that had been the foundation of design in the great age.   Upon this I would remark only that it is right to associate Lysippos with the succeeding, rather than the preceding, epoch.   The position thus assigned him is a very high one, so far as influence is concerned; the succeeding epoch was formed by him more than by any other artist.

All that we know of Lysippos suggests great vigor in the man.   Largely self-taught, he disregarded to a great extent the traditions prevailing in his home, and

---

[6] Never expressed in print so far as I know; I learn it through the kindness of Mr. Howard Giles.

rather followed the work of a foreign master, though by no means slavishly. He studied his art for himself, and made various important innovations. He shrank from no subject susceptible of treatment in bronze: gods, men, women, and animals were all treated by him with conspicuous success, and goddesses too, if we have not erred in attributing to him the original of the Medici Aphrodite. He was equally successful in his execution of colossi and of statuettes a foot high; in his expression of the majesty of Zeus, the pathos of the weary Herakles, the fiery heart of Alexander, and the exultant pride of a spirited horse; while the boyish grace of Eros, the youthful grace of the apoxyomenos, and the seductive beauty of a young woman whom he called Aphrodite found adequate representation at his hands. Assuredly, a man who could produce such a variety of works in so satisfactory a manner must have brought to his work an extraordinary amount of intellectual vigor. He must have brought also a phenomenal command of technique. We can not see in him a profoundly spiritual artist, who put his soul into every work. Skopas may have been such a man, but Lysippos worked too easily.

His life suggests that of Titian. Titian died—probably—at the age of ninety-nine; he painted unweariedly and well to the last. Throughout his career he was recognized generally as the greatest painter of the time, and as one of the first gentlemen of his time: kings were his guests and friends. The meager records sketch for us a not dissimilar life in the case of Lysippos. He lived to a great age; Alexander, Kassander, and Seleukos were his patrons. We may imagine him in his last days as an old man with such strength as belongs to the aged, full of honors and contented in his fame.

ADDENDA

Page 46, line 11: Doubts have been expressed as to the interpretation of the Conservatori "charioteer"; cf. Jones, *Palazzo dei Conservatori,* p. 211 and addenda. Nudity was so usual in Greek sculpture, however, that a nude charioteer should not excite surprise.

Page 137, line 8 from bottom: On the Hellenistic portrait statue see Carpenter, in *A.J.A.,* XXXI, 1927, pp. 160-168. He denies all Lysippian character and regards the statue, except the head, as a tolerably close imitation of an original of the fifth century, similar to the Ares Borghese. This I take to be wrong. The best analogies for the position are those mentioned in the text; compare also the Farnese Herakles and the Meleager. I know no figure of the fifth century in which the hand holding the lance is raised so high. It is true that the details of the torso are not treated as Lysippos would have treated them; but the various followers of a great master do not all show his influence in all ways.—In connection with the Argive coin, the Poseidon of Melos should be mentioned: except for the garment around the lower part of the body, it corresponds well to the coin-type. The body is slender, and perhaps Mme. Maviglia was right in referring it to a Lysippian original, though it certainly is not an exact copy.

Page 188, line 4: It should be stated that this "Prudence" belongs to the pulpit made by Giovanni Pisano and his pupils, 1302-1311. The pulpit has recently been put together in the cathedral at Pisa.

Page 194, note 25: Add references: *Memoirs of the American Academy in Rome,* Vol. VI; *A. J. A.,* XXXI, 1927, pp. 163 f. (Carpenter).

Page 232, last paragraph: Amelung (*A. J. A.,* XXXI, 1927, pp. 281-86) states that the original of the statuette in the British Museum is represented also by a life-size herm in Naples (Bernoulli, *Griech. Ikonographie,* I, p. 187, no. 11, pl. XXIV); and he publishes two reliefs, representing the conversation of Socrates with Diotima, in which the figure of Socrates resembles the statuette somewhat. It does not appear to be sure, however, that the reliefs are imitated directly from the original of the statuette. Amelung feels sure of the genuineness of the statuette.

APPENDIX I

BIOGRAPHICAL AND GENERAL

TRANSLATIONS

1. Pliny, N. H., XXXIV, 37. (Trans. Jex-Blake.)

   Still I should like to touch on the most famous [statues], and those which any particular circumstance has made noteworthy, and to name the illustrious artists. Even the works of individual sculptors are too numerous to be catalogued; Lysippos, for example, is said to have made fifteen hundred pieces of statuary, all of such merit that any one alone would bring him fame. Their number was discovered when his heir broke open his money-box after his death, for it was his custom to lay by a piece of gold out of the price he received for each statue.

2. Pliny, N. H., XXXIV 51. (Trans. Jex-Blake.)

   Lysippos lived in the hundred and thirteenth [328-325 B. C.], in the days of Alexander the Great; so also did his brother Lysistratos.

3. Pliny, N. H., XXXIV 61-67. (Trans. Jex-Blake.)

   61 Duris declares that Lysippos of Sikyon was no man's pupil; that he was originally a coppersmith, and was encouraged to venture on a higher path by the words of Eupompos. That painter when asked which of the earlier artists he followed, pointed to a crowd of people, and replied that nature should be imitated and not any artist.

   62 Lysippos produced more works than any other artist, possessing, as I have said, a most prolific genius. Among them is the man scraping himself, which Marcus Agrippa dedicated in front of his baths. In this statue the Emperor Tiberius took a marvellous delight, and though capable of self-control in the first years of his reign, he could not refrain from having the statue removed into his private chamber, substituting another in its place. The populace of Rome resented this so deeply that they raised an outcry in the theatre, demanding the restitution of the Ἀποξυόμενον

   63 to which the emperor was fain to yield, in spite of the passion he had conceived for the statue. Lysippos has also won fame by his drunken flute-player, his dogs and huntsman, and above all by the four-horse chariot and the figure of the Sun made for the Rhodians. He also made a number of portraits of Alexander the Great, beginning with one of him as a boy, which the Emperor Nero, who was

APPENDIX I

BIOGRAPHICAL AND GENERAL

1. **Pliny, N. H., XXXIV 37. (Ed. Sellers and Jex-Blake.)**

   Insignia maxime et aliqua de causa notata voluptarium sit attigisse artificesque celebratos nominavisse, singulorum quoque inexplicabili multitudine, cum Lysippus MD opera fecisse prodatur, tantae omnia artis ut claritatem possent dare vel singula, numerum apparuisse defuncto eo, cum thensaurum effregisset heres, solitum enim ex manipretio cuiusque signi denarios seponere aureos singulos.

2. **Pliny, N. H., XXXIV 51. (Ed. Sellers and Jex-Blake.)**

   CXIII Lysippus fuit, cum et Alexander Magnus, item Lysistratus frater eius.

3. **Pliny, N. H., XXXIV 61-67. (Ed. Sellers and Jex-Blake.)**

   Lysippum Sicyonium Duris negat ullius fuisse dis- *61* cipulum, sed primo aerarium fabrum audendi rationem cepisse pictoris Eupompi responso. eum enim interrogatum, quem sequeretur antecedentium, dixisse monstrata hominum multitudine naturam ipsam imitandam esse, non artificem. plurima ex omnibus signa fecit, ut diximus, *62* fecundissimae artis, inter quae destringentem se quem M. Agrippa ante Thermas suas dicavit mire gratum Tiberio principi. non quivit temperare sibi in eo, quamquam imperiosus sui inter initia principatus, transtulitque in cubiculum alio signo substituto, cum quidem tanta populi Romani contumacia fuit ut theatri clamoribus reponi apoxyomenon flagitaverit princepsque quamquam adamatum resposuerit. nobilitatur Lysippus et temulenta tibicina et canibus ac *63* venatione, in primis vero quadriga cum Sole Rhodiorum. fecit et Alexandrum Magnum multis operibus a pueritia eius orsus. quam statuam inaurari iussit Nero princeps delectatus admodum illa, dein, cum pretio perisset gratia artis, detractum est aurum, pretiosiorque talis existimabatur etiam cicatricibus operis atque concisuris in quibus aurum haeserat remanentibus. idem fecit Hephaestionem Alex- *64* andri Magni amicum, quem quidam Polyclito adscribunt,

greatly charmed with the statue, ordered to be gilded.
Then, as this costly addition spoiled the beauty of the
work, the gold was removed, and the statue was considered
more valuable without it, in spite of the scars upon it and
the incisions for fixing the gold. Further he made a
64   statue of Hephaistion, the friend of Alexander the Great,
which some ascribe to Polykleitos, although that artist
lived almost a hundred years earlier. We have also from
his hand an Alexander in a hunting group, which is conse-
crated at Delphoi, a Satyr at Athens and a troup of Alexander's bodyguard, in which all his friends' portraits are
rendered with great fidelity. This group was transported
to Rome by Metellus after the conquest of Makedonia. By
Lysippos also are various four-horse chariots. His chief
65   contributions to the art of sculpture are said to consist
in his vivid rendering of the hair, in making the heads
smaller than older artists had done, and the bodies slimmer
and with less flesh, thus increasing the apparent height of
his figures. There is no Latin word for the canon of symmetry [συμμετρία] which he was so careful to preserve,
bringing innovations which had never been thought of before into the square canon of the older artists, and he often
said that the difference between himself and them was that
they represented men as they were, and he as they appeared
to be. His chief characteristic is extreme delicacy of execution even in the smallest details.

He left artists of high reputation in his sons and pupils,
66   Laippos, Boedas, and above all Euthykrates; the latter
however imitated not so much the refinement as the perse-
verance of his father, choosing to win approval by an austere rather than a lighter style of execution. In this manner
he made for Delphoi an admirable statue of Herakles, for
Thespiai an Alexander hunting, a group of the Thespiades
and a combat between horsemen, a statue of Trophonios
within his oracular cave, several chariots with four horses,
a horse carrying hunting prongs, and hunting dogs.

His pupil was Teisikrates, also a native of Sikyon, who
67   followed more closely the school of Lysippos, so that many
of his works can hardly be distinguished from those of the
master: witness his portrait of an old man at Thebes, of
king Demetrios and of Peukestes, who saved Alexander's
life and well deserves the honour of a statue.

4. Pliny, N. H., XXXV 153. (Trans. Jex-Blake.)
Lysistratos of Sikyon, brother of the Lysippos whom I

cum is centum prope annis ante fuerit, item Alexandri
venationem quae Delphis sacrata est, Athenis Satyrum, turmam Alexandri in qua amicorum eius imagines summa omnium similitudine expressit—hanc Metellus Macedonia su-
bacta transtulit Romam—fecit et quadrigas multorum gen-
erum. statuariae arti plurimum traditur contulisse capillum
exprimendo, capita minora faciendo quam antiqui, corpora   65
graciliora siccioraque, per quae proceritas signorum maior
videretur. non habet Latinum nomen symmetria quam
diligentissime custodit nova intactaque ratione quadratas
veterum staturas permutando, vulgoque dicebat ab illis
factos quales essent homines, a se quales viderentur esse.
propriae huius videntur esse argutiae operum custoditae in
minimis quoque rebus. filios et discipulos reliquit laudatos   66
artifices Laippum, Boedan, sed ante omnes Euthycraten,
quamquam is constantiam potius imitatus patris quam ele-
gantiam austero maluit genere quam iucundo placere.
itaque optime expressit Herculem Delphis et Alexandrum
Thespis venatorem et Thespiadas, proelium equestre, simu-
lacrum ipsum Trophonii ad oraculum, quadrigas com-
plures, equum cum fuscinis, canes venantium. huius porro   67
discipulus fuit Tisicrates et ipse Sicyonius, sed Lysippi
sectae propior, ut vix discernantur complura signa, ceu
senex Thebanus et Demetrius rex, Peucestes Alexandri
Magni servator, dignus tanta gloria.

4. Pliny, N. H., XXXV 153. (Ed. Sellers and Jex-Blake.)
   Hominis autem imaginem gypso e facie ipsa primus

have mentioned in an earlier book, was however the first who obtained portraits by making a plaster mould on the actual features, and introduced the practice of taking from the plaster a wax cast on which he made the final corrections. He also first first rendered likenesses with exactitude, for previous artists had only tried to make them as beautiful as possible.

4a. Anth. Pal. XVI (Plan. App. IV), 344. (Trans. Paton.)

A. Who art thou, dear young man, the point of thy chin just marked with down? *B.* Stranger, I am Porphyrius. *A.* Thy country? *B.* Africa. *A.* Who hath honored thee? *B.* The Emperor, on account of my driving. *A.* Who testifies to it? *B.* The faction of the Blues. *A.* Porphyrius, thou shouldst have had Lysippus, a skilled sculptor, to testify to so many victories.

5. Athenaios, Deipnosophistai, XI 784; Kaibel vol. III p. 24.

They say that the sculptor Lysippos, for the gratification of Kassander, when he founded Kassandria, since he was ambitious and desired to find some peculiar vessel, on account of the great quantity of Mendaean wine that was exported from the city, made great efforts and, having brought together many vessels of various kinds and taken something of the pattern from each, made his own individual form.

6. Cicero, Brutus, 86, 296.

As Lysippos used to say that the Doryphoros of Polykleitos was a master to him, so you say that the advocacy of the Servilian Law was a master to you.

7. Cicero, De Oratore, III 7, 26.

There is one art of moulding, in which Myron, Polykleitos, and Lysippos were preeminent; these were all unlike one another, but in such a way that you do not wish any one of them to be unlike himself.

8. Pseudo-Cicero, Ad Herennium, IV 6.

It was not in that way that Chares learned from Lysippos to make statues—that Lysippos showed a Myronic head, arms of Praxiteles, and a Polykleitan breast—but he saw the master making everything in his presence; he could

omnium expressit ceraque in eam formam gypsi infusa emendare instituit Lysistratus Sicyonius, frater Lysippi de quo diximus. hic et similitudines reddere instituit, ante eum quam pulcherrimas facere studebatur.

4a. Anth. Pal. XVI (Plan. App. IV), 344. (Ed. Paton.)

α. Τίς τελέθεις, φίλε κοῦρε, γενειάδος ἄκρα χα-
ράσσων;
β. Ὦ ξένε, Πορφύριος. α. Τίς πατρίς; β. Ἡ
Λιβύη.
α. Τίς δέ σε νῦν τίμησεν; β. Ἄναξ, χάριν ἱππο-
συνάων.
α. Τίς μάρτυς τελέθει; β. Δῆμος ὁ τῶν Βενέτων.
α. Ἔπρεπέ σοι Λύσιππον ἔχειν ἐπιμάρτυρα νίκης
τοσσατίης, πλάστην ἴδμονα, Πορφύριε.

5. Athenaios, Deipnosophistai, XI 784. (Ed. Kaibel, vol.
III, p. 24.)

Λύσιππον τὸν ἀνδριαντοποιόν φασι Κασάνδρῳ χαριζόμενον, ὅτε συνῴκισε τὴν Κασάνδρειαν, φιλοδοξοῦντι καὶ βουλομένῳ ἴδιόν τινα εὑρέσθαι κέραμον διὰ τὸ πολὺν ἐξάγεσθαι τὸν Μενδαῖον οἶνον ἐκ τῆς πόλεως, φιλοτιμηθῆναι καὶ πολλὰ καὶ παντοδαπὰ γένη παραθέμενον κεραμίων ἐξ ἑκάστου ἀποπλασάμενον ἴδιον ποιῆσαι πλάσμα.

6. Cicero, Brutus, 86, 296. (Ed. Friedrich.)
Ut Polycliti doryphorum sibi Lysippus aiebat, sic tu suasionem legis Serviliae tibi magistram fuisse.

7. Cicero, De Oratore, III 7, 26. (Ed. Friedrich.)
Una fingendi est ars, in qua praestantes fuerunt Myro Polyclitus Lysippus; qui omnes inter se dissimiles fuerunt, sed ita tamen, ut neminem sui velis esse dissimilem.

8. Pseudo-Cicero, Ad Herennium, IV 6. (Ed. Friedrich.)
Chares ab Lysippo statuas facere non isto modo didicit, ut Lysippus caput ostenderet Myronium, brachia Praxitelae, pectus Polycletium, sed omnia coram magistrum facientem videbat, ceterorum opera vel sua sponte poterat

certainly study the works of others by himself.   Those people believe that students who wish to learn these things can be taught more conveniently by another scheme.

9. Columella, De Re Rustica, I, praefatio, 31.

Nor were those of a later age—Bryaxis, Lysippos, Praxiteles, and Polykleitos—bewildered by the beauty of the Olympian Zeus or of the Pheidiac Athena and ashamed to make trial of what they could accomplish or of how far they could advance.

9a. Nikephoros Choumnos (Boissonade, Anecdot. III, p. 357).

(Lysippos and Apelles made) living images, lacking only breath and movement.

10. Petronius, Satirikon, 88.   (Trans. Heseltine.)

Lysippus died of starvation as he brooded over the lines of a single statue.

11. Propertius, Elegiae, III 9, 9.   (Trans. Butler.)

'Tis Lysippus' glory to mould statues with all the fire of life.

12. Quintilian, De Institutione Oratoria, XII 10, 9.   (Trans. Butler.)

Lysippus and Praxiteles are asserted to be supreme as regards faithfulness to nature.   For Demetrius is blamed for carrying realism too far, and is less concerned about the beauty than the truth of his work.

13. Suidas, Lexicon, v. Ἀγαλματοποιοί.

That is, artists; consummate statuaries are Lysippos, Polykleitos, and Pheidias.

14. Suidas, Lexicon, v. Χειρουργοί.

The best and consummate artists are Pheidias, Lysippos, and Polykleitos.

15. Varro, De Lingua Latina, IX, 18.

For Lysippos did not follow the vices rather than the art of earlier artists.

15a. "Laterculi Alexandrini."

Sculptors making primarily statues of gods: Pheidias, Praxiteles, Skopas.

Sculptors making primarily statues of mortals: Myron, Lysippos, Polykleitos, Phyromachos.

considerare: isti credunt eos, qui haec velint discere, alia ratione doceri posse commodius.

9. Columella, De Re Rustica, I, praefatio, 31. (Ed. Lundström.)

Nec pulchritudine Iovis Olympii Minervaeque Phidiacae sequentis aetatis adtonitos piguit experiri Bryaxin, Lysippum, Praxitelen, Polycletum, quid efficere aut quo usque progredi possent.

9a. Nikephoros Choumnos (Boissonade, Anecdot. III, p. 357).[1]

(Lysippos and Apelles made) ζώσας εἰκόνας καὶ πνοῆς μόνης καὶ κινήσεως ἀπολειπομένας.

10. Petronius, Satirikon, 88. (Ed. Heseltine.)

Lysippum statuae unius lineamentis inhaerentem inopia extinxit.

11. Propertius, Elegiae, III 9, 9. (Ed. Butler.)

Gloria Lysippo est animosa effingere signa.

12. Quintilian, De Institutione Oratoria, XII 10, 9. (Ed. Butler.)

Ad veritatem Lysippum ac Praxitelen accessisse optime adfirmant. Nam Demetrius tanquam nimius in ea reprehenditur et fuit similitudinis quam pulchritudinis amantior.

13. Suidas, Lexicon, v. Ἀγαλματοποιοί. (Ed. Bekker.)

Τουτέστι χειρουργοί, οὗτοι ἀκριβεῖς, Λύσιππος, Πολύκλειτος, Φειδίας.

14. Suidas, Lexicon, v. Χειρουργοί. (Ed. Bekker.)

Ἐγένοντο ἄριστοι καὶ ἀκριβεῖς Φειδίας, Λύσιππος, Πολύκλειτος.

15. Varro, De Lingua Latina, IX, 18. (Ed. Goetz and Schoell.)

Neque enim Lysippus artificum priorum potius secutus est vitiosa quam artem.

15a. "Laterculi Alexandrini" (Abh. Preuss. Akad. Wiss., 1904; p. 7 of Abhandlung). (Ed. Diels.)

ΑΓΑΛΜΑΤΟΠΟΙΟΙ
Φειδίας, Πραξιτέλης, Σκόπας.
ΑΝΔΡΙΑΝΤΟΠΟΙΟΙ
Μύρων, Λύσιππος, Πολύκλειτος, Φυρόμαχος.

[1] This passage is known to me only through the citation in Smith's Dictionary of Greek and Roman Biography and Mythology, II, p. 871.

16. Varro, De Re Rustica, III 2, 5.   (Trans. Storr-Best.)

Why, its walls [those of your mansion] are plastered with pictures, and statues as well, while mine shows never a trace of Lysippus or Antiphilus, though many of the hoer and the shepherd.

17. Vitruvius, De Architectura, III, Praefatio, 2. (Trans. Morgan.)

In particular we can learn this from the case of the sculptors and painters of antiquity. Those among them who were marked by high station or favourably recommended have come down to posterity with a name that will last forever; for instance, Myron, Polyclitus, Phidias, Lysippus, and the others who have attained to fame by their art. For they acquired it by the execution of works for great states or for kings or for citizens of rank.

Zeus at Tarentum

18. Lucilius, in Nonius Marcellus, De Indiscretis Generibus, v. Cubitus (Lindsay, vol. I p. 296).

That Zeus of Lysippus, at Tarentum, was over forty cubits in height.

19. Pliny, N. H., XXXIV 40. (Trans. Jex-Blake.)

Yet another is the Zeus at Tarentum by Lysippus, which is 40 cubits [58 ft.] in height and is noteworthy because the weight is so nicely balanced that the colossus can, they say, be turned round by a touch of the hand, and yet cannot be overthrown by the wind. The artist is said to have provided against this by placing a column a little way off, on the side where it was most necessary to break the violence of the wind. The size of the statue and the difficulty of transporting it prevented Fabius Verrucosus from touching it, although he brought the Herakles in the Capitol from Tarentum.

20. Strabo, Geographica, VI 278.   (Trans. Hamilton.)

It [Tarentum] possesses a noble gymnasium and a spacious forum, in which there is set up a brazen colossus of Jupiter, the largest that ever was, with the exception of that of Rhodes. The citadel is situated between the forum and the entrance of the harbor; it still preserves some slight relics of its ancient magnificence and gifts, but the chief of them were destroyed either by the Carthaginians when they took the city, or by the Romans when they took it by force and sacked it. Amongst other booty taken on this occasion

16. Varro, De Re Rustica, III 2, 5. (Ed. Goetz.)
Tua enim oblita tabulis pictis nec minus signis; at mea, vestigium ubi sit nullum Lysippi aut Antiphilu, at crebra sartoris et pastoris.

17. Vitruvius, De Architectura, III, Praefatio, 2. (Ed. Rose.)
Maxime autem id animadvertere possumus ab antiquis statuariis et pictoribus, quod ex his qui dignitatis notas et commendationis gratiam habuerunt, aeterna memoria ad posteritatem sunt permanentes, uti Myron Polycletus Phidias Lysippus ceterique qui nobilitatem ex arte sunt consecuti. namque ut civitatibus magnis aut regibus aut civibus nobilibus opera fecerunt, ita id sunt adepti.

ZEUS AT TARENTUM

18. Lucilius, in Nonius Marcellus, De Indiscretis Generibus, v. Cubitus. (Ed. Lindsay, vol. I, p. 296.)
Lysippi Iuppiter ista
transibit quadraginta cubita altu' Tarento.

19. Pliny, N. H., XXXIV 40. (Ed. Sellers and Jex-Blake.)
. . . Talis et Tarenti factus a Lysippo XL cubitorum. mirum in eo quod manu, ut ferunt, mobilis—ea ratio libramenti est—nullis convellatur procellis. id quidem providisse et artifex dicitur modico intervallo, unde maxime flatum opus erat frangi, opposita columna. itaque magnitudinem propter difficultatemque moliendi non attigit eum Fabius Verrucosus, cum Herculem qui est in Capitolio inde transferret.

20. Strabo, Geographica, VI 278. (Ed. Meineke.)
"Εχει δὲ γυμνάσιόν τε κάλλιστον καὶ ἀγορὰν εὐμεγέθη, ἐν ᾗ καὶ ὁ τοῦ Διὸς ἵδρυται κολοσσὸς χαλκοῦς, μέγιστος μετὰ τὸν 'Ροδίων. μεταξὺ δὲ τῆς ἀγορᾶς καὶ τοῦ στόματος ἡ ἀκρόπολις μικρὰ λείψανα ἔχουσα τοῦ παλαιοῦ κόσμου τῶν ἀναθημάτων· τὰ γὰρ πολλὰ τὰ μὲν κατέφθειραν Καρχηδόνιοι λαβόντες τὴν πόλιν, τὰ δ' ἐλαφυραγώγησαν 'Ρωμαῖοι κρατήσαντες βιαίως· ὧν ἐστι καὶ ὁ 'Ηρακλῆς ἐν τῷ Καπετωλίῳ χαλκοῦς κολοσσικός, Λυσίππου ἔργον, ἀνάθημα Μαξίμου Φαβίου τοῦ ἑλόντος τὴν πόλιν.

was the brazen colossus of Hercules, the work of Lysippus, now in the Capitol, which was dedicated as an offering by Fabius Maximus, who took the city.

20a. Livy, Ab Urbe Condita, XXVII 16, 8.

But, with more magnanimity than Marcellus, Fabius refrained from taking booty of this sort. When a scribe asked what he wished to be done with the statues of great size—these are gods, all of whom, in their individual attitudes, are represented as if fighting—he ordered that the angry gods be left to the Tarentines.

Zeus at Sikyon

21. Pausanias, Graeciae Descriptio, II 9, 6. (Trans. Frazer.)

In the open part of the market-place is a bronze Zeus, a work of Lysippus.

Zeus at Argos

22. Pausanias, Graeciae Descriptio, II 20, 3. (Trans. Frazer.)

Opposite to it there is a sanctuary of Nemean Zeus: the bronze image of the god, who is represented standing, is a work of Lysippus.

Zeus and Muses at Megara

23. Pausanias, Graeciae Descriptio, I 43, 6. (Trans. Frazer.)

And in the neighboring temple are images of the Muses and a bronze Zeus, both by Lysippus.

Poseidon

24. Lucian, Zeus Tragoedus, 9. (Trans. Harmon.)

Hermes [addressing Poseidon]: That's all very well, but Lysippus made you of bronze and a pauper because the Corinthians had no gold at that time.

25. Pausanias, Graeciae Descriptio, II 1, 7-9. (Trans. Frazer.)

On the temple [in the Isthmian sanctuary], which is not very large, stand bronze Tritons. In the fore-temple are images, two of Poseidon, one of Amphitrite, and one of the Sea, which is also of bronze. The images inside the temple were dedicated in my time by the Athenian Herodes. They include four horses gilded all over except the hoofs, which are of ivory. Beside the horses are two Tritons: from the waist upward they are of gold, but from the waist downward they are of ivory. On the chariot stand

20a. Livy, Ab Urbe Condita, XXVII 16, 8. (Ed. Müller.)

Sed maiore animo generis eius praeda abstinuit Fabius quam Marcellus; qui interroganti scriba, quid fieri signis vellet ingentis magnitudinis—di sunt, suo quisque habitu in modum pugnantium formati—deos iratos Tarentinis relinqui iussit.

ZEUS AT SIKYON

21. Pausanias, Graeciae Descriptio, II 9, 6. (Ed. Schubart.)

Τῆς δὲ ἀγορᾶς ἐστιν ἐν τῷ ὑπαίθρῳ Ζεὺς χαλκοῦς, τέχνη Λυσίππου.

ZEUS AT ARGOS

22. Pausanias, Graeciae Descriptio, II 20, 3. (Ed. Schubart.)

Τούτων δὲ ἀπαντικρὺ Νεμείου Διός ἐστιν ἱερόν, ἄγαλμα ὀρθὸν χαλκοῦν, τέχνη Λυσίππου.

ZEUS AND MUSES AT MEGARA

23. Pausanias, Graeciae Descriptio, I 43, 6. (Ed. Schubart.)

Καὶ ἐν τῷ ναῷ τῷ πλησίον Μούσας καὶ χαλκοῦν Δία ἐποίησε Λύσιππος.

POSEIDON

24. Lucian, Zeus Tragoedus, 9. (Ed. Harmon.)

Ναί, ἀλλὰ σὲ μέν, ὦ ἐννοσίγαιε, χαλκοῦν ὁ Λύσιππος καὶ πτωχὸν ἐποίησεν, οὐκ ἐχόντων τότε Κορινθίων χρυσόν.

25. Pausanias, Graeciae Descriptio, II 1, 7-9. (Ed. Schubart.)

Τῷ ναῷ δὲ ὄντι μέγεθος οὐ μείζονι ἐφεστήκασι Τρίτωνες χαλκοῖ. καὶ ἀγάλματά ἐστιν ἐν τῷ προνάῳ, δύο μὲν Ποσειδῶνος, τρίτον δὲ ᾿Αμφιτρίτης, καὶ θάλασσα, καὶ αὕτη χαλκῆ. τὰ δὲ ἔνδον ἐφ᾿ ἡμῶν ἀνέθηκεν Ἡρώδης ᾿Αθηναῖος, ἵππους τέσσαρας ἐπιχρύσους πλὴν τῶν ὁπλῶν· ὁπλαὶ δέ σφισίν εἰσιν ἐλέφαντος. καὶ Τρίτωνες δύο παρὰ τοὺς ἵππους εἰσὶ χρυσοῖ, τὰ μετ᾿ ἰξὺν ἐλέφαντος καὶ οὗτοι· τῷ δὲ ἅρματι ᾿Αμφιτρίτη καὶ Ποσειδῶν ἐφεστήκασι, καὶ παῖς ὀρθός ἐστιν ἐπὶ δελφῖνος ὁ Παλαίμων· ἐλέφαντος δὲ καὶ χρυσοῦ καὶ οὗτοι πεποίηνται. τῷ βάθρῳ δέ, ἐφ᾿ οὗ τὸ ἅρμα, μέση μὲν

Amphitrite and Poseidon, and the boy Palaemon is erect on a dolphin. These statues also are made of ivory and gold. On the pedestal on which the chariot stands are figures sculptured in relief: in the middle is the Sea holding up the child Aphrodite, and on either side are the Nereids, as they are called. I know that there are altars to the Nereids elsewhere in Greece, and that some people have dedicated precincts to them beside harbours, where honours are paid to Achilles also. Doto has a holy sanctuary at Gabala, where is still preserved the robe by which, as the Greeks say, Eriphyle was bribed to wrong her son Alcmaeon. On the pedestal of Poseidon's statue are wrought in relief the sons of Tyndareus, because they too are saviours of ships and of seafaring men. The other votive offerings consist of images of Calm and of the Sea, and a horse fashioned in the likeness of a sea-monster from the breast onward; also statues of Ino and Bellerophon and the horse Pegasus.

26. Pausanias, Graeciae Descriptio, II 35, 1. (Trans. Frazer.)
There is also [at Hermione] a sanctuary of Artemis surnamed Iphigenia, and a bronze Poseidon with one foot on a dolphin.

27. Pausanias, Graeciae Descriptio X 36, 8. (Trans. Frazer.)
And at the harbour [at Anticyra] there is a small sanctuary of Poseidon built of unhewn stones: the interior is coated with stucco. The image is of bronze, and represents the god standing with one foot on a dolphin; on this side he has his hand on his thigh, in the other hand he holds a trident.

DIONYSOS

28. Pausanias, Graeciae Descriptio, IX 30, 1. (Trans. Frazer.)
There is also on Helicon a bronze Apollo fighting with Hermes for the lyre. Also there is a Dionysus by Lysippus: the standing image of Dionysus was dedicated by Sulla, and is the finest of all the works of Myron, next to his statue of Erechtheus at Athens.

29. Lucian, Zeus Tragoedus, 12. (Trans. Harmon.)
Hermes: Here is still another question that is hard to solve. Both of them are of bronze and of the same artistic merit, each being by Lysippus, and what is more they are equals in point of family, for both are sons of Zeus—I mean Dionysus here and Heracles. Which of them has precedence? For they are quarrelling, as you see.

ἐπείργασται θάλασσα ἀνέχουσα Ἀφροδίτην παῖδα, ἑκατέρωθεν δέ εἰσιν αἱ Νηρηίδες καλούμεναι. ταύταις καὶ ἑτέρωθι τῆς Ἑλλάδος βωμοὺς οἶδα ὄντας, τοὺς δὲ καὶ τεμένη σφίσιν ἀναθέντας ποιμαίνισιν, ἔνθα καὶ Ἀχιλλεῖ τιμαί· Δωτοῦς δὲ ἐν Γαβάλοις ἱερόν ἐστιν ἅγιον, ἔνθα πέπλος ἔτι ἐλείπετο, ὃν Ἕλληνες Ἐριφύλην λέγουσιν ἐπὶ τῷ παιδὶ λαβεῖν Ἀλκμαίωνι. τοῦ Ποσειδῶνος δέ εἰσιν ἐπειργασμένοι τῷ βάθρῳ καὶ οἱ Τυνδάρεω παῖδες, ὅτι δὴ σωτῆρες καὶ οὗτοι νεῶν καὶ ἀνθρώπων εἰσὶ ναυτιλλομένων. τὰ δὲ ἄλλα ἀνάκειται Γαλήνης ἄγαλμα καὶ Θαλάσσης, καὶ ἵππος εἰκασμένος κήτει τὰ μετὰ τὸ στέρνον, Ἰνώ τε καὶ Βελλεροφόντης καὶ ὁ ἵππος ὁ Πήγασος.

26. Pausanias, Graeciae Descriptio, II 35, 1. (Ed. Schubart.)
Καὶ Ἀρτέμιδος ἐπίκλησιν Ἰφιγενείας ἐστὶν ἱερόν, καὶ Ποσειδῶν χαλκοῦς τὸν ἕτερον πόδα ἔχων ἐπὶ δελφῖνος.

27. Pausanias, Graeciae Descriptio, X 36, 8. (Ed. Schubart.)
Ἔστι δέ σφισιν ἐπὶ τῷ λιμένι Ποσειδῶνι οὐ μέγα ἱερόν, λογάσιν ᾠκοδομημένον λίθοις· κεκονίαται δὲ τὰ ἐντός. τὸ δὲ ἄγαλμά ὀρθὸν χαλκοῦ πεποιημένον, βέβηκε δὲ ἐπὶ δελφῖνι τῷ ἑτέρῳ τῶν ποδῶν· κατὰ τοῦτο δὲ ἔχει καὶ τὴν χεῖρα ἐπὶ τῷ μηρῷ, ἐν δὲ τῇ ἑτέρᾳ χειρὶ τρίαινά ἐστιν αὐτῷ.

DIONYSOS

28. Pausanias, Graeciae Descriptio, IX 30, 1. (Ed. Schubart.)
καὶ Ἀπόλλων χαλκοῦς ἐστιν ἐν Ἑλικῶνι καὶ Ἑρμῆς μαχόμενοι περὶ τῆς λύρας, καὶ Διόνυσος ὁ μὲν Λυσίππου, τὸ δὲ ἄγαλμα ἀνέθηκε Σύλλας τοῦ Διονύσου τὸ ὀρθόν, ἔργον τοῦ Μύρωνος θέας μάλιστα ἄξιον μετά γε τὸν Ἀθήνησιν Ἐρεχθέα.

29. Lucian, Zeus Tragoedus, 12. (Ed. Harmon.)
Ἰδοὺ πάλιν ἄλλο δύσλυτον καὶ τοῦτο· χαλκῶ μὲν ἀμφοτέρω ἐστὸν καὶ τέχνης τῆς αὐτῆς, Λυσίππου ἑκάτερόν τὸ ἔργον, καὶ τὸ μέγιστον, ὁμοτίμω τὰ ἐς γένος, ἄτε δὴ Διὸς παῖδε, ὁ Διόνυσος οὑτοσὶ καὶ Ἡρακλῆς. πότερος οὖν αὐτῶν προκαθίζει; φιλονεικοῦσι γάρ, ὡς ὁρᾷς.

Helios

30. Cassius Dio, XLVII 33, 4. (Trans. Cary.)

Afterwards Cassius himself crossed over to their island, where he met with no resistance, possessing, as he did, their good-will because of the stay he had made there while pursuing his education; and though he did the people no harm, yet he appropriated their ships, money, and public and sacred treasures, with the exception of the chariot of the Sun.

Eros

31. Pausanias, Graeciae Descriptio, II 5, 1. (Trans. Frazer.)

On the summit of the Acro-Corinth there is a temple of Aphrodite. Her image represents the goddess armed, and there are images of the Sun, and of Love, the latter bearing a bow.

32. Pausanias, Graeciae Descriptio, IX 27, 3 (Trans. Frazer.)

Afterwards Lysippus made a bronze statue of Love for the Thespians: Praxiteles had previously made one of Pentelic marble.

Kairos

33. Ausonius, Epigrammata, XXXIII. (Trans. Evelyn-White.)

"Whose work art thou?" "Pheidias's: his who made Pallas' statue, who made Jove's: his third masterpiece am I. I am a goddess seldom found and known to few, Opportunity my name." "Why stand'st thou on a wheel?" "I cannot stand still." "Why wearest thou winged sandals?" "I am ever flying. The gifts which Mercury scatters at random I bestow when I will." "Thou coverest thy face with thy hair." "I would not be recognized." "But— what!—art thou bald at the back of thy head?" "That none may catch me as I flee." "Who is she who bears thee company?" "Let her tell thee." "Tell me, I beg, who thou art." "I am a goddess to whom not even Cicero himself gave a name. I am a goddess who exacts penalties for what is done and what undone, to cause repentance. So I am called Metanoea." "Do thou now tell me what does she along with thee?" "When I have flown away she remains: she is retained by those I have passed by. Thou also whilst thou keepest asking, whilst thou tarriest with questioning wilt say that I have slipped away out of thy hands."

HELIOS

30. Cassius Dio, Historia Romana, XLVII 33, 4. (Ed. Cary.)
Καὶ μετὰ τοῦτο καὶ αὐτὸς ἐς τὴν νῆσον περαιωθεὶς ἄλλο μὲν κακὸν οὐδὲν αὐτοὺς ἔδρασεν (οὔτε γὰρ ἀντέστησάν οἱ, καὶ εὔνοιαν αὐτῶν ἐκ τῆς διατριβῆς ἣν ἐκεῖ κατὰ παιδείαν ἐπεποίητο εἶχε), τὰς δὲ δὴ ναῦς καὶ τὰ χρήματα καὶ τὰ ὅσια καὶ τὰ ἱερά, πλὴν τοῦ ἅρματος τοῦ Ἡλίου, παρεσπάσατο.

EROS

31. Pausanias, Graeciae Descriptio, II 5, 1. (Ed. Schubart.)
Ἀνελθοῦσι δὲ ἐς τὸν Ἀκροκόρινθον ναός ἐστιν Ἀφροδίτης· ἀγάλματα δὲ αὐτή τε ὡπλισμένη καὶ Ἥλιος καὶ Ἔρως ἔχων τόξον.

32. Pausanias, Graeciae Descriptio, IX 27, 3. (Ed. Schubart.)
Θεσπιεῦσι δὲ ὕστερον χαλκοῦν εἰργάσατο Ἔρωτα Λύσιππος, καὶ ἔτι πρότερον τούτου Πραξιτέλης λίθου τοῦ Πεντέλησι.

KAIROS

33. Ausonius, Epigrammata, XXXIII. (Ed. Evelyn-White.)
Cuius opus? Phidiae: qui signum Pallados, eius
  quique Iovem fecit; tertia palma ego sum.
sum dea quae rara et paucis Occasio nota.
  Quid rotulae insistis? Stare loco nequeo.
Quid talaria habes? Volucris sum. Mercurius quae
  fortunare solet, trado ego, cum volui.
Crine tegis faciem. Cognosci nolo. Sed heus tu
  occipiti calvo es? Ne tenear fugiens.
Quae tibi iuncta comes? Dicat tibi. Dic rogo, quae sis.
  Sum dea, cui nomen nec Cicero ipse dedit.
sum dea, quae factique et non facti exigo poenas,
  nempe ut paeniteat: sic Metanoea vocor.
Tu modo dic, quid agat tecum. Quandoque volavi,
  haec manet: hanc retinent quos ego praeterii.
tu quoque dum rogitas, dum percontando moraris,
  elapsam dices me tibi de manibus.

34. Kallistratos, Descriptiones, VI.

I wish to describe to you the work of Lysippos, the fairest of statues, which the artist made and offered to the view of the Sikyonians. Kairos it was, modelled into an image out of bronze with art that rivalled nature. Kairos was a boy just becoming a man, blooming from head to foot with the flower of youth. He was fair to behold, shaking his fledgeling beard and leaving his hair loose for the breeze to wave wherever it wished; and his flesh was blooming, showing its bloom in the luster of his body. (2) For the most part he was like to Dionysos; his forehead shone with loveliness and his cheeks, reddened into youthful bloom, were fair, casting a gentle glow upon his eyes; and he stood on tiptoe on a sort of sphere, and his feet were winged. His hair had not grown in the usual way; but the long hair, falling down over the eyebrows, waved its curl against the cheeks, while the back part of Kairos's head was void of tresses, showing only the newborn sprouts of the hair. (3) We stood stricken with speechlessness at the spectacle, seeing the bronze contriving works of nature and departing from its own order; for though bronze it was reddened, and though naturally hard it was cast so as to appear soft, yielding to art as it should wish; and though lacking animate feeling it was believed to possess it indwelling, and really it was supported by its firmly set foot; and though standing still it showed that it had the possibility of starting off, and deceived one's eye, conveying the impression that it possessed the power of motion forward and had received from the artist the ability to cut the air with its wings, if it should wish. (4) So great was our wonder; but one of those that are learned in matters of art and know how, with more artistic feeling, to trace out the marvels of the artists, acclaimed also the design of the statue, explaining how the power of Kairos was retained in the work of art: that the wings on the feet conveyed a hint of swiftness; and as causing the revolutions of ages he is represented as riding on the seasons; and as for the bloom of youth, that is because all that is timely is beautiful and Kairos is the only creator of beauty, while everything that is faded is outside the nature of Kairos; and as for the long hair in front, that is because he can easily be seized when he is coming on, but when he has passed the moment for action has gone with him and it is not possible to catch Kairos when he has been disregarded.

34. Kallistratos, Descriptiones, VI. (Ed. Schenkl and Reisch.)

Ἐθέλω δέ σοι καὶ τὸ Λυσίππου δημιούργημα τῷ λόγῳ παραστῆσαι, ὅπερ ἀγαλμάτων κάλλιστον ὁ δημιουργὸς τεχνησάμενος Σικυωνίοις εἰς θέαν προῦθηκε. Καιρὸς ἦν εἰς ἄγαλμα τετυπωμένος ἐκ χαλκοῦ πρὸς τὴν φύσιν ἁμιλλωμένης τῆς τέχνης. παῖς δὲ ἦν ὁ Καιρὸς ἡβῶν ἐκ κεφαλῆς ἐς πόδας ἐπανθῶν τὸ τῆς ἥβης ἄνθος. ἦν δὲ τὴν μὲν ὄψιν ὡραῖος σείων ἴουλον καὶ ζεφύρῳ τινάσσειν, πρὸς ὃ βούλοιτο καταλιπὼν τὴν κόμην ἄνετον, τὴν δὲ χρόαν εἶχεν ἀνθηρὰν τῇ λαμπηδόνι τοῦ σώματος τὰ ἄνθη δηλῶν. (2) ἦν δὲ Διονύσῳ κατὰ τὸ πλεῖστον ἐμφερής· τὰ μὲν γὰρ μέτωπα χάρισιν ἔστιλβεν, αἱ παρειαὶ δὲ αὐτοῦ εἰς ἄνθος ἐρευθόμεναι νεοτήδιον ὡραίζοντο ἐπιβάλλουσαι τοῖς ὄμμασιν ἁπαλὸν ἐρύθημα, εἱστήκει δὲ ἐπί τινος σφαίρας ἐπ' ἄκρων τῶν ταρσῶν βεβηκὸς ἐπτερωμένος τὼ πόδε. ἐπεφύκει δὲ οὐ νενομισμένως ἡ θρίξ, ἀλλ' ἡ μὲν κόμη κατὰ τῶν ὀφρύων ὑφέρπουσα ταῖς παρειαῖς ἐπέσειε τὸν βόστρυχον, τὰ δὲ ὄπισθεν ἦν τοῦ Καιροῦ πλοκάμων ἐλεύθερα μόνην τὴν γενέσεως βλάστην ἐπιφαίνοντα τῆς τριχός. (3) ἡμεῖς μὲν οὖν ἀφασίᾳ πληγέντες πρὸς τὴν θέαν εἰστήκειμεν τὸν χαλκὸν ὁρῶντες ἔργα φύσεως μηχανώμενον καὶ τῆς οἰκείας ἐκβαίνοντα τάξεως· χαλκὸς μὲν γὰρ ὢν ἠρυθαίνετο, σκληρὸς δὲ ὢν τὴν φύσιν διεχεῖτο μαλακῶς εἴκων τῇ τέχνῃ πρὸς ὃ βούλοιτο, σπανίζων δὲ αἰσθήσεως ζωτικῆς ἔνοικον ἔχειν ἐπιστοῦτο τὴν αἴσθησιν καὶ ὄντως ἐστήρικτο πάγιον τὸν ταρσὸν ἐρείσας, ἑστὼς δὲ ὁρμῆς ἐξουσίαν ἔχειν ἐδείκνυτο καί σοι τὸν ὀφθαλμὸν ἠπάτα, ὡς καὶ τῆς εἰς τὸ πρόσω κυριεύων φορᾶς, καὶ παρὰ τοῦ δημιουργοῦ λαβὼν καὶ τὴν ἀέριον λῆξιν τέμνειν εἰ βούλοιτο ταῖς πτέρυξι. (4) καὶ τὸ μὲν ἡμῖν θαῦμα τοιοῦτον ἦν, εἰς δέ τις τῶν περὶ τὰς τέχνας σοφῶν καὶ εἰδότων σὺν αἰσθήσει τεχνικωτέρᾳ τὰ τῶν δημιουργῶν ἀνιχνεύειν θαύματα καὶ λογισμὸν ἐπῇδε τῷ τεχνήματι, τὴν τοῦ καιροῦ δύναμιν ἐν τῇ τέχνῃ σωζομένην ἐξηγούμενος· τὸ μὲν γὰρ πτέρωμα τῶν ταρσῶν αἰνίττεσθαι τὴν ὀξύτητα, καὶ ὡς τὸν πολὺν ἀνελίττων αἰῶνα φέρεται ταῖς ὥραις ἐποχούμενος, τὴν δὲ ἐπανθοῦσαν ὥραν, ὅτι πᾶν εὔκαιρον τὸ ὡραῖον καὶ μόνος κάλλους δημιουργὸς ὁ καιρός, τὸ δὲ ἀπηνθηκὸς ἅπαν ἔξω τῆς καιροῦ φύσεως, τὴν δὲ κατὰ τοῦ μετώπου κόμην, ὅτι προσιόντος μὲν αὐτοῦ λαβέσθαι ῥάδιον, παρελθόντος δὲ ἡ τῶν πραγμάτων ἀκμὴ συνεξέρχεται καὶ οὐκ ἔστιν ὀλιγωρηθέντα λαβεῖν τὸν καιρόν.

35. Kedrenos, Historiarum Compendium, 322.

(B) There was [in the Lauseum at Constantinople] the image of Lindian Athens, four cubits in height and made of smaragdus, a work of the sculptors Skyllis and Dipoinos, which Sesostris, ruler of Egypt, once sent as a gift to Kleoboulos, the Lindian ruler; and the Knidian Aphrodite of white marble, nude and covering only the pudenda with her hand, a work of the Knidian Praxiteles; and the Samian Hera, a work of Lysippos and Boupalos the Chian; and the winged Eros with the bow, coming from Myndos; (C) and the ivory Zeus of Pheidias, which Perikles dedicated in the temple at Olympia; and the statue representing time, bald behind and long-haired in front, a work of Lysippos.

36. Himerios, Eclogae, XIV 1. (Wernsdorf p. 240.)

Lysippos was skilled not only in hand, but also in mind. What kind of projects did he venture on, through his cleverness?   He enrolled Kairos among the gods and made a statue of him, expounding his nature through the image. The marvel is something like this, as I remember: he represents a youth, extremely handsome in appearance, an ephebos, with long hair from the temples to the forehead, but bare from the forehead back; armed with a knife in his right hand, and holding a balance in his left; and winged on his ankles, not in order that he may move lightly through the air above the earth, but so that, though seeming to touch the ground, he may successfully conceal the fact that his weight does not rest on the earth.

37. Phaedrus, Fabulae, V 8.

The runner hovering upon a winged knife, with hair on his forehead but with the back part of his head bare— whom you may hold if you seize him, but once passed Jupiter himself could not catch—represents the brief period of opportunity in affairs. In order that slow delay might not hinder achievements, the ancients fashioned such an image of Time.

38. Poseidippos: Anth. Pal. XVI (Plan. App. IV), 275. (Trans. Paton.)

A. Who and whence was the sculptor? B. From Sicyon. A. And his name? B. Lysippus. A. And who are thou? B. Time who subdueth all things. A. Why dost thou stand on tip-toe? B. I am ever running. A. And why hast thou a pair of wings on thy feet? B. I fly

35. Kedrenos, Historiarum Compendium, 322. (Ed. Bekker.)

(B) Ἵστατο δὲ καὶ τὸ ἄγαλμα τῆς Λινδίας Ἀθηνᾶς τετράπηχυ ἐκ λίθου σμαράγδου, ἔργον Σκύλλιδος καὶ Διποίνου τῶν ἀγαλματουργῶν, ὅπερ ποτὲ δῶρον ἔπεμψε Σέσωστρις Αἰγύπτου τύραννος Κλεοβούλῳ τῷ Λινδίῳ τυράννῳ. καὶ ἡ Κνιδία Ἀφροδίτη ἐκ λίθου λευκῆς, γυμνή, μόνην τὴν αἰδῶ τῇ χειρὶ περιστέλλουσα, ἔργον τοῦ Κνιδίου Πραξιτέλους. καὶ ἡ Σαμία Ἥρα, ἔργον Λυσίππου καὶ Βουπάλου τοῦ Χίου. καὶ Ἔρως τόξον ἔχων, πτερωτός, Μυνδόθεν ἀφικόμενος. (C) καὶ ὁ Φειδίου ἐλεφάντινος Ζεύς, ὃν Περικλῆς ἀνέθηκεν εἰς νεὼν Ὀλυμπίων. καὶ τὸ τὸν χρόνον μιμούμενον ἄγαλμα, ἔργον Λυσίππου, ὄπισθεν μὲν φαλακρόν, ἔμπροσθεν δὲ κομῶν.

36. Himerios, Eclogae, XIV 1 (Wernsdorf p. 240). (Ed. Dübner.)

Δεινὸς δὲ ἦν ἄρα οὐ χεῖρα μόνον, ἀλλὰ καὶ γνώμην ὁ Λύσιππος. Οἷα γοῦν ἐκεῖνος διὰ τῆς ἑαυτοῦ γνώμης τετόλμηκεν! ἐγγράφει τοῖς θεοῖς τὸν Καιρόν, καὶ μορφώσας ἀγάλματι τὴν φύσιν αὐτοῦ διὰ τῆς εἰκόνος ἐξηγήσατο. Ἔχει δὲ ὧδέ πως, ὡς ἐμὲ μνημονεύειν, τὸ δαίδαλμα. Ποιεῖ παῖδα τὸ εἶδος ἀβρόν, τὴν ἀκμὴν ἔφηβον, κομῶντα μὲν τὸ ἐκ κροτάφων εἰς μέτωπον, γυμνὸν δὲ τὸ ὅσον ἐκεῖθεν ἐπὶ τὰ νῶτα μερίζεται· σιδήρῳ τὴν δεξιὰν ὡπλισμένον, ζυγῷ τὴν λαιὰν ἐπέχοντα, πτερωτὸν τὰ σφυρά, οὐχ ὡς μετάρσιον ὑπὲρ γῆς ἄνω κουφίζεσθαι, ἀλλ' ἵνα δοκῶν ἐπιψαύειν τῆς γῆς, λανθάνῃ κλέπτων τὸ μὴ κατὰ γῆς ἐπερείδεσθαι.

37. Phaedrus, Fabulae, V 8. (Ed. Havet.)

Cursor volucri pendens in novacula,
Calvus comosa fronte, nudo occipitio
(Quem si occuparis teneas; elapsum semel
Non ipse possit Iuppiter reprehendere),
Occasionem rerum significat brevem;
Effectus impediret ne segnis mora,
Finxere antiqui talem effigiem Temporis.

38. Poseidippos: Anth. Pal. XVI (Plan. App. IV), 275. (Ed. Paton.)

α. Τίς πόθεν ὁ πλάστης; β. Σικυώνιος. α. Οὔνομα δὴ τίς; β. Λύσιππος. α. Σὺ δὲ τίς; β. Καιρὸς ὁ πανδαμάτωρ. α. Τίπτε δ' ἐπ' ἄκρα βέβηκας; β. Ἀεὶ τροχάω. α. Τί δὲ ταρσοὺς ποσσὶν ἔχεις διφυεῖς; β. Ἵπταμ' ὑπηνέμιος.

with the wind. A. And why dost thou hold a razor in thy
right hand? B. As a sign to men that I am sharper than
any sharp edge. A. And why does thy hair hang over thy
face? B. For him who meets me to take me by the fore-
lock. A. And why, in Heaven's name, is the back of thy
head bald? B. Because none whom I have once raced by
on my winged feet will now, though he wishes it sore,
take hold of me from behind. A. Why did the artist
fashion thee? B. For your sake, stranger, and he set me
up in the porch as a lesson.

39. Tzetzes, Chiliades, X 266-272.

The Macedonian Alexander, the great king, grieved
when he had once neglected the favorable time in his affairs.
Then Lysippos the sculptor perfected an image of time
and sculptured it with his clever sagacity; he represented
him as deaf, bald on the back of the head, standing with
winged feet on a sphere, and presenting a knife to any one
attempting to seize him from behind; in this way advis-
ing every one not to disregard time.

(The statue is mentioned also in X 280.)

HERAKLES AT TARENTUM

40. Niketas Choniates, De Signis Constantinopolitanis, 5.
(Trans. Jones.)

The great Herakles then begotten of three nights lies
mighty and mightily fallen, he who was seated on a basket,
whereon was strewn the lion's skin. There he sat with
no quiver hung about him, with no bow in his hand and no
club to defend him, but extending his right leg and right
arm as far as he could, and with his left leg bent at the
knee. His left arm was supported at the elbow and the
forearm raised, and on the palm of the left hand he was
resting his head gently, full of despondency. His breast
and shoulders were broad, his hair thick, his buttocks fat,
and his arms brawny, and his height was such as Lysimachos might have supposed the original Herakles to
reach, when he fashioned of bronze this, the choicest jewel
of his art, first and last, of such colossal bulk that the
string which enclosed its thumb might serve as a man's
girdle and the shin of its leg was tall as a man.

41. Niketas Choniates, De Alexio Isaaci Angeli Fratre, III
335 C-D.

[The Empress Euphrosyne] decided to scourge on the

α. Χειρὶ δὲ δεξιτερῇ τί φέρεις ξυρόν; β. Ἀνδράσι δεῖγμα,
ὡς ἀκμῆς πάσης ὀξύτερος τελέθω.
α. Ἡ δὲ κόμη, τί κατ' ὄψιν; β. Ὑπαντιάσαντι λαβέσθαι.
α. Νὴ Δία, τἀξόπιθεν δ' εἰς τί φαλακρὰ πέλει;
β. Τὸν γὰρ ἅπαξ πτηνοῖσι παραθρέξαντά με ποσσὶν
οὔτις ἔθ' ἱμείρων δράξεται ἐξόπιθεν.
α. Τοὔνεχ' ὁ τεχνίτης σε διέπλασεν; β. Εἵνεκεν ὑμέων,
ξεῖνε· καὶ ἐν προθύροις θῆκε διδασκαλίην.

39. Tzetzes, Chiliades, X 266-272. (Ed. Kiessling.)
Ὁ Μακεδὼν Ἀλέξανδρος, ὁ βασιλεὺς ὁ μέγας,
Ἤσχαλλε χρόνον ἐκδραμών ποτε τῶν προσηκόντων.
Τότε τελῶν δ' ὁ Λύσιππος ἀνδριαντοεργάτης
Τὸν χρόνον ἠγαλμάτωσε σοφῇ τῇ διανοίᾳ,
Κωφόν, ὀπισθοφάλακρον, πτερόπουν ἐπὶ σφαίρας,
Πρὸς τὸ κατόπιν μάχαιράν τινι διδόντα πλάσας,
Πάντας ἐντεῦθεν νουθετῶν, χρόνον μὴ παρατρέχειν.

HERAKLES AT TARENTUM

40. Niketas Choniates, De Signis Constantinopolitanis, 5. (Ed. Bekker.)
Κατήρειπτο τοίνυν Ἡρακλῆς ὁ τριέσπερος μέγας μεγαλωστὶ κοφίνῳ ἐνιδρυμένος, τῆς λεοντῆς ὑπεστρωμένης ἄνωθεν. ἐκάθητο δὲ μὴ γωρυτὸν ἐξημμένος, μὴ τόξον ταῖν χεροῖν φέρων, μὴ τὸ ρόπαλον προβαλλόμενος, ἀλλὰ τὴν μὲν δεξιὰν βάσιν ἐκτείνων ὥσπερ καὶ τὴν αὐτὴν χεῖρα εἰς ὅσον ἐξῆν, τὸν δὲ εὐώνυμον πόδα κάμπτων εἰς τὸ γόνυ καὶ τὴν λαιὰν χεῖρα ἐπ' ἀγκῶνος ἐρείδων, εἶτα τὸ λοιπὸν τῆς χειρὸς ἀνατείνων, καὶ τῷ πλατεῖ ταύτης ἀθυμίας πλήρης καθυποκλίνων ἠρέμα τὴν κεφαλήν... ἦν δὲ τὸ στέρνον εὐρύς, τοὺς ὤμους πλατύς, τὴν τρίχα οὖλος, τὰς πυγὰς πίων, βριαρὸς τοὺς βραχίονας, καὶ εἰς τόσον προέχων μέγεθος εἰς ὅσον, οἶμαι, καὶ τὸν ἀρχέτυπον Ἡρακλῆν εἴκασεν ἂν ἀναδραμεῖν ὁ Λυσίμαχος ὁ πρῶτον ἅμα καὶ ὕστατον τῶν ἑαυτοῦ χειρῶν πανάριστον φιλοτέχνημα τουτονὶ χαλκουργήσας, καὶ οὕτω μέγιστον ὡς τὴν περιελοῦσαν τὸν αὐτοῦ ἀντίχειρα μήρινθον εἰς ἀνδρεῖον ζωστῆρα ἐκτείνεσθαι καὶ τὴν κνήμην τοῦ ποδὸς εἰς ἀνδρόμηκες.

41. Niketas Choniates, De Alexio Isaaci Angeli Fratre, III 335 C-D. (Ed. Bekker.)
Καὶ τὸν καλλίνικον Ἡρακλῆν τοῦ Λυσιμάχου ἔργων τὸ

back, with many whips, the glorious Herakles, the most
beautiful of Lysimachos's works; the work in which the
lion-skin is spread over a basket, and the hero rests his
head on his hand and grieves over his own misfortunes.
Alas, Herakles, for the absurdity; and alas for the outrage
against you, mighty and great-hearted hero! What Eurys-
theus ever proposed for you such a trial? Or what Om-
phale, worn-out prey of passions and vilely artful wench,
treated you so arrogantly as this?

42. Plutarch, Fabius Maximus, 22, 6. (Trans. Perrin.)
However, he [Fabius Maximus] removed the colossal
statue of Herakles from Tarentum, and set it up on the
Capitol, and near it an equestrian statue of himself, in
bronze.

43. Suidas, Lexicon, v. βασιλική.
There [in the Basilica in Constantinople] a statue of
Herakles was worshipped. It was transferred to the Hippodrome. It came to Constantinople from Rome in the
consulship of Julian; it was conveyed by ship and wagon,
along with ten marbles. (This is repeated almost verbatim
in Παραστάσεις σύντομοι χρονικαί, 37.)

43a. Constantine Manasses, Ecphrasis I, lines 21-32.
Many are the works in painting and sculpture from
which Pheidiases, Praxiteleses, Lysippoi and Parrhasioi
are famous even until now. Hence was wrought the cow
of Myron, absolutely alive, so as to deceive even the young
calf and entice the bellowing bull into love; hence Herakles
the son of Zeus was wrought in bronze, noble and great
and a hero and mighty, seated on a woven basket, with
the right hand . . . supporting the head bent in despondency; one would say that he was lamenting his own misfortunes; so living is the work in bronze, so truly alive the
image.

Herakles at Sikyon

44. Pausanias, Graeciae Descriptio, II 9, 8. (Trans. Frazer.)
Here is a bronze Hercules, made by Lysippus, the
Sicyonian.

Herakles Epitrapezios

45. Martial, Epigrammata, IX 43. (Trans. Ker.)
He who seated makes softer the hard stones by a
stretched lion's skin, a huge god in small shape of bronze,
and who, with face upturned, regards the stars he shoul-

κάλλιστον ὄντα, χειρὶ βαλόντα τὴν κεφαλὴν τῆς λεοντῆς
ὑπεστρωμένης κοφίνῳ καὶ τὰς ἰδίας τύχας ὀλοφυρόμενον,
πολλαῖς κατὰ νώτου ξᾶναι διενοεῖτο. Ἡράκλεις τοῦ ἀτοπή-
ματος, καὶ παπαὶ τῶν ἐπὶ σοὶ τολμωμένων, ἥρως ἄλκιμε καὶ
μεγαλόθυμε. τίς σοι Εὐρυσθεὺς τοιοῦτον πώποτε προύθηκεν
ἆεθλον; ἢ τίς Ὀμφάλη, ἐπίτριμμα ἐρώτων καὶ κακότεχνον
γύναιον, οὕτω σοι ὑπερηφάνως προσενήνεκται;

42. Plutarch, Fabius Maximus, 22, 6. (Ed. Perrin.)
Οὐ μὴν ἀλλὰ τὸν κολοσσὸν τοῦ Ἡρακλέους μετακομί-
σας ἐκ Τάραντος ἔστησεν ἐν Καπιτωλίῳ, καὶ πλησίον ἔφιπ-
πον εἰκόνα χαλκῆν ἑαυτοῦ.

43. Suidas, Lexicon, v. Βασιλική. (Ed. Bekker.)
Ἔνθα καὶ Ἡρακλῆς ἐλατρεύθη, πολλὰς θυσίας δεξάμε-
νος, ὃς ἐν τῷ ἱπποδρομίῳ μετετέθη. ἐπὶ δὲ Ἰουλιανοῦ ὑπατι-
κοῦ ἀπὸ Ῥώμης ἦλθεν εἰς τὸ Βυζάντιον, καὶ εἰσήχθη ἐν
ἀπήνῃ καὶ νηὶ καὶ στῆλαι δέκα.

43a. Constantine Manasses, Ecphrasis I, lines 21-32. (Ed.
Sternbach, in *Jh. Oest. Arch. I.*, V, 1902, Beiblatt, col. 75.)
Πολλὰ μὲν ἔργα καὶ ζωγραφίας καὶ πλαστικῆς, ἐξ ὧν
Φειδίαι καὶ Πραξιτέλεις καὶ Λύσιπποι καὶ Παρρήσιοι μέχρι
καὶ νῦν περιλάλητοι· ἐντεῦθεν ἡ Μύρωνος βοῦς ἄντικρυς
ἔμπνους δεδημιούργηται, ὡς καὶ μόσχον ἁπαλὸν ἀπατῆσαι
καὶ ταῦρον μυκητὴν εἰς ἔρωτα ἐφελκύσασθαι· ἐντεῦθεν
Ἡρακλῆς ὁ Διὸς ἐσφυρηλάτηται καλὸς καὶ μέγας καὶ ἥρως
καὶ βριαρὸς πλεκτῷ μὲν καλάθῳ ἐπικαθήμενος, τῇ δεξιᾷ......
δὲ τὴν κεφαλὴν ὑπανέχων ὑπὸ βαρυθυμίας ὀκλάζουσαν·
εἴποι τις αὐτὸν τὰς ἑαυτοῦ τύχας ὀδύρεσθαι· οὕτως ἔμψυ-
χον τὸ χαλκούργημα, οὕτως αὐτόχρημα ἔμπνουν τὸ ἄγαλμα.

HERAKLES AT SIKYON
44. Pausanias, Graeciae Descriptio, II 9, 8. (Ed. Schubart.)
Ἐνταῦθα Ἡρακλῆς χαλκοῦς ἐστί· Λύσιππος ἐποίησεν
Σικυώνιος.

HERAKLES EPITRAPEZIOS
45. Martial, Epigrammata, IX 43. (Ed. Ker.)
Hic qui dura sedens porrecto saxa leone
mitigat, exiguo magnus in aere deus,
quaeque tulit spectat resupino sidera vultu,

dered, whose left hand is aglow with strength, his right
with wine—no recent work of fame is he, nor the glory of
Roman chisel: Lysippus' noble gift and handiwork you
see. This deity the board of Pella's tyrant displayed, he
who lies in a world he swiftly subdued; by him Hannibal,
then a boy, swore at Libyan altars; he bade fierce Sulla
resign his power. Vexed by the boastful threats of fickle
courts, he is glad now to dwell beneath a private roof;
and, as he was of old the guest of gentle Molorchus, so
has he now chosen to be the god of learned Vindex.

46. Martial, Epigrammata, IX 44. (Trans. Ker.)
    I asked Vindex lately whose art and happy toil fash-
ioned Alcides. He laughed, for this is his way—and
slightly nodding, said: "Don't you, a poet, know your
Greek? The base has an inscription and shows the name."
I read "of Lysippos": I thought it was of Phidias!

47. Statius, Silvae, IV, 6. (Trans. Slater.)
    One day as I was idly loitering at sundown in the
broad Enclosure, a truant from my task, for the fit was
not upon me, I was borne off to feast with generous Vindex; and still in my inmost heart lives unforgotten the
memory of that night. It was not idle cheer that regaled
us, dainties fetched from divers climes and vintages old
as the Public Charter Chest.
    Wretched indeed are they whose delight is to tell the
flavour of the pheasant from the crane of Thrace; what
goose has the richest vitals; why the Umbrian boar has
less breed about him than the boar of Tuscany; and on
what shore the succulent oyster finds his softest bed. The
feast of reason was ours and talk from the heart of
Helicon, with merry jests, that lured us to sit out the mid-
winter night and banish gentle sleep from our eyes, until
Castor's brother-twin peeped out from his Elysian home
and Dawn mocked the feast of yesternight. Ah, honest
night; and would that then as once in Tiryns two moons
had been joined in one! A night to be marked with sea-
pearls from Erythraean deeps; a night to treasure long
and the spirit of it to live for evermore! There it was
and then that I learnt so well those thousand shapes of
classic ivory and bronze, and waxen forms so shrewdly
counterfeited they seemed upon the brink of speech. For
where will you find the peer of Vindex to discern in

cuius laeva calet robore, dextra mero,
non est fama recens nec nostri gloria caeli;
   nobile Lysippi munus opusque vides.
hoc habuit numen Pellaei mensa tyranni,
   qui cito perdomito victor in orbe iacet;
hunc puer ad Libycas iuraverat Hannibal aras;
   iusserat hic Sullam ponere regna trucem.
offensus variae tumidis terroribus aulae
   privatos gaudet nunc habitare lares,
utque fuit quondam placidi conviva Molorchi,
   sic voluit docti Vindicis esse deus.

46. Martial, Epigrammata, IX 44. (Ed. Ker.)
   Alcides modo Vindicem rogabam
   esset cuius opus laborque felix.
   risit, nam solet hoc, levique nutu
   "Graece numquid" ait "poeta nescis?
   inscripta est basis indicatque nomen."
   Λυσίππου lego, Phidiae putavi.

47. Statius, Silvae, IV, 6. (Ed. Klotz.)
   Forte remittentem curas Phoeboque levatum
   pectora, cum patulis tererem vagus otia Saeptis
   iam moriente die, rapuit me cena benigni
   Vindicis. haec imos animi perlapsa recessus
   inconsumpta manet. neque enim ludibria ventris   *5*
   hausimus aut epulas diverso a sole petitas
   vinaque perpetuis aevo certantia fastis.
   a miseri! quos nosse uvat, quid Phasidis ales
   distet ab hiberna Rhodopes grue, quis magis anser
   exta ferat, cur Tuscus aper generosior Umbro,   *10*
   lubrica qua recubent conchylia mollius alga:
   nobis verus amor medioque Helicone petitus
   sermo hilaresque ioci brumalem absumere noctem
   suaserunt mollemque oculis expellere somnum,
   donec ab Elysiis prospexit sedibus alter   *15*
   Castor et hesternas risit Tithonia mensas.
   o bona nox iunctaque utinam Tirynthia luna!
   nox et Erythraeis Thetidis signanda lapillis
   et memoranda diu geniumque habitura perennem!
   mille ibi tunc species aerisque eborisque vetusti   *20*
   atque locuturas mentito corpore ceras
   edidici. quis namque oculis certaverit usquam
   Vindicis, artificum veteres agnoscere ductus
   et non inscriptis auctorem reddere signis?

classic work a master's hand, or to name the artist of an
unsigned piece? Vindex alone can say which bronzes
were fashioned with sleepless care by cunning Myro:
which marble was conjured into life by the chisel of in-
dustrious Praxiteles; what ivory carving took the last
touches from the man of Pisa's finger; what breathing
bronze was cast by Polycletus; what line reveals even at
a distance the hand of bygone Apelles? Whenever he lays
down the lute, it is thus that Vindex makes holiday; this
is the passion that lures him from the grottos of the Muses.
Amid his treasures, guardian and god of his temperate
board, was a Hercules that with deep delight took my
heart captive, and with long gazing I could not satisfy my
sight, such a majesty was in the work, such a power was
framed within those narrow confines: the god, the god was
there! Aye, he vouchsafed himself, Lysippus, to thine
eyes, a dwarf to the eye, a giant to the mind. And though
that wondrous stature be confined within a foot's space,
yet look the figure up and down and you will be fain to
cry: 'That is the breast that crushed the ravager of Nemea;
those the arms that swung the fatal club and snapped the
Argo's oars!' It is not bulk: tiny is the form that has this
wizard power! What subtlety, what skill was in the
cunning master's hand, that had the power as well to conceive in his mind a colossal statue as to fashion an ornament for the table. Never could the Telchines in the caves
of Ida have devised in tiny bronze so dainty a counter-
feit,—no nor brawny Brontes, nor he of Lemnos, who
makes radiant the gleaming armour of the gods. Nor is
his presentment repulsive and unsuited to the easy moods
of feasting. That is the Hercules at whom the house of
frugal Molorchus marvelled; that the Tegean priestess
beheld in Alea's groves; that rose from the cinders on Oeta
to the sky, and sipped his nectar with joy while Juno still
frowned. The very air of heartfelt jollity invites to the
feast. One hand holds his brother's languorous cup, the
other still grips the club. And see, a rugged seat upbears
him, a rock with the Nemean lion's skin for covering.

Inspired is the work, and worthy has been its lot.
Once the lord of Pella possessed it to be the worshipful
deity of his joyous board, and bore it, his companion, East
and West. In the hand that but now had crowned and un-
crowned kings and overthrown great cities, blithely would
he clasp it. From this Hercules he would seek courage

haec tibi quae docto multum vigilata Myroni 25
aera, laboriferi vivant quae marmora caelo
Praxitelis, quod ebur Pisaeo pollice rasum,
quid Polycliteis iussum spirare caminis,
linea quae veterem longe fateatur Apellen,
monstrabit: namque haec, quotiens chelyn exuit, illi 30
desidia est, hic Aoniis amor avocat antris.
haec inter castae genius tutelaque mensae
Amphitryoniades multo mea cepit amore
pectora nec longo satiavit lumina visu:
tantus honos operi finesque inclusa per artos 35
maiestas! deus ille, deus! seseque videndum
indulsit, Lysippe, tibi parvusque videri
sentirique ingens! et cum mirabilis intra
stet mensura pedem, tamen exclamare libebit,
si visus per membra feres: 'hoc pectore pressus 40
vastator Nemees, haec exitiale ferebant
robur et Argoos frangebant brachia remos.'
ac spatium! tam magna brevi mendacia formae!
quis modus in dextra, quanta experientia docti
artificis curis, pariter gestamina mensae 45
fingere et ingentes animo versare colossos!
tale nec Idaeis quicquam Telchines in antris
nec stolidus Brontes nec, qui polit arma deorum,
Lemnius exigua potuisset ludere massa.
nec torva effigies epulisque aliena remissis, 50
sed qualem parci domus admirata Molorchi
aut Aleae lucis vidit Tegeaea sacerdos;
qualis et Oetaeis emissus in astra favillis
nectar adhuc torva laetus Iunone bibebat:
sic mitis vultus, veluti de pectore gaudens, 55
hortatur mensas. tenet haec marcentia fratris
pocula, at haec clavae meminit manus; aspera sedis
sustinet et cultum Nemeaeo tegmine saxum.
digna operi fortuna sacro. Pellaeus habebat
regnator laetis numen venerabile mensis 60
et comitem occasus secum portabat et ortus,
praestabatque libens modo qua diademata dextra
abstulerat dederatque et magnas verterat urbes.
semper ab hoc animos in crastina bella petebat,
huic acies semper victor narrabat opimas, 65
sive catenatos Bromio detraxerat Indos
seu clusam magna Babylona refregerat hasta

for the morrow's fray: to Hercules he would tell, a conqueror ever, his gorgeous victories, whether he had won
from Bromius the credit of putting the Indians in chains,
or with strong spear burst the gates of Babylon, or over-
whelmed in battle Pelasgian liberty and the land of Pelops.
Of all the long array of his triumphs men say he sought
excuse only for one—the overthrow of Thebes.   And
when Fate snapped the thread of achievement and the
king drank the deadly wine, heavy as he was with the dark
shades of death, he was afraid at the changed countenance
of the god he loved and the bronze that at that last feast
broke into sweat.

Thereafter the priceless treasure fell to the Nasamo-
nian king; aye, and Hannibal of the dread right hand, in
the pride of his faithless sword poured libations to the God
of Valour, who, for all that, hated a master drenched with
Italian blood and menacing with fell fires the towers of
Romulus; yes, hated him even when he vowed Him banquets and the bounty of Lenaeus, and sighed to follow in
his accursed camp; but most when with sacrilegious flames
he destroyed His own fanes, defiling hearth and shrine
of innocent Saguntus and kindling in her people a noble
frenzy.

Then after the passing of the Phoenician leader the
princely bronze fell into no common hands.   Now the
trophy adorned the feasts of Sulla, accustomed as it was
to enter into the homes of the great, and happy in the
pedigree of its masters.

To-day,—if gods deign to read the hearts and souls of
men,—though neither court nor kingly purple surround
thee, yet white and stainless, lord of Tiryns, is thy master's
soul.   An old-world loyalty is his, a heart true for all time
to friendship once vowed.   Vestinus is my witness, who
even in the heyday of youth yet vied with his great fore-
fathers.   It is his spirit that Vindex breathes night and
day, and lives ever in the arms of that noble shade.   Here
then, Alcides, bravest of all gods, is welcome repose for
thee.   Not on war and proud battle thou gazest but upon
lyre and fillet and song-loving bays.   Vindex in ceremonial
lays shall tell in what strength thou didst strike terror into
the halls of Ilium and of Thrace, into snowy Stymphalos
and the rainy hills of Erymanthus: what manner of foe-
man thou wast to the owner of the Spanish herds and to
the Egyptian potentate of the altar merciless; he shall tell

seu Pelopis terras libertatemque Pelasgam
obruerat bello; magnoque ex agmine laudum
fertur Thebanos tantum excusasse triumphos.   *70*
ille etiam, magnos Fatis rumpentibus actus,
cum traheret letale merum, iam mortis opaca
nube gravis vultus alios in numine caro
aeraque supremis timuit sudantia mensis.
mox Nasamoniaco decus admirabile regi   *75*
possessum; fortique deo libavit honores
semper atrox dextra periuroque ense superbus
Hannibal. Italicae perfusum sanguine gentis
diraque Romuleis portantem incendia tectis
oderat, et cum epulas, et cum Lenaea dicaret   *80*
dona, deus castris maerens comes ire nefandis,
praecipue cum sacrilega face miscuit arces
ipsius immeritaeque domos ac templa Sagunti
polluit et populis furias immisit honestas.
nec post Sidonii letum ducis aere potita   *85*
egregio plebeia domus. convivia Syllae
ornabat semper claros intrare penates
adsuetum et felix dominorum stemmate signum.
nunc quoque, si mores humanaque pectora curae
nosse deis; non aula quidem, Tirynthie nec te   *90*
regius ambit honos, sed casta ignaraque culpae
mens domini, cui prisca fides coeptaeque perenne
foedus amicitiae. scit adhuc florente sub aevo
par magnis Vestinus avis, quem nocte dieque
spirat et in carae vivit complexibus umbrae.   *95*
hic igitur tibi laeta quies, fortissime divum,
Alcide, nec bella vides pugnasque feroces,
sed chelyn et vittas et amantes carmina laurus.
hic tibi solemni memorabit carmine, quantus
Iliacas Geticasque domos quantusque nivalem   *100*
Stymphalon quantusque iugis Erymanthon aquosis
terrueris, quem te pecoris possessor Hiberi,
quem tulerit saevae Mareoticus arbiter arae.
hic penetrata tibi spoliataque limina mortis
concinet et flentes Libyae Scythiaeque puellas.   *105*
nec te regnator Macetum nec barbarus unquam
Hannibal aut saevi posset vox horrida Syllae
his celebrare modis. certe tu, muneris auctor,
non aliis malles oculis, Lysippe, probari.

how thou didst pierce and plunder the halls of Death, and
leave the daughters of Libya and of Scythia in tears.
Neither the Emperor of Macedon nor savage Hannibal
nor the rude voice of savage Sulla could ever have hymned
thee in such strains. Thou, assuredly, Lysippus, who
didst devise the masterpiece, wouldst not have chosen to
find favour in other eyes than his.

The Labors of Herakles, in Alyzia

48. Strabo, Geographica, X 459. (Trans. Falconer.)

Next to Leucas followed Palaerus and Alyzia, cities of
Acarnania, of which Alyzia is distant from the sea fifteen
stadia. Opposite to it is a harbor sacred to Hercules, and
a grove from whence a Roman governor transported to
Rome "the labors of Hercules," the workmanship of Lysippus, which was lying in an unsuitable place, being a
deserted spot.

49. Anth. Pal. XVI (Plan. App. IV), 96. (Trans. Paton.)

What first and what next shall my mind marvel at,
what lastly shall my eyes admire in the portraiture of the
man and hind? He, mounting on the beast's loins, rests
all the weight of his knee on her, grasping with his hands
her beautifully branched antlers, while she, panting hard
with open jaws and forced breath, tells of her heart's
anguish by her tongue. Rejoice, Heracles; the whole hind
now glitters, not her horns alone golden, but fashioned all
of gold by Art.

Herakles, Without Weapons

50. Geminus: Anth. Pal. XVI (Plan. App. IV), 103. (Trans.
Paton.)

Heracles, where is thy great club, where thy Nemean
cloak and thy quiver full of arrows, where is thy stern
glower? Why did Lysippus mould thee thus with dejected
visage and alloy the bronze with pain? Thou art in distress, stripped of thy arms. Who was it that laid thee
low? Winged Love, of a truth one of thy heavy labours.

51. Philip: Anth. Pal. XVI (Plan. App. IV), 104. (Trans.
Paton.)

So Hera, then, wished for this to crown all his labors,
the sight of doughty Heracles stripped of his arms!
Where is the lion-skin cloak, where the quiver of loud-
whizzing arrows on his shoulder and the heavy-footed

The Labors of Herakles, in Alyzia

48. Strabo, Geographica, X 459. (Ed. Meineke.)
Ἀπὸ δὲ Λευκάδος ἑξῆς Πάλαιρος καὶ Ἀλυζία τῆς
Ἀκαρνανίας εἰσὶ πόλεις, ὧν ἡ Ἀλυζία πεντεκαίδεκα ἀπὸ
θαλάττης διέχει σταδίους, καθ᾿ ἥν ἐστι λιμὴν Ἡρακλέους
ἱερὸς καὶ τέμενος, ἐξ οὗ τοὺς Ἡρακλέους ἄθλους, ἔργα Λυσίππου, μετήνεγκεν εἰς Ῥώμην τῶν ἡγεμόνων τις, παρὰ
τόπον κειμένους διὰ τὴν ἐρημίαν.

49. Anth. Pal. XVI (Plan. App. IV), 96. (Ed. Paton.)
Τί πρῶτον, τί δ᾿ ἔπειτα φρεσίν, τί δὲ λοίσθιον ὅσσοις
θαυμάσομαι τέχνης ἀνέρος ἠδ᾿ ἐλάφου;
ὧν ὁ μὲν ἰξύϊ θηρὸς ἐπεμβεβαὼς γόνυ βρίθει,
εὐπτόρθων παλάμαις δραξάμενος κεράων·
ἡ δ᾿ ὑπὸ χάσματι πολλὰ καὶ ἄσθματι φυσιόωσα
γλώσσῃ σημαίνει θλιβομένην κραδίην.
Ἡρακλες, γήθησον, ὅλη κεμὰς ἄρτι τέθηλεν
οὐ κέρασιν μούνοις, ἀλλὰ τέχνῃ χρυσέη.

Herakles, without weapons

50. Geminus: Anth. Pal. XVI (Plan. App. IV), 103. (Ed.
Paton.)
Ἡρακλες, ποῦ σοι πτόρθος μέγας, ἦ τε Νέμειος
χλαῖνα, καὶ ἡ τόξων ἔμπλεος ἰοδόκη;
ποῦ σοβαρὸν βρίμημα; τί σ᾿ ἔπλασεν ὧδε κατηφῆ
Λύσιππος, χαλκῷ τ᾿ ἐγκατέμιξ᾿ ὀδύνην;
ἄχθῃ γυμνωθεὶς ὅπλων σέο· τίς δέ σ᾿ ἔπερσεν;
ὁ πτερόεις, ὄντως εἷς βαρὺς ἄθλος, Ἔρως.

51. Philip: Anth. Pal. XVI (Plan. App. IV), 104. (Ed.
Paton.)
Ἥρη τοῦτ᾿ ἄρα λοιπὸν ἐβούλετο πᾶσιν ἐπ᾿ ἄθλοις,
ὅπλων γυμνὸν ἰδεῖν τὸν θρασὺν Ἡρακλέα.
ποῦ χλαίνωμα λέοντος, ὅ τ᾿ εὐροΐζητος ἐπ᾿ ὤμοις
ἰός, καὶ βαρύπους ὅζος ὁ θηρολέτης;

branch, the slayer of beasts? Love has stripped thee of all, and it is not strange that, having made Zeus a swan, he deprived Heracles of his weapons.

THE FARNESE HERAKLES

51a. Libanios, Ecphraseis, XV.

It was not possible for Herakles, when he had ceased his work, to stand without praise, nor to cease to be an object of wonder when he ceased from his labors, but to remain represented in sculpture, for those who saw, both toiling and after toil. 2. Thus represented, then, the artist set him in a conspicuous place. For Herakles was set up not as Nemea saw him when he was braving danger, but as Argos received him after the slaying of the lion. 3. He was set up, then, bearing tokens of his feats, but having passed the critical point of his trials. In the first place his head is bent toward the ground and is looking, I think, to see if he can slay something else. Then the neck is bent along with the head. 4. And all his body is bare of covering, for Herakles, with his attention fixed on valor, could not concern himself about modesty. Of the arms the right is tensed and bent behind his back, while the left is relaxed and extends toward the ground. 5. The club, set on the ground and enjoying the same ease as its master, supports him under the armpit; the club supports him again while he rests, as it saved him in fighting. In my judgment the artist determined the position of the club well. For in his labors Herakles uses his right hand for it, but his left while he rests in time of ease. He has given him an idle hand also. The lion-skin is set on the club; it covers both the lion and that by which the lion was destroyed. 6. Of the feet the right is starting into motion, while the left is placed under the body and set firmly on the basis, and permits the spectators to learn what kind of man Herakles was even when resting from his labors.

ALEXANDER

52. Anth. Pal. XVI (Plan. App. IV), 120. (Trans. Paton.)

Lysippus modelled Alexander's daring and his whole form. How great is the power of this bronze! The brazen king seems to be gazing at Zeus and about to say, "I set Earth under my feet; thyself, Zeus, possess Olympus."

πάντα σ᾽ Ἔρως ἀπέδυσε· καὶ οὐ ξένον, εἰ Δία κύκνον
ποιήσας, ὅπλων νοσφίσαθ᾽ Ἡρακλέα.

The Farnese Herakles

51a. Libanios, Ecphraseis, XV.   (Ed. Foerster.)

Οὐκ ἦν ἄρα τὸν Ἡρακλέα πεπαυμένον τῶν ἔργων ἐπαί
νου καταστῆναι χωρὶς οὐδὲ λῆξαι τοῦ θαύματος, ὡς τῶν
ἄθλων ἐπαύσατο, μένειν δὲ τοῖς ὁρῶσι καὶ πονοῦντα καὶ
μετὰ πόνον πλαττόμενον. 2. οἷον γοῦν ὁ δημιουργὸς εἰς
περιφανῆ χῶρον ἀνέστησεν. ἀνάκειται γὰρ Ἡρακλῆς οὐχ
οἷον εἶδεν ἡ Νεμέα προκινδυνεύοντα, ἀλλ᾽ οἷον Ἄργος ἀπέ
λαβεν ἐπ᾽ ἀναιρέσει τοῦ λέοντος. 3. ἀνέστηκε γοῦν φέρων
μὲν τῶν ἀγωνισμάτων γνωρίσματα, λήξας δὲ ὅμως τῆς
ἀγώνων ἀκμῆς. πρῶτον μὲν γὰρ αὐτῷ ἡ κεφαλὴ νεύει πρὸς
γῆν καὶ δοκεῖ μοι σκοπεῖν εἴ τι κτείνειεν ἕτερον. ἔπειτα
δειρὴ συναπονεύει τῇ κεφαλῇ. 4. καὶ ἅπαν τὸ σῶμα γυμνὸν
κροκαλύμματος, οὐ γὰρ ἦν Ἡρακλεῖ μέλειν αἰδοῦς σκοπου
μένῳ πρὸς ἀρετήν. τῶν δὲ δὴ χειρῶν ἡ μὲν δεξιὰ τέταται
καὶ συγκέκαμπται κατόπιν εἰς νῶτον, παρεῖται δὲ ἡ λαιὰ
καὶ τείνει πρὸς γῆν. 5. ἀνέχει δὲ αὐτὸν ὑπὸ μάλης τὸ ῥό
παλον ἐνιδρυμένον εἰς γῆν καὶ τῇ αὐτῇ ῥαστώνῃ χρησάμε
νον. καὶ τὸ ῥόπαλον ἀνέχει παυόμενον πάλιν, ὡς μαχόμενον
ἔσωζεν. εὖ δέ μοι δοκεῖ ὁ δημιουργὸς διηρηκέναι τοῦ ῥο
πάλου τὴν τάξιν. δεξιῷ μὲν γὰρ χρῆται πονῶν, λαιῷ δὲ
παυόμενος ἐν ἡσυχίας καιρῷ. καὶ χεῖρα δέδωκεν ἄπρακτον.
ἡ δὲ δὴ λεοντῆ τῷ ῥοπάλῳ προσίδρυται καὶ καλύπτει τόν τε
λέοντα καὶ δι᾽ οὗ διέφθαρται. 6. τοῖν δὲ δὴ ποδοῖν ὁ μὲν
δεξιὸς ὁρμᾷ πρὸς ὁρμήν, ὁ δὲ λαιὸς ὑποβέβηκε καὶ τῷ βά
θρῳ προσήρεισται καὶ παρέχει τοῖς ὁρῶσι μαθεῖν οἷος Ἡρα
κλῆς καὶ πόνων παυόμενος.

Alexander

52. Anth. Pal. XVI (Plan. App. IV), 120.   (Ed. Paton.)

Τόλμαν Ἀλεξάνδρου καὶ ὅλαν ἀπεμάξατο μορφὰν
Λύσιππος· τίν᾽ ὁδὶ χαλκὸς ἔχει δύναμιν;
αὐδασοῦντι δ᾽ ἔοικεν ὁ χάλκεος ἐς Δία λεύσσων·
«Γᾶν ὑπ᾽ ἐμοὶ τίθεμαι· Ζεῦ, σὺ δ᾽ Ὄλυμπον ἔχε.»

53. Anth. Pal. XVI (Plan. App. IV), 121. (Trans. Paton.)

Imagine that thou seest Alexander himself; so flash his very eyes in the bronze, so lives his dauntless mien. He alone subjected to the throne of Pella all the earth which the rays of Zeus look on from heaven.

54. Anth. Pal. XVI (Plan. App. IV), 122. (Trans. Paton.)

Here seest thou newly-born Alexander, the son of great-hearted Philip, him the bold-spirited to whom Olympias of old gave birth, to whom from his cradle Ares taught the labours of war and whom Fortune called to the throne.

55. Apuleius, Florida, VII. (Bohn translation.)

Now this is a most signal fact respecting Alexander, that in order to have his image descend the more authentically to posterity, he would not allow it to be vulgarised by many artists, but commanded throughout all his empire, that no one should presumptuously make the king's likeness in brass, or in painting, or with the graver; but that Polycletus alone should mould it in brass, Apelles alone delineate it in colours, Pyrgoteles alone should elaborate it with the graver. Besides these three artists, far the most eminent in their several kinds, if any other was found to have put his hands to the king's most sacred image, he should be punished just as one who had committed sacrilege. The consequence of that fear imposed on all was, that Alexander was presented with singular excellence in all his likenesses; so that in all statues, pictures, and engraved gems, he appears with the same vigorous aspect of a most intrepid warrior, the same genius of a mighty hero, the same beauty and freshness of youth, the same noble expansion of forehead.

56. Choricius; Madrid Codex fol. 174 v; *Jb. Arch. I.*, IX, 1894, p. 168.

If Lysippos had portrayed Alexander as like Lysippos in stature, do you think that the image would have pleased the Macedonian, who thought himself superior to all men in everything?

57. Choricius; Madrid Codex fol. 164 v; *Jb. Arch. I.*, IX, 1894, p. 173.

Alexander, the son of Philip—for he was the son of Philip, even though he wished to be thought the son of Zeus—was portrayed by many sculptors and many painters. The works of all except Lysippos he praised but little, whether the material was color or bronze, because

53. Anth. Pal. XVI (Plan. App. IV) 121. (Ed. Paton.)
Αὐτὸν 'Αλέξανδρον τεκμαίρεο· ὧδε τὰ κείνου
ὄμματα, καὶ ζωὸν θάρσος ὁ χαλκὸς ἔχει·
ὃς μόνος, ἣν ἐφορῶσιν ἀπ' αἰθέρος αἱ Διὸς αὐγαί,
πᾶσαν Πελλαίῳ γῆν ὑπέταξε θρόνῳ.

54. Anth. Pal. XVI (Plan. App. IV), 122. (Ed. Paton.)
Τοῦτον 'Αλέξανδρον, μεγαλήτορος υἷα Φιλίππου,
δέρκεαι ἀρτιλόχευτον, 'Ολυμπιὰς ὅν ποτε μήτηρ
καρτερόθυμον ἔτικτεν· ἀπ' ὠδίνων δέ μιν "Αρης
ἔργα μόθων ἐδίδασκε, Τύχη δ' ἐκέλευσεν ἀνάσσειν.

55. Apuleius, Florida, VII. (Ed. Van der Vliet.)
Sed cum primis Alexandri illud praeclarum, quod imaginem suam, quo certior posteris proderetur, noluit a multis artificibus vulgo contaminari, sed edixit universo orbi suo, ne quis effigiem regis temere adsimularet aere, colore, caelamine: quin saepe solus eam Polycletus aere duceret; solus Apelles coloribus deliniaret, solus Pyrgoteles caelamine excuderet: praeter hos tris multo nobilissimos in suis artificiis si quis uspiam, repperiretur alius sanctissimae imagine regis manus admolitus, haud secus in eum quam in sacrilegium vindicaturum. eo igitur omnium metu factum, solus Alexander ut ubique imaginum similis esset, utique omnibus statuis et tabulis et toreumatibus idem vigor acerrimi bellatoris, idem ingenium maximi honoris, eadem forma viridis iuventae, eadem gratia relicinae frontis cerneretur.

56. Choricius; Madrid Codex fol. 174v; Jb. Arch. I., IX, 1894, p. 168. (Ed. Förster.)
Εἰ δὲ Λύσιππος τὸν 'Αλέξανδρον ἔπλασεν ἐοικότα Λυσίππῳ τὸ μῆκος, οἴει ἂν κεχαρισμένον εἶναι τὸν ἀνδριάντα τῷ Μακεδόνι πάντων ἐν ἅπασιν οἰομένῳ προέχειν;

57. Choricius; Madrid Codex fol. 164v; Jb. Arch. I., IX, 1894, p. 168. (Ed. Förster.)
'Αλέξανδρον, τὸ Φιλίππου μειράκιον, Φιλίππου γὰρ ἦν, εἰ καὶ τοῦ Διὸς δοκεῖν ἐβούλετο εἶναι, πολλοὶ μὲν εἰργάζοντο πλάσται, πολλοὶ δὲ ἔγραφον ζωγράφοι.. ὁ δὲ τῶν μὲν ἄλλων ἧττον ἐπήνει τὰ ἔργα, εἴτε χρώματα ἦν εἴτε χαλκὸς ἡ ὕλη, ὅτι τὰ μὲν αὐτοῦ μιμεῖσθαι ἐδόκουν, τὰ δὲ οὐ πάνυ, ἥδεται

they seemed to represent some features faithfully, but others not very well; but he was always pleased when he saw the statue by Lysippos. 2. For Alexander son of Philip was keen, manly, majestic, and resolute; so also was Alexander the work of Lysippos. So he ordered other artists to represent other men, but himself he determined to entrust to Lysippos only. 3. So exceedingly well did the Sikyonian portray the man of Macedon.

58. Cicero, Epistulae ad Familiares, V 12, 7. (Trans. Shuckburgh.)

For the famous Alexander himself did not wish to be painted by Apelles, and to have his statue made by Lysippos above all others, merely from personal favor to them, but because he thought that their art would be a glory at once to them and to himself.

59. Himerios, Orationes, XIV 14 (Wernsdorf p. 634.)

Did not Alexander give Lysippos a name and reputation, when he had been portrayed by him so well that even Poetry herself marvelled greatly at the masterpiece? Or have you not heard the epigram that is spoken about the statue of Alexander? This:

Lysippus, sculptor of Sicyon, bold hand, cunning craftsman, its glance is of fire, that bronze thou didst cast in the form of Alexander. No longer do we blame the Persians: cattle may be pardoned for flying before a lion. (Trans. Paton.)

60. Himerios, Eclogae, XXXI 2 (Wernsdorf p. 286.)

They say that Alexander became an object of competition for the arts of former times, so that Lysippos and Apelles shared his person between them; and one interpreted the nature of the king in paint, the other in bronze.

61. Horace, Epistulae II 1, 237-241. (Trans. Masom.)

That same monarch, who in his extravagance spent so much on so ridiculous a poem, by an edict forbade that anyone but Apelles should paint him, or that any statuary besides Lysippus should mould the brass which was to represent the features of the valiant Alexander.

62. Pliny, N. H., VII 125. (Trans. Jex-Blake.)

The emperor Alexander also issued an edict that none but Apelles might paint his portrait, none but Pyrgoteles engrave it, and none but Lysippus cast his statue in bronze. Several famous likenesses of him exist of these three kinds.

δὲ ὁρῶν τὴν Λυσίππου εἰκόνα 'Αλέξανδρος· (2) τὸ γὰρ ὀξὺ καὶ ἀρρενωπὸν καὶ γαῦρον καὶ ἄοκνον εἶχε μὲν ὁ Φιλίππου, εἶχε δὲ ὁ Λυσίππου· ὥστε τοῖς μὲν ἄλλοις ἄλλους δημιουργεῖν ἐνετέλλετο, ἑαυτὸν δὲ ἠξίου μόνῳ Λυσίππῳ πιστεύειν. (3) οὕτω μὲν εὖ μάλα ἐποίει τὸν Μακεδόνα ὁ Σικυώνιος.

58. Cicero, Epistulae ad Familiares, V 12, 7. (Ed. Purser.)
Neque enim Alexander ille gratiae causa ab Apelle potissimum pingi et a Lysippo fingi volebat, sed quod illorum artem cum ipsis tum etiam sibi gloriae fore putabat.

59. Himerios, Orationes, XIV 14 (Wernsdorf, p. 634). (Ed. Wernsdorf.)
Οὐ γὰρ δὴ Λυσίππῳ ὄνομά τε ἐδίδου καὶ δόξαν 'Αλέξανδρος ὑπ' ἐκείνου πλαττόμενος, ὡς καὶ αὐτὴν τὴν ποίησιν σφόδρα θαυμάσαι τὸ φιλοτέχνημα; ἢ οὐκ ἀκούετε τὸ ἐπίγραμμα τὸ ἐπὶ εἰκόνος τῆς 'Αλεξάνδρου λεγόμενον; τὸ
Λύσιππε, πλάστα Σικυώνιε, θαρσαλέη χείρ,
δάϊε τεχνῖτα, πῦρ τοι ὁ χαλκὸς ὁρῇ,
ὃν κατ' 'Αλεξάνδρου μορφᾶς χέες· οὐκέτι μεμπτοὶ
Πέρσαι· συγγνώμη βουσὶ λέοντα φυγεῖν.

60. Himerios, Eclogae, XXXI 2 (Wernsdorf, p. 286). (Ed. Dübner.)
Γενέσθαι μὲν καὶ 'Αλέξανδρον λόγος ταῖς πάλαι τέχναις ἀγώνισμα, ὥστε δὴ καὶ νειμάμενοι τὴν μορφὴν αὐτοῦ Λύσιππος καὶ 'Απελλῆς, ὁ μὲν φαρμάκοις, ὁ δὲ χαλκῷ τὴν φύσιν τοῦ βασιλέως ἡρμήνευσαν.

61. Horace, Epistulae, II 1, 237-241. (Ed. Mueller.)
Idem rex ille, poema
Qui tam ridiculum tam care prodigus emit,
Edicto vetuit, nequis se praeter Apellen
Pingeret aut alius Lysippo duceret aera
Fortis Alexandri voltum simulantia.

62. Pliny, N. H., VII 125. (Ed. Sellers and Jex-Blake.)
Idem hic imperator edixit ne quis ipsum alius quam Apelles pingeret, quam Pyrgoteles scalperet, quam Lysippus ex aere duceret, quae artes pluribus inclaruere exemplis.

63. Plutarch, Alexander, 4, 1. (Trans. Perrin.)

The outward appearance of Alexander is best represented by the statues of him which Lysippus made, and it
was by this artist alone that Alexander himself thought it
fit that he should be modelled. For those peculiarities
which many of his successors and friends afterwards tried
to imitate, namely, the poise of the neck, which was bent
slightly to the left, and the melting glance of his eyes, this
artist has accurately observed.

64. Plutarch, De Alexandri Magni Fortuna aut Virtute, II 2.
(Trans. Philips, revised by Goodwin.)

. Furthermore, there were also Apelles the painter and
Lysippus the statuary both living under the reign of
Alexander. The first of which painted him grasping
Jupiter's thunderbolt in his hand, so artfully and in such
lively colors, that it was said of the two Alexanders that
Philip's was invincible, but Apelles's inimitable. Lysippus, when he had finished the first statue of Alexander
looking up with his face to the sky (as Alexander was
wont to look, with his neck slightly bent), not improperly
added to the pedestal the following lines:

The statue seems to look to Jove and say,
Take thou Olympus; me let Earth obey!

For which Alexander gave to Lysippus the sole patent for
making all his statues; because he alone expressed in brass
the vigor of his mind, and in his lineaments represented
the lustre of his virtue; while others, who strove to imitate
the turning of his neck and softness and brightness of his
eyes failed to observe the manliness and lion-like fierceness
of his countenance.

65. Plutarch, De Iside et Osiride, 24. (Trans. Baxter, revised
by Goodwin.)

And Lysippus the carver had good reason to quarrel
with the painter Apelles for drawing Alexander's picture
with a thunder-bolt in his hand, whereas himself had made
him but with a spear, which (he said) was natural and
proper for him, and a weapon the glory of which no time
would rob him of.

66. Poseidippos: Anth. Pal. XVI (Plan. App. IV) 119.

(This epigram is quoted by Himerius; see no. 59
above.)

67. Tzetzes, Chiliades, VIII 416-434.

This Lysippos also was a sculptor in bronze. He was
of the city Sikyon, which is very near Corinth, and was

63. Plutarch, Alexander 4, 1. (Ed. Perrin.)

Τὴν μὲν οὖν ἰδέαν τοῦ σώματος οἱ Λυσίππειοι μάλιστα τῶν ἀνδριάντων ἐμφαίνουσιν, ὑφ' οὗ μόνου καὶ αὐτὸς ἠξίου πλάττεσθαι. καὶ γὰρ μάλισθ' ἃ πολλοὶ τῶν διαδόχων ὕστερον καὶ τῶν φίλων ἀπεμιμοῦντο, τήν τε ἀνάτασιν τοῦ αὐχένος εἰς εὐώνυμον ἡσυχῇ κεκλιμένου καὶ τὴν ὑγρότητα τῶν ὀμμάτων, διατετήρηκεν ἀκριβῶς ὁ τεχνίτης.

64. Plutarch, De Alexandri Magni Fortuna aut Virtute, II 2. (Ed. Bernardakis.)

Ἦν δὲ καὶ Ἀπελλῆς ὁ ζωγράφος καὶ Λύσιππος ὁ πλάστης κατ' Ἀλέξανδρον· ὧν ὁ μὲν ἔγραψε τὸν κεραυνοφόρον οὕτως ἐναργῶς καὶ κεκραμένως, ὥστε λέγειν, ὅτι δυεῖν Ἀλεξάνδρων ὁ μὲν Φιλίππου γέγονεν ἀνίκητος, ὁ δ' Ἀπελλοῦ ἀμίμητος. Λυσίππου δὲ τὸν πρῶτον Ἀλέξανδρον πλάσαντος, ἄνω βλέποντα τῷ προσώπῳ πρὸς τὸν οὐρανὸν (ὥσπερ αὐτὸς εἰώθει βλέπειν Ἀλέξανδρος ἡσυχῇ παρεγκλίνων τὸν τράχηλον) ἐπέγραψέ τις οὐκ ἀπιθάνως

αὐδασοῦντι δ' ἔοικεν ὁ χάλκεος εἰς Δία λεύσσων,
Γᾶν ὑπ' ἐμοὶ τίθεμαι· Ζεῦ, σὺ δ' Ὄλυμπον ἔχε.

διὸ καὶ μόνον Ἀλέξανδρος ἐκέλευε Λύσιππον εἰκόνας αὐτοῦ δημιουργεῖν. μόνος γὰρ οὗτος, ὡς ἔοικε, κατεμήνυε τῷ χαλκῷ τὸ ἦθος αὐτοῦ καὶ συνεξέφαινε τῇ μορφῇ τὴν ἀρετήν· οἱ δ' ἄλλοι τὴν ἀποστροφὴν τοῦ τραχήλου καὶ τῶν ὀμμάτων τὴν διάχυσιν καὶ ὑγρότητα μιμεῖσθαι θέλοντες οὐ διεφύλαττον αὐτοῦ τὸ ἀρρενωπὸν καὶ λεοντῶδες.

65. Plutarch, De Iside et Osiride, 24. (Ed. Bernardakis.)

Εὖ δὲ καὶ Λύσιππος ὁ πλάστης Ἀπελλῆν ἐμέμψατο τὸν ζωγράφον, ὅτι τὴν Ἀλεξάνδρου γράφων εἰκόνα κεραυνὸν ἐνεχείρισεν· αὐτὸς δὲ λόγχην, ἧς τὴν δόξαν οὐδὲ εἷς ἀφαιρήσεται χρόνος ἀληθινὴν καὶ ἰδίαν οὖσαν.

66. Poseidippos: Anth. Pal. VI (Plan. App. IV), 119.
(This epigram is quoted by Himerius; see no. 59 above.)

67. Tzetzes, Chiliades, VIII 416-434. (Ed. Kiessling.)

Καὶ οὗτος πλάττων τὰ χαλκᾶ ὁ Λύσιππος ὑπῆρχεν.
Ἦν ἐκ τῆς Σικυῶνος δὲ τῆς ἔγχιστα Κορίνθου,

contemporary with Alexander son of Philip. He made statues perfectly like the originals. Alexander was pleased with his works of art; for he represented him with his head on one side, seeming to look toward the sky, and accurately in every respect as Alexander that famous Macedonian was, so that the onlookers thought that they saw Alexander, not a block of marble. On the marble some student of epigrams inscribed this:

The brazen king seems to be gazing at Zeus and about to say, "I set Earth under my feet; thyself, Zeus, possesses Olympus."[2]

This Sikyonian, Lysippos the sculptor, when once Alexander had neglected a favorable time and was deeply discouraged by its passing, very cleverly sculptured the image of Time, representing him as deaf, bald on the back of his head, standing with winged feet on a sphere, and presenting a knife to any one attempting to seize him from behind; in this way warning every one not to disregard time.

68. Tzetzes, Chiliades, XI 97-108.

The great king Alexander, son of Philip, is said by every one to have had one eye gray and the other black. Such he was as to his eyes. His neck was slanting and turned to one side, so that he seemed to gaze toward the heavens. As such Lysippos represented him in bronze. His images pleased Alexander, rather than the false statues by Stasikrates,[3] with their look of being puffed up with vain conceit. That Alexander's appearance was such is shown by the epigram, which runs as follows:

The brazen king seems to be gazing at Zeus and about to say, "I set Earth under my feet; thyself, Zeus, possess Olympus."[4]

69. Valerius Maximus, VIII 11, ext. 2.

Furthermore how much value, do we think, was ascribed to art by King Alexander, who wished to be portrayed in painting only by Apelles and in sculpture only by Lysippos?

---

[2] Paton's translation; see nos. 52 and 64.

[3] This sculptor is mentioned also in Chiliades, VIII 408-415, and XI 94-96; other citations in Pauly-Wissowa under Deinokrates. Cf. Kurt Müller, *Der Leichenwagen Alexanders des Grossen*, p. 74.

[4] Paton's translation; see nos. 52, 64, and 67.

Τῷ τοῦ Φιλίππου σύγχρονος υἱῷ τῷ Ἀλεξάνδρῳ,
Πανεμφερῆ ἀγάλματα ποιῶν τοῖς πρωτοτύποις.
Ἐπέχαιρε δ' Ἀλέξανδρος ταῖς τούτου πλαστουργίαις.   420
Καὶ γὰρ καὶ παρατράχηλον ἐποίησεν ἐκεῖνον,
Δοκοῦντα βλέπειν οὐρανὸν καὶ πᾶν ἠκριβωμένως,
Ὁποῖος ἦν Ἀλέξανδρος ὁ Μακεδὼν ἐκεῖνος,
Ὥστε δοκεῖν τοὺς βλέποντας Ἀλέξανδρον, οὐ στήλην.
Ἦι στήλῃ τις ἐπέγραψεν ἐπιγραμματοφόρος·   425
«Αὐδάσοντι δ' ἔοικεν ὁ χάλκεος, ἐς Δία λεύσων,
Γᾶν ὑπ' ἐμὲ τίθεμαι, Ζεῦ, σὺ δ' Ὄλυμπον ἔχε».
Οὗτος ὁ Σικυώνιος ὁ Λύσιππος ὁ πλάστης,
Καὶ Ἀλεξάνδρου πώποτε χρόνον παραδραμόντος,
Καὶ ἀθυμοῦντος δὲ δεινῶς τῇ παροιχήσει τούτου,   430
Πανσόφως ἠγαλμάτωσε τοῦ χρόνου τὴν εἰκόνα,
Πάντας ἐντεῦθεν νουθετῶν, χρόνον μὴ παρατρέχειν,
Κωφόν, ὀπισθοφάλακρον, πτέροπουν ἐπὶ σφαίρας,
Πρὸς τὸ κατόπιν μάχαιράν τινι διδόνα πλάσας.

68. Tzetzes, Chiliades, XI 97-108. (Ed. Kiessling.)
    Ὁ βασιλεὺς ὁ μέγιστος Ἀλέξανδρος Φιλίππου,
    Γλαυκὸν τὸν ἕνα ὀφθαλμὸν ἔχειν θρυλλεῖται πᾶσι,
    Μέλανα δὲ τὸν ἕτερον. τοῖς ὀφθαλμοῖς τοιοῦτος.
    Ἦν δὲ καὶ σιμοτράχηλος καὶ παρατραχηλῶν δέ,   100
    Ὥστε δοκεῖν πρὸς οὐρανὸν ἐνατενίζειν τοῦτον.
    Τοιοῦτον καὶ ὁ Λύσιππος ἐκεῖνον ἐχαλκούργει.
    Καὶ τούτου δὲ Ἀλέξανδρος ἐπέχειρεν εἰκόσιν,
    Ἡ Στασικράτους πλάσμασι ψευδέσι, τυφουμένοις.
    Ὅτι δ' ἦν ὁ Ἀλέξανδρος τοιοῦτος τὴν ἰδέαν,   105
    Δηλοῖ καὶ τὸ ἐπίγραμμα ὅπερ τυγχάνει τόδε,
    «Αὐδάσοντι δ' ἔοικεν ὁ χάλκεος, ἐς Δία λεύσων,
    Γᾶν ὑπ' ἐμὲ τίθεμαι, Ζεῦ, σὺ δ' Ὄλυμπον ἔχε».

69. Valerius Maximus, VIII 11, ext. 2. (Ed. Halm.)
    Quantum porro dignitatis a rege Alexandro tributum
    arti existimamus, qui se et pingi ab uno Apelle et fingi a
    Lysippo tantummodo voluit?

The Granikos Monument

70. Arrian, Anabasis, I 16, 4. (Trans. Chinnock.)

Of the Macedonians, about twenty-five of the Companions were killed at the first onset; brazen statues of whom were erected at Dium, executed by Lysippus, at Alexander's order. The same statuary also executed a statue of Alexander himself, being chosen by him in preference to all other artists.

71. Justin, Historiae, XI 6, 12-13.

Of Alexander's army nine foot-soldiers and a hundred twenty horsemen perished. For the consolation of the others, the king adorned their tomb with equestrian statues at great cost, and gave to their kinsmen immunity from public services.

72. Plutarch, Alexander, 16, 7. (Trans. Perrin.)

But on Alexander's side Aristobulus says there were thirty-four dead in all, of whom nine were footmen. (8) Of these, then, Alexander ordered statues to be set up in bronze, and Lysippus wrought them.

73. Velleius Paterculus, Historia Romana, I 11, 3-4. (Trans. Watson.)

This is the Metellus Macedonicus who erected the porticos around the two temples without an inscription, now encircled by the porticos of Octavia, and who brought from Macedonia the group of equestrian statues that face the front of the temples, and form at present the chief ornament of the place. Of this group the following origin is related. Alexander the Great, it is said, desired Lysippus, an eminent artist in such performances, to make statues of such horsemen of his own troop as had fallen at the River Granicus, representing their likenesses in the figures, and placing one of Alexander himself among them.

The Krateros Group

74. Plutarch, Alexander, 40, 4. (Trans. Jones.)

Krateros erected a memorial of this hunt at Delphi. He caused figures of bronze to be made, representing the lion, the dogs, the king in combat with the lion, and himself coming to the rescue; some of these were made by Lysippos, the rest by Leochares.

Socrates

75. Diogenes Laertius, De Vitis Philosophorum, II 5, 43. (Trans. Yonge.)

THE GRANIKOS MONUMENT

70. Arrian, Anabasis, I 16, 4. (Ed. Roos.)

Μακεδόνων δὲ τῶν μὲν ἑταίρων ἀμφὶ τοὺς εἴκοσι καὶ πέντε ἐν τῇ πρώτῃ προσβολῇ ἀπέθανον· καὶ τούτων χαλκαῖ εἰκόνες ἐν Δίῳ ἑστᾶσιν, Ἀλεξάνδρου κελεύσαντος Λύσιππον ποιῆσαι, ὅσπερ καὶ Ἀλέξανδρον μόνος προκριθεὶς ἐποίει.

71. Justin, Historiae, XI 6, 12-13. (Ed. Rühl.)

De exercitu Alexandri novem pedites, centum XX equites cecidere, quos rex inpense ad ceterorum solacia humatos statuis equestribus donavit cognatisque eorum inmunitatem dedit.

72. Plutarch, Alexander, 16, 7. (Ed. Perrin.)

Τῶν δὲ περὶ τὸν Ἀλέξανδρον Ἀριστόβουλός φησι τέσσαρας καὶ τριάκοντα νεκροὺς γενέσθαι τοὺς πάντας, ὧν ἐννέα πεζοὺς εἶναι. (8) τούτων μὲν οὖν ἐκέλευσεν εἰκόνας ἀνασταθῆναι χαλκᾶς, ἃς Λύσιππος εἰργάσατο.

73. Velleius Paterculus, Historia Romana I 11, 3-4. (Ed. Haase.)

Hic est Metellus Macedonicus, qui porticus, quae fuere circumdatae duabus aedibus sine inscriptione positis, quae nunc Octaviae porticibus ambiuntur, fecerat, quique hanc turmam statuarum equestrium, quae frontem aedium spectant, hodieque maximum ornamentum eius loci ex Macedonia detulit. Cuius turmae hanc causam referunt, Magnum Alexandrum impetrasse a Lysippo, singulari talium auctore operum, ut eorum equitum, qui ex ipsius turma apud Granicum flumen ceciderant, expressa similitudine figurarum faceret statuas et ipsius quoque iis interponeret.

THE KRATEROS GROUP

74. Plutarch, Alexander, 40, 4. (Ed. Perrin.)

Τοῦτο τὸ κυνήγιον Κρατερὸς εἰς Δελφοὺς ἀνέθηκεν, εἰκόνας χαλκᾶς ποιησάμενος τοῦ λέοντος καὶ τῶν κυνῶν καὶ τοῦ βασιλέως τῷ λέοντι συνεστῶτος καὶ αὐτοῦ προσβοηθοῦντος, ὧν τὰ μὲν Λύσιππος ἔπλασε, τὰ δὲ Λεωχάρης.

SOCRATES

75. Diogenes Laertius, De Vitis Philosophorum, II 5, 43. (Ed. Hübner.)

So he died; but the Athenians immediately repented of their action, so that they closed all the palaestrae and gymnasia; and they banished his accusers, and condemned Meletus to death; but they honoured Socrates with a brazen statue, which they erected in the place where the sacred vessels are kept; and it was the work of Lysippus.

PRAXILLA

76. Tatian, Contra Graecos, 52 (Worth p. 113). (Trans. Pratten.)

For Lysippus cast a statue of Praxilla, whose poems contain nothing useful.

AESOP

77. Agathias: Anth. Pal. XVI (Plan. App. IV), 332. (Trans. Paton.)

Thou didst well, old Lysippus, sculptor of Sicyon, in placing the portrait of Samian Aesop in front of the Seven Sages, since they for their part put force, and not persuasion, into their saws, but he, saying the right thing in his wise fables and inventions, playing in serious earnest, persuades men to be sensible. Rough expostulation is to be avoided, but the sweetness of the Samian's fables makes a pretty bait.

78. Pliny, N. H., XXXIV 86. (Trans. Jex-Blake.)

Aristodemos also made wrestlers, two-horse chariots with charioteer, and figures of philosophers, of old women, and of King Seleukos; his Spear-bearer too has a charm of its own.

79. Tatian, Contra Graecos, 55 (Worth p. 119). (Trans. Pratten.)

And not only have his tales kept the fabulist Aesop in everlasting remembrance, but also the plastic art of Aristodemus has increased his celebrity.

PYTHES

80. Pausanias, Graeciae Descriptio, VI 14, 12. (Trans. Frazer.)

The two statues of Pythes, son of Andromachus, a man of Abdera, are by Lysippus: they were dedicated by his soldiers. Pythes seems to have been a captain of freelances, or a good soldier in some capacity.

APPENDIX I 311

Ὁ μὲν οὖν ἐξ ἀνθρώπων ἦν· Ἀθηναῖοι δ' εὐθὺς μετέγνωσαν, ὥστε κλεῖσαι καὶ παλαίστρας καὶ γυμνάσια. καὶ τοὺς μὲν ἐφυγάδευσαν, Μελίτου δὲ θάνατον κατέγνωσαν· Σωκράτη δὲ χαλκῆς εἰκόνος ἐτιμήσαντο, ἣν ἔθεσαν ἐν τῷ πομπείῳ, Λυσίππου ταύτην ἐργασαμένου.

PRAXILLA

76. Tatian, Contra Graecos, 52 (Worth, p. 113). (Ed. Kalkmann, *Rh. Mus.* XLII, 1887, p. 489.)
Πράξιλλαν μὲν γὰρ Λύσιππος ἐχαλκούργησεν, μηδὲν εἰποῦσαν διὰ τῶν ποιημάτων χρήσιμον.

AESOP

77. Agathias: Anth. Pal. XVI (Plan. App. IV), 332. (Ed. Paton.)
Εὖγε ποιῶν, Λύσιππε γέρων, Σικυώνιε πλάστα,
δείκελον Αἰσώπου στῆσαο τοῦ Σαμίου
ἑπτὰ σοφῶν ἔμπροσθεν· ἐπεὶ κεῖνοι μὲν ἀνάγκην
ἔμβαλον, οὐ πειθώ, φθέγμασι τοῖς σφετέροις,
ὃς δὲ σοφοῖς μύθοις καὶ πλάσμασι καίρια λέξας,
παίζων ἐν σπουδῇ, πείθει ἐχεφρονέειν.
φευκτὸν δ' ἡ τρηχεῖα παραίνεσις· ἡ Σαμίου δὲ
τὸ γλυκὺ τοῦ μύθου καλὸν ἔχει δέλεαρ.

78. Pliny, N. H., XXXIV 86. (Ed. Sellers and Jex-Blake.)
. . . Aristodemus et luctatores bigasque cum auriga, philosophos, anus, Seleucum regem. habet gratiam suam huius quoque doryphorus.

79. Tatian, Contra Graecos, 55 (Worth, p. 119). (Ed. Kalkmann, *Rh. Mus.* XLII, 1887, p. 491.)
Καὶ τὸν ψευδολόγον Αἴσωπον ἀείμνηστον οὐ μόνον τὰ μυθολογήματα ἀλλὰ καὶ ἡ κατὰ τὸν Ἀριστόδημον πλαστικὴ περισπούδαστον ἀπέδειξεν.

PYTHES

80. Pausanias, Graeciae Descriptio, VI 14, 12. (Ed. Schubart.)
Πύθου δὲ τοῦ Ἀνδρομάχου, γένος ἀνδρὸς ἐξ Ἀβδήρων, ἐποίησε μὲν Λύσιππος, ἀνέθεσαν δὲ οἱ στρατιῶται δύο εἰκόνας· εἶναι δὲ ἡγεμών τις ξένων ἢ καὶ ἄλλως τὰ πολεμικὰ ἀγαθὸς ὁ Πύθης ἔοικε.

POLYDAMAS

81. Pausanias, Graeciae Descriptio, VI 5, 1-7. (Trans. Frazer.)

The statue on the lofty pedestal is a work of Lysippos: the man it represents was the tallest of men, if we except the heroes and the mortal race, if such there were, that preceded the heroes. Certainly of this present race of men this Pulydamas, son of Nicias, was the tallest. Scotusa, the native town of Pulydamas, is now no longer inhabited. For Alexander, tyrant of Pherae, seized it in time of truce. Some of the townspeople were gathered in the theatre, for it happened that they were holding a public assembly. So Alexander surrounded them with targeteers and archers, and shot them all down, and he butchered all the rest of the men, and sold the women and children in order to pay his mercenaries. This calamity befell Scotusa when Phrasiclides was archon at Athens, in the second year of the hundred and second Olympiad, the Olympiad in which Damon of Thurii was victorious for the second time. The handful that escaped abode for a little while in the city, but afterwards they too were obliged, by their weak and forlorn condition, to abandon it at the time when God visited the whole Greek nation with a second overthrow in the war with Macedonia. Other men besides Pulydamas have won famous victories in the pancratium, but besides the crowns he won in the pancratium, Pulydamas performed the following exploits of a different sort. The highlands of Thrace, on this side the river Nestus, which flows through the land of Abdera, are the home of wild animals, including lions. These lions attacked the army of Xerxes of old, and made havoc of the camels which were carrying the provisions. Often they roam into the country about Mount Olympus, one side of which is turned to Macedonia, and the other to Thessaly and the river Peneus. Here on Mount Olympus Pulydamas unarmed slew a lion, a great and mighty beast. He was incited to the feat by a desire to emulate the deeds of Hercules, because the story goes that Hercules also conquered the Nemean lion. Yet another marvellous exploit of Pulydamas is on record. He went among a herd of cattle, and catching the largest and most savage bull by one of its hind feet, he held fast its hoof, and though the beast plunged and struggled he did not let go,

POLYDAMAS

81. Pausanias, Graeciae Descriptio, VI, 5, 1-7. (Ed. Schubart.)

Ὁ δὲ ἐπὶ τῷ βάθρῳ τῷ ὑψηλῷ Λυσίππου μέν ἐστιν ἔργον, μέγιστος δὲ ἁπάντων ἐγένετο ἀνθρώπων πλὴν τῶν ἡρώων καλουμένων καὶ εἰ δή τι ἄλλο ἦν πρὸ τῶν ἡρώων θνητὸν γένος· ἀνθρώπων δὲ τῶν καθ' ἡμᾶς οὗτός ἐστιν ὁ μέγιστος Πουλυδάμας Νικίου. Σκότουσα δὲ ἡ τοῦ Που- 2 λυδάμαντος πατρὶς οὐκ ᾠκεῖτο ἔτι ἐφ' ἡμῶν· Ἀλέξανδρος γὰρ τὴν πόλιν ὁ Φεραίων τυραννήσας κατέλαβεν ἐν σπονδαῖς, καὶ Σκοτουσαίων τούς τε ἐς τὸ θέατρον συνειλεγμένους, ἔτυχε γάρ σφισιν ἐκκλησία τηνικαῦτα οὖσα, τούτους τε ἅπαντας κατηκόντισε πελτασταῖς ἐν κύκλῳ περισχὼν καὶ τοξόταις, καὶ τὸ ἄλλο ὅσον ἐν ἡλικίᾳ κατεφόνευσε, γυναῖκας δὲ ἀπέδοτο καὶ παῖδας, μισθὸν εἶναι τὰ χρήματα τοῖς ξένοις. αὕτη Σκοτουσαίοις ἡ συμφορὰ Φρασικλείδου μὲν Ἀθήνῃ- 3 σιν ἐγένετο ἄρχοντος, δευτέρᾳ δὲ ὀλυμπιάδι ἐπὶ ταῖς ἑκατόν, ἣν Δάμων Θούριος ἐνίκα τὸ δεύτερον, ταύτης ἔτει δευτέρῳ τῆς ὀλυμπιάδος. καὶ ὀλίγον τε ἔμενε τὸ διαφυγὸν τῶν Σκοτουσαίων, καὶ αὖθις ὑπὸ ἀσθενείας ἐξέλιπον καὶ οὗτοι τὴν πόλιν, ὅτε καὶ τοῖς πᾶσιν Ἕλλησι προσπταῖσαι δεύτερα ἐν τῷ πρὸς Μακεδόνας πολέμῳ παρεσκεύασεν ὁ δαίμων. Παγκρατίου μὲν δὴ καὶ ἄλλοις ἤδη γεγόνασιν ἐπιφανεῖς νῖκαι· Πουλυδάμαντι δὲ τάδε ἀλλοῖα παρὰ τοὺς ἐπὶ 4 τῷ παγκρατίῳ στεφάνους ὑπάρχοντά ἐστιν. ἡ ὀρεινὴ τῆς Θρᾴκης, ἡ ἔνδον Νέστου ποταμοῦ τοῦ ῥέοντος διὰ τῆς Ἀβδηριτῶν, καὶ ἄλλα θηρία, ἐν δὲ αὐτοῖς παρέχεται καὶ λέοντας, οἳ καὶ τῷ στρατῷ ποτὲ ἐπιθέμενοι τῷ Ξέρξου τὰς ἀγούσας καμήλους τὰ σιτία ἐλυμήναντο. οὗτοι πολλάκις οἱ 5 λέοντες καὶ ἐς τὴν περὶ τὸν Ὄλυμπον πλανῶνται χώραν· τούτου δὲ τοῦ ὄρους ἡ μὲν ἐς Μακεδονίαν πλευρά, ἡ δὲ ἐπὶ Θεσσαλοὺς καὶ τὸν ποταμὸν τέτραπται τὸν Πηνειόν. ἐνταῦθα ὁ Πουλυδάμας λέοντα ἐν τῷ Ὀλύμπῳ, μέγα καὶ ἄλκιμον θηρίον, κατειργάσατο οὐδενὶ ἐσκευασμένος ὅπλῳ. προήχθη δὲ ἐς τὸ τόλμημα φιλοτιμίᾳ πρὸς τὰ Ἡρακλέους ἔργα, ὅτι καὶ Ἡρακλέα ἔχει λόγος κρατῆσαι τοῦ ἐν Νεμέᾳ λέοντος. ἕτερον δὲ ἐπὶ τούτῳ θαῦμα ὑπελίπετο ὁ Πουλυ- 6 δάμας ἐς μνήμην· ἐς ἀγέλην ἐσελθὼν βοῶν, τὸν μέγιστον καὶ ἀγριώτατον ταῦρον λαβὼν τοῦ ἑτέρου τῶν ὄπισθεν ποδῶν τὰς χηλὰς κατεῖχεν ἄκρας, καὶ πηδῶντα καὶ ἐπειγόμενον οὐκ ἀνίει, πρίν γε δὴ ὁ ταῦρος ὀψέ ποτε καὶ ἐς ἅπαν ἀφικόμενος βίας ἀπέφυγεν ἀφεὶς ταύτῃ τῷ Πουλυδάμαντι τὰς χηλάς. Λέγεται δὲ καὶ ὡς ἄνδρα ἡνίοχον ἐλαύνοντα σπουδῇ τὸ ἅρμα ἐπέσχε τοῦ πρόσω· λαβόμενος γὰρ τῇ ἑτέρᾳ τῶν χειρῶν ὄπισθε τοῦ ἅρματος, ὁμοῦ καὶ τοὺς ἵππους πε-

till at last the bull putting forth all its strength escaped, leaving its hoof in the hands of Pulydamas. It is said, too, that he stopped a chariot driven at speed; for, seizing it from behind with one hand, he held as in a vice the horses and their driver. Hearing of his exploits, Darius, a bastard son of Artaxerxes, who, supported by the commons of Persia, had dethroned Sogdius, the legitimate son of Artaxerxes, and reigned in his stead, sent messengers, and by the promise of gifts persuaded Pulydamas to go up to Susa and see him. There he challenged three of the band called Immortals to fight him all at once, and slew them all. Of the feats I have enumerated, some are represented on the pedestal of his statue at Olympia, others are mentioned in the inscription.

81a. Lucian, Deorum Concilium, 12.

Then too the statue of the athlete Polydamas, in Olympia, cures persons ill with fever.

TROILOS

82. Pausanias, Graeciae Descriptio, VI 1, 4-5. (Trans. Frazer.)

Troilus gained victories in the chariot-races at the same time that he was umpire: one was a victory with a full-grown pair, the other was with a team of foals. These victories were gained by him in the hundred and second Olympiad. After that the Eleans made a law that for the future none of the umpires should enter chariots for a race. The statue of Troilus is by Lysippus.

CHEILON

83. Pausanias, Graeciae Descriptio, VI 4, 6-7. (Trans. Frazer.)

Chilon, an Achaean of Patrae, won two Olympic victories in wrestling among the men, one at Delphi, four at the Isthmus, and three at Nemea. He died in battle, and was buried by the Achaean state. The inscription at Olympia proves it:

Twice in wrestling alone I conquered the men at Olympia and at Pytho,
Thrice at Nemea, and four times at the Isthmus by the sea:
I am Chilon of Patrae, the son of Chilon; I perished in war,

δήσας καὶ τὸν ἡνίοχον εἶχε. Δαρεῖος δὲ ᾿Αρταξέρξου παῖς 7
νόθος, ὃς ὁμοῦ τῷ Περσῶν δήμῳ Σόγδιον καταπαύσας παῖδα
᾿Αρταξέρξου γνήσιον ἔσχεν ἀντ᾽ ἐκείνου τὴν ἀρχήν, οὗτος
ὡς ἐβασίλευσεν ὁ Δαρεῖος, ἐπυνθάνετο γὰρ τοῦ Πουλυδάμαντος τὰ ἔργα, πέμπων ἀγγέλους ὑπισχνούμενος δῶρα
ἀνέπεισεν αὐτὸν ἐς Σοῦσά τε καὶ ἐς ὄψιν ἀφικέσθαι τὴν
αὑτοῦ. ἔνθα δὴ κατὰ πρόκλησιν Περσῶν ἄνδρας τῶν καλουμένων ἀθανάτων ἀριθμὸν τρεῖς, ἀθρόους οἱ μονομαχή-
σαντας, ἀπέκτεινεν. ἔργων δὲ τῶν κατειλεγμένων οἱ τὰ μὲν
ἐπὶ τῷ βάθρῳ τοῦ ἀνδριάντος ἐν ᾿Ολυμπίᾳ, τὸ δὲ καὶ δηλού-
μενά ἐστιν ὑπὸ τοῦ ἐπιγράμματος.

81a. Lucian, Deorum Concilium, 12. (Ed. Jacobitz.)
᾿Ήδη καὶ ὁ Πουλυδάμαντος τοῦ ἀθλητοῦ ἀνδριὰς ἰᾶται
τοὺς πυρέττοντας ἐν ᾿Ολυμπίᾳ.

TROILOS

82. Pausanias, Graeciae Descriptio, VI 1, 4-5. (Ed. Schubart.)
... ἀλλὰ τῷ μὲν ἑλλανοδικεῖν τε ὁμοῦ καὶ ἵππων ὑπῆρξεν
ἀνελέσθαι νίκας, τῷ Τρωΐλῳ, τελείᾳ τε συνωρίδι καὶ πώλων
ἅρματι· ὀλυμπιάδι δὲ ἐκράτει δευτέρᾳ πρὸς ταῖς ἑκατόν.
ἀπὸ τούτου δὲ καὶ νόμος ἐγένετο ᾿Ηλείοις μηδὲ ἵππους τοῦ 5
λοιποῦ τῶν ἑλλανοδικούντων καθιέναι μηδένα. τούτου μὲν
δὴ τὸν ἀνδριάντα ἐποίησε Λύσιππος.

CHEILON

83. Pausanias, Graeciae Descriptio, VI 4, 6-7. (Ed. Schubart.)
Χείλωνι δὲ ᾿Αχαιῷ Πατρεῖ δύο μὲν ᾿Ολυμπικαὶ νῖκαι
πάλης ἀνδρῶν, μία δὲ ἐγένετο ἐν Δελφοῖς, τέσσαρες δὲ ἐν
᾿Ισθμῷ καὶ Νεμείων τρεῖς. ἐτάφη δὲ ὑπὸ τοῦ κοινοῦ τῶν
᾿Αχαιῶν, καὶ οἱ καὶ τοῦ βίου συνέπεσεν ἐν πολέμῳ τὴν τε-
λευτὴν γενέσθαι. μαρτυρεῖ δέ μοι καὶ τὸ ἐπίγραμμα τὸ ἐν
᾿Ολυμπίᾳ·
Μουνοπάλης νικῶ δὶς ᾿Ολύμπια Πύθιά τ᾽ ἄνδρας,
τρὶς Νεμέᾳ, τετράκις δ᾽ ᾿Ισθμῷ ἐν ἀγχιάλῳ,
Χείλων Χείλωνος Πατρεύς, ὃν λαὸς ᾿Αχαιῶν
ἐν πολέμῳ φθίμενον θάψ᾽ ἀρετῆς ἕνεκεν.
Τὸ μὲν δὴ ἐπίγραμμα ἐπὶ τοσοῦτο ἐδήλωσεν· εἰ δὲ Λυσίπ- 7
που τοῦ ποιήσαντος τὴν εἰκόνα τεκμαιρόμενον τῇ ἡλικίᾳ

And was buried for my valour's sake by the Achaean
people.
Thus far the inscription. If I may guess the war in which
Chilon fell by reference to the date of Lysippus, the
sculptor who made the statue, I should say either that he
marched to Chaeronea with the whole body of the Achaeans, or that, prompted by his personal valour and courage,
he alone of all the Achaeans fought against Antipater and
the Macedonians at Lamia in Thessaly.

84. Pausanias, Graeciae Descriptio, VII 6, 5. (Trans. Frazer.)
The guide at Patrae said that the wrestler Chilon was
the only Achaean who took part in the fighting at Lamia.

KALLIKRATES

85. Pausanias, Graeciae Descriptio, VI 17, 3. (Trans. Frazer.)
There is also a statue of a boxer who was victorious
among the boys, Butas, a Milesian, son of Polynices; and
a statue of Callicrates, a native of Magnesia, on the Leth-
aeus, who won two crowns in the armed race: the statue
of Callicrates is a work of Lysippus.

XENARCHES?

86. Pausanias, Graeciae Descriptio, VI 2, 1. (Trans. Frazer.)
There is a statue of a pancratiast by Lysippus. This
man the first not only from Stratus, but from the whole of
Acarnania, who won a victory in the pancratium. . . . he
was called [Xenarches], son of Philandrides.

"JASON"

87. Christodoros, Ecphrasis (Anth. Pal. II), 297-302. (Trans.
Paton.)
There, too, was Hermes with his rod of gold. He was
standing, but was tying with his right hand the lace of
his winged shoe, eager to start on his way. His right leg
was already bent, over it was extended his left hand and his
face was upturned to the sky, as if he were listening to the
orders of his father.

LION

88. Strabo, Geographica, XIII 590. (Trans. Falconer.)
It was from Lampsacus that Agrippa transported the
Prostrate Lion, the workmanship of Lysippus, and placed
it in the sacred grove between the lake and the strait.

συμβαλέσθαι δεῖ με τὸν πόλεμον ἔνθα ὁ Χείλων ἔπεσεν, ἤτοι
ἐς Χαιρώνειαν ᾿Αχαιοῖς τοῖς πᾶσιν ὁμοῦ στρατεύσασθαι ἢ
ἰδίᾳ κατ᾿ ἀρετήν τε καὶ τόλμαν ᾿Αχαιῶν μόνος ᾿Αντιπάτρου
μοι καὶ Μακεδόνων ἐναντία ἀγωνίσασθαι περὶ Λαμίαν φαί-
νεται τὴν ἐν Θεσσαλίᾳ.

84. Pausanias, Graeciae Descriptio, VII 6, 5. (Ed. Schubart.)
    ῾Ο δὲ τῶν ἐπιχωρίων Πατρεῦσιν ἐξηγητὴς τὸν παλαι-
    στὴν Χείλωνα ᾿Αχαιῶν μόνον μετασχεῖν ἔφασκε τοῦ ἔργου
    τοῦ περὶ Λαμίαν.

KALLIKRATES

85. Pausanias, Graeciae Descriptio, VI 17, 3. (Ed. Schubart.)
    ᾿Ανάκειται δὲ καὶ πύκτης κρατήσας ἐν παισί, Βούτας
    Πολυνείκους Μιλήσιος, καὶ Καλλικράτης ἀπὸ τῆς ἐπὶ Λη-
    θαίῳ Μαγνησίας, ἐπὶ τῷ ὁπλίτῃ δρόμῳ στεφάνους δύο ἀνη-
    ρημένος· Λυσίππου δὲ ἔργον ἡ τοῦ Καλλικράτους ἐστιν
    εἰκών.

XENARCHES?

86. Pausanias, Graeciae Descriptio, VI 2, 1. (Ed. Schubart.)
    Παγκρατιαστοῦ δὲ ἀνδρὸς τὸν μὲν ἀνδριάντα εἰργά-
    σατο Λύσιππος· ὁ δὲ ἀνὴρ οὗτος ἀνείλετο ἐπὶ παγκρατίῳ
    νίκην τῶν ἄλλων τε ᾿Ακαρνάνων καὶ τῶν ἐξ αὐτῆς Στράτου
    πρῶτος... [Ξενάρχης] τε ἐκαλεῖτο Φιλανδρίδου.

"JASON"

87. Christodoros, Ecphrasis (Anth. Pal. II), 297-302. (Ed.
    Paton.)
    ῏Ην δὲ καὶ ῾Ερμείας χρυσόρραπις· ἱστάμενος δὲ
    δεξιτερῇ πτερόεντος ἀνείρυε δεσμὰ πεδίλου,
    εἰς ὁδὸν ἀΐξαι λελιημένος· εἶχε γὰρ ἤδη
    δεξιὸν ὀκλάζοντα θοὸν πόδα, τῷ ἔπι λαιὴν
    χεῖρα ταθεὶς ἀνέπεμπεν ἐς αἰθέρα κύκλον ὀπωπῆς,
    οἷά τε πατρὸς ἄνακτος ἐπιτρωπῶντος ἀκούων.

LION

88. Strabo, Geographica, XIII 590. (Ed. Meineke.)
    ᾿Εντεῦθεν δὲ μετήνεγκεν ᾿Αγρίππας τὸν πεπτωκότα
    λέοντα, Λυσίππου ἔργον· ἀνέθηκε δὲ ἐν τῷ ἄλσει τῷ μεταξὺ
    τῆς λίμνης καὶ τοῦ εὐρίπου.

Free Horse

89. Niketas Choniates, De Signis Constantinopolitanis, 7.

[The Latins, when they took Constantinople in 1204, destroyed along with other statues] the unbridled horse, pricking up its ears and snorting, stepping forward exultant, with head held high.[5]

90. Philip: Anth. Pal., IX 777. (Trans. Paton.)

Look how proudly the art of the worker in bronze makes this horse stand. Fierce is his glance as he arches his neck and shakes out his wind-tossed mane for the course. I believe that if a charioteer were to fit the bit to his jaws and prick him with the spur, thy work Lysippus, would surprise us by running away; for Art makes it breathe.

91. Psellos: Anth. Gr., App. III, 267.

On the bronze horse with raised foot, in the Hippodrome.

This bronze horse that you see is full of life;—verily he is alive and he will soon leap about; and raising this forefoot he will strike and kick you if you go near him. He is starting to run: stay back, do not approach him; but rather flee, lest you receive such injury as I mentioned.

Cow

92. Prokopios, De Bello Gothico, IV 21.

There is a certain ancient fountain-house in front of this market-place, and a cow of bronze stood near it, which I think was the work of Pheidias the Athenian or of Lysippos. For many statues made by these two men are in that place.

Horse in Rome

93. Pliny, N. H., VIII 155. (Trans. Bostock and Riley.)

It is said, also, that Caesar, the Dictator, had a horse, which would allow no one to mount but himself, and that its forefeet were like those of a man; indeed it is thus represented in the statue before the temple of Venus Genetrix.

---

[5] An unparalleled meaning for εὐήνιον, but apparently the only one possible, if the word is retained. The translation is kindly suggested by Professor C. W. E. Miller. ἀνήνιον, as suggested by Professor Robinson, would be an easy emendation; but it gives a painfully bathetic sense.

FREE HORSE

89. Niketas Choniates, De Signis Constantinopolitanis, 7. (Ed. Bekker.)

...καὶ τὸν ἀχάλινον ἵππον ὀρθιάζοντα τὸ οὖς καὶ φριμάσσοντα, γαῦρόν τε καὶ εὐήνιον προποδίζοντα.

90. Philip: Anth. Pal., IX 777. (Ed. Paton.)

Ἴδ' ὡς ὁ πῶλος χαλκοδαιδάλῳ τέχνᾳ
κορωνιῶν ἕστηκε· δριμὺ γὰρ βλέπων
ὑψαυχενίζει, καὶ διηνεμωμένας
κορυφῆς ἐθείρας οὐρίωκεν ἐς δρόμον.
δοκέω, χαλινοὺς εἴ τις ἡνιοστρόφος
ἐναρμόσῃ γέννυσι κἀπικεντρίσῃ,
ὁ σὸς πόνος, Λύσιππε, καὶ παρ' ἐλπίδας
τάχ' ἐκδραμεῖται· τᾷ τέχνᾳ γὰρ ἐμπνέει.

91. Psellos: Anth. Gr., App. III, 267. (Ed. Cougny, vol. III, p. 334.)

Εἰς τὸν χαλκοῦν ἵππον, τὸν ἐν τῷ Ἱπποδρόμῳ, ἀπηωρημένον τὸν πόδα ἔχοντα.

Ἔμπνους ὁ χαλκοῦς ἵππος οὗτος, ὃν βλέπεις,
ἔμπνους ἀληθῶς, καὶ φριμάξεται τάχα·
τὸν πρόσθιον δὲ τοῦτον ἐξαίρων πόδα,
βαλεῖ σε καὶ λάξ, εἰ παρέλθῃς πλησίον.
Δραμεῖν καθορμᾷ, στῆθι, μὴ προσεγγίσῃς·
μᾶλλον δὲ φεῦγε, μὴ λάβῃς τὸ τοῦ λόγου.

Cow

92. Prokopios, De Bello Gothico, IV 21. (Ed. Haury.)

Ἔστι δέ τις ἀρχαία πρὸ ταύτης δὴ τῆς ἀγορᾶς κρήνη, καὶ βοῦς ἐπὶ ταύτης χαλκοῦς ἕστηκε, Φειδίου, οἶμαι, τοῦ Ἀθηναίου ἢ Λυσίππου ἔργον. ἀγάλματα γὰρ ἐν χώρῳ τούτῳ πολλὰ τούτοιν δὴ τοῖν ἀνδροῖν ποιήματά ἐστιν.

93. Pliny, N. H., VIII 155. (Ed. Mayhoff.)

Nec Caesaris dictatoris quemquam alium recepisse dorso equus traditur, idemque similes humanis pedes priores habuisse, hac effigie locatus ante Veneris Genetricis aedem.

94. Statius, Silvae, I 1, 84-87. (Trans. Slater.)

Henceforth let the steed give place that over against the temple of our Lady of Latium stands in Caesar's forum, the steed which men say Lysippus hazarded for the lord of Pella, and which anon in amazement bore on its back a sculptured Caesar.

95. Suetonius, Caesar, 61. (Trans. Rolfe.)

He [Caesar] rode a remarkable horse, too, with feet that were almost human; for its hoofs were cloven in such a way as to look like toes. This horse was foaled on his own place, and since the soothsayers had declared that it foretold the rule of the world for its master, he reared it with the greatest care, and was the first to mount it, for it would endure no other rider. Afterwards, too, he dedicated a statue of it before the temple of Venus Genetrix.

96. Gnomologium Vaticanum (*Wiener Studien*, XI, 1889, p. 62, nos. 399-400).

The sculptor Lysippos was asked by somebody: "Why, in making your statue, did you not provide Demos (the People) with ears?" He said: "Demos never forms opinions by hearing, but rather by wilfulness." The same man, seeing a badly made statue, said that it was difficult to criticize; for he was at a loss, because of the multitude of faults, as to where he should begin.

94. Statius, Silvae, I 1, 84-87. (Ed. Klotz.)
Cedat equus, Latiae qui contra templa Diones
Caesarei stat sede fori—quem traderis ausus
Pellaeo, Lysippe, duci, mox Caesaris ora
mirata cervice tulit—

95. Suetonius, Caesar, 61. (Ed. Rolfe.)
Utebatur autem equo insigni, pedibus prope humanis
et in modum digitorum ungulis fissis, quem natum apud se,
cum haruspices imperium orbis terrae significare domino
pronuntiassent, magna cura aluit nec patientem sessoris
alterius primus ascendit; cuius etiam instar pro aede
Veneris Genetricis postea dedicavit.

96. Gnomologium Vaticanum (Wiener Studien, XI, 1889, p.
62, nos. 399-400. (Ed. Sternbach.)
Λύσιππος ὁ ἀνδριαντοποιὸς ἐρωτηθεὶς ὑπό τινος «διὰ τί
δήμῳ, ἀνδριάντα ποιῶν, ὦτα οὐ περιέθηκας;» εἶπε· «δῆμος
ἀκοῇ οὔποτε τίθεται, αὐθαδείᾳ δὲ μᾶλλον». Ὁ αὐτὸς ἰδὼν
ἀνδριάντα κακῶς πεπλασμένον δυσκατηγόρητον ἔφη εἶναι·
διὰ γὰρ τὸ πλῆθος τῶν ἁμαρτημάτων ἀπορεῖν, πόθεν
ἄρξεται.

APPENDIX II

BIBLIOGRAPHY

WORKS DEALING WITH LYSIPPOS SPECIFICALLY

Amelung, Walther: Statuette der Artemis. *Röm. Mitt.*, XX, 1905, 136-155.

Collignon, Maxime: Lysippe. Paris, 1905.

Cultrera, Giuseppe: Una statua di Ercole. *Memorie dell' Accademia dei Lincei*, XIV, 1910, 179-276.

Gardner, Percy: The Apoxyomenos of Lysippus. *J.H.S.*, XXV, 1905, 234-259.

Lippold, Georg: Lysippos. (Article in Pauly-Wissowa.)

Loewy, Emanuel: Lysipp und seine Stellung in der griechischen Plastik. Hamburg, 1891.

Maviglia, Ada: L'Attività di Lisippo ricostruita su nuova base. Rome, 1914.

Preuner, E.: Ein delphisches Weihgeschenk. Leipzig, 1900.

Waldhauer, Oscar: Lisipp, Berlin, 1923. (In Russian.)

MUSEUMS

Athens, National Museum:

Γλυπτὰ τοῦ 'Εθνικοῦ Μουσείου, by P. Kavvadias.
Athens, 1890-1892. Includes nos. 1-1044; no illustrations.

Γλυπτὰ τοῦ 'Εθνικοῦ Μουσείου, by P. Kastriotis.
Athens, 1908. Includes nos. 1-2725; briefer discussions than in Kavvadias; no illustrations.

Guide illustré du Musée National d' Athènes. Vol. 1: Marbres et bronzes. By V. Stais. Athens, 1908. Selected monuments.

Τὸ ἐν 'Αθήναις 'Εθνικὸν Μουσεῖον, by I. Svoronos.
Athens, 1903-1911. Two vols. text, two vols. plates; a third of each supposed to have been prepared by Svoronos. So far includes the Antikythera finds and the reliefs, excluding grave-reliefs. There is also a German edition.

Athens, Acropolis Museum:

Catalogue of the Acropolis Museum. Vol. 1 by Guy Dickins; vol. 2 by Stanley Casson. Cambridge, 1912 and 1921. Fully illustrated, but in vol. 1 only by drawings.

Berlin:

Beschreibung der antiken Skulpturen. Berlin, 1891. Fully illustrated by drawings.

Kurze Beschreibung der antiken Skulpturen im alten
Museum. 3rd ed. Berlin, 1922. Handbook with 80 plates.
Führer durch das Antiquarium. I. Bronzen. By K. A.
Neugebauer. Berlin, 1924.
Boston:
Catalogue of Greek and Roman Sculptures, by L. D.
Caskey. Cambridge, 1925. Fully illustrated.
Brussels:
Musées Royaux: Catalogue des sculptures et inscrip-
tions antiques, by Franz Cumont. 2nd ed. Brussels, 1913.
Sammlung Somzée: Antike Kunstdenkmäler. By
Adolf Furtwängler. Munich, Bruckmann, 1897. 80 pp.,
43 plates.
Cassel:
Die antiken Skulpturen und Bronzen des Königl. Mu-
seum Fridericianum in Cassel, by Margarete Bieber. Mar-
burg, 1915.
Constantinople:
Musées Impériaux Ottomans: Catalogue des sculptures
grecques, romaines et byzantines, by Gustave Mendel. 3
vols. Constantinople, 1912-1914. Drawings of everything.
Copenhagen, Ny Carlsberg Glyptotek:
Fortegnelse over de Antike Kunstvaerker, by Carl
Jacobsen. Copenhagen, 1907. No illustrations, but accom-
panied by an atlas: Billedtavler til Kataloget over Antike
Kunstvaerker.
Tillaeg til Katalog over Ny Carlsberg Glyptoteks
Antike Kunstvaerker, by Frederik Poulsen. Copenhagen,
1914. No illustrations. Bound with the 1907 catalogue.
La Glyptothèque Ny-Carlsberg: Les monuments an-
tiques, by Paul Arndt. Munich, 1896-1912. 230 pp., 220
plates.
Antike Skulpturen der Glyptothek Ny Carlsberg, by
Georg Lippold. Selected monuments.
Dresden, Albertinum:
Verzeichnis der antiken Original-Bildwerke. Dresden,
1915. Handbook, 20 illustrations, no references. There
is now a later edition.
Florence, Museo Archeologico:
I: Storia e Guida Ragionata. II: Guida Figurata.
Florence, 1912. Handbook, 160 plates.
Florence, Uffizi:
Elenco delle Sculture. Florence, 1921. Handbook with
some references; valuable chiefly for its 48 illustrations.

Frankfurt am Main, Städtische Galerie:
Kurzes Verzeichnis der Bildwerke. 3rd ed. Frankfurt, 1915. Handbook, no illustrations, some references.
Geneva, Musée d' art et d' histoire:
Catalogue des sculptures antiques, by W. Deonna. Geneva, 1924. Some illustrations.
Catalogue des bronzes figurés antiques, by W. Deonna. Geneva, 1915-1916. Many illustrations.
Leningrad, Hermitage:
Sculptures in the Hermitage, by G. von Kieseritzky (in Russian). St. Petersburg, 1901. Many small illustrations.
Brief Catalogue of the Hermitage, by Oskar Waldhauer (in Russian). St. Petersburg, 1912.
London, British Museum:
A Catalogue of Sculpture in the Department of Greek and Roman Antiquities, by A. H. Smith. 3 vols. London, 1892-1904. Some illustrations.
Catalogue of the Bronzes, Greek, Etruscan, and Roman, by H. B. Walters. London, 1899. Some illustrations.
Marbles and Bronzes: Fifty Plates from Selected Subjects, with brief text. 2nd ed. London, 1922.
Select Bronzes, Greek, Roman, and Etruscan. 73 plates with text, by H. B. Walters. London, 1915.
Madrid, Prado:
Catálogo de la Escultura, by Eduardo Barròn. Madrid, 1910. Handbook, some illustrations.
Marbres antiques du Musée du Prado à Madrid, by R. Ricard. Bordeaux-Paris, 1923. (Bibliothèque de l' école des hautes études hispaniques, 7.)
Munich:
Beschreibung der Glyptothek Königs Ludwigs I, by Adolf Furtwängler, revised by Paul Wolters. Munich, 1910. Full discussions, no illustrations.
Führer durch die Glyptothek Königs Ludwigs I, by Paul Wolters. Munich, 1922. Handbook, no references, 64 illustrations.
Naples:
Guida Illustrata del Museo Nazionale di Napoli, compilata . . . per cura di A. Ruesch. 2nd ed. Naples, n.d. Handbook with good discussions and references; 129 illustrations.

New York, Metropolitan Museum:
Handbook of the Classical Collection, by Gisela M. A. Richter. New York, 1917. New ed., 1927.
Paris, Bibliothèque Nationale:
Catalogue des bronzes antiques, by E. Babelon and J.-A. Blanchet. Paris, 1895. Poor illustrations of everything.
Paris, Louvre:
Catalogue sommaire des marbres antiques. Paris, Braun, 1918. Handbook, valuable chiefly for its 64 illustrations.
Notice de la sculpture antique du Musée Impérial du Louvre, by W. Fröhner. Paris, 1869. No illustrations.
Les bronzes antiques du Louvre, by A. de Ridder. 2 vols. (of which the first contains all the figurines). Paris, 1913-1915. Full illustrated catalogue.
Les bronzes antiques, by A. de Ridder. Paris, 1913. Handbook, 64 illustrations.
Philadelphia, University Museum:
Catalogue of the Mediterranean Section, by Stephen Bleecker Luce. Philadelphia, 1921.
Rome, Museo Barracco:
La collection Barracco, publié par Fr. Bruckmann d'apres la classification et avec le texte de G. Barracco et W. Helbig. Munich, 1894. 80 plates.
Rome, Museo Capitolino:
The Sculptures of the Museo Capitolino, by Members of the British School at Rome, edited by H. Stuart Jones. Oxford, 1912. 1 vol. text, 1 vol. plates.
Musei Capitolini, by Settimo Bocconi. Rome, 1914. Handbook, including both the Museo Capitolino and the Palazzo dei Conservatori; valuable chiefly for its illustrations.
Rome, Lateran:
Die antike Bildwerke des lateranensischen Museums beschrieben, by O. Benndorf and R. Schöne. Leipzig, 1867. A few drawings.
Rome, Museo Nazionale:
Le Terme di Diocleziano e il Museo Nazionale Romano, by R. Paribeni. 4th ed. Rome, 1922. Handbook with good discussions and references; 16 illustrations.
Rome, Museo Torlonia:
Il Museo Torlonia Riprodotto in Fototipia (with text by Visconti). Rome. 161 plates.

Rome, Palazzo dei Conservatori:
The Sculptures in the Palazzo dei Conservatori, by members of the British School at Rome, edited by H. Stuart Jones. Oxford, 1926. 1 vol. text, 1 vol. plates.
Rome, Vatican:
Die Skulpturen des Vaticanischen Museums, by Walther Amelung. 2 vols. text, 2 vols. plates. Berlin, 1903-1908.
Rome, Villa Albani:
Description de la Villa Albani, by S. Morcelli, C. Fea, and P. E. Visconti. Rome, 1869. No illustrations, little value.
Vienna:
Sculpturen des K. K. Munz- und Antiken-Cabinets in Wien, by E. von Sacken. Vienna, 1873. Illustrations.
Die antiken Bronzen des K. K. Munz- und Antiken-Cabinets in Wien, by E. von Sacken. Vienna, 1871. Drawings.

General Works

Amelung, Walther: Führer durch die Antiken in Florenz. Munich, 1897.
Arndt, Paul, and Amelung, Walther: Photographische Einzelaufnahmen antiker Skulpturen. Munich, 1893—. (Einzelaufnahmen.)
Griechische und römische Porträts, nach Auswahl und Anordnung von Heinrich Brunn und Paul Arndt. Munich, 1891—. (Arndt-Bruckmann.)
Denkmäler der griechischen und römischen Skulptur, herausgegeben von H. Brunn, fortgesetzt von P. Arndt. Munich, 1888—. (Brunn-Bruckmann.)
Bernoulli, J. J.: Die erhaltene Darstellungen Alexanders des Grossen. Munich, 1905.
Bulle, H.: Der schöne Mensch: Altertum. Munich and Leipzig. 2nd edition, 1912; 3rd edition (somewhat abridged), 1922.
Collignon, Maxime: Histoire de la sculpture grecque. 2 vols. Paris, 1892 and 1897.
Dickins, Guy: Hellenistic Sculpture. Oxford, 1920.
Dütschke, H.: Antike Bildwerke in Oberitalien. 5 vols. Leipzig, 1874-1882.
Friederichs, Carl: Königliche Museen zu Berlin: Die Gipsabgüsse antiker Bildwerke. 2nd edition, revised by Paul Wolters. Berlin, 1885.
Furtwängler, Adolf: Meisterwerke der griechischen Plastik.

Leipzig and Berlin, 1893. (Masterpieces of Greek Sculpture; translated and edited by Eugénie Sellers. London, 1895.)

Gardner, Ernest A.: Six Greek Sculptors. London, 1910. Reprinted 1924. (*S.G.S.*)

Gardner, Ernest A.: A Handbook of Greek Sculpture. 2nd edition. London, 1915.

Hekler, Anton: Die Bildniskunst der Griechen und Römer. (Greek and Roman Portraits. New York, Putnam, 1912.)

Hekler, Anton: Römische weibliche Gewandstatuen. In: Münchener archäologische Studien dem Andenken Adolf Furtwänglers gewidmet. Munich, 1909.

Helbig, Wolfgang: Führer durch die öffentlichen Sammlungen klassischen Altertümer in Rom. 2 vols. 2nd ed.: Leipzig, 1899. 3rd ed., revised by Amelung and others: Leipzig, 1912-1913.

Hyde, Walter Woodburn: Olympic Victor Monuments and Greek Athletic Art. Washington, 1921. (*OVM.*)

Kekulé von Stradonitz, Reinhard: Die Bildnisse des Sokrates. In: *Abh. Preuss. Akad. Wiss.*, 1908.

Klein, Wilhelm: Geschichte der griechischen Kunst. 3 vols. Leipzig, 1904-1907.

Koepp, Friedrich: Ueber das Bildniss Alexanders des Grossen. Berlin: Archaeol. Gesells. Winckelmannsfest, Programm 52, 1892.

Lange, Julius: Die menschliche Gestalt in der Geschichte der Kunst von der zweiten Blütezeit der griechischen Kunst bis zum XIX Jahrhundert. Herausgegeben von P. Köbke. Aus dem Dänischen übertragen von Mathilde Mann. Strassburg, 1903.

Loewy, Emanuel: Inschriften griechischer Bildhauer. Leipzig, 1885.

Matz, Friedrich: Antike Bildwerke in Rom, mit Ausschluss der grösseren Sammlungen. Nach des Verfassers Tode weitergeführt und herausgegeben von F. von Duhn. 3 vols. Leipzig, 1881.

Michaelis, Adolph: Ancient Marbles in Great Britain. Cambridge, 1882.

Overbeck, Johannes: Geschichte der griechischen Plastik. 2 vols. 4th ed. Leipzig, 1892-1894.

Overbeck, Johannes: Die antiken Schriftquellen zur Geschichte der bildenden Künste bei den Griechen. Leipzig, 1868. (*SQ*).

Overbeck, Johannes: Griechische Kunstmythologie. Leipzig, 1871-1889. (*KM*).

Pauly's Real-Encyclopädie der klassischen Altertumswissenschaft. Neu Bearbeitung. Unter Mitwirkung zahlreicher Fachgenossen herausgegeben von Georg Wissowa und Wilhelm Kroll. Stuttgart, 1894—.

The Elder Pliny's Chapter on the History of Art, translated by K. Jex-Blake; with Commentary and Historical Introduction by E. Sellers. London, 1896.

Poulsen, Frederik: Delphi. Translated by G. C. Richards. London, 1920. There is a new Danish edition, 1922; I have not seen it.

Reinach, Salomon: Recueil de Têtes antiques idéales ou idéalisées. Paris, 1903.

Reinach, Salomon: Repertoire de Reliefs grecs et romains. Paris, 1909.

Reinach, Salomon: Répertoire de la Statuaire grecque et romaine. 5 vols. Paris, 1897-1924.

Roscher, W. H.: Ausführliches Lexikon der griechischen und römischen Mythologie. Leipzig, 1884—.

Schreiber, Theodor: Studien über das Bildniss Alexanders des Grossen. In: *Abh. Sächs. Gesells. d. Wissenschaften*, XXI, 1903.

Springer, Anton: Die Kunst des Altertums. 12th ed., revised by Paul Wolters. Leipzig, 1923.

Ujfalvy, Charles de: Le type physique d' Alexandre le Grand. Paris, 1902.

Von Mach, Edmund: University Prints, Series A: Greek and Roman Sculpture. Boston, 1916.

Von Mach, Edmund: A Handbook of Greek and Roman Sculpture (to accompany the University Prints). Boston, 1905.

Waldmann, Emil: Griechische Originale. 2nd ed. Leipzig, 1923.

Willers, Heinrich: Studien zur griechischen Kunst. Leipzig, 1914.

INDEX

(Under names of places are entered only matters that might not easily be found under other headings.)

Aesop, by Lysippos, 234; in Villa Albani, 234

Agasias, warrior of, 177

Ageladas, sculptor, 4

Agenor, athlete, by younger Polykleitos, 21

Agias, at Delphi, 123-33; compared with apoxyomenos, 128-30; compared with "Mercure Richelieu", 183; compared with "Philandridas" and Ilissos stele, 237; compared with youth in Berlin, 238; compared with Herakles Epitrapezios, 104

Agias, at Pharsalos, 123 f., 127 f., 130 ff.

Aisypos, athlete, by Daidalos, 18

Akousilaos, athlete, 5

Alexander, Aboukir medallions, 223 f.; with aegis, 229; Azara, 213 ff.; British Museum head, 220; Capitol head, 222; crystal head, 229; Cyrene, 223; equestrian statue, 228; Evans intaglio, 227; Frankfurt head, 214 f.; Geneva head, 214; with the lance, 218 f., 223; by Leochares, 46; Louvre bronze, 216 f., 219; Louvre marble statuette, 218 f.; relations with Lysippos, 65 f.; Messene relief, 227; Naples horseman, 225 f.; Nelidow bronze, 217 f.; Pergamon head, 221; Priene statue, 220 f.; in quadriga, by Euphranor, 41, 45 f.; Rondanini, 45 f.; sarcophagus, 228; Tarsos medallions, 227

Alexander of Epeiros, 66

Alexis, sculptor, 27

Alkaios(?), portrait, 247 f.

Alketos, athlete, by Kleon, 20

Alypos, sculptor, 5, 10, 12 f., 27

Alyzia, reliefs near, 137, 202, 205

Amazons, statues of, 28-31

Amertas, athlete, by Phradmon, 28

Amphion, sculptor, 9 f.

Anatomical knowledge shown in statues, 83, 176 f.

Antidotos, painter, 40

Antignotos, sculptor, 74

Antipatros, athlete, by Polykleitos, 22 f.

Antiphanes, sculptor, 9, 14-16, 19, 27, 39

Anzio figure, 233

Apelles, painter, 72

Aphrodite, of Amyklai, by Polykleitos, 22; anadoumene, 55; Capitol, 55-57; of Capua, 57; crouching, 55; by Kleon, 19 f.; Knidian, 55 f.; Medici, 55-57, 186-89, 250, 254; by Skopas, 50 f., 55-57

Apollo, two statues by Skopas, 50

Apollo and Hermes, group, 151 f.

Apoxyomenos, Athens relief, 78; Athens torso, 83; Cortona bronze, 77, 89, 92; by Daidalos, 19, 75, 88 f.; from Ephesos, 88 f.; Loeb bronze, 75 f.; by Lysippos, chapter IV; Paris bronzes, 75, 77; by Polykleitos, 75-77; on steles, 75, 77; Trèves bronze, 79; Uffizi type, 78-80, 85-89; on vase, 78

Apoxyomenos, Vatican type, attribution to Lysippos, 89-91; lack of copies, 85; compared with Agias, 128-30; compared with Eros, 114; compared with

[329]

Herakles Epitrapezios, 103 f.; description, 81-83
Ares, Borghese, 44; Ludovisi type, 166-70; by Skopas, 167 ff.
Aristandros, name of two sculptors, 48 f.
Aristeides, sculptor, 27
Aristeides of Thebes, painter, 42
Aristion, athlete, by Polykleitos, 24 f.
Aristippos, portrait, 240
Aristodemos, athlete, by Daidalos, 17
Aristodemos, sculptor, 230, 234
Aristotle, portrait, 234 f.
Asia Minor, Lysippos's work in, 73
Asopodoros, sculptor, 27
Athena Rospigliosi, 51
Athenodoros, sculptor, 9, 13
Athens, church: relief with two female figures, 162
Athens, National Museum: Antikythera or Cerigotto bronze, 44 f.; "Atalanta" head from Tegea, 54 f.; fragments from Mt. Helikon, 151 f.; head resembling Ares Ludovisi, 166; relief, female figure, 158; relief, figure resembling Idolino, 35; torso of apoxyomenos, 83
Autolykos, athlete, by Leochares or Lykios, 36

Bari, silver dish at, 172
Beneventum, head from, 31-33
Berlin: youth, 238; dancer, 249 f.
Bias, portrait, 248
Boedas, son of Lysippos, 149 f.
Boxer, bronze, in Rome, 194, Addenda
Brussels: head of Uffizi apoxyomenos type, 80
Bryaxis, sculptor, portrayer of Seleukos, 230; possible author of Albani Herakles, 206; of Lateran Poseidon, 144; of Otricoli Zeus, 141
Bull, by Lysippos, 253
Bykelos, athlete, by Kanachos, 11

Cassel, male head at, 87
Cassius, captor of Rhodes, 69
Chares, pupil of Lysippos, 73, 126, 222 f.
Cheilon, athlete, by Lysippos, 66 f., 235
Cheimon, athlete, by Naukydes, 4
Coins: Amastris (Herakles Epitrapezios), 100 f.; ("Jason"), 171; Argos (Poseidon), 145; (Zeus), 137; Bruttium (Poseidon), 145; Corinth (Isthmian temple) 143; (Poseidon), 145; (seated Poseidon), 143; Demetrios Poliorketes (Poseidon), 145; Hermione (Poseidon), 145; Kydonia (Eros), 108; Marcianapolis ("Jason"), 171; Megara (Zeus), 138; Patrai (Poseidon), 146; Pergamon (Herakles), 191; Phokaia (Poseidon), 146; Sikyon (Herakles), 53 f., 208; (Zeus), 134; Sybrita, 172; Tarentum (Praying Boy), 149; Trapezus ("Jason"), 171; Troy (Hector), 219; with Herakles Farnese, 204 f.
Colossus of Rhodes, 139
Constantinople, bronze statue at, 192
Copenhagen: bearded head, 240, 254; Hermes, 183 f.; poet, 247 f.; terracotta relief, 79 f.
Corinth, signed base at, 64, 92; renewed signature at, 70

Daidalos, Sikyonian sculptor, 14 f., 17-19, 27, 31, 37; his apoxyomenos, 75, 87-89
Daippos, son of Lysippos, 74, 90 f.
Damagetos, athlete, 5
Dameas, sculptor, 9
Daochos group, 117-123
Deinolochos, athlete, by Kleon, 20

Delphi: Aigospotamoi group, 7-13; Arcadian group, 13-15; Argive group, 15-17; Daochos group, 117-23; Krateros group, 67, 226 ff.; Rhodian chariot, 68 f.; tholos, 49; Trojan horse, 7

Demeter ("grande Herculanaise"), 154 ff., 254

Demeter of Knidos, 211 f.

Demetrios, sculptor, 260

Demetrios Phalereus, portrait, 240

Demos, by Lysippos(?), 233

Design, Lysippian, 257 f.

Diagoras, athlete, 5

Dionysios of Syracuse, at Olympia, 22 f.

Dionysos, head in Lateran, 151; head in Palazzo dei Conservatori, 151; by Lysippos, 151

Diskobolos of Naukydes, 5 f.

Dogs, by Lysippos, 249, 251

Doidalsas, sculptor, 55

Dorieus, athlete, 5

Douris of Samos, 58

Dresden, four athletes at, 239

Eros with bow, attributed to Lysippos, 113-15; attributed to Praxiteles, 112 f.; comparison with apoxyomenos, 113 f.; copies, 105-108; copy in Athens, 108; differences in copies and interpretation, 109-111; as Hellenistic, 112 f.; mentioned by Kedrenos, 115

Eros at Myndos, by Lysippos, 115; at Thespiai, by Lysippos, 72, 112

Eukles, athlete, by Naukydes, 5

Euphranor, sculptor and painter, 40-48, 65; possible author of Albertini Herakles, 207; of Lateran Poseidon, 144; influence on Lysippos, 256

Eupolemos, athlete, by Daidalos, 17

Eupolos, athlete, 19

Eupompos, painter, 59

Euripides, portrait, 248

Euthenos, statue by Daidalos, 19

Euthykrates, son of Lysippos, 90, 177, 245

Eutychides, sculptor, 126

Florence, Uffizi: bearded portrait head, 240

Flute-girl, by Lysippos, 234, 249-50

Frankfurt: head resembling Munich bronze head, 37

Ganymede, in Florence, 248, 254; possible subject of type called Paris, 43 f.

Glaukon, athlete, by Daidalos, 18

Granikos monument, 66, 224-26

Grave-stele from Ilissos, 237

Hagesipolis, Spartan king, by Kleon, 20

Hebe, by Naukydes, 5

Helios, by Lysippos, 152 f.; head in Copenhagen, 153

Hephaistion, by Polykleitos or Lysippos, 25, 230

Hera, by Polykleitos, 4

Herakles Albertini, 206-209; with bow, Lateran, 193; bronze, Louvre, 205; bronze, Villa Albani, 206; with club, Mykonos, 209; Chiaramonti, 212; Conservatori, 191 f.; with deer, 191; at Delos, 101 f.; at Dresden, 101; Epitrapezios, 97-104

Herakles, Farnese type, 197 ff.; precursers, 200 f.; imitations wth Telephos, 202

Herakles, Genzano, 53, 208; in groups, 193; herm, Conservatori, 53; labors, at Alyzia, 190-93; Lansdowne, 53, 208-211; with lion, 190 f.; in Louvre, 212; Malatesta, 206; Ny Carlsberg, 205; Pitti, Farnese type, 197, 203; Schick's type, 212

Herakles, seated, Cherchell, 102;

Hermitage, 192; Loeb, 179; Naples, 102; Olympia, 102; Roanne, 179
Herakles, at Sikyon, 196; at Tarentum, 193 f.; without weapons, 195 f.
"Herculanaises", 154-63
Hermes, of Atalanti, 183; bronze in Berlin, 184; bronze in British Museum, 182; bronze in Geneva, 184; resembling Idolino, 33; at Lysimachia, by Polykleitos, 25 f.; "Mercure Richelieu", 182 f.; at Merida, 179; Naples, 177-82
Horse, with abnormal hoofs, 228; Conservatori, 252; Naples, 226; of Troy, by Antiphanes, 7
Horses, by Lysippos, 251 f.
Hysmon, athlete, by Kleon, 20

Idealism of Lysippos, 259
Idolino, 33-35, 38
"Isthmius", 40

"Jason", 83, 91, 170-77

Kairos, by Lysippos, 163-65
Kallikles, sculptor, 36
Kallikrates, athlete, by Lysippos, 235
Kanachos the younger, sculptor, 10 f., 27
Kantharos, sculptor, 126
Kassander, general, 67, 73
Kedrenos, mention of Eros and Kairos, 115
Kephisodotos the elder, 39
Kephisodotos the younger, 185
Kleon, sculptor, 19-21
Koreidas, athlete, by Lysippos, 62-64, 93
Kos, base with epigram, 70-72
Krateros group, 67, 226-28
Kritios, sculptor, 10
Kritodamos, athlete, by Kleon, 20
Kyniskos, athlete, by Polykleitos, 4

Lead fastenings for feet, 8
Leochares, sculptor, 46, 57, 65, 69, 228
Leto and children, by Euphranor, 42-43
Lindos, signature of Lysippos at, 69
Lion, by Lysippos, 252
London, British Museum: Fagan head, 171, 176; Westmacott athlete, 75 f.
Lykinos, athlete, by Kleon, 20
Lykios, sculptor, 36
Lysistratos, brother of Lysippos, 261

Madrid, Prado: Kairos(?), 164; female figure, 161
Maenad, Berlin, 249 f.; of Skopas, 54; Villa Albani, 250
Martial, doubtful reading in, 98 f.
Megara, signed base at, 69, 93-96
Meleager, 240-45, 254
Munich: bronze head of boy, 35-38; female head, 250
Muses, by Lysippos, 153 ff.
Myron, Ladas of, 247
Myron of Thebes, drunken woman of, 249

Naples: head of Asklepios(?), 142; bronze horseman, 225 f., 254; torso resembling Eros, 108; wrestlers, 245-47
"Narkissos", 31
Naukydes, sculptor, 4-6, 21, 31; diskobolos of, 89; possible second of the name, 5, 26
Nemea, temple, 49 f.
Nero, colossus of, 139
Nikias, painter, 40
Olympia: base in form of knuckle-bone, 164 f.; bronze head from, 236; Elean trophy, 17; "Philandridas" head, 236 f.
Oxen, by Phradmon, 48
Paintings: Argos and Io, 171 f.; Eros, 108; Poseidon, 146; Py-

lades, 172; Zeus, 139 f.
Paris, by Euphranor, 43-45
Paris, Louvre: head of Askle-
pios(?), 142; athlete resembl-
ing Uffizi apoxyomenos, 78 f.;
female figure, 161
Patrokles, sculptor, 10, 11 f., 17,
27, 38; father of Naukydes,
5 f., 7
Pausanias, sculptor, 14 f.
Perikleitos, Periklytos, sculptor,
6
Perixyomenos, by Daippos, 74,
76, 90 f.; by Antignotos, 74
Persephone ("petite Hercula-
naise"), 158-63, 254
Phanias, Phanis, sculptor, 126
Pharsalos, signature at, 65, 123
Philandridas(?), athlete, by Ly-
sippos, 235-37
Phradmon, sculptor, 27-31
Phrynon, sculptor, 27
Pison, sculptor, 9
Piston, sculptor, 168
Polydamas, athlete, by Lysippos,
65; base, 96 f., 163
Polycharmos, sculptor, 55
Polykleitos the elder, sculptor,
3 f., 262; his Amazon, 28-31;
his influence on Lysippos, 84 f.,
256; his sons, 26 f.
Polykleitos the younger, sculp-
tor, 21-26; signature at The-
bes, 62 f.; as teacher of Ly-
sippos, 58
Polykleitos, possible third, 26
Portraits by Lysippos, 230-36,
247 f., 260 f.
Poseidon, British Museum, 137;
Budapest, 147; Dresden, 147;
Eleusis type, 147 f.; Lateran
type, 143-49, 187; Loeb
bronze, 150; by Lysippos, at
Corinth, 142 f.; of Melos, 151,
Addenda; Porcigliano, 150;
temple statue at the Isthmus,
142 f.; Vienna, 147; Vienna,
cameo, 146 f.
Pozzuoli, female figure at, 163
Praxilla, by Lysippos, 233 f.

Praxiteles, chronology, 72; con-
trast with Lysippos, 257 f.;
Hermes, contrast with Seile-
nos, 185; Mantineia base, 97;
style in statues of Aphrodite,
56
Praying boy, 149, 182
Praying woman, by Euphranor,
46 f.
Productiveness of Lysippos, 72
Ptolichos, sculptor, 10
Pyrgoteles, gem-cutter, 229, 234
Pythes, warrior, by Lysippos,
235

Realism of Lysippos, 260f.
Rhodes, quadriga by Lysippos at,
68 f.
Rome, S. Agnese Fuori: alabaster statuette, 157
Rome, Lateran: head resembling Munich bronze head, 36
Rome, Museo Nazionale: athlete
head, 238; basalt head, 37; basalt statue, 36 f.; Hellenistic
prince, 137, Addenda; seated
figure, 247
Rome, Museo Torlonia: athlete
heads, 238
Rome, Palazzo dei Conservatori:
nude charioteer, 46, Addenda;
Herakles, fighting, 191 f.
Rome, Vatican: female figure,
161; "Fortuna", 163; head resembling Munich bronze head,
35
Rome, Villa Colonna: sarcophagus, 157

Samolas, sculptor, 14
Satyr, Barberini Faun, 179;
dancing, 152; flute-playing,
152; by Lysippos, 152, 186;
playing with tail, 152; sleeping, 179
Seilanion, sculptor, 183
Seilenos and Dionysos, 184-86,
254
Seleukos Nikator, 67 f., 230 f.,
254

Signatures of Lysippos, at Corinth, 64, 70; at Lindos, 69; at Megara, 69; at Pharsalos, 65; at Thebes, 62 f.; at Thermon, 64
Sisyphos I, of Daochos group, ascribed to Phradmon, 31
Skopas, sculptor, 48-57, 262; Alexander sarcophagus, 228; Aphrodite, 55-57; as architect, 49-51; Ares Ludovisi, 166 ff.; Genzano Herakles, 53 f., 208 f.; Lansdowne Herakles, 208-11; Herakles at Sikyon, 53 f., 208; influence on Lysippos, 256 f.; maenad, 54; sculptures at Tegea, 51-54; versatility, 50 f.; works, 50 f.
Socrates, 231-33, Addenda
Sostratos, sculptor, 40
Sthennis, sculptor, 47, 69
Stones, as accessories with statues, 203
Strongylion, sculptor, 28 f.
Susa (Tunis), female figure at, 157
Symmetry, dynamic and static, 262

Tarentum, male head at, 194 f.; work of Lysippos at, 66
Tegea, temple at, 49-52, 54
Teisandros, sculptor, 10, 13, 27
Teisikrates, sculptor, 126, 168
Tharykidas, athlete, by Daidalos, 17 f.
Theater at Epidauros, 23 f.
Thebes, base at, 62-64, 92 f.; relations with Phocians, 21 f.
Theokosmos, sculptor, 9 f.
Thermon, signed base at, 64
Tholos at Delphi, 49
Tholos at Epidauros, 23 f.
Timokles, athlete, by Polykleitos, 26, 62
Timon, athlete, by Daidalos, 18
Tintoretto, analogy with Lysippos, 261 f.
Troilos, athlete, by Lysippos, 59-62, 235
Tunis, Musée Alaoui: sarcophagus, 157
Turin: portrait head, 177

Vienna: athlete in prayer, 38; cameo with Poseidon, 147 f.

"Westmacott athlete", 75 f.
Wrestlers, Naples, 245-47

Xanten, Byzantine chest at, 195
Xenokles, athlete, by Polykleitos, 24
Xenokrates, sculptor, 126

Zeus, at Argos, by Lysippos, 136 f.; Berlin head, 150; Blundell Hall, 39; bronze in Berlin, 137 f.; bronzes in British Museum, 135, 141 f.; bronze in Catania, 136; bronze in Constantinople, 141; bronze in Copenhagen, 136; bronze in Evreux, 136; bronze in Frankfurt, 136; bronze in Munich, 38 f.; bronze in Naples, 135; bronzes in Paris, 136; bronze in Syracuse, 136; bronze in Vienna, 135; Dresden, 141; from Khamissa, 142; at Megara, by Lysippos, 95 f., 138; Meilichios, by Polykleitos, 4; statues at Olympia, by Kleon, 19 f.; of Otricoli, 140 f., 204; Palazzo dei Conservatori, 142; Philios, by Polykleitos, 23; at Sikyon, by Lysippos, 134; at Tarentum, by Lysippos, 139 f.

PLATE 1

DORYPHOROS AFTER POLYKLEITOS, NAPLES

PLATE 2

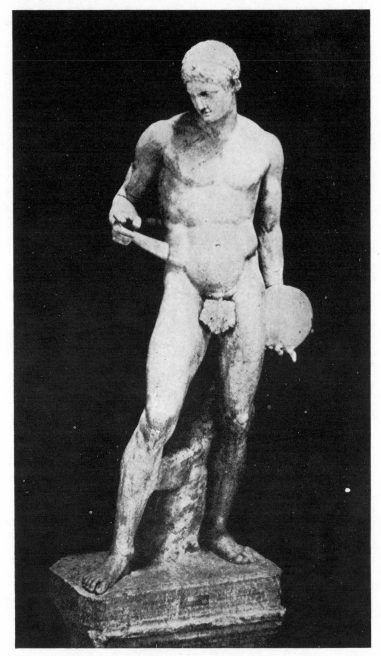

Photo Bruckmann

DISKOBOLOS AFTER NAUKYDES, VATICAN

PLATE 3

A

Photo. Bruckmann

DORIA-PAMPHILI AMAZON

B

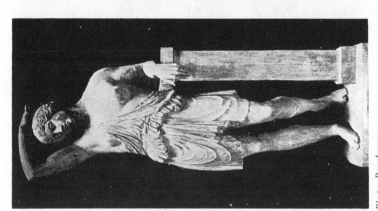

Photo. Bruckmann

BERLIN AMAZON

C

Photo. Bruckmann

CAPITOL AMAZON

PLATE 4

Photo. Bruckmann

STATUE IN VIENNA

PLATE 5

STATUE FOUND AT ANTIKYTHERA

PLATE 6

Photo. Bruckmann

ALEXANDER RONDANINI

PLATE 7

Photo. Bruckmann

HEAD OF ALEXANDER RONDANINI

PLATE 8

A

HELMETED HEAD FOUND AT TEGEA

B

HEAD OF HERAKLES FOUND AT TEGEA

PLATE 9

A

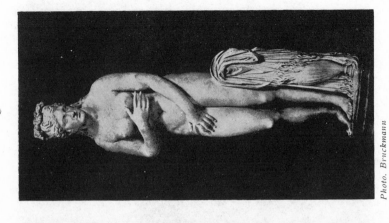

MEDICI APHRODITE

B

KNIDIAN APHRODITE, COPY IN MUNICH

C

CAPITOL APHRODITE

PLATE 10

STATUE FOUND AT EPHESOS

PLATE 11

A

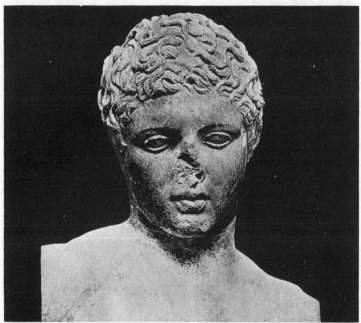

Photo. Bruckmann

HEAD OF DISKOBOLOS AFTER NAUKYDES, MUNICIPAL
ANTIQUARIUM, ROME

B

Photo. Bruckmann

HEAD OF STATUE FOUND AT EPHESOS

PLATE 12

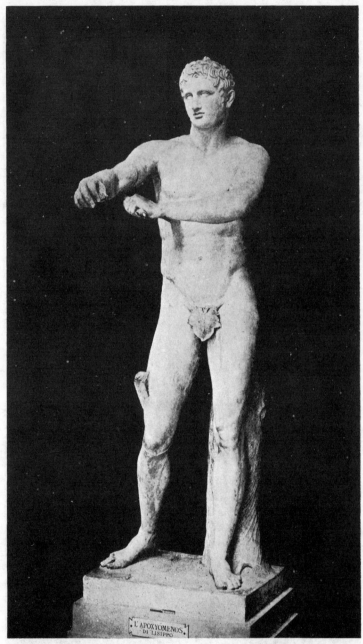

L'APOXYOMENOS
DI LISIPPO

Photo. Bruckmann

APOXYOMENOS, VATICAN

PLATE 13

Photo. Bruckmann

Photo. Bruckmann   HEAD OF THE VATICAN APOXYOMENOS

PLATE 14

A

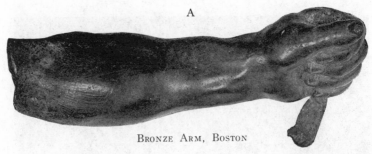

BRONZE ARM, BOSTON

B

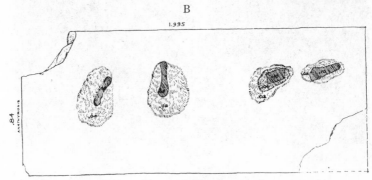

BASE AT THEBES

C

BASE AT MEGARA

PLATE 15

HERAKLES EPITRAPEZIOS, CAST IN DRESDEN

PLATE 16

HERAKLES EPITRAPEZIOS, CAST IN DRESDEN

PLATE 17

EROS, BRITISH MUSEUM

PLATE 18

Photo. Bruckmann

Photo. Bruckmann

HEAD OF EROS, COPENHAGEN

PLATE 19

Torso of Eros, Hillyer Art Gallery, Smith College

PLATE 20

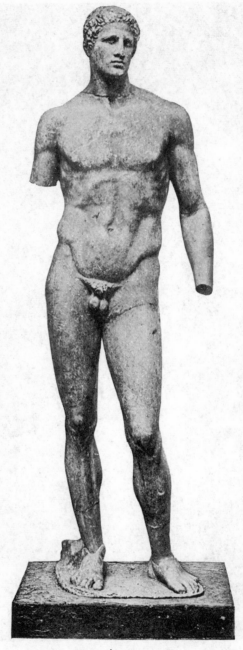

AGIAS

PLATE 21

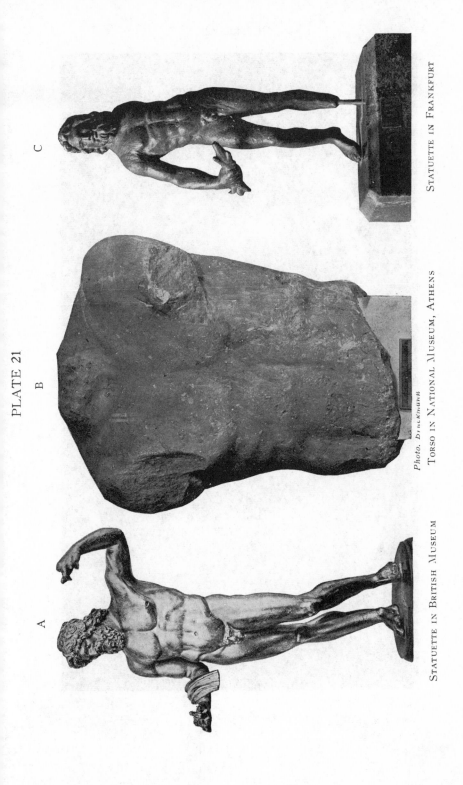

A   B   C

STATUETTE IN BRITISH MUSEUM   TORSO IN NATIONAL MUSEUM, ATHENS   STATUETTE IN FRANKFURT

Photo. Bruckmann

PLATE 22

Photo. Bruckmann

ZEUS OF OTRICOLI

PLATE 23

ZEUS, DRESDEN

PLATE 24

POSEIDON, LATERAN

PLATE 25

POSEIDON, CANDIA

PLATE 26

Photo. Bruckmann "GRANDE HERCULANAISE"

PLATE 27

Photo. Bruckmann "PETITE HERCULANAISE"

PLATE 28

Photo. Bruckmann

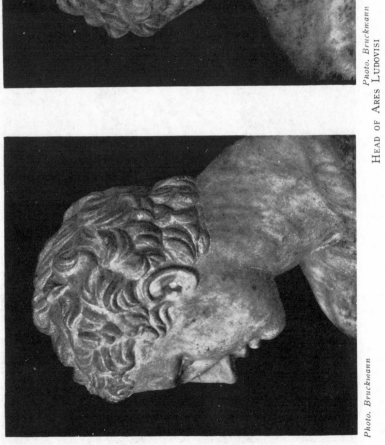

Photo. Bruckmann

HEAD OF ARES LUDOVISI

PLATE 29

Photo. Bruckmann

Photo. Bruckmann

TORSO OF ARES, NAPLES

PLATE 30

Lansdowne "Jason," Cast

PLATE 31

LANSDOWNE "JASON," CAST

PLATE 32

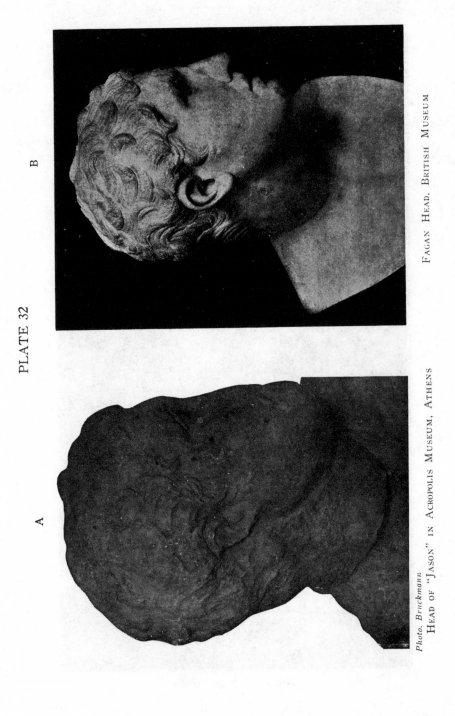

A

B

Photo. Bruckmann
HEAD OF "JASON," IN ACROPOLIS MUSEUM, ATHENS

FAGAN HEAD, BRITISH MUSEUM

PLATE 33

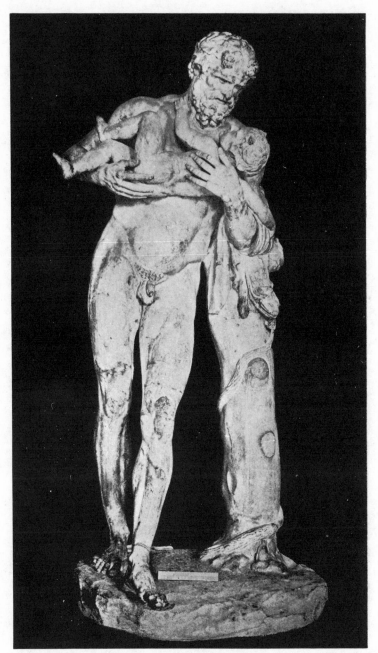

SEILENOS AND DIONYSOS, LOUVRE

PLATE 34

Photo. Alinari
HEAD OF SEILENOS, MUSEO NAZIONALE, ROME

PLATE 35

Photo. Bruckmann

HERMES, NAPLES

PLATE 36

PLATE 37

Photo. Bruckmann

HERAKLES FARNESE

PLATE 38

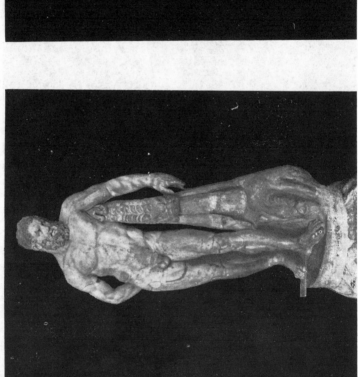

A

Photo. Bruckmann HERAKLES, UFFIZI

B

Photo. Bruckmann HERAKLES, VILLA BORGHESE

PLATE 39

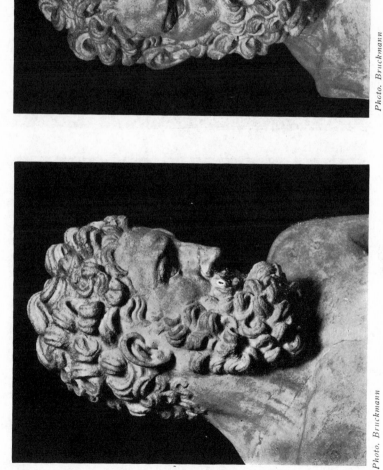

Photo. Bruckmann

Photo. Bruckmann

HEAD OF HERAKLES, VILLA BORGHESE

PLATE 40

A

B

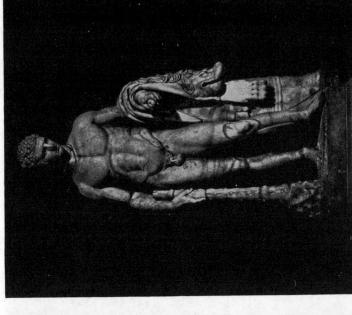

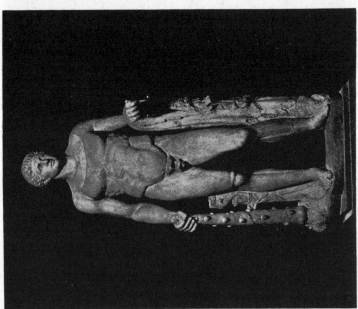

Two Statues of Herakles, Palazzo Pitti

PLATE 41

LANSDOWNE HERAKLES

PLATE 42

Photo. Giraudon

HERAKLES IN LOUVRE, STATUETTE

PLATE 43

Photo. Bruckmann

ALEXANDER AZARA

PLATE 44

Photo. Bruckmann

ALEXANDER AZARA

PLATE 45

HEAD OF ALEXANDER, GENEVA

PLATE 46

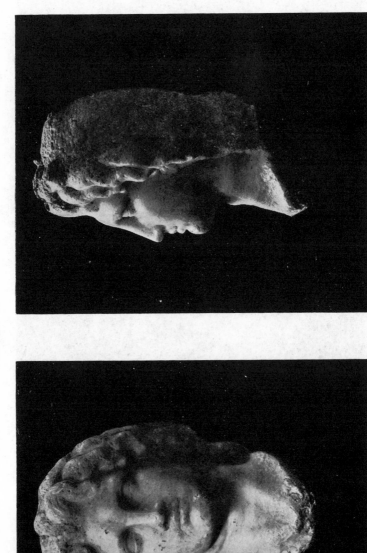

PLATE 47

ALEXANDER IN LOUVRE, STATUETTE

PLATE 48

A

Photo. Bruckmann

Bronze Horseman, Naples

B

Statues in Church of St. George, Saloniki

PLATE 49

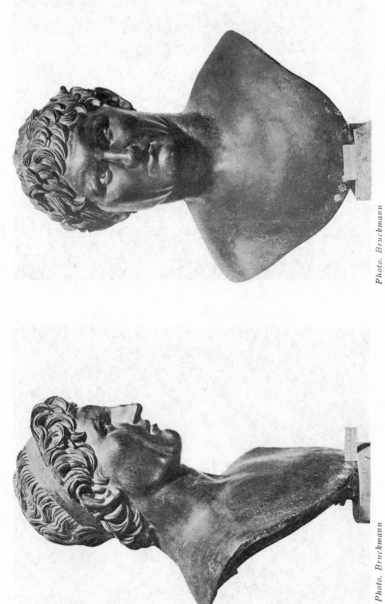

Photo. Bruckmann

Photo. Bruckmann

BUST OF SELEUKOS NIKATOR, NAPLES

PLATE 50

Photo. Bruckmann

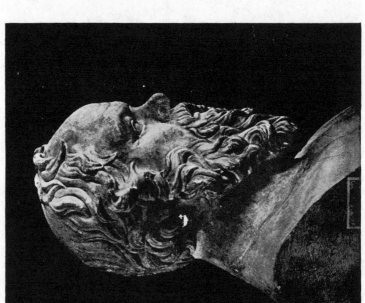

Photo. Bruckmann

BUST OF SOCRATES, LOUVRE

PLATE 51

Photo. Bruckmann

Photo. Bruckmann

BRONZE HEAD FOUND AT OLYMPIA

PLATE 52

A   B

"PHILANDRIDAS" HEAD

C   D

Photo. Bruckmann   *Photo. Bruckmann*

HEAD OF YOUTH ON STELE

PLATE 53

Photo. Bruckmann.

A

GANYMEDE, FLORENCE

B

Photo. Bruckmann.

HERMES IN GENEVA, STATUETTE

C

HEAD OF STATUE IN BERLIN

PLATE 54

STATUE IN BERLIN

PLATE 55

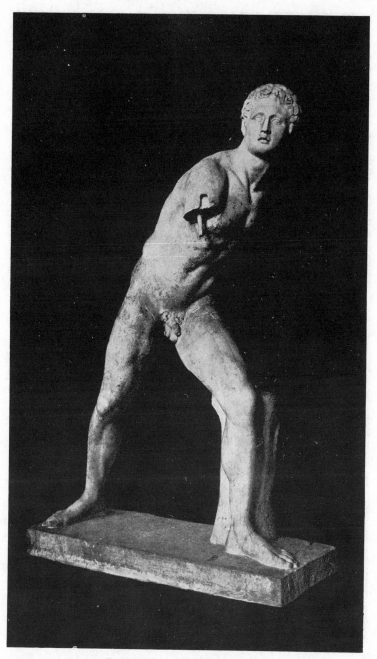

BEARDLESS ATHLETE, DRESDEN

PLATE 56

BEARDED ATHLETE, DRESDEN

PLATE 57

HEAD IN COPENHAGEN

PLATE 58

MELEAGER, VATICAN

PLATE 59

Photo. Bruckmann

Photo. Bruckmann

HEAD OF MELEAGER, COPENHAGEN

PLATE 60

Photo. Bruckmann

WRESTLERS

PLATE 61

Dancer, Frankfurt